The Econometrics of Demand Systems

With Applications to Food Demand in the Nordic Countries

by

David L. Edgerton
Lund University, Sweden

Bengt Assarsson
Uppsala University, Sweden

Anders Hummelmose
Landbocentret, Brønderslev, Denmark

Ilkka P. Laurila
University of Helsinki, Finland, and
Agricultural Economics Research Institute, Helsinki, Finland

Kyrre Rickertsen
Agricultural University of Norway, Ås, Norway

Per Halvor Vale
Agricultural University of Norway, Ås, Norway

KLUWER ACADEMIC PUBLISHERS
DORDRECHT / BOSTON / LONDON

Distributors for North America:
Kluwer Academic Publishers
101 Philip Drive
Assinippi Park
Norwell, Massachusetts 02061 USA

Distributors for all other countries:
Kluwer Academic Publishers Group
Distribution Centre
Post Office Box 322
3300 AH Dordrecht, THE NETHERLANDS

Library of Congress Cataloging-in-Publication Data
The econometrics of demand systems : with applications to food demand in the Nordic countries / by David L. Edgerton ... [et al.].
p. cm. -- (Advanced studies in theoretical and applied econometrics ; 34)
Includes index.
ISBN 0-7923-4106-6
1. Food industry and trade--Scandinavia--Econometric models.
2. Food supply--Scandinavia--Econometric models. 3. Demand (Economic theory)--Econometric models. I. Edgerton, David L.
II. Series.
HD9015.S342E27 1996
339.4'86413'00948--dc20 96-23237
CIP

Printed on acid-free paper.

Printed in the United States of America

CONTENTS

Part II: Special Studies

GLOSSARY

Definitions of Basic Variables

$i, j, k = 1, \ldots, n$	Index for commodities
p_i	Price of the ith good
q_i	Quantity consumed of the ith good
$x_i = q_i p_i$	Expenditure on the ith good
$x = \sum_i x_i$	Total expenditure
$w_i = x_i / x$	Budget share of the ith good
y	Disposable income
ε_i	Stochastic error term in the equation for the ith good

Vectors and matrices are printed in bold face, for example

$\boldsymbol{p} = (p_1, \ldots, p_n)'$	Price vector
$\boldsymbol{q} = (q_1, \ldots, q_n)'$	Quantity vector

Definitions of Basic Functions

$u = \upsilon(\boldsymbol{q})$	(Direct) utility function
$u = \psi(x, \boldsymbol{p})$	Indirect utility function
$x = c(u, \boldsymbol{p})$	Expenditure function
$q_i = g_i(x, \boldsymbol{p})$	Marshallian demand function
$q_i = h_i(u, \boldsymbol{p})$	Hicksian demand function
$E_i = \dfrac{\partial \ln g_i}{\partial \ln x}$	Total expenditure elasticity
$e_{ij} = \dfrac{\partial \ln g_i}{\partial \ln p_j}$	Uncompensated (Marshallian) price elasticity
$\tilde{e}_{ij} = \dfrac{\partial \ln h_i}{\partial \ln p_j}$	Compensated (Hicksian) price elasticity

Definitions in Two-Stage Budgeting

In two-stage budgeting the commodities are divided up into a number of groups. The following notation is used.

Q_r	*Group* expenditure for the rth group of goods
$E_{(r)i}$	*Within group* expenditure elasticity for the ith good within the rth group of goods
$E_{(r)}$	*Group* expenditure elasticity for the rth group of goods
E_i	*Total* expenditure elasticity for the ith good

with similar notation for the budget shares, w. The price elasticities are defined as

$e_{(r)ij}$	*Within group* uncompensated price elasticity between the jth and i^{th} goods within the rth group of goods
$e_{(r)(s)}$	*Group* uncompensated price elasticity between the sth and r^{th} groups of goods
e_{ij}	*Total* uncompensated price elasticity between the jth and i^{th} goods

with similar notation for the compensated price elasticities $\tilde{e}$.

Definitions in Aggregate Time-Series

$t = 1, \ldots, T$	Index for time periods

The index t is only used when we need to distinguish between different time periods and/or different aggregation levels. Variables are now defined q_{it}, p_{it}, w_{it}, *etc.*

Definitions in Household Studies

$h = 1, \ldots, H$	Index for households

The index h is only used when we need to distinguish between different households and/or different aggregation levels. Variables are now defined q_{ih}, p_{ih}, w_{ih}, *etc.*

In Chapter 10, the results for time-series and household studies are compared. In this chapter time-series and household variables are denoted in upper case, while individual variables are denoted in lower case.

Notational System

The notational system used in this book is organised chapterwise. All equations, tables, *etc.*, are numbered starting from one in each chapter. References within a chapter simply use the relevant number, whilst references between chapters use both chapter and number.

PREFACE

This book contains some of the results from the research project "Demand for Food in the Nordic Countries", which was initiated in 1988 by Professor Olof Bolin of the Agricultural University in Ultuna, Sweden and by Professor Karl Johan Weckman, of the University of Helsinki, Finland. A pilot study was carried out by Bengt Assarsson, which in 1989 led to a successful application for a research grant from the NKJ (The Nordic Contact Body for Agricultural Research) through the national research councils for agricultural research in Denmark, Finland, Norway and Sweden. We are very grateful to Olof Bolin and Karl Johan Weckman, without whom this project would not have come about, and to the national research councils in the Nordic countries for the generous financial support we have received for this project.

We have received comments and suggestions from many colleagues, and this has improved our work substantially. At the start of the project a reference group was formed, consisting of Professor Olof Bolin, Professor Anders Klevmarken, Agr. lic. Gert Aage Nielsen, Professor Karl Johan Weckman and Cand. oecon. Per Halvor Vale. Gert Aage Nielsen left the group early in the project for a position in Landbanken, and was replaced by Professor Lars Otto, while Per Halvor Vale soon joined the research staff. The reference group has given us useful suggestions and encouraged us in our work. We are very grateful to them.

A large number of research reports have been published in a separate working paper series for this project, a list of which can be found in Appendix 1. These reports have been presented at our local departments and at various national and international conferences, for example the Econometric Society's World Congresses in Barcelona and Tokyo, the Econometric Society's European Meeting in Uppsala, The American Agricultural Economics Association's Annual Meetings in Baltimore and Indianapolis, The International Conference of Agricultural Economics in Harare, The European Congress of Agricultural Economists in Stresa, The Romanian-Swedish Economic Symposium in Bucharest, The Annual Meeting of the Nordic Society of Agricultural Researchers in Uppsala, and Ekonometridagarna (The Econometric Days) in Gothenburg, Lund, Stockholm, Umeå and Uppsala. We are very grateful to the participants in these events for all the comments and suggestions that we have received.

The authors share the responsibility for this book, and work on all the chapters has been discussed thoroughly among the research staff at workshops that have been arranged on a regular basis. Nevertheless, different members of the research staff bear the main responsibility for the various components of the book, which is divided into three parts.

Parts one and three are the joint responsibility of all the authors, while the individual authors bear separate responsibility for the second part. Part one consists of chapters one to five, which describe our joint data base, the underlying microeconomic model, the econometric specification and the empirical analysis of a common model. The data analysis for this part has been performed by David Edgerton for Sweden, Anders Hummelmose for Denmark, Ilkka Laurila for Finland and Kyrre Rickertsen for Norway, using a TSP programme provided by David Edgerton. Part two consists of chapters six to eleven, which are on specific topics that one or more of the authors have addressed separately, while the third part consists of the conclusions in chapter twelve.

The authorship of the various chapters is distributed as follows:

Bengt Assarsson. Chapters 1 and 7.
Bengt Assarsson and David Edgerton. Chapters 2 and 5.
David Edgerton. Chapters 4, 6, 11, 12, Appendix 1 and bibliography file.
Ilkka Laurila. Chapter 8, Appendix 2 and data files.
Kyrre Rickertsen. Chapter 3.
Kyrre Rickertsen and Per Halvor Vale. Chapter 9.
Per Halvor Vale. Chapter 10.

David Edgerton has also had responsibility for the final editing process.

In conclusion, we hope that this book, or at least parts of it, can be used as a textbook in applied demand analysis. For that purpose we have included a data appendix, in which the reader will find details of how the data and computer programmes used in this study can be obtained through the internet. These files can be used to directly replicate our work, provided the reader has the computer package TSP (version 4.2 or later) available. The reader is of course free to further improve the specifications presented in this book. The files also include an extended bibliography concerning the econometric analysis of food demand.

March, 1996

David Edgerton
Lund

Bengt Assarsson
Uppsala

Anders Hummelmose
Brønderslev

Ilkka Laurila
Helsinki

Kyrre Rickertsen
Ås

Per Halvor Vale
Ås

Part I

A MODEL FOR FOOD CONSUMPTION IN THE NORDIC COUNTRIES

Advanced Studies in Theoretical and Applied Econometrics

Volume 34

The titles published in this series are listed at the end of this volume.

THE ECONOMETRICS OF DEMAND SYSTEMS

1

INTRODUCTION*

The theory of consumer demand has been a central topic in economics for many years, and modern formalised economic theory has dealt with consumer demand for some considerable time. The formalised theory of consumer demand has led the way towards econometric applications, and it is such applications that form the main theme of the present study. We are hereby pursuing a tradition which, from a Nordic perspective, has been followed by some of our most prominent applied economists, of whom the most well known are Ragnar Frisch, Gunnar Myrdal, Trygve Haavelmo and Herman Wold[1].

The development of new econometric techniques has been very rapid during recent years. New methods for estimation and testing have been developed, which are potential tools for applications in many fields. In the case of consumer demand theory, and in particular in the study of food demand, new models and specifications have been developed that encompass older models. Application of these models may well throw new light on the properties of consumer demand.

During the last decades the search for a better specification of demand systems has paid much attention to the choice of functional form, and in particular to so called "flexible functional forms" that can approximate arbitrarily chosen preferences. Two of the most well known of these systems are the translog model, developed by Christensen *et al.* (1979), and the Almost Ideal Demand System (AIDS), developed by Deaton and Muellbauer (1980b). These systems have been used, and are still used, in numerous applications. They are used to test theoretical conditions derived from consumer demand theory; homogeneity, symmetry and negativity. The systems are also used to provide estimated elasticities, that is the percentage change in the quantity demanded of a certain good in relation to the percentage change in (i) the relative price of that good or some other good, or (ii) the total (real) outlay of the consumer(s).

A thorough textbook treatment of the economic theory of demand analysis can be found in Deaton and Muellbauer (1980a), while the more recent Theil and Clements (1987) and Pollak and Wales (1992) attempt to bridge the gap between economic theory and econometric application. The book by Bewley (1986) concentrates in more detail, however, on the econometric aspects of demand systems. A number of comprehensive reports concerning American food demand have been published in recent years, the most general being those of Capps and Senauer

---

* This chapter, which is the shared responsibility of all the authors, has been written by Bengt Assarsson.

[1] Herman Wold was actually a statistician, but he wrote extensively on economic and econometric matters.

(1986), Rauniker and Huang (1987) and Haung (1993). These use a modern systems approach, something that is sadly lacking in the analysis of Nordic food demand, with the primary exception of Klevmarken (1981).

The purpose of the present study is to analyse the demand for food in the Nordic countries. This is done through an econometric analysis of systems of demand equations, based on the neoclassical theory of consumer demand. The original versions of the translog and the AIDS were static models, which was clearly a deficiency, as noted for example by Deaton and Muellbauer (1980b) in their original evaluation of the AIDS model. We can therefore expect significant improvements to be possible regarding the *specification* of new demand systems, in particular with respect to dynamics, parameter stability and (possibly) functional form.

We have also incorporated the latest developments in econometrics, to help us *estimate* and *evaluate* the systems more efficiently than has previously been usual. In particular, the modern theory of misspecification testing allows us to evaluate more thoroughly the demand systems we are using, with respect to the assumptions that have been made to allow estimation and testing of restrictions. A further aim is to construct well-specified demand systems that explain the *historical development* of the consumption of different food items in the Nordic countries.

The alternative specifications and modern econometric techniques we use make it likely that the results we obtain, concerning tests of economic theory and estimated elasticities, will differ from those obtained in previous studies. The models we derive should statistically outperform most of the specifications previously used in the literature when applied to the data set used in this study, *i.e.* annual food consumption in the Nordic countries. We therefore expect new results to emerge in the course of this study.

In the next chapter the book starts with a description of food consumption in the Nordic countries. The development of volume indices, budget shares, relative prices and physical quantities for different food items during the last three decades is presented. This chapter provides a preliminary and sketchy examination of the possible causes behind the changes in food consumption, where interest is focused on relative price changes as the primary cause. A number of charts are presented that show the development of food consumption over time in the different countries. Further charts can easily be obtained from the data provided on the files described in Appendix 2, using any standard graphical programme such as Microsoft Excel.

The empirical analysis is based on neoclassical theoretical models. In Chapter 3 basic theoretical notions are discussed, defining for example the concepts of utility maximisation and duality, which are important for our econometric analysis. In Chapter 4, the problem of explicitly formulating a demand model is addressed, and the specification, estimation and evaluation of estimated models are discussed.

In order to compare the different countries empirically, we use a common model for all of them in Chapter 5, this being a fairly simple dynamic extension of the AIDS model. The common model is further extended in various ways in Chapter 6, with respect to separability structure, parameter stability, dynamic structure and with respect to functional form. The most general system derived here is a dynamic switching regression model, where parameters are allowed to change over time. In Chapter 7 we develop another dynamic form; an error correction model based on the AIDS flexible functional form. This general model is then used to test some popular but more restrictive forms, such as the partial adjustment and the auto-regressive error forms.

Chapters 8-11 are more disparate in character and reflect the various interests of researchers in the different Nordic countries. Chapter 8 is devoted to constructing forecasts for the Finnish economy for the period 1990-2000. Forecasting models are chosen from the menu of models that appeared in Chapters 4 to 6. In Chapters 9 and 10 household expenditure data is used in addition to the aggregate national accounts in an analysis of Norwegian food consumption. The analysis is used to compare results previously obtained with aggregate data and the common model, with results for different household groups. The importance of demographic and socio-economic variables is also evaluated. Chapter 11 takes up the rather technical problem concerning when estimated demand systems *automatically* satisfy the adding up requirement of economic theory. The results of this theoretical analysis are applied to the common model.

2

THE CONSUMPTION OF FOOD IN THE NORDIC COUNTRIES*

2.1 INTRODUCTION

In this chapter we shall describe the development of food consumption in Denmark, Finland, Norway and Sweden. The descriptive part of our analysis aims at getting a feeling for the trends and general development of food consumption and relative prices, as well as being a means of detecting peculiarities in the data.

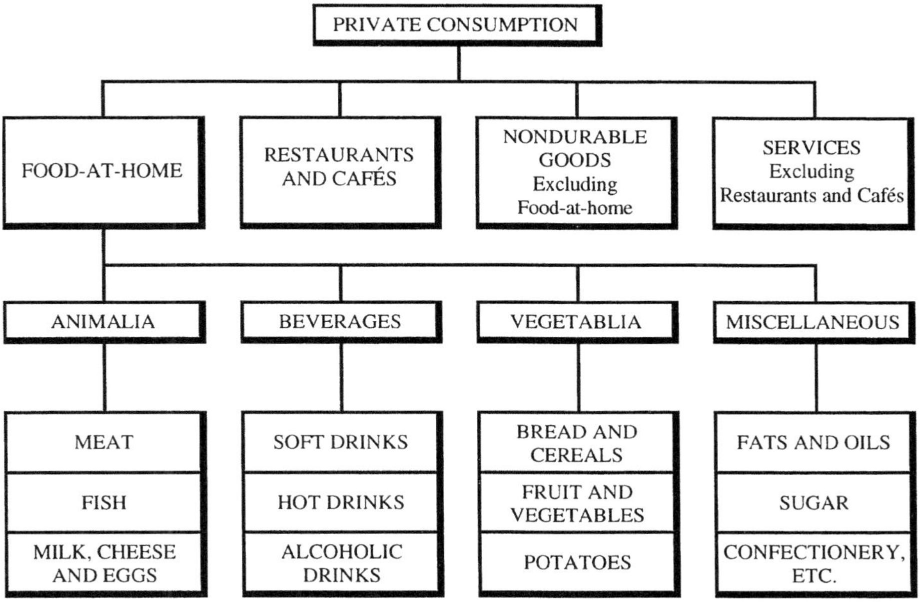

Figure 1: Utility Tree Used in This Study

Our data consists of consumption statistics for food and other goods and services. The data is divided into categories as shown in Figure 1, which is defined according to a three-stage budgeting demand model that is presented in Chapter 4.

* This chapter, which is the shared responsibility of all the authors, has been written by Bengt Assarsson and David Edgerton.

At the highest level of aggregation total *private consumption* is determined. The particular problems associated with the treatment of durable goods are not dealt with in this book, however, and private consumption is thus defined as the consumption of nondurables and services. This definition is the most commonly used in applied work concerning consumption behaviour under the life cycle hypothesis. At the next level of aggregation the categories are *food-at-home*, *restaurants and cafés*, *other nondurable goods* and *other services*. The aggregation level below this divides *food-at-home* into the categories *animalia*, *vegetablia*, *beverages* and *miscellaneous*. Finally, these categories are divided into the subgroups shown in the figure.

A demand analysis, whether performed informally or through a formal econometric analysis, needs to take into account the *quantities* of the various goods that are consumed, the *prices* of those goods and the *income* of the consumers.

One problem that we meet when analysing consumption at the level of aggregation shown in Figure 1 is what units to use when measuring quantity. The use of physical quantities is appealing for disaggregated goods, but as the Swedish saying goes "You can't compare apples and pears". In fact we might be prepared to consider aggregate weight as a measure of fruit consumption, but aggregate weight is hardly appropriate for combining, say, fillet steak and offal let alone fillet steak and visits to the dentist. The unit of quantity used in this study is therefore *real consumption* (*RC*), measured in thousands of units of the local currency at 1985 year's prices. Since we are comparing trends over time we will be looking at *per capita* consumption in the descriptive analysis of this chapter, and, for reasons that will become clear in the next two chapters, also in the econometric analysis presented in the rest of the book.

The *current consumption* (*CC*) of a good measures its value, and is defined in this book as the *per capita* money expenditure on that good, measured in thousands of units of the local currency at contemporary prices. Since prices are measured in different currencies, there is no obvious unit-free measure that can be used for the cross-country comparison of prices, quantities and values. Currency conversions are subject to the volatility of the exchange rate, and while purchasing power parities could be used, some goods are not traded internationally so that the real exchange rates are also volatile. To compare consumption patterns across countries, we shall instead compare the budget shares and relative prices for the different food items.

While the real consumption of different goods tends to increase with income, the budget shares may either increase or decrease as the case may be. Goods for which budget shares decrease with income are denoted necessities and goods for which budget shares increase with income are denoted luxuries. Note that we only occasionally use income directly as a variable in this study, using for the most part total private consumption expenditure instead. This follows from our decision to ignore intertemporal effects, such as savings and the purchase of durables.

In the next section we give a short formal description of how our data is constructed and the sources that are used. The third section contains an analysis of the development of real consumption and relative prices (shown graphically in

Appendix A to this chapter), and of budget shares (shown in Appendix B). The consumption patterns across countries can be compared using these chartts. The trends are discussed for both total consumption and each of the food items in Figure 1. The final section contains a short discussion concerning the physical consumption of various foodstuffs.

2.2 THE DATA

2.2.1 Data Construction

The data used in this study is in general based upon the annual time-series of consumption statistics, found in the national accounts published by the various governmental statistical offices.[1] These statistics are constructed in slightly different ways in the different countries. All countries use both retail trade statistics, collected at a disaggregated level, and wholesale and manufacturing statistics. The balance between these different sources varies between the countries, however. The method used for converting wholesale and manufacturing statistics (so called disappearance data) into consumption statistics is the following commodity flow method,

$$C = IP + HP - IC + NI + \Delta S - W, \tag{1}$$

where C represents the household consumption of a foodstuff, IP agricultural/industrial production, HP home production, IC industrial consumption, NI net imports, ΔS change of stocks and W waste.

As described in the Glossary at the beginning of the book, we will be using the following notation. Real consumption of the ith commodity is denoted by q_i, the price of which is denoted by p_i. Total consumption is denoted by x.

The level of aggregation used in the national accounts implies that the consumption statistics that are published are themselves derived from data at a more disaggregated level. This in turn has been obtained from information on physical quantities and average prices (often based on subindicies of the consumer price index). We therefore formally define our measure of quantity as real consumption, given by

$$q = RC = \textstyle\sum_k RC_k \,. \tag{2}$$

Implicit price indices are then constructed from the series of current and real consumption through the formula

$$p = CC / RC = \textstyle\sum CC_k / \sum RC_k \,. \tag{3}$$

---

[1] Cross-sectional analyses for Norway are considered in Chapters 9 and 10, however.

We are thus using Paasche indices, as opposed to the chained Laspeyres or Edgeworth indices commonly used in the construction of national consumer price indices. In the charts presented in the next section we define the relative price of a food item as

$$p_i^* = p_i / P, \tag{4}$$

where P denotes the general price level, which in this case is defined as the price index for total consumption including durables and semi-durables.

Budget shares are defined relative to their aggregation level. *Food-at-home's* share is thus the expenditure on food-at-home relative to total private expenditure on nondurables and services, *beverages'* budget share is relative to the expenditure on food-at-home, whilst the budget share of *alcoholic drinks* is defined relative to the expenditure on *beverages*. If the ith commodity is a member of the rth commodity group (given at the aggregation level nearest above the commodity in question), then the within group budget share is defined as

$$w_{ri} = \frac{p_i q_i}{x_r}, \tag{5}$$

where x_r denotes the total money expenditure for the rth commodity group. The relationships between different within group, between group and total quantities are further discussed in Chapter 4.2.4.

2.2.2 Data Sources for the Nordic Countries

Data for the commodity groups described in Figure 1 is available for different periods in the different countries: 1953-1990 for Denmark, 1960-1990 for Finland, 1962-1988 for Norway and 1963-1989 for Sweden. In some countries data for additional periods is available for a number of categories. In the following subsections we will discuss some details concerning data collection and construction for the various Nordic countries. In all countries the population data has been obtained from the central statistical authorities.

Danish Food Consumption Data

The annual data used in the Danish study has been obtained from the consumption statistics, published by Danish Statistics in the national accounts. This data covers the period from 1953 to 1990. From 1966 to 1990 the annual time-series data for current and real consumption are taken directly from the Statistical Yearbook.

Data covering the years 1953 to 1966 was obtained for the first stage from the databank *ADAM*. The data for the second and third stages were constructed using some older national accounts' data from Danish Statistics. To make these values consistent with the post-1966 values, some small adjustments were made. A further discussion concerning the construction of the Danish data can be found in Hummelmose (1991).

Finnish Food Consumption Data

The annual data consists of value and quantity series of goods and services for household consumption in Finland, covering the years 1950-1990. The national account's time-series for 1970-1990 were obtained from the Central Statistical Office of Finland. Because the volume series using the base year 1985 are only available from 1975, a level adjustment for the years 1970-1974 was made.

Some of the data covering the years 1960-1969 was obtained from the Research Institute of the Finnish Economy. The rest of the data for 1960-1969, and all the data for 1950-1959, has been constructed directly using the series presented in Laurila (1985). A level adjustment was performed to make these values agree with the post-1960 values, and the base year is thus 1985 for all the series. For further discussion on consumption data in the national accounts, see Söder (1984).

The data covering 1950-1990 is used to describe the development of consumption patterns, whereas the econometric analysis employs only the data covering 1960-1990. The reasons for not using the data from the 1950's in the econometric analysis are as follows: (a) a number of series are only available from 1960, (b) most of the post-1960 values are derived from a uniform data source that is different from the data source utilised when deriving the pre-1960 values, and (c) consumer preferences tend to change over time, and consequently the observation period should not cover too long a time period (most econometric methods implicitly assume constant consumer preferences).

Norwegian Food Consumption Data

The data consists of annual time-series of current and real consumption, given in the national accounts published by the Central Bureau of Statistics of Norway. The figures for 1960 and 1961 do not exist for the complete commodity breakdown used in this study, and these years are excluded from the estimation of some stages.

Norwegian consumption statistics are, in principle, based on retail trade statistics. Wholesale trade and manufacturing statistics are also used in some cases, however, although the commodity flow method (1) is modified in such a way that constructed margins are used to derive retail values. The retail values thus obtained are then verified against disappearance data (for which the discussion in the section on Swedish consumption data is highly relevant). The data for *fish*, *potatoes*, *vegetables*, *fruit*, *berries* and *alcoholic drinks* have a relatively large source of error since the estimates of home production are rather uncertain.

Swedish Food Consumption Data

The data used in the Swedish study has been obtained from the consumption statistics published in the national accounts. The calculations for these statistics are performed by the National Agricultural Market Board (*SJV*), Statistics Sweden (*SCB*) and other sources.

Consumption statistics are mainly obtained in Sweden by the use of manufacturing statistics using the method of commodity flow, the main exception to this being *alcoholic drinks*, where retail trade statistics are used directly. Note that several of the components in (1) have considerable sources of error. Home production is only estimated periodically from survey data (this particularly affects potatoes and fruit) and does not include the illegal production of alcohol. Net imports exclude unregistered tax-free imports and other legal and illegal border trade. Stock changes have never been registered for households or retail traders, and since 1985 not even for wholesale traders. Finally, wastage is only periodically estimated and excludes household waste.

SJV calculate two consumption series: *total consumption*, where *IC* excludes the production of more highly processed foodstuffs, and *direct consumption*, where this is not the case. For example, the sugar used in the production of alcohol, conserves *etc*, is *included* in the total consumption of sugar, but *excluded* from the direct consumption. It is the figures for direct consumption that are relevant for this study, since these more closely reflect the choices that face the consumer. Finally, SCB extract private (household) consumption from direct consumption, by using periodically estimated budget shares that separate the private, public and catering sectors.[2] See Edgerton (1989) for a detailed description of the construction of Swedish food consumption statistics.

Quarterly statistics are published by SCB, but are merely extrapolations at this level of disaggregation. Annual data for real and current consumption for 1963-1989 are used for the econometric analysis in this study, where we have corrected for the changes of base year that occur in the official statistics. In the charts we also use data from 1950-1962 regarding total consumption and total food. This data is of poor quality, and does not allow for any disaggregation into more detailed food categories. More recent data from 1990 is also used in the charts.

2.3 REAL CONSUMPTION, RELATIVE PRICES AND BUDGET SHARES

In this section we discuss the charts for different food items, *etc.*, given in the appendices to this chapter. In Appendix A (Charts 1 to 20) we present country by country results concerning real consumption and relative prices. Real consumption

[2] Statistics on the private consumption of foodstuffs can be found in Appendix 1 of SCB's National Accounts Annual Reports.

is measured as the *per capita* consumption in terms of 1,000 units of the local currency in 1985 year's prices, while relative prices are defined by (5). The only exception to this is the chart concerning total consumption, where the actual price index is given. In Appendix B (Charts 21 to 24) we present the budget shares for all countries, these being calculated relative to the next stage of the utility tree given in Figure 1.

The purpose of the analysis in this section is to give some preliminary indications concerning the development of food consumption in the Nordic countries. We are not hoping for any quantitative answers, these will have to wait for the econometric analysis in the remaining chapters of the book. We are, however, hoping to be able to compare (a) different countries and (b) different foodstuffs, and this raises a number of delicate questions concerning the scaling of the charts.

Our primary concern is the comparison between countries. The same scale is therefore being used for all countries regarding the relative prices of any specific foodstuff, which allows us to compare relative price levels and volatility between countries. To compare real consumption we must look at graphs that use different currencies. Since the relevant exchange rates have varied over time, we have chosen to always use a relation that, though never holding exactly, will not be too "incorrect" for any time period. The ratio 1:1:1 is used between the Danish, Norwegian and Swedish *krona*, while the ratio between the Scandinavian currencies and the Finnish *markka* varies, for reasons of presentational convenience, for the most part between 1:0.6 to 1:0.7 in the different charts. Finally, the comparison between different national budget shares is accomplished by including all countries in the same chart.

To standardise the comparisons between foodstuffs we proceed as follows. As far as possible we let relative prices have the same scale for as many goods as possible, *i.e.* a spread of one unit. This enables simple comparisons of price volatility to be made. In many cases an interval of 0.5 - 1.5 is used, but this is not always appropriate in situations with heavily falling or rising prices, or with different price developments in the different countries. Care must therefore always be taken when comparing relative price levels. In a number of cases, where relative prices have varied greatly over time, we have had to use a different scale altogether.[3] These cases are noted at the relevant points in the text.

Choosing the scale for real consumption is somewhat more difficult. In many ways, it is not a comparison of the absolute consumption of different foodstuffs that is interesting, but rather a comparison of their rates of growth. This would indicate an advantage in using a logarithmic scale, something that unfortunately would also lead to a loss of information regarding levels. We therefore employ the usual arithmetic scales, but these are dimensioned in such a way that the range of the axis is roughly equivalent to a growth of 500 percent over the time interval. This is not an unambiguous decision rule, and some latitude has been allowed for visual

---

[3] A few foodstuffs have extreme price variations for one or more countries. Using the same scale for all goods would thus lead to very uninformative charts for most goods.

configuration (*i.e.*, we have tried to centre the graph lines). The charts should, however, give a good general impression regarding high or low rates of growth. In some cases, with large rates of growth, this scaling is inappropriate, and we have therefore used a smaller scale. These cases are noted in the text in same way as for relative prices.

Total Private Consumption (Chart 1)

As can be seen in Appendix A to this chapter, *total consumption* followed a rising trend for all countries during the period under study. This trend became weaker, however, for all countries in the middle of the 70's. This was particularly so for Denmark and Sweden, and less so for Finland and Norway. It is notable that there was even a decline in total consumption in Sweden and Denmark, during the period 1976-1982,[4] while Norway maintained almost the same growth rate in this period as during the 60's. The signs of poor macroeconomic performance during the 70's show up mostly for Denmark and Sweden, a little less for Finland and Norway. Common for all countries is the downturn during the late 70's and the somewhat lower growth rate experienced after the crisis. All the countries have also experienced a downturn in the late 80's, this starting somewhat earlier in Denmark and Norway. These experiences are likely to affect the consumption of food and the different food items.

Total Food Consumption (Charts 2 and 21)

Looking at Chart 2 we can see that *total food consumption* has increased in all countries. The average annual growth rates (*AAGR*) differ considerably between the countries. During the period that is common to all countries (1963-1988) the largest increase was in Finland, where the *per capita* consumption increased by 2.2 percent annually. The lowest *AAGR* is for Sweden, at only 0.5 percent, while Denmark and Norway lay in-between at 1.3 percent and 1.4 percent respectively. We can also note that there was a decline in food consumption in Sweden during the period 1976-82. For the other countries, food consumption had an upward trend, although there was also a decline in Norway in 1980-82. Relative prices have tended to fall in Denmark since the beginning of the 70's, and have fluctuated up and down in Norway and Finland. In Sweden, there was a sharp increase in prices in the beginning of the 60's, since when the trend has been in general downwards. In general, however, except for Denmark and the one sharp increase in Sweden, there are only small variations in the relative prices.

It seems likely that the upward trend in total food consumption in Finland,

[4] Total private consumption fell by 0.3 percent in Denmark and by 0.1 percent in Sweden. The growth rate fell in Finland and Norway during the same time period.

Norway and Sweden is mainly due to the increase in the standard of living. In Sweden, the changes in food consumption seem to have been strongly affected by changes in income, in particular the decline in food consumption between 1976 and 1982 was accompanied by a decline in total consumption. In Denmark the declining relative prices appear to have also contributed to the strong growth in food consumption as well as a sharp drop in its budget share. The decline in total consumption during this long period was most marked in Denmark and Sweden, though the growth rate also declined in the other countries.

The budget shares of *total food consumption* are found in Chart 21. These have declined more or less continuously for all countries during the period of observation. This is to be expected, since food must be considered a necessity and incomes have increased during this period. Note that the decline has been most marked for Denmark. The high budget share for Finland, and the low share for Sweden in the beginning of the period, also agree with our preconception of the relative wealth of the Nordic countries.

Restaurants and Cafés (Charts 3 and 21)

There has been a large increase in the relative price of *restaurants and cafés* in all countries, with the exception of Denmark since the late 60's. Nevertheless, consumption increased in all countries except for Sweden, which exhibited the largest price rise. For the period 1963-1988 the *AAGR* was positive for Finland[5] (4.4 percent), Norway (2.4 percent) and Denmark (2.2 percent). The decline in Sweden was 0.4 percent. The short-run price changes are also reflected in consumption changes, which can be particularly seen for Finland, Norway and Sweden. The price declines in Finland 1980 and Norway 1979-80 were accompanied by increases in consumption, while the sharp price increase in Sweden 1974-77 was followed by a marked decline in consumption. It should also be noted that the growth in consumption decreased substantially in all countries during the stagnation period 1976-1982.

The budget share for *restaurants and cafés*, as a proportion of *total food*, shows an upward trend in all countries, indicating its luxury character. The upward trend is strongest in Finland and weakest in Sweden, which probably reflects that Finland is catching up with the standard of living in the other Nordic countries, particularly with Sweden. The weak upward trend in Sweden is due to the relatively slow growth of income and the relatively high increases in prices. As can be seen from Chart 21, the budget shares at the end of the period are highest in Denmark and Finland (over 20 percent) and lowest in Norway and Sweden (about 15 percent).

[5] The Finnish real consumption scales have been modified slightly in Charts 3 and 4 to improve the visual configuration. The changes are minor and do not affect comparisons.

Food-at-Home (*Chart 4*)

The development of consumption of *food-at-home* shows an upward trend in all countries, which flattened out in Sweden, however, in the middle of the 70's. For the period 1963-1988 the *AAGR* was 1.7 percent in Finland, 1.3 percent in Norway, 1.0 percent in Denmark and 0.7 percent in Sweden. Relative prices declined in Denmark, Finland and Sweden, but rose slightly in Norway. The decline has been quite sharp in Denmark since the middle of the 70's, when the influence of Denmark's membership of the EEC began to take effect. Comparing the peaks and troughs in prices and consumption, some short-run consumption changes may be traced to corresponding changes in relative prices. In particular, the peaks in Finland in 1957 and 1977 are matched by troughs in consumption, and the troughs in prices in 1955 and 1979 by peaks in consumption. For Norway, the price decline in 1980 was matched by an increase in consumption. A similar pattern is revealed for Sweden, but is less clear for Denmark. There is also a decline in consumption in all countries during the recession period 1976-1982.

Animalia (*Charts 5 and 22*)

The consumption of *animalia* shows an upward trend in all the countries. During the period 1963-1988 the *AAGR* was 1.6 percent in Finland, 1.2 percent in Norway, 1.1 percent in Denmark and 0.7 percent in Sweden. In Denmark, there was also an upward trend in the relative price until the sharp increase in 1973, after which it decreased. Note the decrease in consumption in the early 70's when prices rose considerably. In Finland the upward trend in consumption has been fairly constant, with quite stable relative prices. Since the early 70's the tendency has been towards a steady increase in consumption and decrease in relative prices, with an irregularity in the late 70's. In Norway there has been a strong upward trend in consumption with the exception of the late 70's. Relative prices have only varied slightly, except for the quite sharp fall in the early 70's and rise in the early 80's, which were followed by equivalent effects on consumption. Finally, in Sweden, consumption was almost constant until the early 70's but then increased, while there was a sharp decrease in the relative price at the same time.

The budget shares for *animalia*, as a proportion of *food-at-home*, show no uniform trend for the different countries. In Finland there was a steady increase during the 50's and 60's, followed by a decrease since the mid 70's, while in Sweden there was a trough in the late 70's. For the other countries there is no marked long-run trend. The Norwegian budget share has been the largest throughout the period, while the Swedish has in general been the lowest. At the end of the period the budget share is lowest in Finland and Sweden (about 35 percent) greatest in Norway (42 percent) and in between in Denmark.

Beverages (*Charts 6 and 22*)

The *beverages* group is dominated to a large extent by *alcoholic drinks*, although prices vary more for non-alcoholic beverages, particularly in Finland, Norway and Sweden. For the group as a whole we can see that there is a general upward trend in consumption in all countries. In Sweden this changes to a marked decline from 1977, which first levelled out five years later. The Swedish decline is probably not wholly due to price increases, however, but rather to legislative changes. The withdrawal from the market of middle strength beer, which had previously been popular (particularly among the youth), caused a qualitative change in the composition of the *beverages* group in Sweden. This change coincided with a sharp rise in the coffee price, which is the cause of the peak in relative prices. Comparing Charts 13 and 14 for Sweden in the late 70's reveals consumption drops for both *hot drinks* and *alcoholic drinks*, but price rises only for the former.

During the period 1963-1988 the *AAGR* for *beverages* as a group was 3.6 percent in Finland, 2.1 percent in Denmark, 2.0 percent in Norway and 0.9 percent in Sweden. Note the decrease in consumption in Denmark in the late 70's when prices rose, and the similar price responses for Finland in 1958 and 1974 and for Norway in 1977. Note also the decline in the *AAGR* for all countries during the recession period 1976-1982. The relative price of *beverages* has changed quite considerably over the period, which is particularly apparent for Denmark and Finland with large relative price decreases during the 50's and 60's.

The budget shares for *beverages* are similar in all the countries. This is remarkable, since budget shares increase until the mid 70's, and then decrease. The only exception to this is Finland, where the budget share also rises in the late 80's to 27 percent. In the other countries the shares are 21-22 percent.

Vegetablia (*Charts 7 and 22*)

We can see that both consumption and relative prices are quite stable over the period. There is a steady upward trend in the consumption of *vegetablia* in Finland, and weak trends in Denmark and Norway. In Sweden the trend is a weakly downward until 1978, after which it increases. For the period 1963-1988 the *AAGR* was 1.5 percent in Finland, 0.7 percent in Norway and 0.4 percent in Denmark and Sweden. Both the Swedish and Norwegian consumption seem to be price responsive, as can be seen from the chart. Short-run price effects can also be noted for Denmark in 1978 and for Finland in 1984.

The budget shares for *vegetablia* exhibit a decreasing trend in Norway, while in Finland the budget share decreases until 1974, and then increases. For Denmark and Sweden the shares are fairly steady. At the end of the period the level is lowest in Denmark and Norway (22 percent) and highest in Sweden and Finland (26-27 percent).

Miscellaneous Foods (*Charts 8 and 22*)

There is an upward trend in consumption in all countries. The increase levelled out and disappeared by the mid 60's in Denmark and Finland, however, while for Norway and Sweden the *AAGR* was 1.5 percent and 1.1 percent, respectively. Short-run price responses are particularly visible for Denmark around 1973, when prices fell and consumption increased. The huge price rise in Norway in 1975 saw a marked decline in consumption, and prices for this group are in general quite volatile for Norway, which for a large part is due to the volatility of sugar prices on the world market. Norway is the only Nordic country with no domestic sugar production. The price decline in 1979 in Sweden was followed by an increase in consumption, and similar short-run changes can also be seen in Finland.

In Denmark, Finland and Norway there are decreasing trends for the *miscellaneous* budget share. In Sweden there is a decline until 1970, after which there is a marked increase. The level at the end of the period is largest for Denmark and Sweden (15-16 percent), but only about 12-13 percent for Finland and Norway.

Meat (*Charts 9 and 23*)

It can be seen that *meat* consumption is sensitive to price changes. There is a general upward trend in consumption for all countries, although in Sweden there was a decrease in the first half of the 80's. The short-run movements are clearly inverse to relative price changes in all countries, with price peaks coinciding with consumption troughs and *vice versa*. For instance, in 1978-79, there was a marked price decrease in Finland accompanied by an increase in consumption. In Norway and Finland the general price level has been relatively stable, but in Denmark and Sweden there has been a more pronounced long-run relationship. In Denmark relative prices have decreased since membership of the EEC in 1973, while in Sweden prices decreased in the mid and late 70's. In both cases a corresponding increase in consumption can be observed. It can also be seen that the *per capita* consumption of *meat* is greatest in Denmark and smallest in Sweden, especially towards the end of the period.

The budget share for *meat* as a proportion of *animalia* increased in Denmark, Finland and Norway during the 60's and early 70's. In Norway the increase continued until the late 70's, but the share has decreased thereafter. In Sweden, there was a steady downward trend for the whole period with the exception of the late 80's. The Danish budget share is consistently the largest, while the graphs for other countries cross each other on several occasions.

Fish (*Charts 10 and 23*)

There is a large difference in the consumption level of *fish* between the countries.

From 1963 onwards, there is an increasing trend in Finland and, to a lesser extent, in Sweden. The trend is decreasing in Denmark, while in Norway consumption decreased until 1974, after which it increased. To some extent these movements in consumption were reflected in price changes. The large relative price increases in Denmark in the late 60's and early 70's were matched by a large reduction in consumption. Likewise, the continuous price increases during the 60's and early 70's in Norway saw a decrease in consumption. For Finland[6] and Sweden the pattern is less obvious, though the trends in consumption and prices move in opposite directions. Price variation is considerable in Finland, but very small in Sweden.

The budget share for *fish* increased in Denmark until 1965 and then decreased, while in Norway it declined until the end of the 70's, but then increased considerably. The budget shares in Finland and Sweden are quite stable, however. The Norwegian and Swedish shares lie consistently over the Danish and Finnish.

Milk, Cheese and Eggs (*Charts 11 and 23*)

There is an upward trend in consumption in Finland, Norway and Sweden. Denmark is the exception, where consumption decreases until 1973 and then increases. These changes in Denmark are matched by opposite trends in relative prices. Price effects are more difficult to detect for the other countries, although the large price decline in Sweden 1972-74 is associated with an accelerated consumption.

The budget share for *milk, cheese and eggs* is greatest in Finland, but is decreasing steadily. In Denmark and Norway it decreased until the middle of the 70's and then increased, while in Sweden the share has remained quite steady.

Soft Drinks (*Charts 12 and 23*)

The consumption of *soft drinks* has increased in all countries. In Denmark and Finland[7] the increase levelled off in the early 70's, while in Sweden the increase has mainly occurred since the mid 80's. The Norwegian rate of increase has been consistently large throughout the period, with the possible exception of the early 80's. There has been a large decrease in relative prices in Sweden since the mid 70's, before that prices first decreased and then increased without having much effect on consumption. In Finland the general trend has been towards lower relative prices, though between the mid 60's and mid 70's the prices first sunk sharply and then rose sharply. In this case the price trough did coincide with a consumption

---

[6] We have adjusted the scale for Finland's real consumption to obtain a better visual presentation. This leads, however, to consumption appearing to be greater than is really the case.

[7] The scale of the Finnish consumption has been adjusted, and the level is in fact lower than is indicated in Chart 12.

peak. In Norway and Denmark the price trend has been quite stable, although the fluctuations have been greater in Denmark. In both these countries the small troughs and peaks in prices and consumption tend to coincide, but without breaking the long term consumption trend. The Norwegian consumption appears to be fairly high compared with the other Nordic countries, however.

The budget share for *soft drinks,* as a proportion of *beverages*, has increased fairly steadily in all countries, except Sweden where there was a decline until the mid 80's followed by a large increase. The level of the budget share is quite similar in Denmark, Finland and Sweden, but is twice as large in Norway.

Hot Drinks (Charts 13 and 24)

There is a similar pattern in the consumption of *hot drinks* in all the countries from the mid 70's. The general trend since this time has been fairly steady, but the very sharp rise in prices in the late 70's corresponds to a trough in consumption in all countries. Note the different scale for relative prices in Chart 13, being roughly three times the standard we are using. This indicates that the aforementioned price rise would have filled the graphs if the usual scale had been possible to use. There was a general increase in consumption until the mid 70's in Denmark and Sweden that was followed by a decline. In Finland[8], there was a strong increasing trend from the early 50's to the mid 70's, accompanied by an equally strong decrease in relative prices.

The budget shares for *hot drinks* are very similar and have decreased in all countries. There is a notable exception during the late 70's when prices and budget shares rose considerably, indicating an inelastic demand.

Alcoholic Drinks (Charts 14 and 24)

Due to the state monopolies concerning the production and sale of alcohol in all the Nordic countries except Denmark, the statistics concerning prices and consumption of registered alcohol are extremely well documented. This should not obscure the fact that illicit distilling and imports, as well as unregistered legal tax-free imports, can cause a significant distortion of the published statistics.

The consumption of *alcoholic drinks* shows a consistent upward trend in all countries except Sweden. This strong trend was broken in all countries in the middle of the 70's, however, and was followed by a weaker increase. Sweden is the exception, since consumption decreased considerably after 1976. This is almost certainly due to the abolishment of middle strength beer (class IIB), which was forbidden for sale outside the state monopoly stores. For the period 1963-88 the

[8] Once again the Finnish consumption scale gives a slightly false impression, the level being somewhat lower than indicated.

AAGR in consumption was almost 5 percent in Denmark, more than 7 percent in Finland, but only 2 percent in Norway and 1 percent in Sweden. The consumption level in Sweden had returned to the 1967 level by 1988, while the consumption in Norway has been fairly stable since the mid-seventies.

Relative prices have declined steadily in Denmark since the late 60's, while showing no clear tendency in the other countries. This is almost certainly a consequence of the fact that all the Nordic countries except Denmark have state monopolies regarding the production and sale of alcohol (with the exception of low strength beer). Especially in Sweden we can see that the price level has been finely tuned to correspond to the general rate of inflation, while the fluctuations are somewhat larger in Finland.

The development of the budget shares are similar in all countries. The budget share for alcohol increased until the mid 70's and then decreased. The decrease was smaller in Finland, however, where there has even been an increase since 1985. These changes are to some extent a reflection of the consumption of other beverages.

Bread and Cereals (Charts 15 and 24)

The consumption of *bread and cereals* has decreased steadily in Denmark since the mid 60's, while in Sweden the consumption decreased until the mid 70's and increased again in the late 80's. The long-run trend in relative prices for these two countries is a reflection of their consumption patterns. In Finland and Norway prices have tended rise without this producing any pronounced effect on consumption, which has remained quite stable. Short term peaks and troughs in prices do not seem to have any noticeable counterpart in consumption for any of the Nordic countries.

The budget share for *bread and cereals*, as a proportion of *vegetablia*, is highest in Finland and lowest Norway, although the shares in the different countries seem to be tending to converge. The budget shares have declined for Finland and Denmark, remained fairly steady for Sweden while having a U-shape in Norway.

Fruit and Vegetables (Charts 16 and 24)

There is an upward trend in the consumption of *fruit and vegetables* in all the countries, especially in Finland where consumption has increased by nearly 800 percent since 1950 (the growth is even greater than indicated in Chart 16, due to the necessary change in scale). There is also a marked downward trend in prices in Denmark and Finland, and a weaker trend in Norway and Sweden. The increase in consumption was also smaller in the latter countries, about 2 percent annually against 3.5 percent in Denmark and more than 7 percent in Finland. We can also note that the short-run price changes seem to correspond to expected short-run changes in consumption.

The budget share for *fruit and vegetables* was fairly constant in all countries, showing a slight upward trend for Finland that still has the lowest share, however. The Swedish and Danish shares are quite similar, while the Norwegian share is greatest.

Potatoes (Charts 17 and 25)

The quality of the *potatoes* statistics is questionable in most countries due to the large home production that is difficult to measure. In Sweden, for example, the total *per capita* consumption of potatoes has been assumed constant during the last decade, and the fluctuations that can be seen in Chart 17 are merely due to varying estimates of public and catering consumption.

In spite of the above qualifier, we can still draw some conclusions from the graphs. Firstly we can see that the price variation over the whole period is much greater than usual for *potatoes*, only *hot drinks* having a larger spread. The year to year fluctuations for *potatoes* are, in fact, the largest of all the food groups. These price fluctuations have a noticeable and expected effect on consumption in Denmark and Finland, a smaller effect in Norway and hardly any at all in Sweden. This, however, might well merely be a product of way the statistics have been gathered. The general level of consumption has been consistently falling in Norway, while the general trend has been two-tiered in Denmark (with a sharp increase in the late 70's). In Finland consumption has taken a U-shape, reaching a minimum in the mid 70's. In Sweden consumption increased somewhat during the 60's and 70's, but as pointed out above this might well be a chimera.

The budget shares for *potatoes* fluctuate considerably about a constant in Denmark and Finland, although the Finnish shares tended to fall in the beginning of the period. In Norway and Sweden there has been a decreasing trend the whole time.

Fats and Oils (Charts 18 and 25)

There is a considerable downward trend in the consumption of *fats and oils* in Finland[9] since the early 60's, though before this there had been an increase. Approximately the same pattern, though less pronounced, can be seen in Denmark, and Norway. In Sweden, the downward trend was broken in the early 70's, and this trend break is matched by a decline in prices. The price variation is much less in Sweden and Finland than in Denmark and Norway, where consumption has

---

[9] The scale for Finnish consumption in Chart 18 is slightly adjusted, but this should not affect the interpretation. The relative price scale has a somewhat larger spread than usual, indicating that the price volatility is greater than it appears to be.

declined. A number of short-run price responses seem clear, but for the most part there is no close agreement between changes in price and consumption.

The budget shares for *fats and oils*, as a proportion of the *miscellaneous* food group, are highest in Finland and lowest in Norway. The budget share has declined considerably in all countries, and at approximately the same rate.

Sugar (Charts 19 and 25)

Sugar consumption has decreased considerably, particularly in Denmark but also in Finland since the early sixties. In fact the decline is even greater than it appears in Chart 19 due to the change of scale that has been made necessary. In Sweden there is a steady decline in consumption, while in Norway consumption decreased until 1975, but has increased after that. The effects of short-run price movements are unclear for Finland and Sweden, but in Denmark and (especially) Norway the price rise in the mid 70's was matched by a decrease in consumption. As previously mentioned the Norwegian price increase was caused by changes in world prices, and the size of this increase has caused us to adjust the normal scale for relative prices. This implies that the changes for the other countries are greater than they appear in the chart. Note that in Sweden there has been a general trend towards decreasing prices, increasing income and decreasing consumption. This can very well reflect changes in the character of food consumption, where more sugar is now being consumed in highly processed foods and less used in home cooking of cakes, deserts and preserves. The general trend towards falling consumption of both *fats and oils* and *sugar* seem otherwise to indicate a trend towards more healthy food in all the Nordic countries.

The budget share for *sugar* is highest in Finland. There is a downward trend in all countries, although there are considerable fluctuations in Norway, due to the enormous volatility of world market and Norwegian prices (the other Nordic countries are large sugar producers).

Confectionery, etc. (Charts 20 and 25)

This group is dominated by *confectionery*, but also includes *ice cream*, *flavourings*, *salt*, *spices* and *honey*. Consumption has increased dramatically in all countries. There has also been a general decline in relative prices in all countries except Sweden, the greatest decline being in Finland.[10] The short term changes in prices do seem to have the expected effects on consumption , but these are not particularly strong.

The healthy trends in the budget shares for *fats and oils* and *sugar* do not hold for *confectionery*. There is an upward trend in consumption and budget shares in

[10] A slight adjustment has been made in the Finnish consumption scale.

Table 1. Average Annual Consumption of Foodstuffs in Denmark and Norway, kilograms or litres per capita.

	DENMARK						NORWAY				
	Average					1990	Average				1988
	1950-59	1960-69	1970-79	1980-89	1950-90		1960-69	1970-79	1980-88	1960-88	
Flour and Grain	93.1	76.0	69.4	73.4	77.9	74.3	75.3	74.5	77.5	75.8	77.5
Sugar	44.2	47.2	47.7	40.1	44.6	37.4	43.5	41.9	41.1	42.2	39.7
Potatoes	120.6	98.8	70.9	72.8	90.3	71.3	102.2	91.2	89.4	94.2	94.7
Fruit and Vegetables	82.2	94.9	106.6	113.3	98.5	126.6	101.7	119.0	133.7	118.2	143.3
Meat	58.5	62.4	68.4	91.4	71.0	105.0	40.7	49.8	52.9	47.9	53.9
beef	17.2	19.5	18.6	16.8	18.1	21.4	15.2	17.2	18.2	16.9	18.7
pork	36.8	38.3	42.0	62.8	45.6	70.2	15.9	20.5	20.2	18.9	20.1
poultry	2.9	3.8	7.1	10.4	6.2	11.6	1.0	2.1	3.1	2.1	4.2
lamb	0.3	0.4	0.4	0.6	0.4.	1.0	4.5	4.9	5.6	5.0	5.3
other meat	1.3	0.4	0.3	0.8	0.7	0.8	4.1	5.1	5.8	5.0	5.6
Fish	13.5	18.5	20.0	20.6	17.8	19.4	20.0	15.9	18.9	18.2	19.0
Fluid Milk, litres	167.5	158.6	139.6	134.5	149.4	123.7	226.0	222.6	215.0	221.2	213.4
whole milk, litres	130.6	120.9	89.7	61.9	99.3	41.2	170.1	162.6	128.5	153.9	79.9
low-fat milk, litres	–	–	26.7	42.9	–	54.3	–	–	36.7	–	63.9
non-fat milk, litres	10.7	12.0	13.5	13.0	12.3	12.4	10.3	21.1	30.1	20.5	29.5
Butter	8.9	10.1	8.3	7.4	8.6	5.8	4.4	5.3	4.7	4.8	4.1
Margarine	18.1	18.3	17.5	16.8	17.6	14.9	21.8	18.2	14.1	18.0	13.0
Cheese	6.3	8.9	9.7	11.9	9.4	14.7	8.6	10.3	12.8	10.6	13.4
Eggs	8.3	11.7	11.5	14.2	11.5	13.9	9.1	9.9	11.7	10.2	11.5
Coffee	6.1	10.5	11.5	10.6	10.8	9.9	–	–	–	–	–
Tea	0.3	0.3	0.4	0.4	0.4	0.4	–	–	–	–	–
Soft Drinks, litres	19.0	34.9	48.8	49.4	44.7	56.4	–	–	–	–	–
Beer, litres	66.7	84.2	120.0	126.1	110.5	123.6	28.2	43.0	48.2	39.9	52.4
Wine, litres	2.7	3.9	10.2	18.3	11.2	21.3	1.6	3.0	4.8	3.1	6.4
Spirits, litres	1.1	2.0	3.7	3.8	3.2	3.2	3.1	4.0	3.3	3.5	2.9

Source. Statistics Denmark and the Central Bureau of Statistics of Norway.

The heading "Fluid Milk" in Tables 1 and 2 includes cream and yoghurt, which are *not* included in the subheadings.

Table 2. Average Annual Consumption of Foodstuffs in Finland and Sweden, kilograms or litres per capita.

	FINLAND						SWEDEN				
	Average					1990	Average				1990
	1950-59	1960-69	1970-79	1980-89	1950-90		1960-69	1970-79	1980-89	1960-90	
Flour and Grain	118.1	94.1	76.2	74.2	90.2	72.2	66.3	60.4	65.6	64.3	68.6
Sugar	37.1	40.8	40.4	35.4	38.3	33.5	40.5	41.5	41.3	41.1	41.4
Potatoes	96.6	97.2	71.6	66.6	82.4	59.1	84.5	82.3	83.6	83.5	83.6
Fruit	20.0	33.9	55.0	68.1	45.1	78.7	78.8	84.8	83.8	82.7	89.7
Vegetables	19.3	16.4	23.9	43.1	26.3	52.5	35.1	41.8	47.6	41.9	55.2
Meat	31.0	38.0	51.5	60.0	45.6	64.2	52.9	59.1	59.8	57.3	59.6
beef	14.4	19.6	22.4	21.5	19.5	21.8	19.0	18.2	16.9	18.0	17.3
pork	13.6	15.7	25.2	31.2	21.7	33.0	25.6	31.6	31.3	29.5	30.6
poultry	–	–	2.0	4.4	3.4	6.7	2.6	4.3	5.3	4.1	5.8
lamb	1.1	0.4	0.3	0.3	0.5.	0.3	0.4	0.6	0.7	0.6	0.8
other meat	1.9	2.3	1.6	2.7	2.1	2.4	5.3	4.5	5.6	5.1	5.1
Fish	11.2	13.8	16.6	18.0	15.0	17.4	20.7	27.5	28.9	25.8	30.1
Fluid Milk, litres	333.4	291.3	273.0	238.6	281.1	216.6	159.7	173.8	174.4	168.7	151.6
whole milk, litres	–	263.7	152.3	88.6	164.3	47.7	141.6	111.9	90.8	112.9	57.1
low-fat milk, litres	–	0.0	77.3	98.0	59.8	101.1	7.5	44.1	53.6	36.2	70.5
non-fat milk, litres	–	5.7	4.2	11.9	8.0	29.3	–	–	–	–	–
Butter	14.6	17.4	13.3	9.8	13.6	5.5	8.6	4.3	3.3	5.3	2.4
Margarine	5.8	4.8	7.9	7.4	6.5	7.6	15.3	18.8	19.4	17.8	18.2
Cheese	2.6	3.6	5.7	9.5	5.5	12.7	7.4	10.6	15.1	11.2	16.5
Eggs	6.8	8.8	10.9	11.1	9.4	11.1	11.6	12.7	13.4	12.6	13.6
Coffee	6.2	9.5	12.2	12.4	10.1	12.1	9.6	10.3	9.2	9.6	9.0
Tea	–	–	–	–	–	–	0.2	0.3	0.4	0.3	0.3
Soft Drinks, litres	–	–	–	–	–	–	31.9	35.9	44.6	38.1	57.6
Beer, litres	6.8	14.9	50.5	61.1	34.5	81.6	42.7	56.0	46.2	48.7	60.3
Wine, litres	1.4	2.5	7.1	9.1	5.2	10.2	4.4	8.1	10.6	7.8	12.2
Spirits, litres	3.4	3.7	6.7	7.6	5.4	7.7	6.3	7.1	5.6	6.3	4.4

Source: The Finnish Central Statistical Office and the Swedish National Agricultural Market Board. *Low-fat milk* includes *non-fat milk* in Sweden.

all countries, mostly due to the rising incomes; *i.e., confectionery* appears to be a luxury good. The budget share is highest in Norway considerably lower in Finland.

2.4 PHYSICAL QUANTITIES

The main interest of this book is concentrated on the *consumption* of food, and the thrust of our analysis is thus centred on categories of food as they are presented to the consumers. In terms of the discussion in section two, our econometric and descriptive analyses are based on *direct* consumption and not *total* consumption. At the same time, the aggregation level of the data has forced us to work with real expenditure as a measure of quantity, which is quite adequate for the above analyses but in some situations lacks intuitive appeal. This is particularly so for those who are interested in nutritional aspects, where the consumption of physical quantities is more relevant. In a similar manner producers will be mainly interested in the total consumption of different foodstuffs, and not the direct consumption. To provide some assistance to these readers, we present some statistics concerning the total consumption of certain specific items of food in Tables 1 and 2. These results are presented in terms of physical quantities (kilograms and litres)

Due to lack of consistent data, the direct consumption of milk and alcoholic products is reported for Sweden. The difference between the direct and total consumption is small in these cases, however, lying between 1 percent and 3 percent for milk and being virtually zero for alcohol. Note also that statistics for total production are only available from 1963 for Sweden (plus for 1960). The average for 1960-1969 has thus been calculated using the years 1960, 1964, 1965 and 1969.

When relating the results if Tables 1 and 2 to those of Charts 9-20 we have to remember a number of things. Firstly differences in the size of the public and catering sectors in the Nordic countries affect the comparison between different countries using private and total consumption. Secondly differences in the proportion of highly processed foods used in different countries also affects comparison between physical quantities and values (a lower proportion of processed foods implies a lower quantity of the raw materials but, in general, a higher value). Thirdly, differences in exchange rates over time affect a comparison of values, but not of physical quantities. Finally, differences in price levels between the Nordic countries in the base year (1985) affect the comparisons when using real expenditure.

From Tables 1 and 2 we can see that the Danes consume twice as much *meat* at the end of the period than the Norwegians, while the Finns and Swedes consume somewhat more than the Norwegians but a lot less than the Danes. In addition the consumption of *meat* is still rising in Denmark, while it has stagnated in the other countries. Looking at Chart 9 we can see that the expenditure on *meat* in 1985 year's prices is roughly the same when measured as real expenditure. This difference is partly due to the fact that *meat* was relatively cheap in Denmark in the base year. Another interesting fact that can be seen from the tables is that the Danes eat mostly cheaper pork (the beef to pork ratio being 0.3) while in Norway, where beef is not so expensive, the ratio is 0.9. This also affects the comparison of values.

The comparison of *fish* also raises some problems. According to the tables it is the Swedes who eat the most fish, while according to Chart 10 (and common knowledge) it is the Norwegians. The difference is to some part be due to how home production is measured, since this is considerable in Norway and *excluded* from the physical quantities but *included* in the national accounts.

Looking at *milk* consumption (including cream and yoghurt) we can see that the Norwegians and Finns drink most milk (over 210-220 litres per person), while the Swedes and Danes drink considerably less (120-150 litres). The consumption is falling in all the Nordic countries. We can also compare the relationship between low and non-fat milk on the one hand and whole milk on the other. The proportion low and non-fat milk is increasing very quickly; in Finland it was 73 percent at the end of the period, in Denmark 62 percent, in Sweden 55 percent and in Norway 54 percent. In Sweden, however, no completely skimmed milk is sold, and even the production of extreme low fat milk is very small. The consumption of *cheese* and *eggs* has been fairly similar and stable in all the Nordic countries.

The consumption of *soft drinks* has been rising quickly in Denmark and Sweden, the two countries where figures are available. *Tea* consumption is low and stable (again in these two countries) whilst *coffee* is rising in Finland and decreasing slowly in Denmark and Sweden. These results agree with the expenditure charts. The same is true for *alcoholic drinks*, if one takes into account the different proportions of the (cheaper) *beer* and (more expensive) *spirits* in the Nordic countries. The Danes drink twice as much beer as the Norwegians and Swedes, and 50 percent more than the Finns. They also drink twice as much *wine* as the Swedes and Finns and more than three times as much as the Norwegians. The consumption of beer and wines is also rising in all the Nordic countries. The consumption of spirits is falling in all countries except Finland, where it has levelled out but where the consumption is twice as high as in the other countries.

The consumption of *flour and grain* is quite similar in the different countries, and is in fact becoming more so. The Swedes eat the most *fruit and vegetables*, but consumption has levelled out for them while it is still rising in the other countries. This more or less agrees with Charts 15 and 16. A comparison of the tables and Chart 17 for *potatoes* shows very little agreement, however. Again, this is most probably due to the fact that home production (which is considerable for potatoes) is poorly estimated and, in addition, treated differently in different countries and in different series of statistics.

The combined figures for *butter* and *margarine* agree quite well with the chart for *fats and oils*. The combined consumption is falling, in Norway due to the fall in margarine consumption and in the other countries because of the fall in butter. The Swedes eat the most margarine and the least butter, while the Danes eat most butter and the Finns least margarine. Finally *sugar* consumption is falling in all countries, at the end of the period consumption being roughly in the interval 35-40 kilograms per person.

A general tendency towards leaner and less fat products can be seen, which is a healthy trend. The fall in the consumption of sugar and increase in fruit and vegetables confirm this. The increase in the consumption of alcohol can be interpreted in the opposite direction, however.

APPENDIX A. Real Consumption and Relative Prices

Chart 1: Total Per Capita Private Consumption (Including Durables)

DENMARK

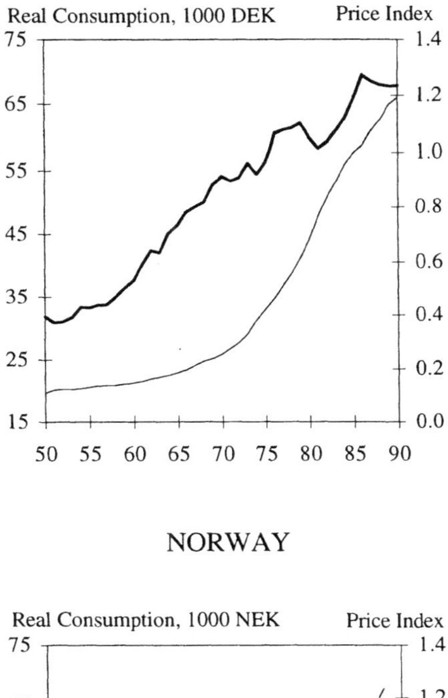

FINLAND

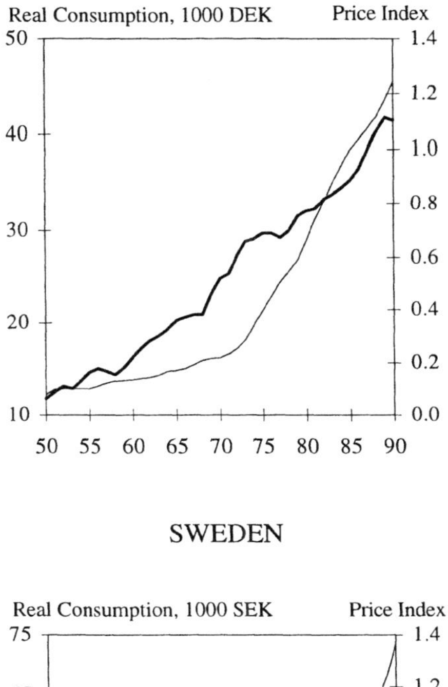

NORWAY

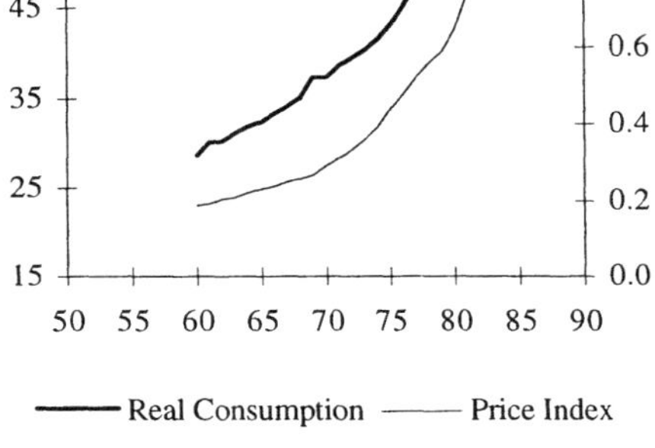

SWEDEN

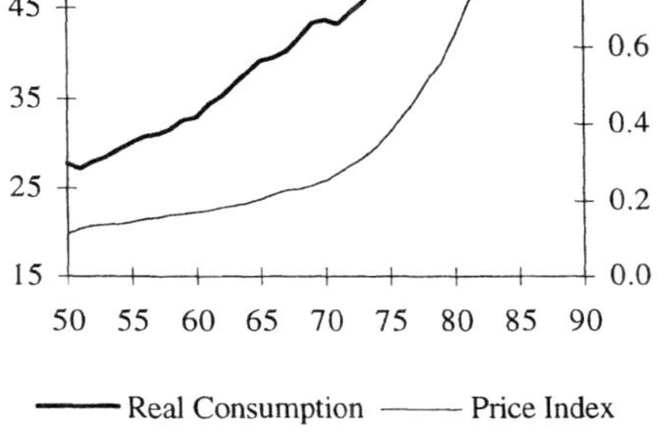

Chart 2: Total Per Capita Food Consumption

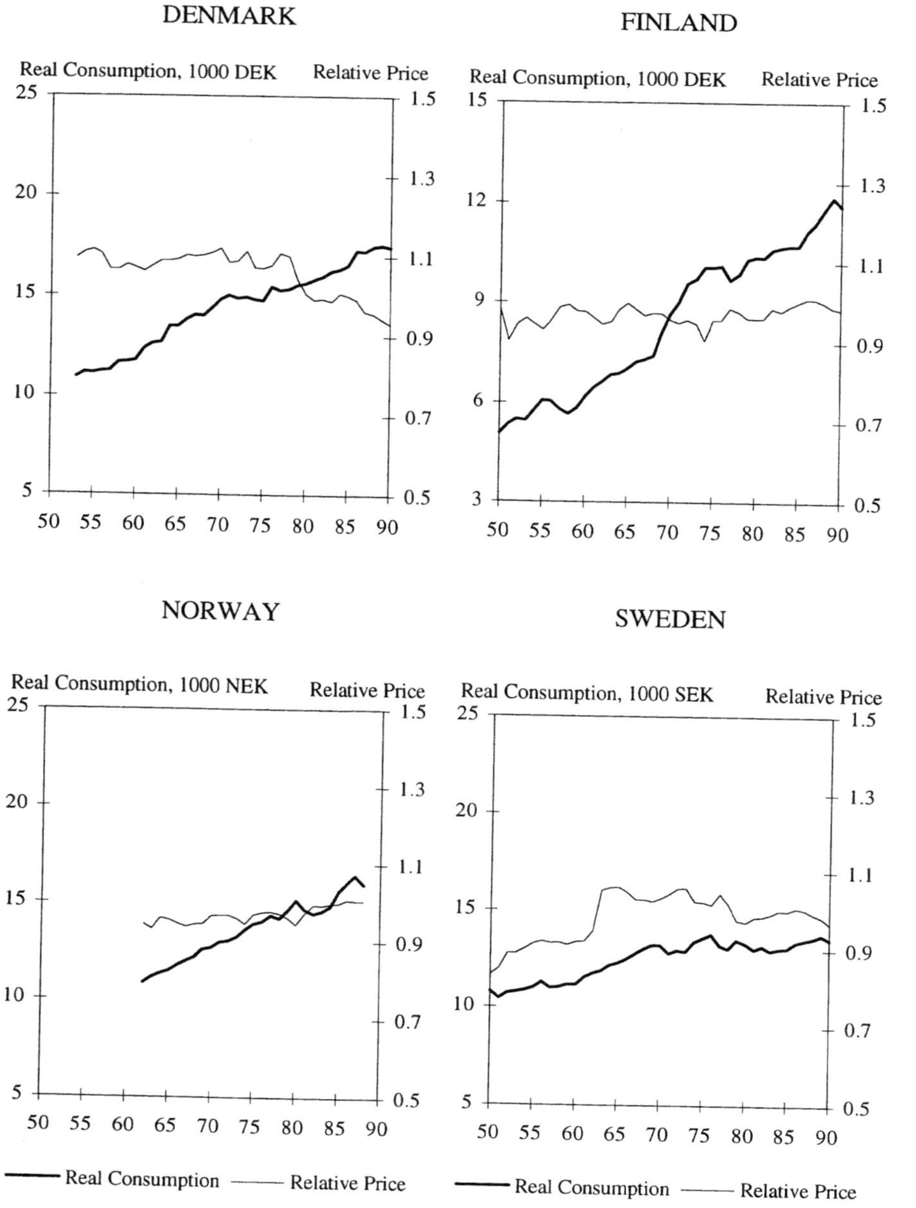

Chart 3: Per Capita Consumption in Restaurants and Cafés

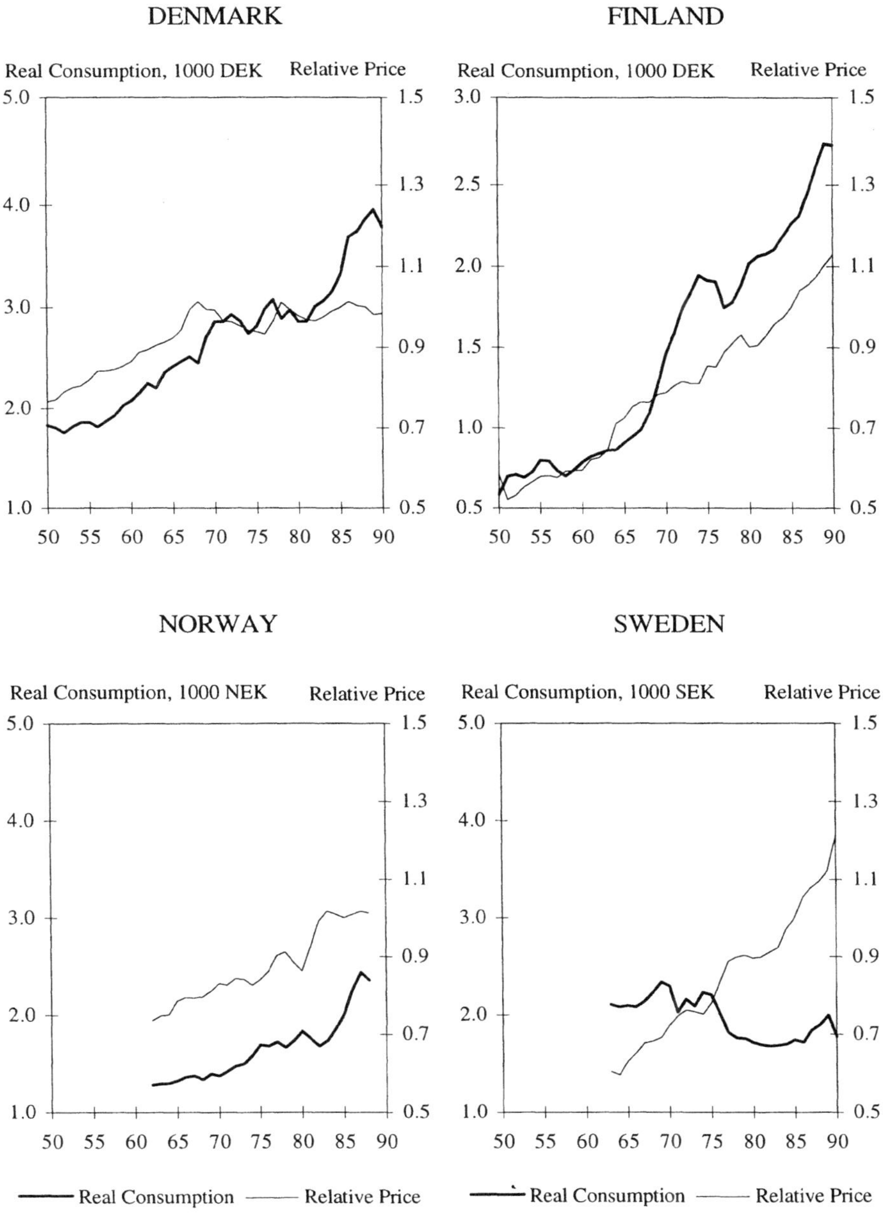

Chart 4: Per Capita Consumption of Food-at-Home

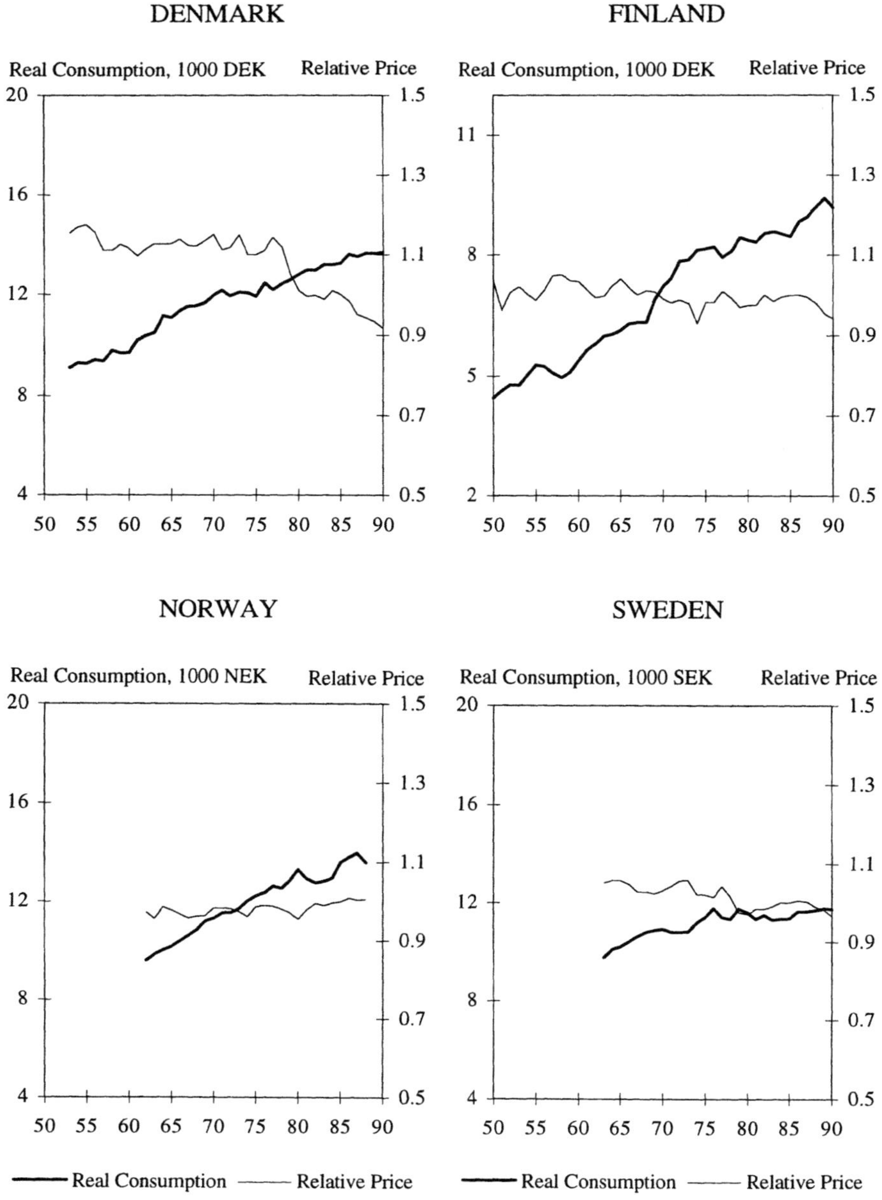

Chart 5: Per Capita Consumption of Animalia

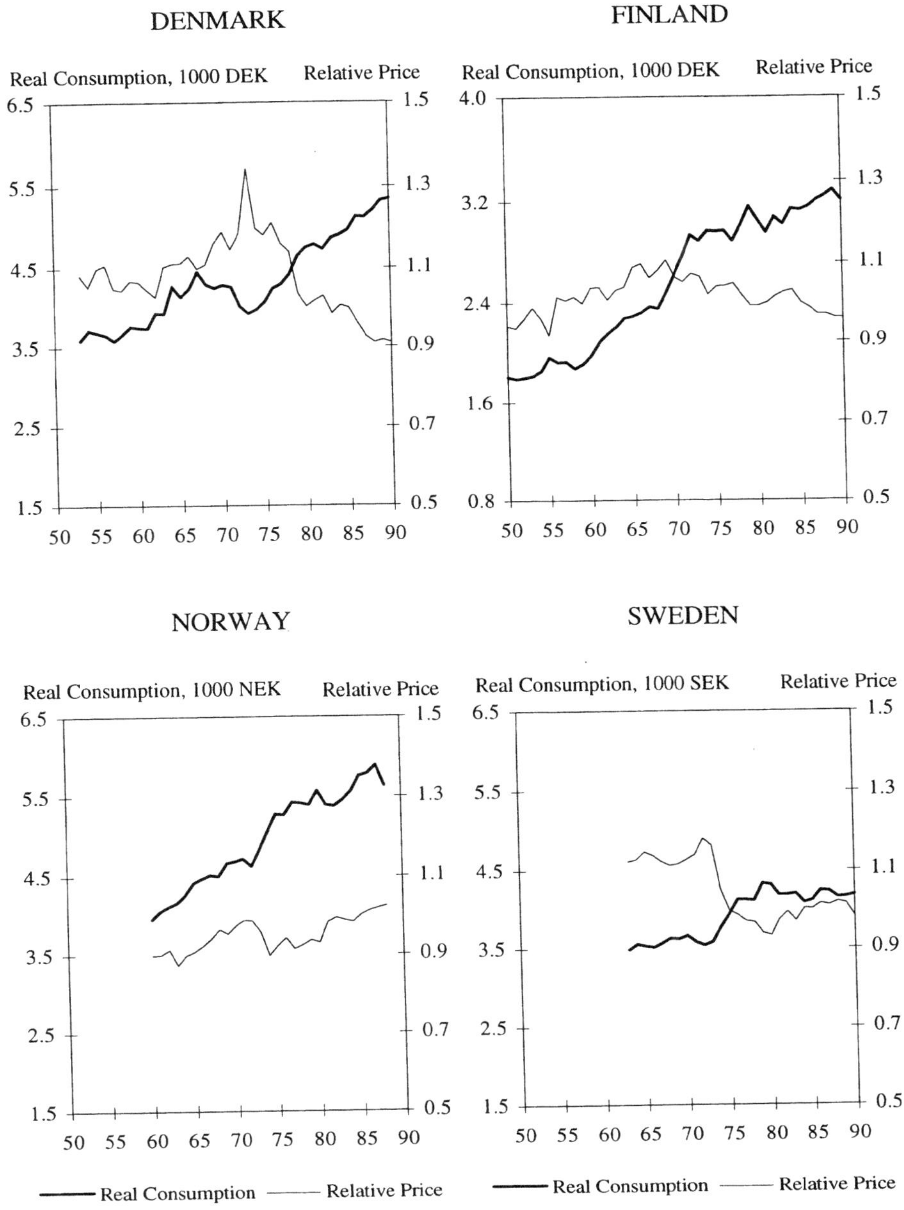

Chart 6: Per Capita Consumption of Beverages

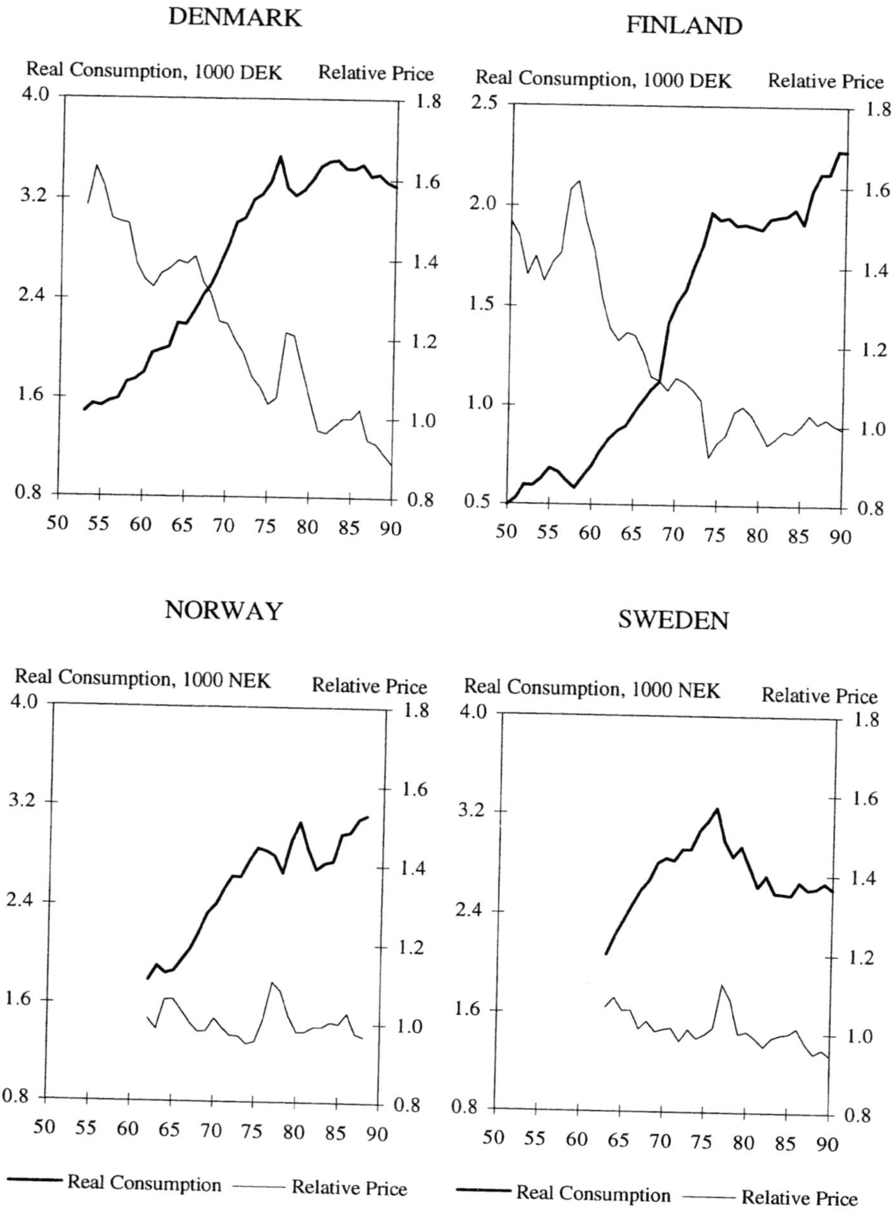

Chart 7: Per Capita Consumption of Vegetablia

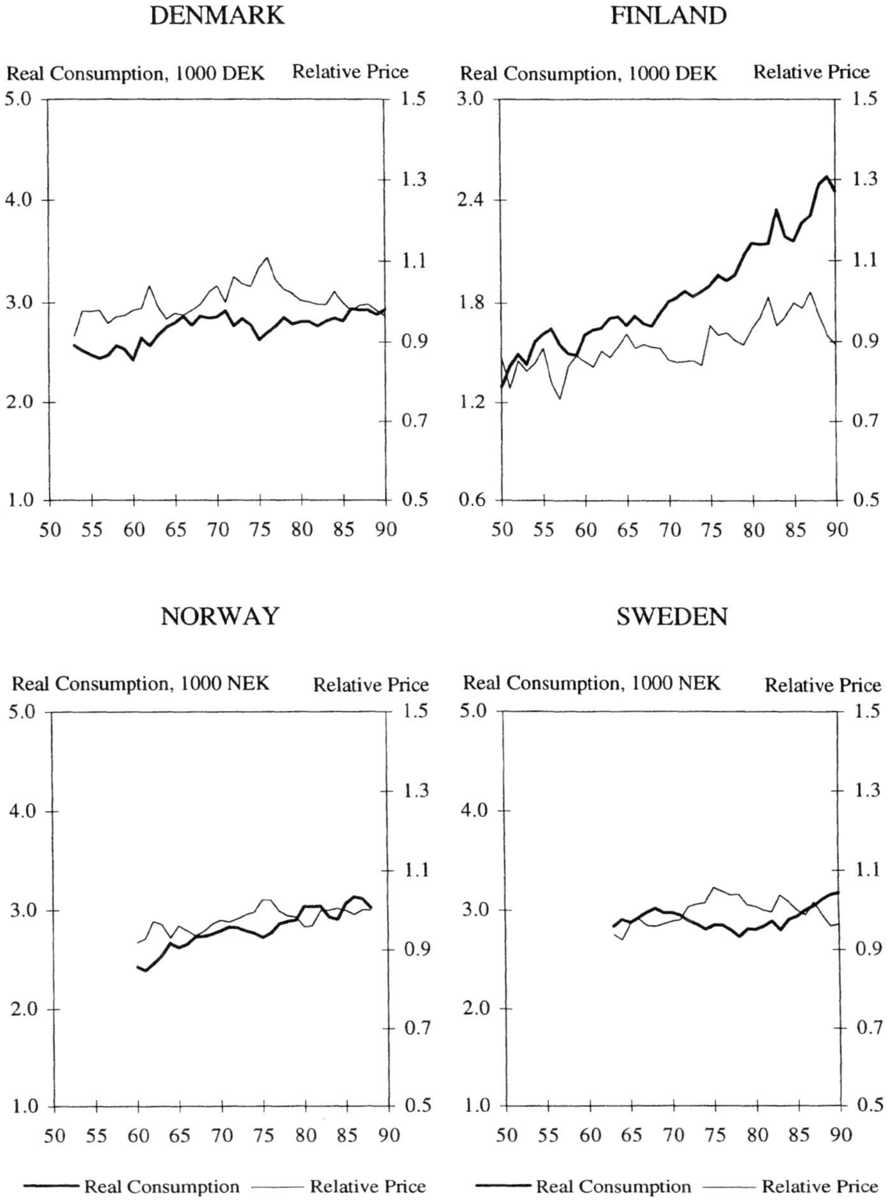

Chart 8: Per Capita Consumption of Miscellaneous Foods

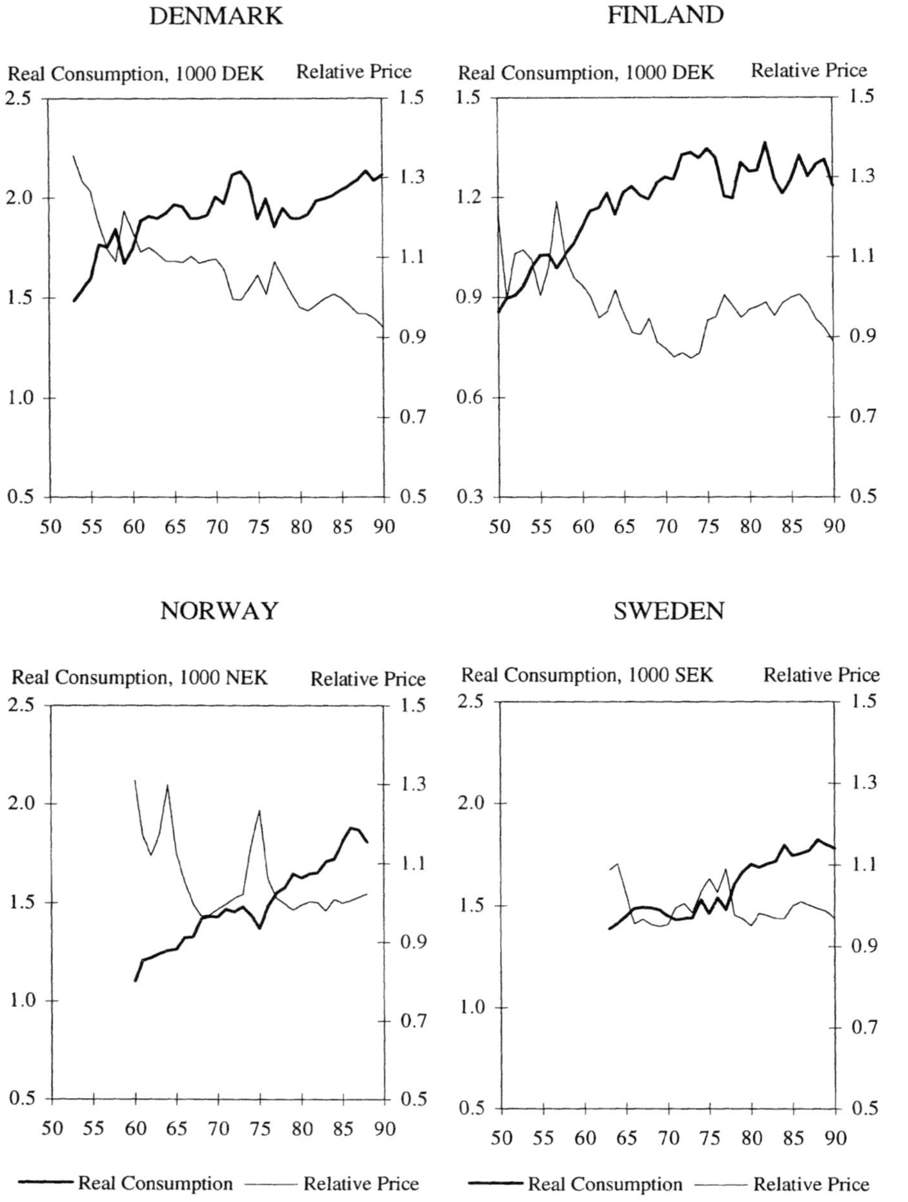

Chart 9: Per Capita Consumption of Meat

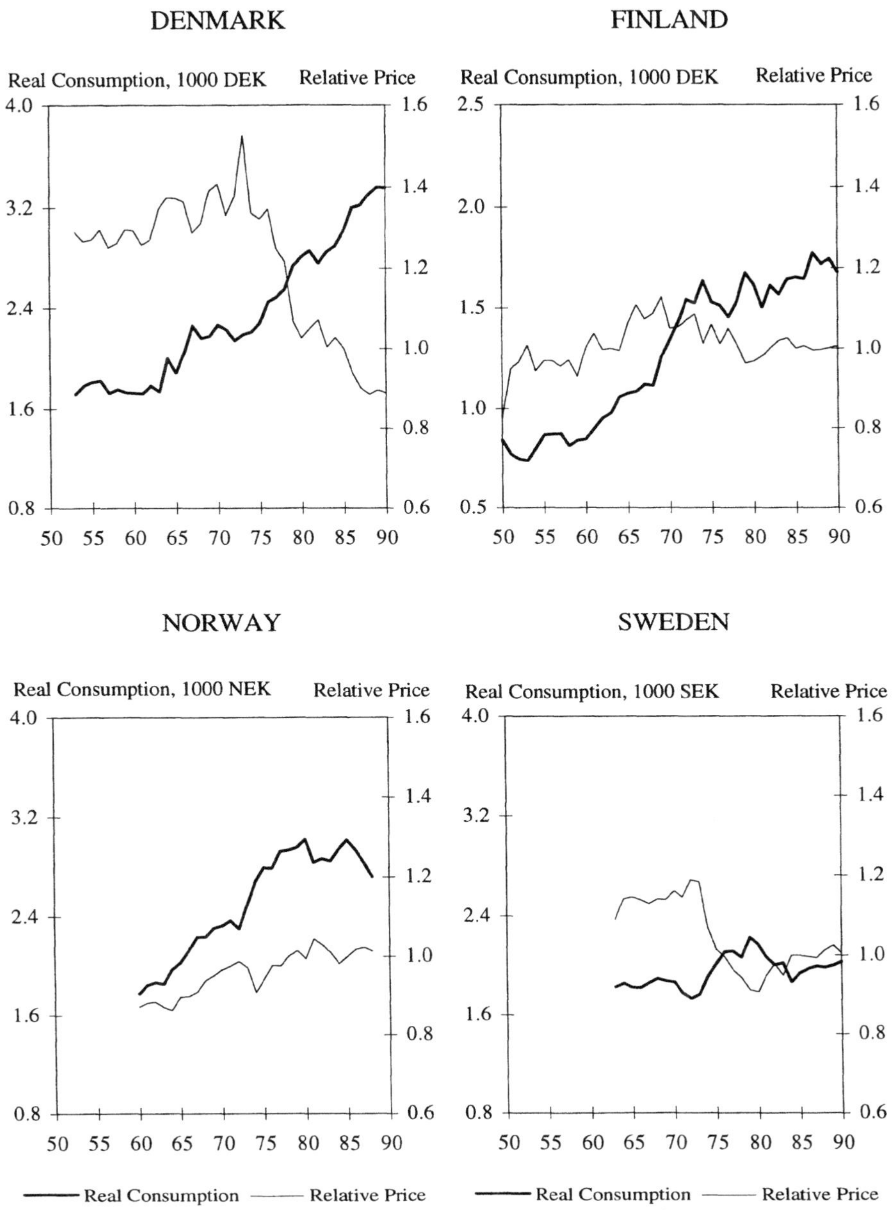

Chart 10: Per Capita Consumption of Fish

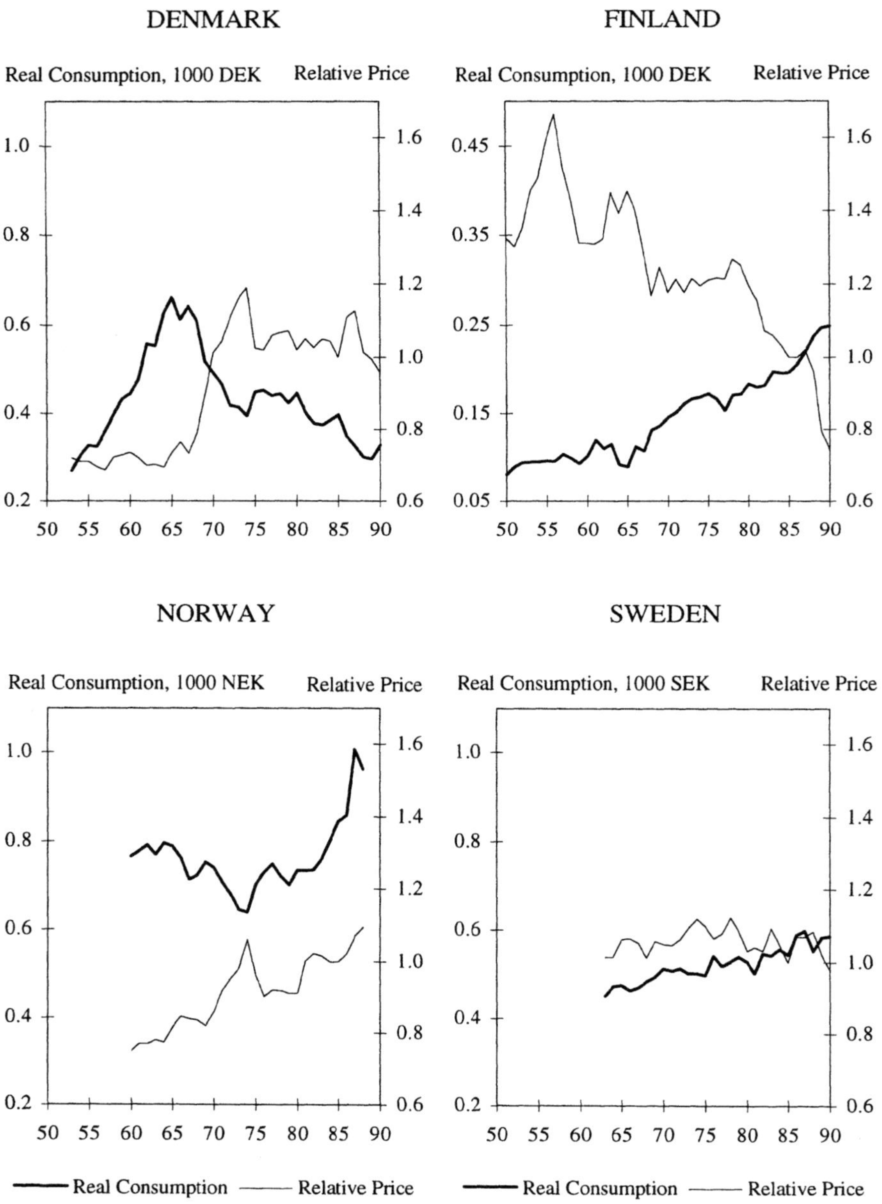

Chart 11: Per Capita Consumption of Milk, Cheese and Eggs

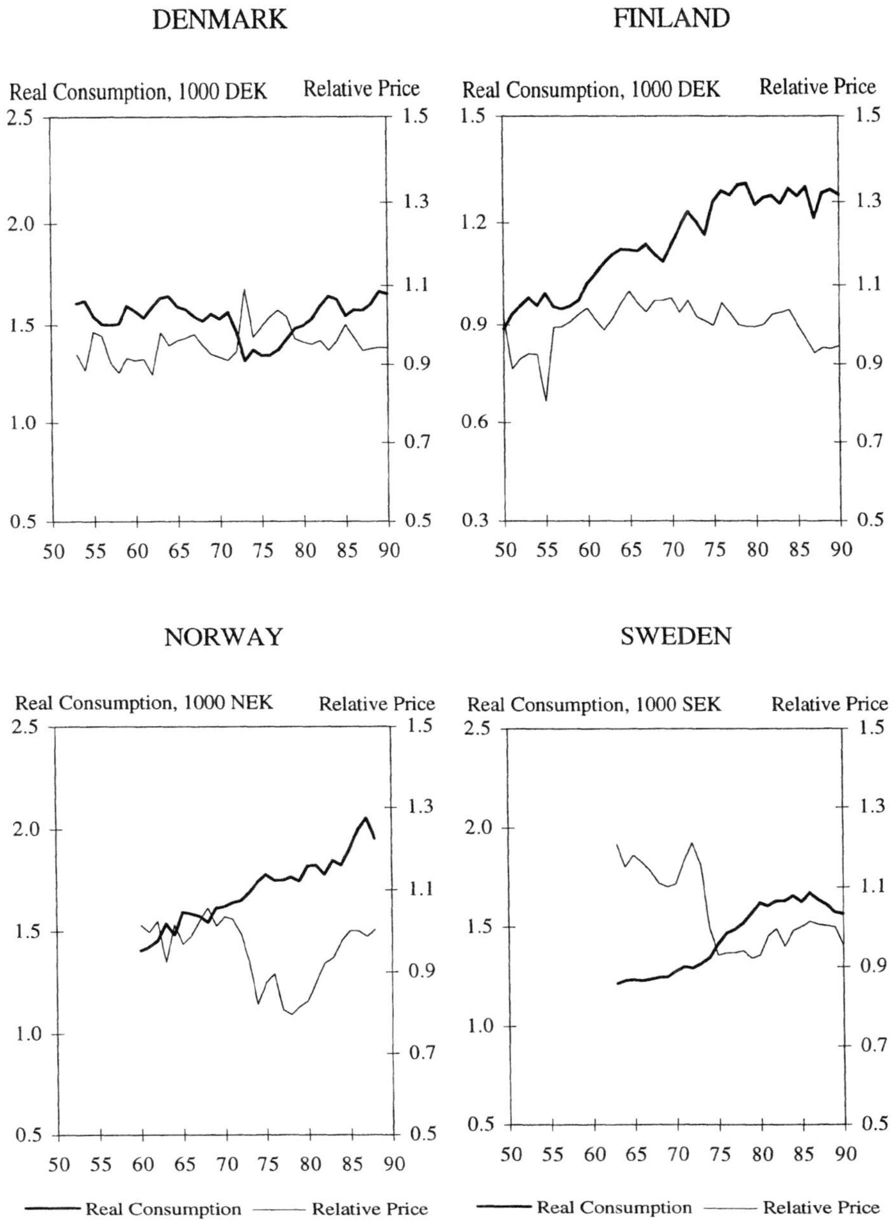

Chart 12: Per Capita Consumption of Soft Drinks

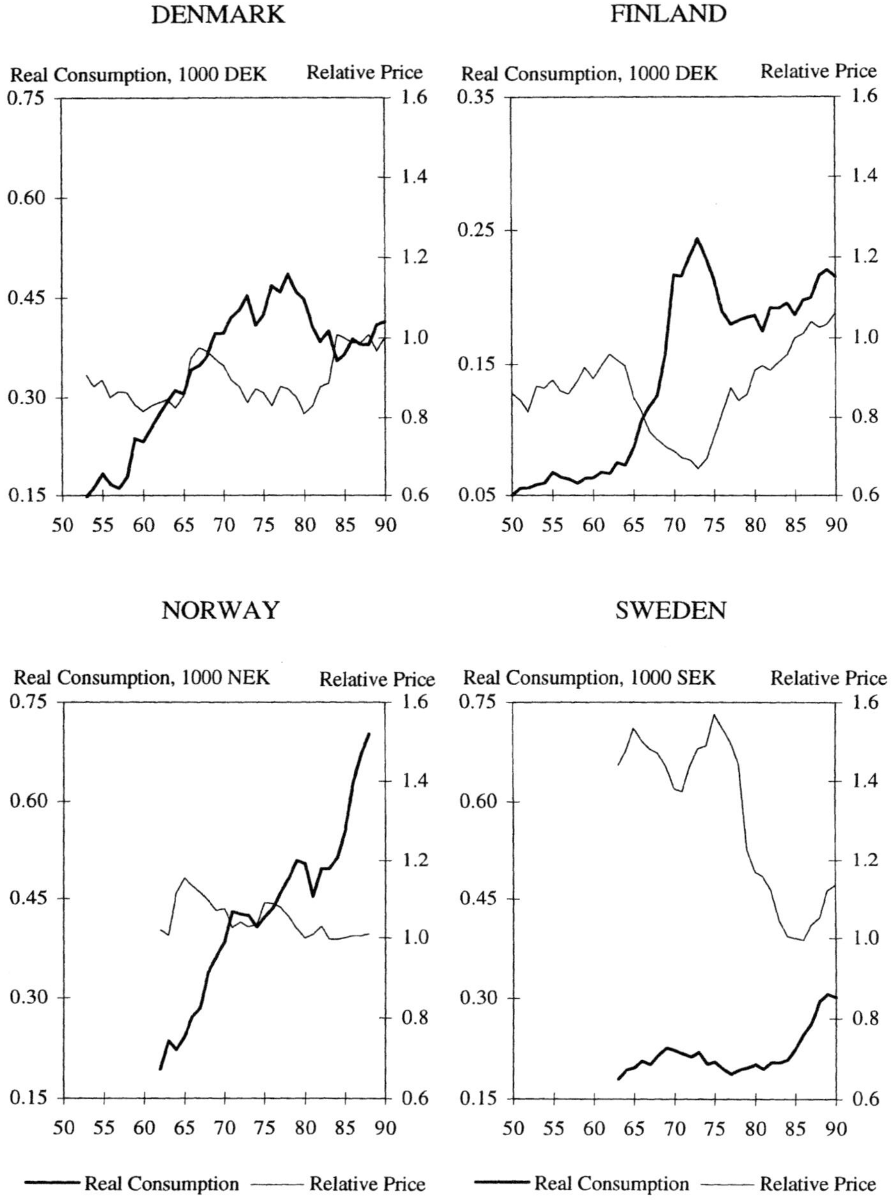

Chart 13: Per Capita Consumption of Hot Drinks

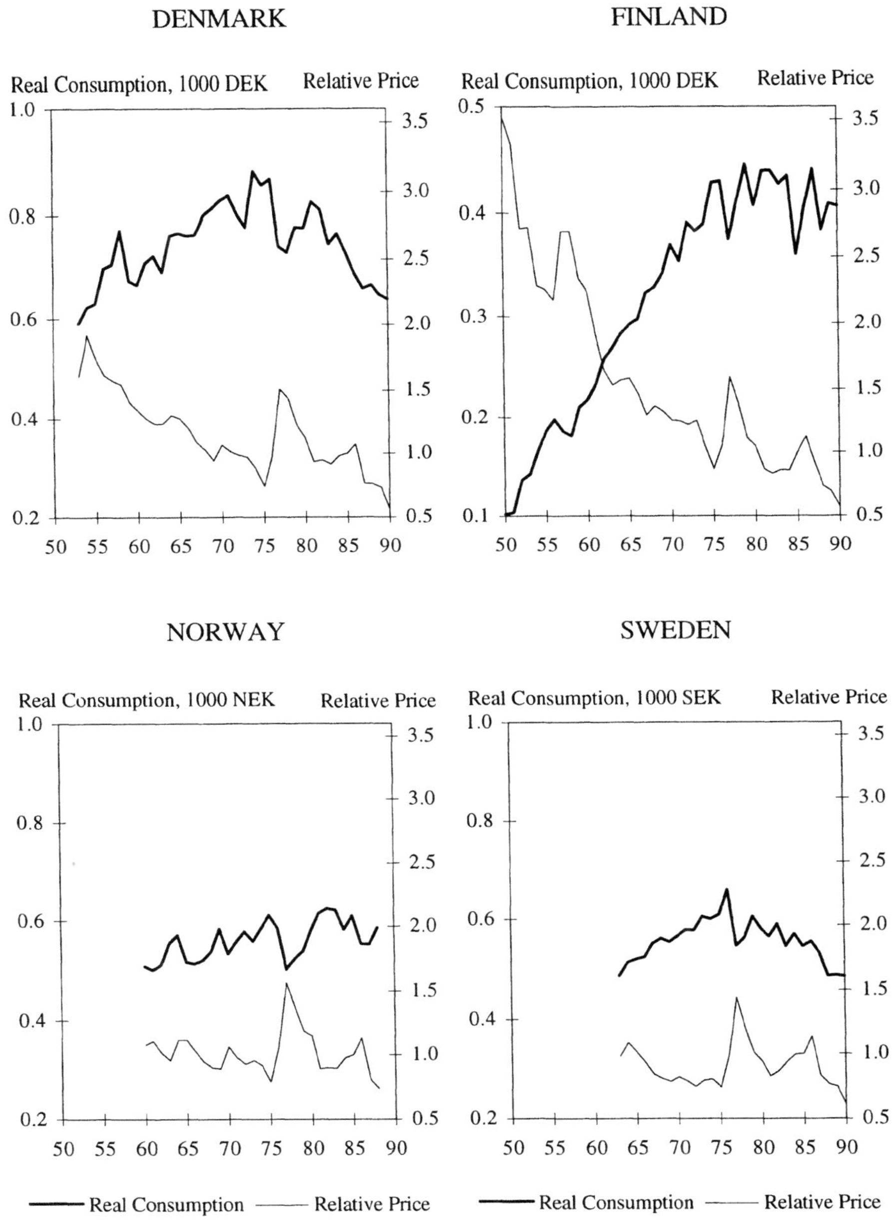

Chart 14: Per Capita Consumption of Alcoholic Drinks

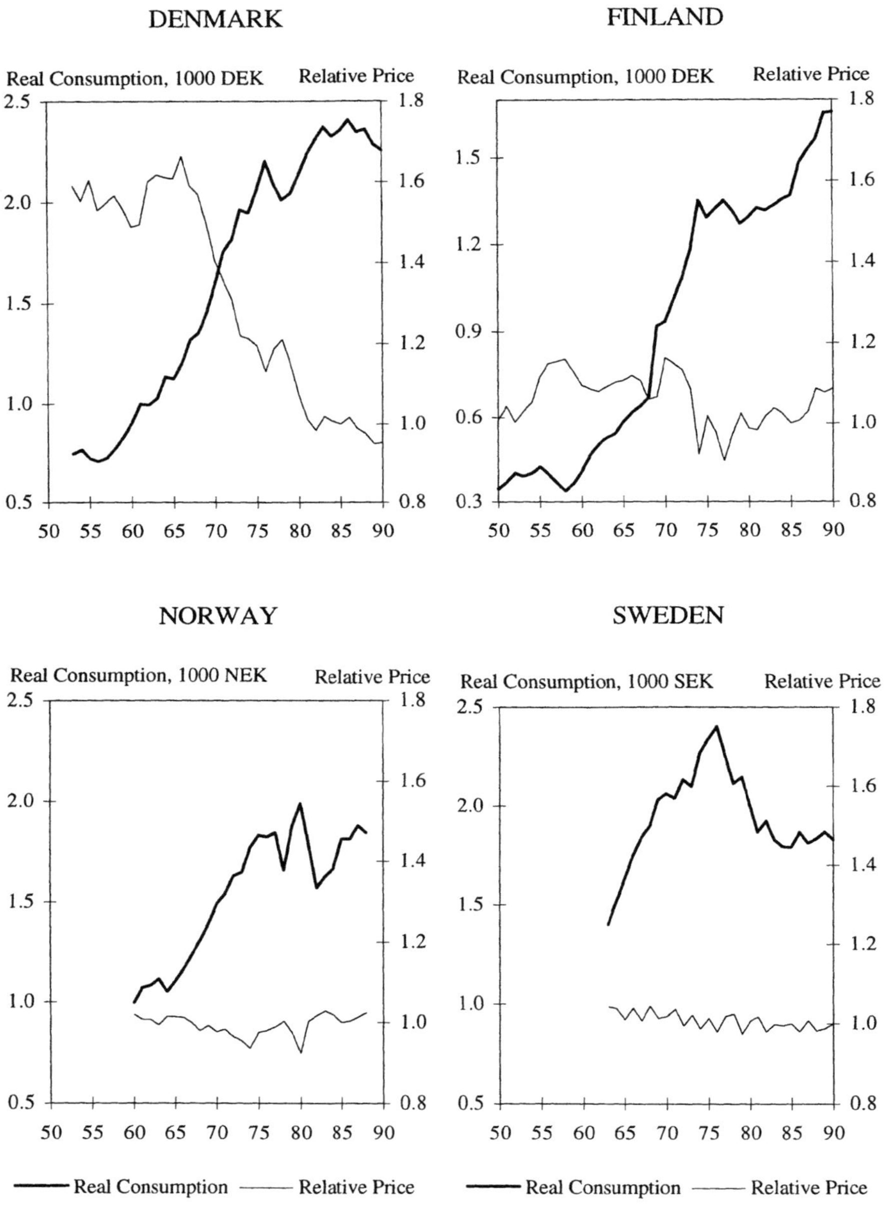

Chart 15: Consumption of Bread and Cereals

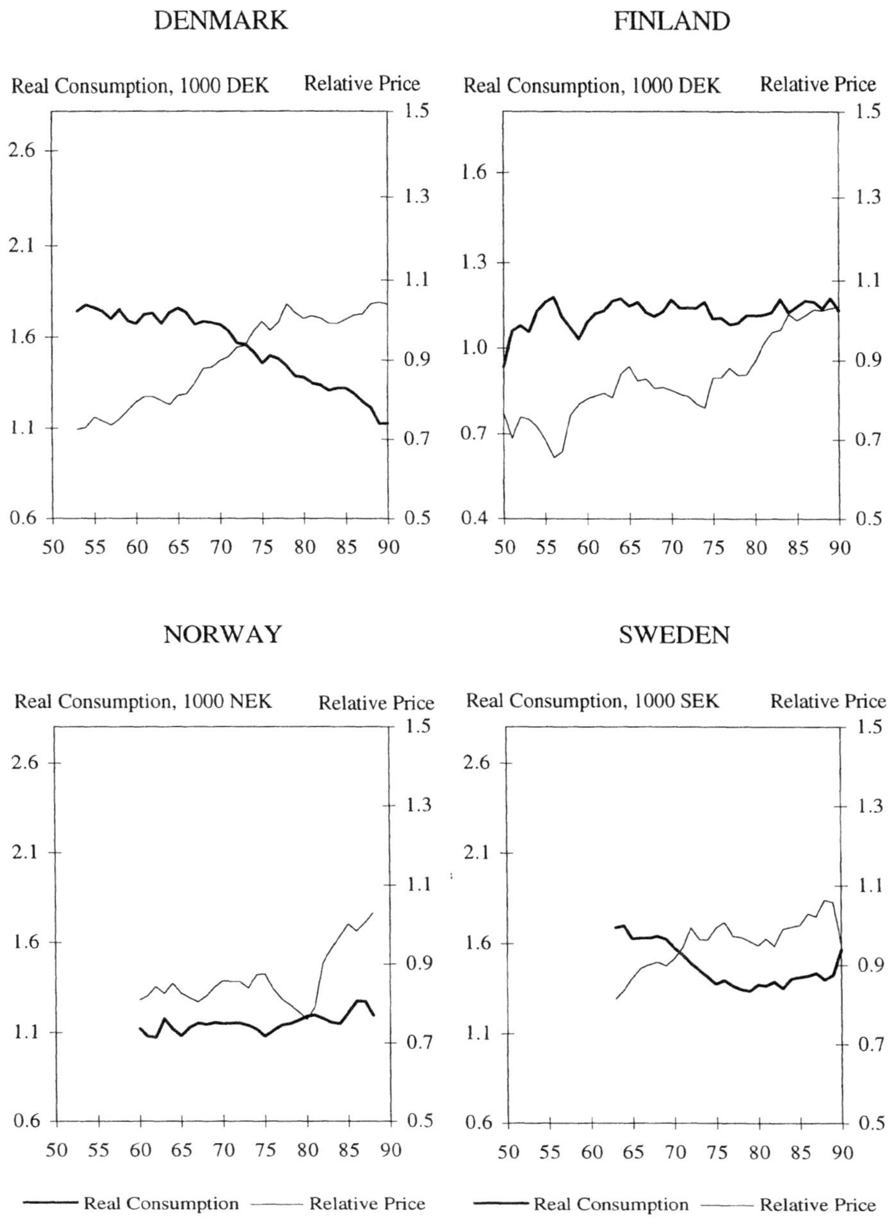

Chart 16: Per Capita Consumption of Fruit and Vegetables

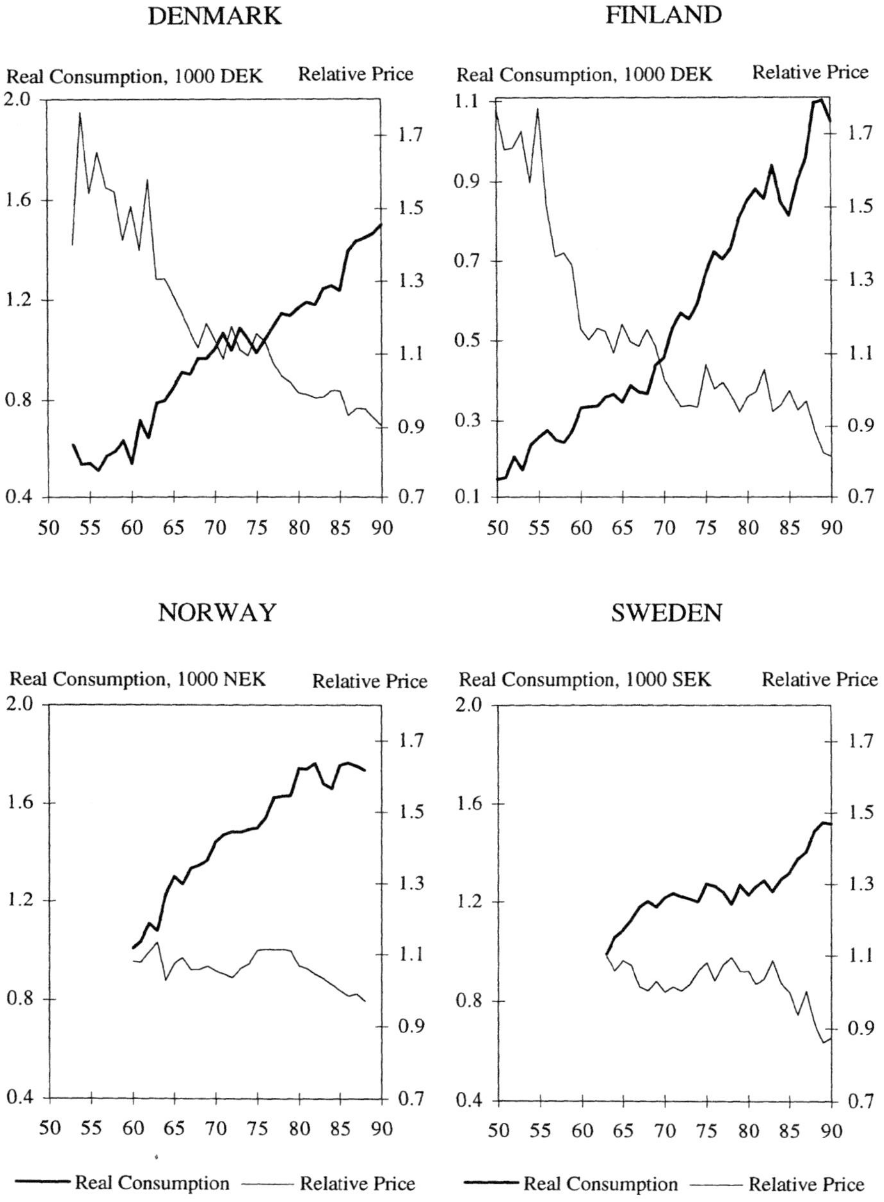

Chart 17: Per Capita Consumption of Potatoes

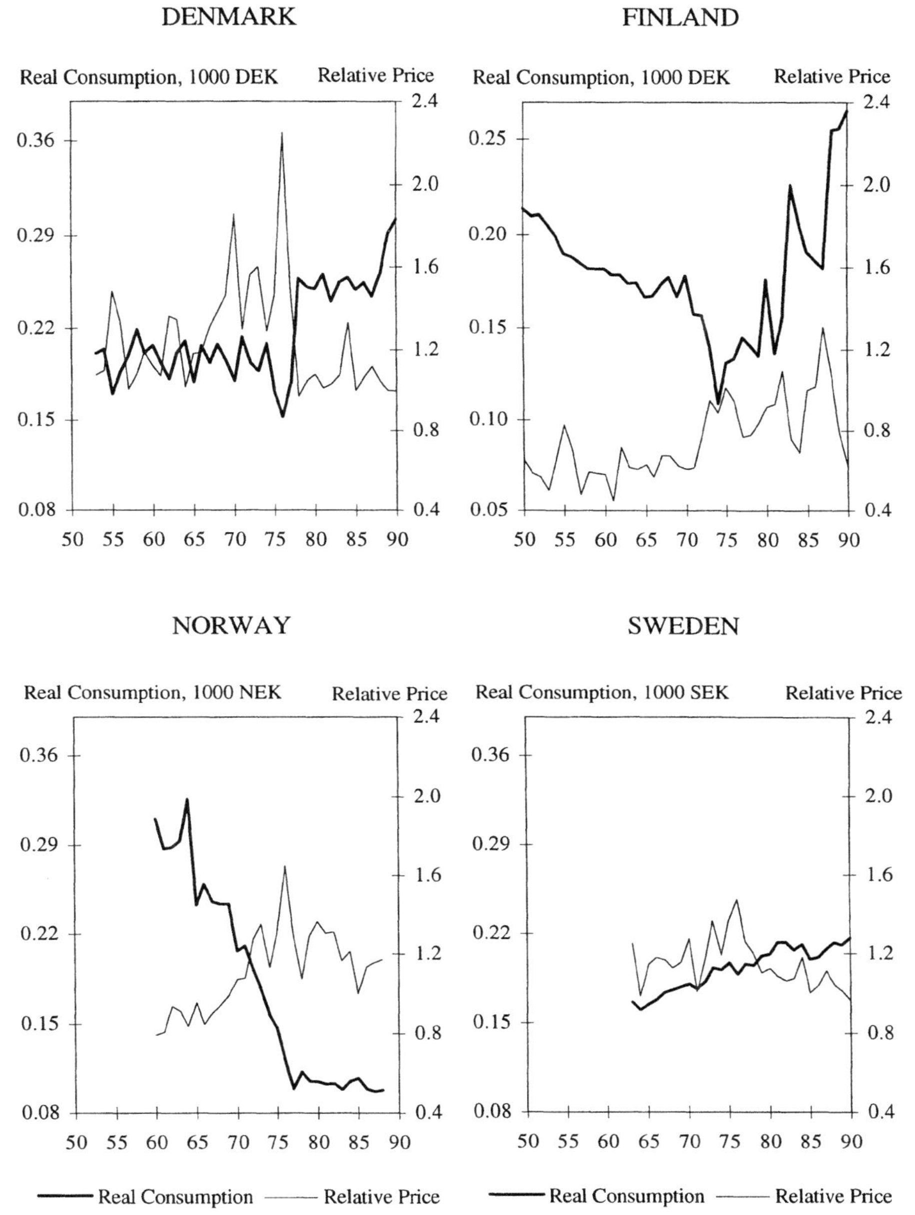

Chart 18: Per Capita Consumption of Fats and Oils

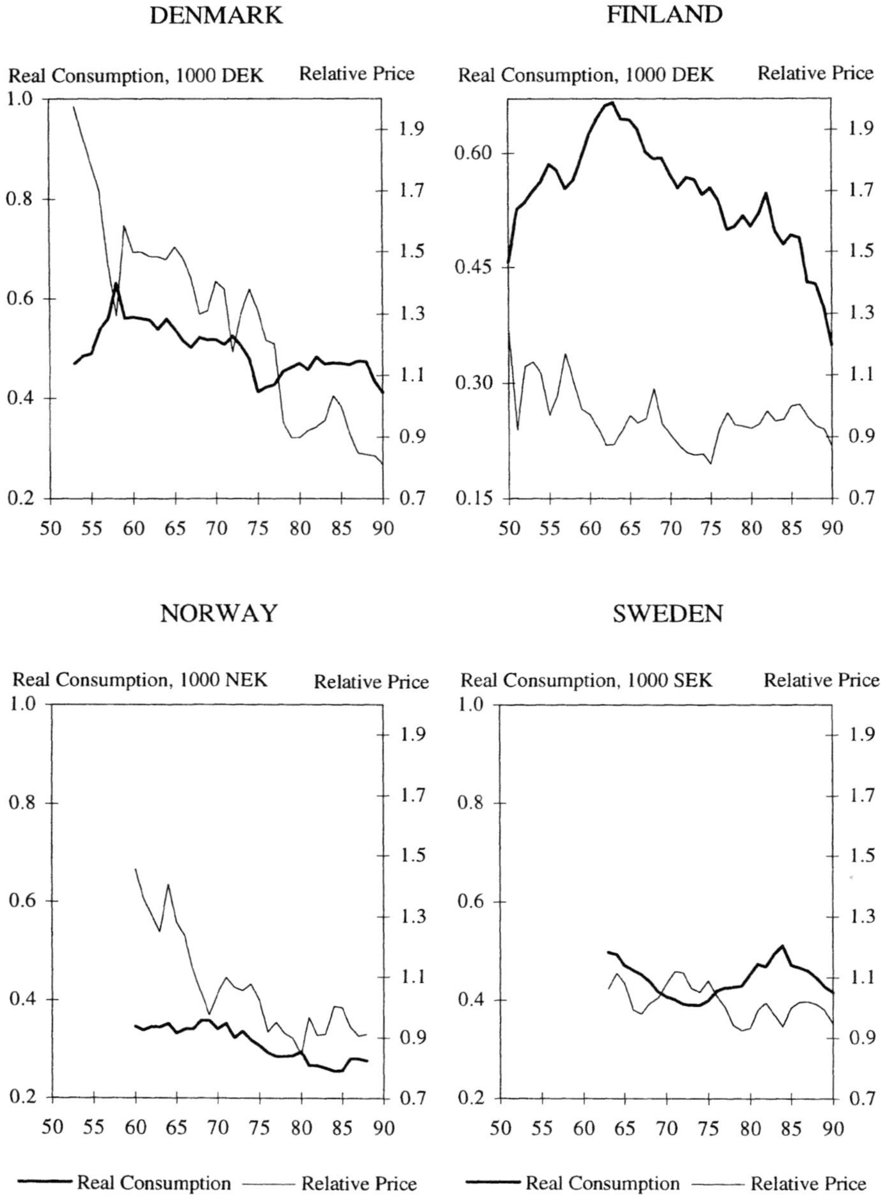

Chart 19: Per Capita Consumption of Sugar

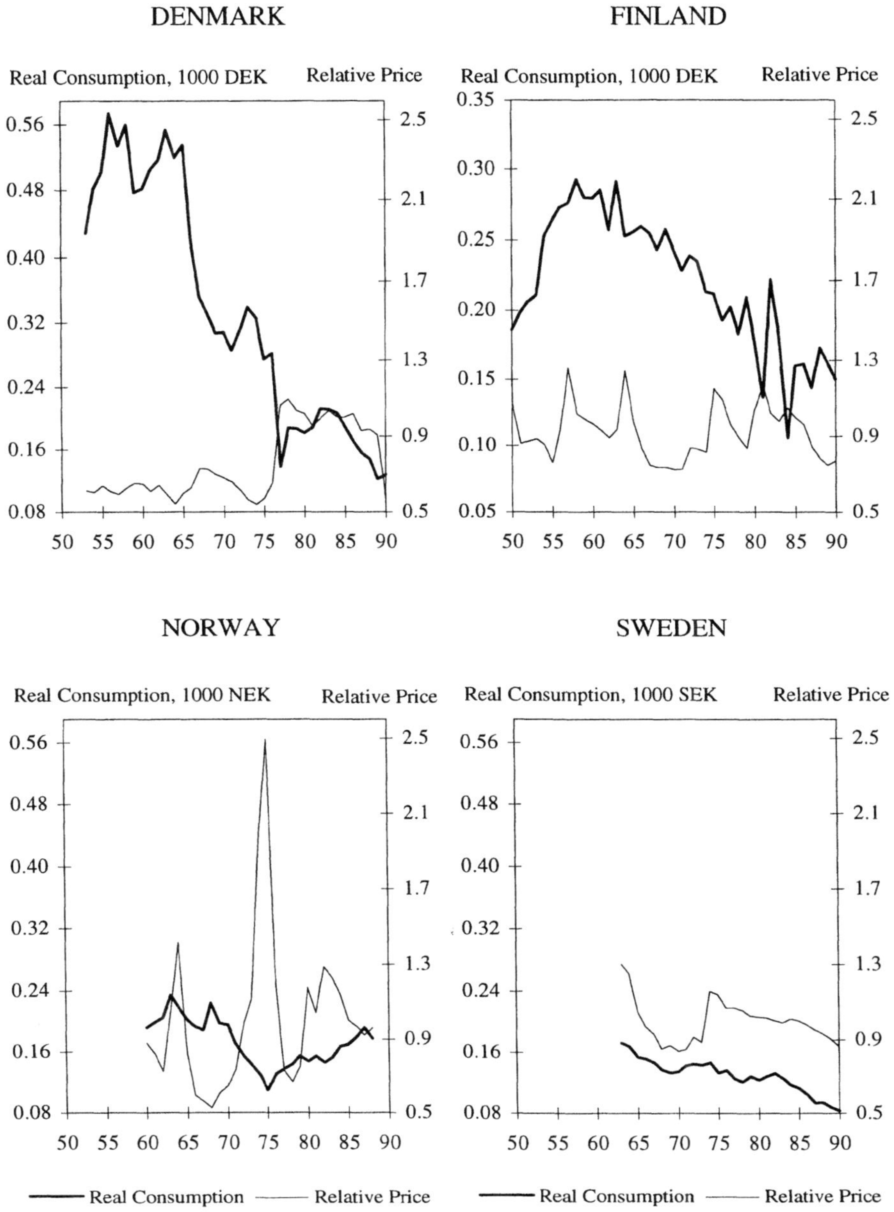

Chart 20: Per Capita Consumption of Confectionery, etc.,

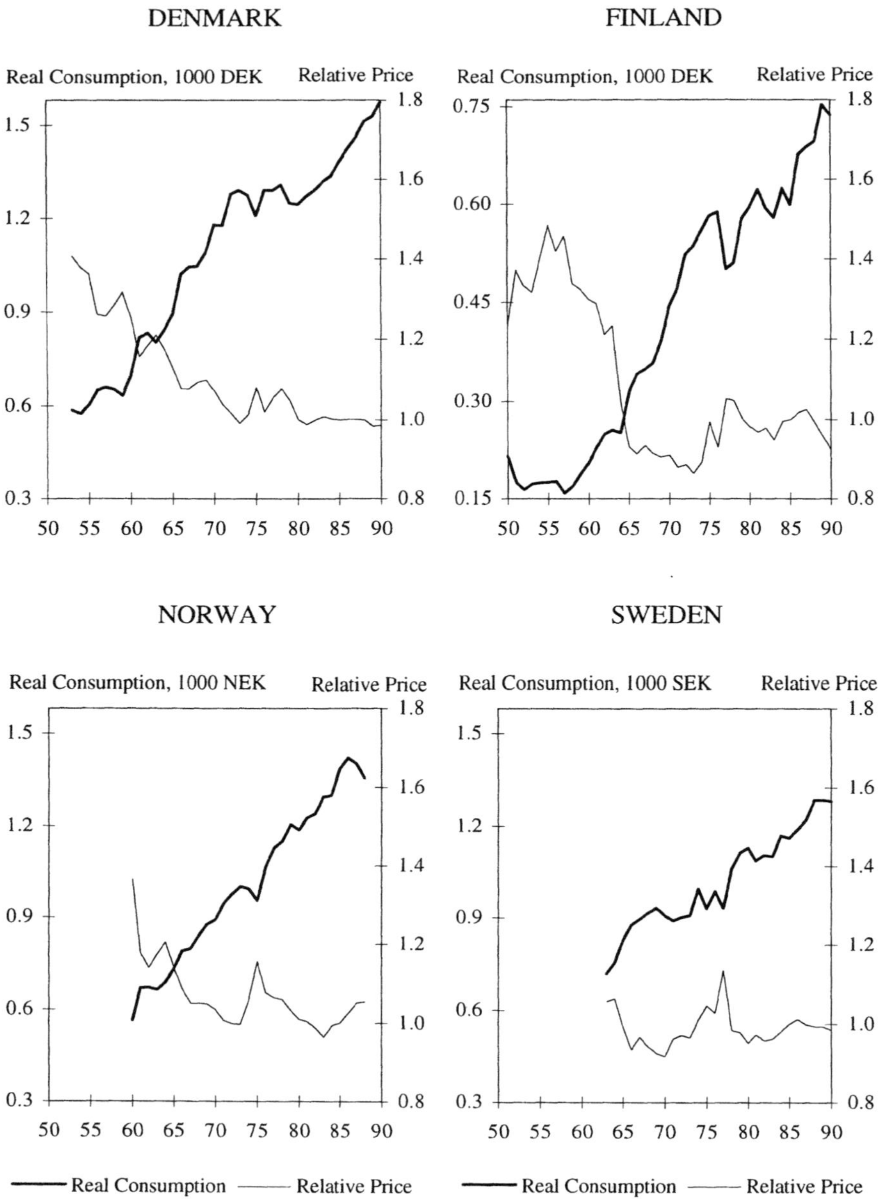

APPENDIX B. Budget Shares

Chart 21: Budget Shares for the First Stage of the Utility Tree

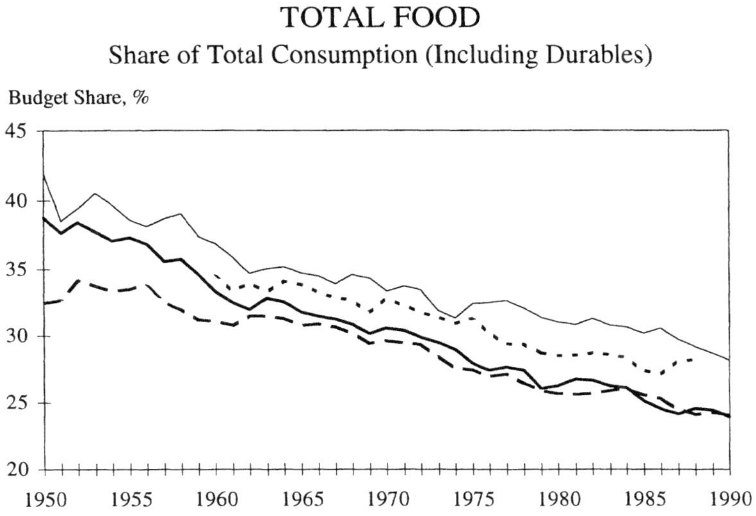

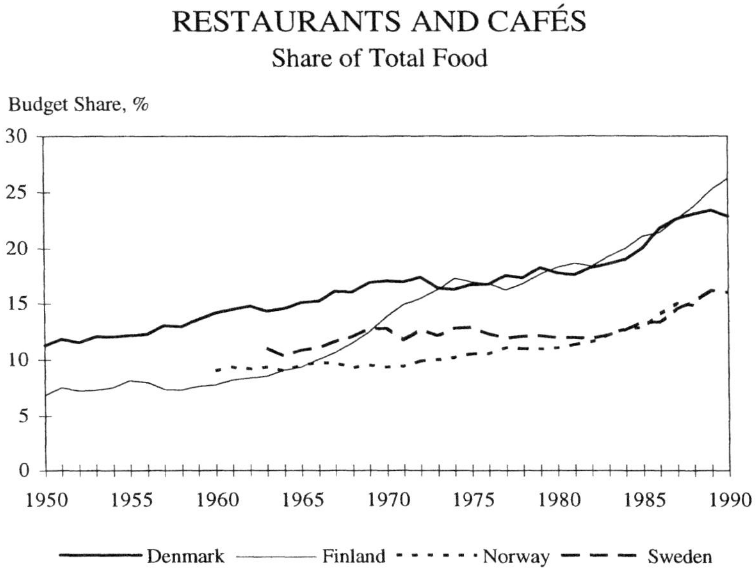

Chart 22: Budget Shares for the Second Stage of the Utility Tree

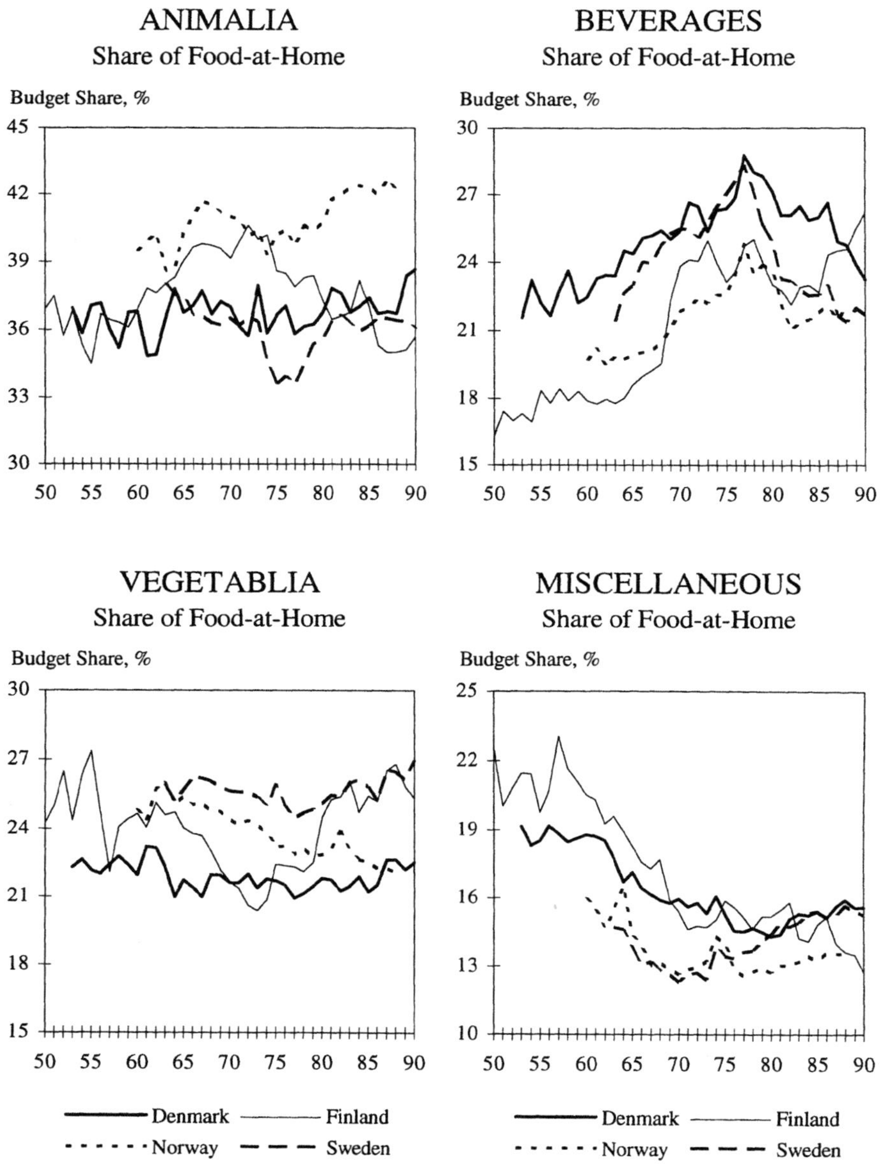

Chart 23: Budget Shares for the Third Stage of the Utility Tree
(i) Meat, (ii) Fish, (iii) Milk, Cheese & Eggs, (iv) Soft Drinks

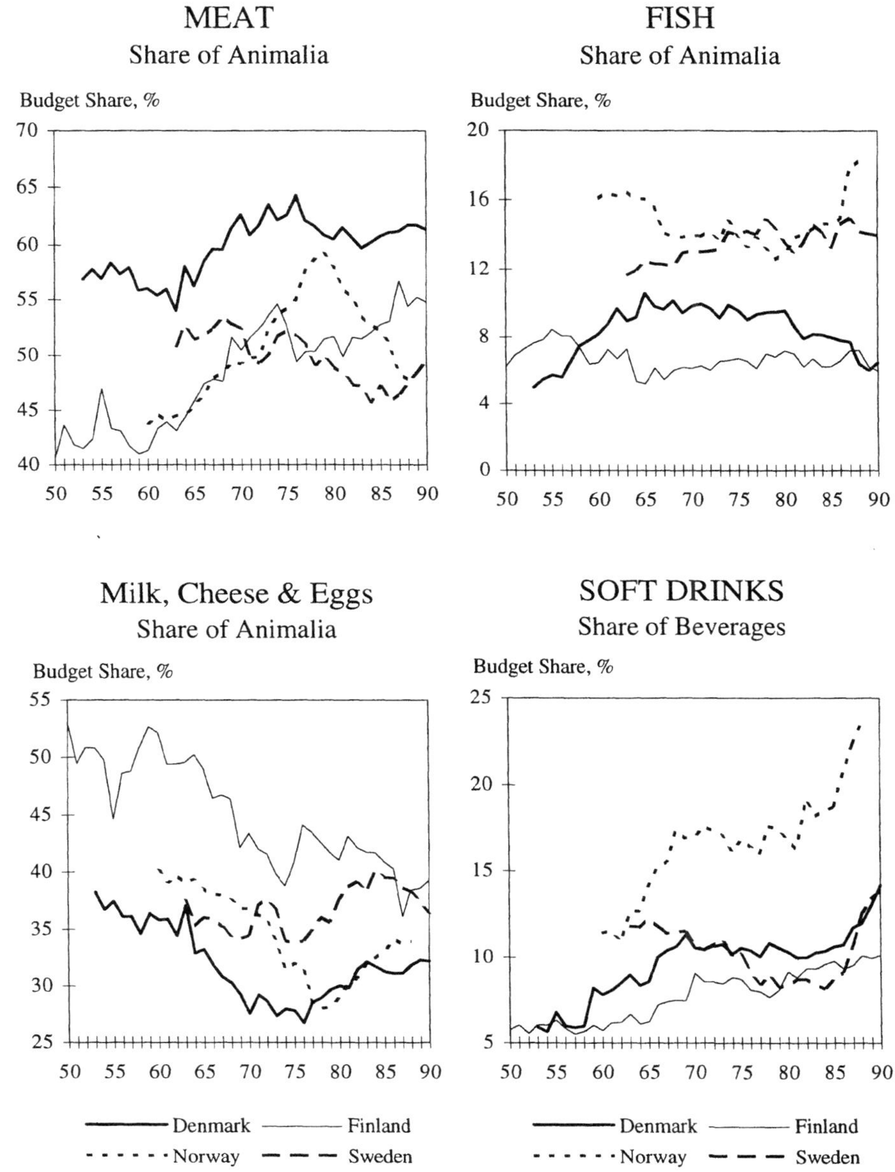

Chart 24: Budget Shares for the Third Stage of the Utility Tree
(i) Hot Drinks, (ii) Alcoholic Drinks, (iii) Bread & Cereals, (iv) Fruit & Veg.

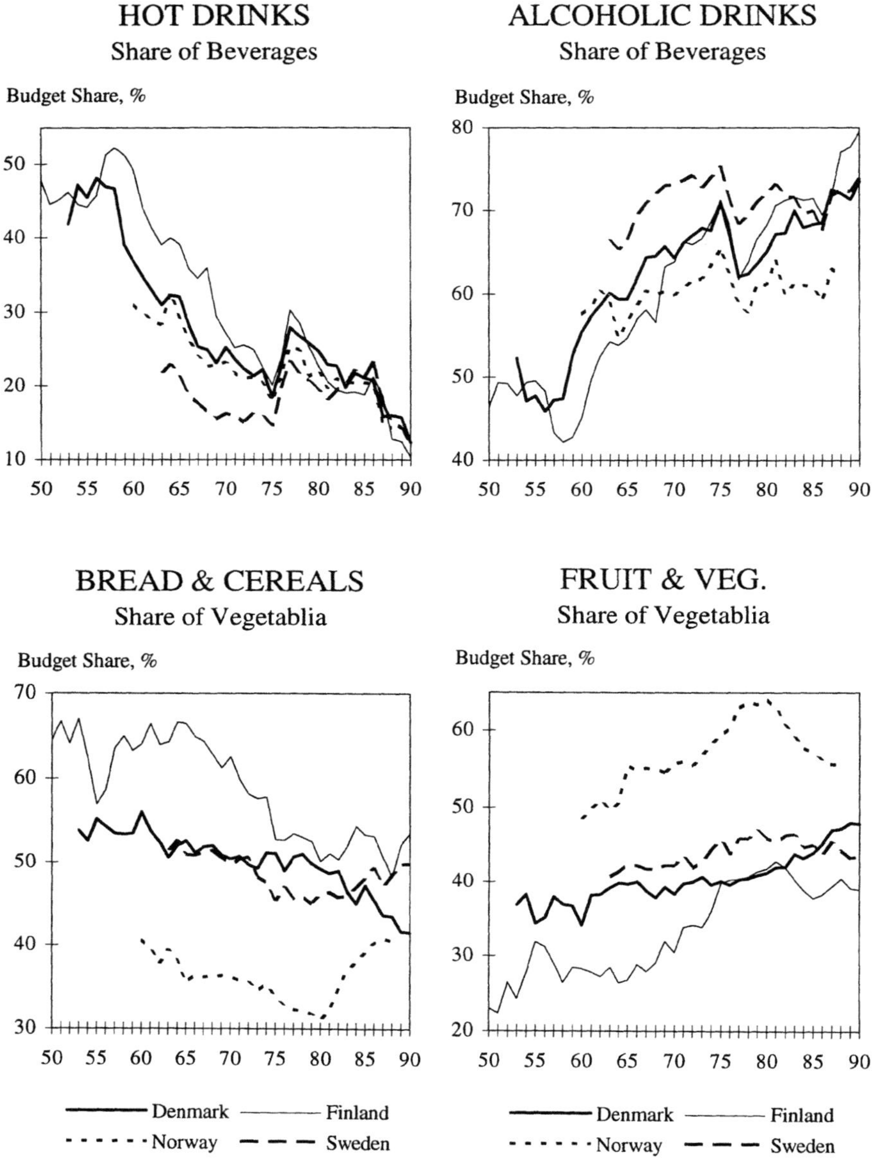

Chart 25: Budget Shares for the Third Stage of the Utility Tree
(i) Potatoes, (ii) Fats & Oils, (iii) Sugar, (iv) Confectionery etc.

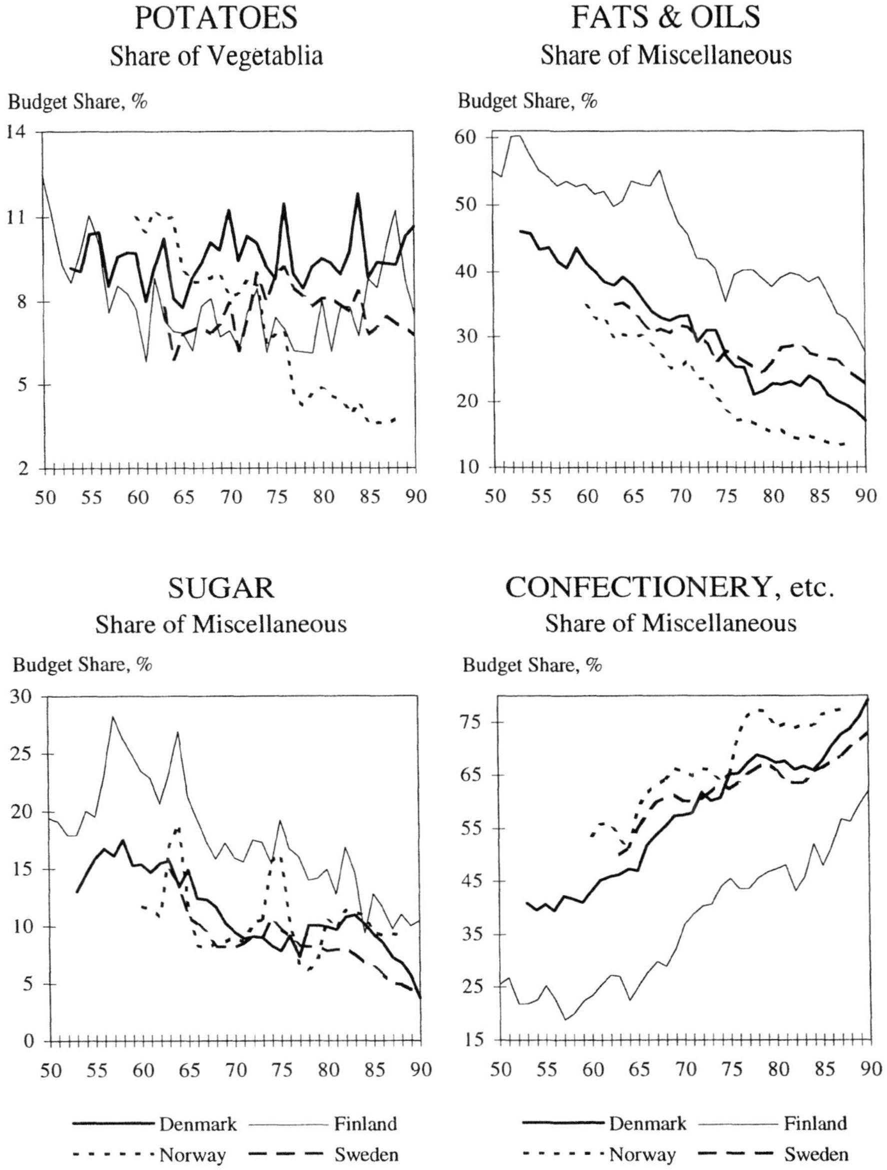

3

CONSUMER DEMAND THEORY*

3.1 INTRODUCTION

The purpose of this chapter is to present the theory underlying our empirical work on the demand for food, and our presentation emphasises those results that are used in the applications. It is based on Deaton and Muellbauer (1980a), Phlips (1983), Deaton (1986) and Varian (1992). The theory is also discussed within the food demand framework by, for example, Johnson *et al.* (1986) and Capps and Havlicek (1987).

The outline of the chapter is as follows. First, consumer preferences and the theory of utility maximisation are introduced. We then describe duality in consumer demand theory, and present empirically testable restrictions of the theory. Finally, the topic of dynamics in consumption is briefly discussed. The particular problems of weak separability and multi-stage budgeting are discussed in Chapter 4.

3.2 PREFERENCES AND UTILITY MAXIMISATION

3.2.1 Preferences and the Utility Function

Consider a consumer facing possible consumption bundles in the consumption set $Q \in R_n^+$, where he (or she) is assumed to have preferences concerning these consumption bundles. Let $q = (q_1, \cdots, q_n) \in Q$ be a vector of n commodities, where q_i denotes the quantity consumed of the ith commodity. Furthermore, let superscripts denote different bundles, and the symbols $\succ$, $\succcurlyeq$ and $\sim$ denote "strictly preferred to", "weakly preferred to" and "indifferent to", respectively. The consumer's preferences are here assumed to be

a) *Reflexive.* Each bundle of commodities is as good as itself for the consumer, *i.e.*, for any bundle q, $q \succcurlyeq q$. This is a trivial but mathematically necessary assumption.

b) *Complete.* The consumer can rank all bundles of commodities and they can be compared, *i.e.*, $q^1 \succcurlyeq q^2$, $q^2 \succcurlyeq q^1$ or $q^1 \sim q^2$.

c) *Transitive.* The consumer's preferences are consistent, *i.e.*, $q^1 \succcurlyeq q^2$ and $q^2 \succcurlyeq q^3$, imply $q^1 \succcurlyeq q^3$. This is a necessary requirement for selecting a best bundle.

---

* This chapter, which is the shared responsibility of all the authors, has been written by Kyrre Rickertsen.

d) *Continuous*. For any q^2 the sets $\{q^1|(q^1 \succcurlyeq q^2)\}$ and $\{q^1|q^2 \succcurlyeq q^1\}$ are closed sets. This rules out certain discontinuous behaviour.

e) *Strongly monotonic*. The consumer is assumed to prefer more to less of all goods, *i.e.*, $q^1 \geq q^2$ and $q^1 \neq q^2$ imply $q^1 \succ q^2$.

f) *Strictly convex*. The consumer prefers averages to extremes, *i.e.*, $q^1 \neq q^2$, $q^1 \succcurlyeq q^3$ and $q^2 \succcurlyeq q^3$ imply $tq^1 + (1-t)q^2 \succ q^3$ for $0 < t < 1$.

It may be shown that if the consumer's preference ordering is reflexive, complete, transitive, continuous and strongly monotonic, then there exists a continuous utility function $\upsilon(q)$ such that $q^1 \succcurlyeq q^2 \Leftrightarrow \upsilon(q^1) \geq \upsilon(q^2)$. This utility function is a purely ordinal measure, *i.e.*, it is a way of assigning a number to every possible consumption bundle such that the more preferred bundles get assigned larger numbers than the less preferred bundles. Given strictly convex preferences, this utility function will be strictly quasi concave, and we assume it is twice differentiable.

3.2.2 Utility Maximisation

A consumer is assumed to allocate his/her total expenditure, x, in a way that maximises the utility function described above, subject to a linear budget constraint. That is,

$$\max u = \upsilon(q_1,\ldots,q_n) \text{ subject to } x = \sum_{i=1}^{n} p_i q_i \,, \tag{1}$$

where p_i denotes the price per unit of the ith good. If we consider all goods and services, the total expenditure is equal to disposable income. Solving the first order conditions of (1) for the quantities, yields the Marshallian demand functions

$$q_i = g_i(x, p_1,\ldots,p_n) \text{ for } i = 1,\ldots,n. \tag{2}$$

3.3 DUALITY AND CONSUMER DEMAND

3.3.1 Introduction

The utility maximisation problem above is frequently called the primal problem. However, the problem may be rephrased to "What is the minimum expenditure required to reach a given utility level?". This is called the dual problem. The solution of the primal problem is identical to the solution of the dual problem, or $q_i \equiv g(x,p) \equiv h\{u[g(x,p),p]\}$, where $h(.)$ denotes the vector of Hicksian demand functions associated with the dual problem. The duality approach to consumer theory is summarised in Figure 1. Maximisation of the direct utility function subject to the budget constraint (a) leads to a system of Marshallian (or uncompen-

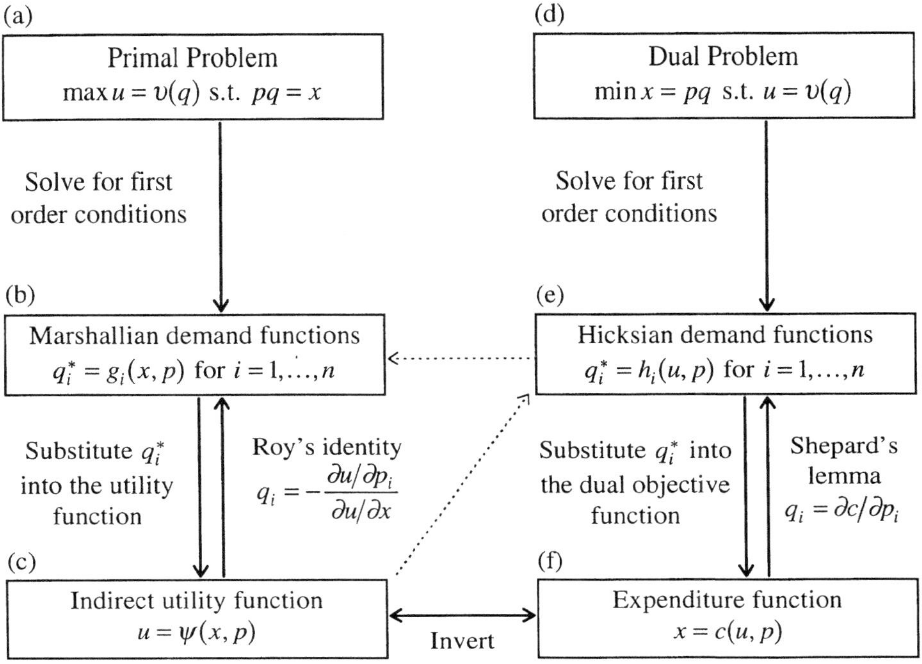

Figure 1: Duality in Consumer Theory

sated) demand functions (b). Substitution of these demand functions into the direct utility function yields the indirect utility function (c). The indirect utility function shows the highest level of utility that may be obtained for alternative prices and income. Furthermore, it is possible to obtain the Marshallian demand functions from the indirect utility function, by using Roy's identity.

The dual problem is to minimise the total expenditure that is required to reach a given level of utility (d). This leads to a system of Hicksian (or income compensated) demand functions (e). Substitution of these functions into the dual objective function yields the expenditure function (f), which shows the minimum expenditure needed to achieve a given level of utility with alternative prices. Moreover, the Hicksian demand functions may be derived by using Shephard's lemma on the expenditure function, *i.e.*, the partial derivatives of the expenditure function with respect to prices are the Hicksian demand functions, assuming these derivatives exist and $p_i > 0$ for all i.

3.3.2 The Expenditure Function

The applications in this book are all based on use of the expenditure function, and its properties are therefore of interest. Any expenditure function that is consistent with utility maximisation has the following properties, namely it is

a) Homogeneous of degree one in prices, *i.e.*, $c(u, tp) = tc(u, p)$ for $t > 0$. If prices are doubled then twice as much outlay is required to stay at the same utility level.
b) Increasing in u, *i.e.*, $u \geq u'$ implies $c(u, p) \geq c(u', p)$. For given prices the consumer has to spend more to be better off.
c) Nondecreasing in prices, *i.e.*, $p \geq p'$ implies $c(u, p) \geq c(u, p')$. If prices increase then at least as much expenditure will be required to stay at the same utility level.
d) Concave in prices, *i.e.*, $c[u, tp + (1 - p')] \geq tc(u, p) + (1 - t)c(u, p')$ for $0 \leq t \leq 1$. When prices rise expenditure will at most rise linearly, since the consumer adjusts purchases away from the relatively more expensive goods.
e) Continuous in prices for $p_i > 0$ for all i.
f) Derivable, yielding the Hicksian demand functions through the use of Shephard's lemma.

3.3.3 Duality and Marshallian Demand Functions

Duality provides a convenient way of deriving demand functions. It is relatively easy to think of specifications of $c(u, p)$ that satisfy the properties a) to f) above. The specified expenditure function can be (i) inverted to give the corresponding indirect utility function, and (ii) partially differentiated to obtain the Hicksian demand functions. The indirect utility function can then be substituted into the derived Hicksian demand functions, which leads to the Marshallian demand functions. This procedure is used to derive the almost ideal demand system that will be discussed in more detail in Chapter 4. An alternative procedure is to use Roy's identity on a specific indirect utility function to derive, for example, the indirect translog model.

Finally, a third possibility is to directly specify a system of demand equations such as the Rotterdam model. The integrability theorem says that any set of demand functions that adds up, is homogeneous of degree zero, and has a symmetric negative semidefinite substitution matrix is, in principle, integrable into a consistent preference ordering.

3.3.4 The Slutsky Equation

In the utility maximisation problem (1), let u^* denote the maximum level of utility which is attained when the commodity vector $q = (q_1^*, \cdots, q_n^*)$ is consumed. Minimising the expenditure needed to achieve the specific utility level, u^*, leads to an identical consumption bundle, that is $q_n^* \equiv h_i(u^*, p) \equiv g_i(x, p)$, where p denotes the price vector $(p_1, \cdots, p_n)$. Substitution of the expenditure function into this identity gives $h_i(u^*, p) \equiv g_i[c(u^*, p), p]$, and differentiating this with respect to p_i yields

$$\frac{\partial h_i(u^*, p)}{\partial p_j} = \frac{\partial g_i(c(u^*, p), p)}{\partial c(u^*, p)} \cdot \frac{\partial c(u^*, p)}{\partial p_j} + \frac{\partial g_i(c(u^*, p), p)}{\partial p_j} . \tag{3}$$

Using Shephard's lemma and rearranging leads to the Slutsky equation

$$\frac{\partial q_i}{\partial p_j} = \frac{\partial h_i}{\partial p_j} - \frac{\partial q_i}{\partial x} q_j . \tag{4}$$

The Slutsky equation divides the total effect of a price change, $\partial q_i / \partial p_j$, into a substitution effect, $\partial h_i / \partial p_j$, and an income effect, $(\partial q_i / \partial x) q_j$. Furthermore, the Slutsky equation is used to define Hicksian substitutes, $\partial h_i / \partial p_j > 0$, and complements, $\partial h_i / \partial p_j < 0$, while gross substitutes are defined as $\partial q_i / \partial p_j > 0$ and gross complements as $\partial q_i / \partial p_j < 0$.

3.4 RESTRICTIONS IN CONSUMER DEMAND

A system of Marshallian demand functions, derived from the maximisation of a specific utility function under a linear budget constraint, automatically satisfies some general restrictions, namely *adding up*, *homogeneity of degree zero*, *negativity* and *symmetry*. Moreover, many common demand systems are derived by duality, or are directly specified, and only satisfy these restrictions under certain conditions. In some cases the conditions are directly testable.

Adding up

The adding up restriction follows from the budget constraint and the monotonicity assumption of preferences, and it implies that the budget is totally used. There are two properties that follow from adding up, that are related to changes in total expenditure and in the price of a single good, respectively. Substitution of the Marshallian demand functions into the budget constraint of the problem (1) leads to

$$x \equiv \sum_i p_i g_i(x, p_1, \ldots, p_n) . \tag{5}$$

Differentiating (5) with respect to x, and defining budget shares as $w_i = p_i q_i / x$ and expenditure elasticities as $E_i = (\partial q_i / \partial x)(q_i / x)$, we obtain the so-called Engel aggregation in elasticity form

$$\sum_i w_i E_i = 1. \tag{6}$$

Next let us differentiate (5) with respect to p_j. If we define the (uncompensated) price elasticities as $e_{ij} = (\partial q_i / \partial p_j)(q_i / p_j)$, we obtain instead Cournot aggregation

$$-w_j = \sum_i w_i e_{ij}\,, \quad \text{for } j = 1,\ldots,n. \tag{7}$$

The restrictions (6) and (7) are impossible to test in many estimated demand systems. The properties of the adding up condition in estimated demand systems are discussed in more detail in Chapter 11.

Homogeneity of Degree Zero

The demand functions (2) are homogeneous of degree zero in total expenditure and prices. To demonstrate this, we may change all prices and total expenditure in the problem (1) by the same proportion t. Neither the budget constraint nor the utility function change. This property is often called the "absence of money illusion", and it implies that a proportional rise in all prices and expenditure has no effect on demand. Using Euler's theorem on the demand functions (2), we obtain the homogeneity of degree zero property in elasticity form,

$$\sum_j e_{ij} + E_i = 0 \quad \text{for } i = 1,\ldots,n, \tag{8}$$

that is, the sum of the price and expenditure elasticities is zero. This restriction is the only one that holds for a single demand function as well as the complete demand system.

Negativity

Two relations of great value in applied work may be derived from the Slutsky equation (4). From Shephard's lemma, we know that $\partial h_i / \partial p_j$ is the matrix of second derivatives of the expenditure function, and this matrix is commonly referred to as the substitution matrix. Note that although $\partial h_i / \partial p_j$ is unobservable, it may be calculated from the observable parts of the Slutsky equation. The fact that the expenditure function is concave in prices implies that the substitution matrix is negative semidefinite, which is the negativity condition. This in turn implies that the diagonal elements of the substitution matrix are nonpositive, *i.e.*, $\partial h_i / \partial p_i \leq 0$, which is necessary but not sufficient for negativity.

The necessary condition can be reformulated in elasticity form by using the Slutsky equation. Setting $i = j$, multiplying by (p_i / q_i) and rearranging leads to

$$e_{ii} + w_i E_i \leq 0. \tag{9}$$

If we define $\tilde{e}_{ij} = (\partial h_i/\partial p_j)(q_i/p_j)$ as the compensated (or Hicksian) price elasticities, then rearranging the Slutsky equation in elasticity form yields $\tilde{e}_{ij} = e_{ij} + w_j E_i$. The condition (9) is thus equivalent to saying that all compensated own-price elasticities must be nonpositive.

Symmetry

A proposition known as Young's theorem (Chiang 1984, p.313) implies that the substitution matrix is symmetric, or

$$\frac{\partial h_i}{\partial p_j} = \frac{\partial^2 c(u,p)}{\partial p_i \partial p_j} = \frac{\partial^2 c(u,p)}{\partial p_j \partial p_i} = \frac{\partial h_j}{\partial p_i}. \tag{10}$$

Using (10) on the Slutsky equation (4) and rearranging in elasticity form yields the so called Hotelling - Juréen relation, which may be written as

$$e_{ij} = \frac{w_j}{w_i} e_{ji} + w_j\left(E_i - E_j\right). \tag{11}$$

Using compensated elasticities we can rearrange this relation as $w_i \tilde{e}_{ij} = w_j \tilde{e}_{ji}$.

The homogeneity, negativity and symmetry restrictions can be tested for and/or imposed in many general demand systems. Imposition of these restrictions reduces the number of elasticities to be estimated, which will be discussed in Chapters 4 and 5.

3.5 DYNAMICS IN CONSUMPTION

The microeconomic theory discussed so far has been set within a static framework. This might be too restrictive, however, since habits or partial adjustment may be important for the consumption of many goods. This is particularly true for goods that are frequently consumed, such as foodstuffs. For example, if a consumer is usually drinks wine with his meals, he will not change this habit instantaneously even if the price of wine is increases. Dynamics are also important in aggregate time-series models, where Johnson *et al.* (1986, p. 1), for example, claim that for almost all demand functions estimated using aggregate time-series data, there is evidence of persistence in the consumption behaviour.

Consumption patterns based on past behaviour are frequently called habit persistence, and according to Pollak and Wales (1992, p. 104) there are two essential features of habit formation. Firstly, past consumption influences current preferences and demand, and secondly a higher level of past consumption of a good implies, *ceteris paribus*, a higher level of current consumption of that good.

Habit formation can be introduced as, for example, lagged consumption in the demand equations (2) or as adjustment costs in the expenditure function, see also Chapters 4 and 5. In applied work, a specific static model is frequently nested within a more general dynamic specification, which allows the simple use of likelihood ratio or Wald procedures to test whether the more complex dynamic model better captures actual behaviour than its static counterpart. We have followed the above approach in this study.

4

THE SPECIFICATION AND ESTIMATION OF DEMAND SYSTEMS*

4.1 INTRODUCTION

In the previous chapter we discussed some of the principal notions behind the theory of consumer demand. In this chapter we consider how to make this theory operational.

The first problem we encounter is how to explicitly formulate the model. Which functional form is appropriate? What are the implications of assuming some sort of separability? How should we take account of dynamic structures? The emphasis here, as in the rest of this chapter, is on those results that are used in the empirical parts of this book - other possible solutions are merely indicated. The second problem we address concerns the estimation of demand models. In particular we concentrate on the alternative estimation methods that are available, and on the assumptions that lie behind these methods. Finally, we discuss the evaluation of estimated demand models. Diagnostic testing of the assumptions used in estimation is considered in some detail, with special regards to the problems connected with testing in systems of equations. Appropriate measures of goodness-of-fit in systems are also introduced. The chapter is completed with a short discussion concerning the testing of such economic hypotheses as homogeneity and symmetry.

4.2 MODEL FORMULATION

4.2.1 Functional Form

Economic theory, as outlined in the previous chapter, merely tells us that, under certain conditions, the existence of consumer preferences implies the existence of a utility function (and expenditure function), which through maximisation (minimisation) leads to a demand function. It does not help us choose any specific functional forms, other than by suggesting certain restrictions that should hold.[1]

In this study we concentrate our attention on the Almost Ideal Demand System (AIDS) first suggested by Deaton and Muellbauer (1980b). Denoting the price of

---

* This chapter, which is the shared responsibility of all the authors, has been written by David Edgerton.

[1] Various intuitively plausible criteria, such as *regularity*, *domain of applicability*, *flexibility*, *etc*., have been suggested to assist us with this choice, see Lau (1986) and Thompson (1988) for example.

the ith good at time t by p_{it}, the column vector of prices by $\boldsymbol{p}_t$ and utility by u_t, then we can write the expenditure function for this model as

$$\ln c(u_t, \boldsymbol{p}_t) = \alpha_0 + \sum_k \alpha_k \ln p_{kt} + \tfrac{1}{2}\sum_k \sum_j \gamma^*_{kj} \ln p_{kt} \ln p_{jt} + u_t \beta_0 \prod_k p_{kt}^{\beta_k} \,. \quad (1)$$

Using the methods described in Chapter 3, this can minimised to yield the AIDS demand function. Denoting budget shares by w_{it} and total expenditure by x_t, this can be written in deterministic form as

$$w_{it} = \alpha_i + \sum_j \gamma_{ij} \ln p_{jt} + \beta_i (\ln x_t - \ln P_t) \quad (2a)$$

$$\ln P_t = \alpha_0 + \sum_k \alpha_k \ln p_{kt} + \tfrac{1}{2}\sum_k \sum_j \gamma_{kj} \ln p_{kt} \ln p_{jt}\,, \quad (2b)$$

where $\gamma_{ij} = \frac{1}{2}(\gamma^*_{ij} + \gamma^*_{ji})$ and where P_t is essentially a price index.

If the regularity conditions, implied by the budget constraint and utility maximisation, are applied to (2), then the following conditions are obtained:

ADDING UP: $\sum_k \alpha_k = 1,\ \sum_k \beta_k = 0$ and $\sum_k \gamma_{kj} = 0,\ \forall i$ (3a)

HOMOGENEITY: $\sum_j \gamma_{ij} = 0,\ \forall i$ (3b)

SYMMETRY: $\gamma_{ij} = \gamma_{ji},\ \forall i, j$ (3c)

NEGATIVITY: The matrices $\boldsymbol{K}_t$ are negative semidefinite, with elements

$$k_{tij} = \gamma_{ij} + \beta_i \beta_j \ln(x_t / P_t) - \delta_{ij} w_{it} + w_{it} w_{jt}\,. \quad (3d)$$

Note that δ_{ij} is Kronecker's delta, equal to one when $i = j$ and zero elsewhere, and that (3c) has been imposed when obtaining (3d). Note also that the parameters in the AIDS model can be interpreted in intuitively pleasing manners. Setting $u = 0$ and $p = 1$ in (1) we can see that α_0 represents the logarithm of subsistence expenditure measured in base year prices. In a similar manner, we can use (2a) to show that α_i represents the budget share of the ith good when expenditure is at the subsistence level. The γ_{ij} and β_i parameters represent the changes in the budget shares caused by changes in prices and real expenditure, and where $\beta_i > 0$ thus implies a luxury good and $\beta_i < 0$ implies a necessity.

The AIDS expenditure function has the flexible functional form property, which means that the demand functions derived from it are first order approximations to any set of demand functions derived from utility maximisation. In addition we can note that simply assuming that demands are continuous functions of budget shares and prices also implies that (2) is a first order approximation. This gives a *raison d'être* for using the AIDS demand function even if, for example, the homogeneity hypothesis is rejected.

The AIDS model, as defined above, is only applicable at the household (individual) level. One of the features of this model, however, is that it can readily be generalised to the aggregate level. If w is now defined as the aggregate budget share and x as aggregate expenditure divided by an appropriate measure of population size, then equations (1) - (3) still hold.

What is now an "appropriate measure of size"? Taking account of different forms of demographic variation leads to quite complicated models, see for example Jorgenson *et al.* (1982), Ray (1986) or Rossi (1988). In time-series data, the rate of demographic change is fairly slow, however, and reasonable approximations to the aggregate demand functions can be obtained by defining x to be the *per capita* or the per household total expenditure. In this study we use *per capita* total expenditure, partly because of the availability of data.

The equation system (2) is nonlinear in the parameters. This is not a real problem when estimating a single demand system using modern computing power. When we want to analyse, for example, structural invariance we may have to estimate hundreds or even thousands of systems, however. The estimation of standard errors (for example for *all* elasticities at *all* time points) can also be time consuming, even for simple nonlinear models. It is thus hardly inappropriate, at least in explanatory analyses, to look for linear approximations to the above demand functions.

The AIDS system is, in fact, not only almost ideal but also almost linear; it is merely the term $\beta_i \ln P_t$ in (2a) that causes the nonlinearity. Deaton and Muellbauer suggested in their seminal article a linear form of the model, obtained by replacing the last two terms of (2b) by Stone's price index. The reasoning behind this is simply that most prices are quite collinear, and that different price indices are thus highly correlated with each other. This is partly an empirical observation, but also follows from a theorem of Wilks (1938) which shows that the correlation between two different weighted averages of correlated series tends to one as the number of series grows, irrespective of the weights being used. Since our price indices are based on aggregates of very large numbers of elementary goods, we expect this result to be applicable here.[2] We therefore sometimes use the following approximate price index,

$$\ln P_t = \alpha_0 + \sum_k w_{kt} \ln p_{kt} \ . \tag{4}$$

The model (2a) plus (4) is known as the Linear Almost Ideal Demand System (LAIDS), and has been extensively applied in the litterature (much more so than the nonlinear version). Note that the parameter α_0 is not identified in the LAIDS model, and is absorbed into the constant terms in (2a). In practice the likelihood function for the nonlinear AIDS model is usually very flat around α_0, causing problems with empirical identification. This prompted Deaton and Muellbauer to suggest equating α_0 to the logarithm of an *a priori* chosen value for real subsistence

[2] *Meat*, for example, is the aggregate of many "elementary" meat products. *Animalia* is the aggregate of all the meat products, the fish products and the dairy products, not just of the three groups defined in stage 3.

expenditure.

Let E_i denote the total expenditure (income) elasticity, e_{ij} the uncompensated price elasticity and $\tilde{e}_{ij}$ the compensated price elasticity. The nonlinear AIDS elasticities can be written as follows, where for the sake of notational simplicity the time subscripts t are dropped.

$$E_i = 1 + \frac{\beta_i}{w_i}, \tag{5}$$

$$e_{ij} = \frac{\gamma_{ij} - \beta_i[\alpha_j + \frac{1}{2}\sum_k(\gamma_{kj} + \gamma_{jk})\ln p_k]}{w_i} - \delta_{ij}, \tag{6a}$$

$$= \frac{\gamma_{ij} + \beta_i[\beta_j \ln(x/P) - w_j - \frac{1}{2}\sum_k(\gamma_{kj} - \gamma_{jk})\ln p_k]}{w_i} - \delta_{ij}, \text{ and} \tag{6b}$$

$$\tilde{e}_{ij} = e_{ij} + w_j E_i. \tag{7}$$

Note that both Green and Alston (1990) and Deaton and Muellbauer (1980b) give the price elasticities under the symmetry hypothesis, that is when $\gamma_{ij} = \gamma_{ji}$.

The problems associated with calculating elasticities in the LAIDS model are fully discussed in Alston *et al.* (1994) and Buse (1994). The formulae proposed by Chalfant (1987) seem to be those that work best, and our own experience has shown these approximations to be quite reliable.[3] The expenditure elasticity is still given by (5), while the uncompensated and compensated price elasticities become

$$e_{ij} = \frac{\gamma_{ij} - \beta_i w_j}{w_i} - \delta_{ij}, \text{ and} \tag{8}$$

$$\tilde{e}_{ij} = \frac{\gamma_{ij}}{w_i} + w_j - \delta_{ij}. \tag{9}$$

4.2.2 Habit Forming and Other Dynamics

The form of the AIDS model proposed in the previous sections is rarely able to explain complex consumer decisions. In particular it ignores the dynamic structure caused by habit forming, adjustment costs *etc*, and assumes that the consumer can immediately and fully adjust to changes in prices and income. Empirically, one often finds that the application of static models to time-series data leads to misspecification (autocorrelated residuals) and relatively low explanatory power.

[3] As far as we know the first article to use this approximation is Goddard (1983).

To obtain a dynamic consumption system consistent with cost minimisation one must adapt the expenditure function in some manner to allow for adjustment costs. This can either be done explicitly, or alternatively by making direct corrections to the demand system and then checking the long-run properties. The former approach is used by Ray (1984) and Blanciforti *et al.* (1986), while Anderson and Blundell (1983) use the latter method.

The simplest way to introduce dynamics is to include the lagged budget share $w_{i,t-1}$ on the right-hand-side of (2). Unfortunately such models do not satisfy adding up, unless we are willing to impose the additional restriction that the parameter of the lagged budget share is the same in all equations.

A more general dynamic AIDS model, which does not involve excessive overparamaterisation, has been suggested by Alessie and Kapteyn (1991), Assarsson (1991) and Kesavan *et al.*(1993), namely

$$w_{it} = \alpha_i + \sum_{j=1}^{n}\theta_{ij} w_{j,t-1} + \sum_{j=1}^{n}\gamma_{ij} \ln p_{jt} + \beta_i(\ln x_t - \ln P_t) \tag{10a}$$

$$\ln P_t = \alpha_0 + \sum_{k=1}^{n}(\alpha_k + \sum_{j=1}^{n}\theta_{kj} w_{j,t-1})\ln p_{kt} + \tfrac{1}{2}\sum_{k=1}^{n}\sum_{j=1}^{n}\gamma_{kj} \ln p_{kt} \ln p_{jt}\,, \tag{10b}$$

where the adding up condition implies that $\Sigma_i \theta_{ij} = 0\ \forall_j$. Further restrictions on the $\boldsymbol{\Theta}$ matrix are necessary to ensure identification, however, since $\Sigma_j w_{jt} \equiv 1\ \forall_t$ otherwise implies an exact collinearity. The most common restrictions are $\alpha_i = 0$ or $\theta_{in} = 0\ \forall_i$, but in our opinion the restriction $\Sigma_j \theta_{ij} = 0\ \forall_i$ is more suitable since the θ parameters can now be interpreted as differences from the average lag effects for the different commodities. Estimating a model with parameter restrictions involves inverting a matrix of the form $\boldsymbol{R}(\boldsymbol{X}'\boldsymbol{X})\boldsymbol{R}'$, which will be nonsingular if $\boldsymbol{R}$ is based on any of the restrictions discussed above. It should be noted that the manner of identifying $\boldsymbol{\Theta}$ does not affect the other parameters, elasticities or test statistics.

This demand system given by (10) is a variant of the interrelated partial adjustment model discussed in Anderson and Blundell (1983).[4] The reasons for using this specification are discussed in more detail in Chapter 5.1. A dynamic version of the LAIDS model is obtained by using (10a), but replacing the definition of the price index by (4). The adequacy of this approximation depends on the degree of collinearity between Stone's index and the exact price index (10b).

The short-run elasticities for AIDS and LAIDS are given by (5) - (9). Note that if the AIDS price elasticities are written in the form (6a), then α_j has to be replaced by $\alpha_j + \Sigma_k \theta_{jk} w_{k,t-1}$, whilst using (6b) implies that $\ln P_t$ must be expressed as in (10b). The form of the price index for LAIDS is left unchanged.

Long-run elasticities can be obtained by setting $w_t = w_{t-1} = w^*$ and solving (10a). If the dynamic effects are large, however, then return to equilibrium can take many

---

[4] Other possibilities for AIDS models are to replace the lagged budget shares by lagged quantities (Ray(1984)), or to take account of demographic factors (Alessie and Kapteyn (1991)). For the translog model Manser (1976) has suggested using lagged total expenditure.

periods and lead to unstable estimated elasticities. We therefore prefer to report medium term simulations instead of long-run elasticities.

4.2.3 Structural Change

One of the major problems in all econometric analysis is the assumption of parameter constancy. The coefficients in a consumption function are, for example, presumed not to vary over time and/or (group of) household.[5] In the analysis of food demand, particular attention has been paid to the possibility of taste (preference) changes as regard levels of fat in meat and dairy produce, see for example Chavas (1983). Much of the literature has been concerned with detecting structural change,[6] but a few articles have addressed the problem of modelling. In particular Dahlgran (1987) and Moschini and Meilke (1989) have suggested different forms of gradually switching regression models, the former using a logit function and the latter a linear function to describe structural change. We follow the approach of Moschini and Meilke in this study, adapting their model to take account of habit forming. A switching dynamic AIDS or LAIDS model is thus written

$$w_{it} = \alpha_i + \alpha_i^* h_t + \sum_{j=1}^{n} (\theta_{ij} + \theta_{ij}^* h_t) w_{j,t-1} + \sum_{j=1}^{n} (\gamma_{ij} + \gamma_{ij}^* h_t) \ln p_{jt} + (\beta_i + \beta_i^* h_t)(\ln x_t - \ln P_t) \tag{11}$$

$$h_t = \begin{cases} 0 & t = 1, \ldots, \tau_1 \\ \dfrac{t - \tau_1}{\tau_2 - \tau_1} & t = \tau_1 + 1, \ldots, \tau_2 \\ 1 & t = \tau_2 + 1, \ldots, T. \end{cases} \tag{12}$$

where $\ln P_t$ is given by either (10b) or (4).[7] Due to lack of degrees of freedom only some of the parameters can be allowed to vary, and we have chosen the β's since these affect both expenditure and price elasticities. The switching regressions model used in Chapter 6 is thus the AIDS system

$$w_{it} = \alpha_i + \sum_{j=1}^{n} \theta_{ij} w_{j,t-1} + \sum_{j=1}^{n} \gamma_{ij} \ln p_{jt} + (\beta_i + \beta_i^* h_t)(\ln x_t - \ln P_t). \tag{13}$$

---

[5] To be more exact, random variation that is independent of the explanatory variables is permissible, in which case one estimates the expected values of the coefficients. This is the point behind the Lucas critique, that is in general the variation is either non random or dependent on policy instruments.

[6] See, for example, Martin and Porter (1985) and Chalfant and Alston (1988) for a parametric and a nonparametric analysis.

[7] As we shall discuss later on, estimation is performed by maximising the likelihood over all possible pairs of τ_1 and τ_2.

Elasticities can be obtained by replacing β_i with $\beta_i + \beta_i^* h_t$ in (5) - (7). Note that (13) is only appropriate for the nonlinear AIDS model. Using the LAIDS price index (4) leads to a switching intercept term $\alpha_0 \beta_i^* h_t$, which is not absorbed into the parameters of the equivalent AIDS model.

In two recent articles Alston and Chalfant (1991a, 1991b) have demonstrated how tests for structural change can have considerable power against other forms of misspecification, in particular against incorrect functional form. Careful interpretation is therefore needed when using the models suggested in this section. A different approach, which will be discussed in Chapter 7, is to formulate an error correction model to allow for differences in long-run and short-run properties.

4.2.4 Separability and Two-Stage Budgeting

An econometrician who wishes to investigate patterns of consumption is always faced with the problems caused by the immense number of goods and services available to the consumer. To be able to analyse a complete demand system consisting of thousands of equations would require huge amounts of data plus a theoretical base for demographic variations. Within the basis of a time-series analysis, such an exercise is nigh on impossible.

The usual way to approach this problem is to assume *a priori* some sort of structure in the consumers' preferences, the most common assumption being that of weak separability.[8] This approach implies that goods can be divided into a number of "separate" groups, where a change of price in a good in one group affects the demand for *all* goods in another group in the same manner.

Following Gorman (1959), Pollak (1971) and Deaton and Muellbauer (1980a, Chapter 5.2), let us more formally consider a two-stage budgeting process, where we assume that the first stage comprises of groups of goods $r = 1,\dots,n$ whilst in the second stage the rth group comprises of goods $i = 1,\dots,m_r$. A consumer's preferences are said to be weakly separable if they can be represented by a utility function of the form, where $\boldsymbol{q}_r$ represents the vector of quantities in the rth group,

$$u = f[\upsilon_1(\boldsymbol{q}_1),\cdots,\upsilon_n(\boldsymbol{q}_n)]. \tag{14}$$

Maximising (14) now implies separately maximising the subutilities $\upsilon_r(\boldsymbol{q}_r)$. Given the allocation of goods between the broad groups, this implies that the second stage of the two-stage budgeting process follows all the usual rules of demand analysis, but with total expenditure replaced by group expenditure. In other words the Marshallian demand functions can be written

$$q_{ri} = g_{ri}(\boldsymbol{p}_1,\dots,\boldsymbol{p}_r,x_r), \tag{15}$$

[8] Other forms of separability, for example implicit or strong separability, are sometimes assumed.

where $\boldsymbol{p}_r$ denotes the price vector for the rth group and $x_r = \Sigma_i p_{ri} q_{ri}$ is the group expenditure. Weak separability also implies that the marginal rate of substitution between any two goods i and j belonging to one group (r) is independent of the consumed quantities of the goods belonging to another group (s), that is

$$\partial\left[\frac{\partial u/\partial q_i}{\partial u/\partial q_j}\right]\Big/\partial q_k = 0 \quad \forall\, i,j \in (r) \text{ and } k \in (s). \tag{16}$$

The allocation of total expenditure into broad groups (stage one) is more problematical, since it is not possible to replace the prices of all goods with a single price index for each group. Deaton and Muellbauer show, however, that the demand function for the rth group of goods can be approximated by

$$Q_r = g_r(P_1, \ldots, P_n, x), \tag{17}$$

where the group expenditure, Q_r, is now expressed in real terms (at base year prices π) and P_r is the true cost of living index for a specific reference utility level u. An assumption implied in the above is that P_r does not to vary too greatly with u, in which case the true cost of living index can be approximated by the usual Paasche or Laspeyres price indices.[9]

The above assumptions thus imply that total expenditure can first be allocated between groups using usual price indices (as approximations to true cost of living indices). When this has been done we can then allocate independently within each group.

There are a number of practical problems involved with the separability assumption. Firstly we must have reasonable *a priori* knowledge that will allow us to divide goods into groups. In practice we often assume a multi-stage decision process, where it is often the last stage that is of primary interest. In this study we use the three-stage budgeting process presented in Chapter 2 and shown in Figure 2.1. We avoid the difficulties connected with the durability of certain goods by ignoring these, and in a first stage assuming a division of the rest of private consumption into four groups - *food-at-home*, *restaurants and cafés*, *other non-durables* and *other services*. *Food-at-home* is then divided into groups representing animal products (*animalia*), vegetable products (*vegetablia*), *beverages* and *miscellaneous*. Finally, each of these groups is divided into three subgroups. The consumer is thus assumed to first decide whether he will eat at home or at a restaurant. If he settles for eating at home, he will then decide how to allocate his consumption between meat products, vegetable products, beverages and other food. Given this allocation, he finally decides what sort of meats, vegetables *etc* he will consume. Note that the inclusion of milk in the animalia group instead of the beverages group is mainly due to the availability of data for Sweden.

[9] The true cost of living index is only exactly independent of u if the group preferences are homothetic. Using the theorem of Wilks (1938) described earlier, we can expect the approximation we have described to be adequate as long as the number of elementary commodities is large, see also Edgerton (1993a).

The second problem we are faced with is how to judge the empirical relevance of the assumed separability structure. Is it reasonable, for example, to assume that a change of restaurant prices effects *all* food goods in the same manner? Is some other form of separability more appropriate? These questions have been addressed by a number of authors, see Pudney (1981), Varian (1982) and Baccouche and Laisney (1991) for various approaches.

Finally, it is obvious that the assumption of (weak) separability implies relationships between price and expenditure elasticities at different levels of the budgeting process. The total expenditure elasticity is obviously affected by both the within group expenditure elasticity and the relevant between group expenditure elasticity. In addition, if the price of a certain good changes, this will cause a direct effect on the quantities purchased of all goods within the same group, given an unchanged group expenditure. The price change will, however, also affect the group price index, and thus the allocation of expenditures between groups. This latter effect will affect all goods, both within and without the same group. Separability does *not* imply that price changes for goods in different groups do not affect each other, but merely that such effects are channelled through the group expenditures, see Deaton and Muellbauer (1980a pp. 127-133).

If we assume that q_{ri} is expressed as real expenditure and that p_{ri} is expressed relative to the base year prices, then denoting the unit vector by ι we can write

$$P_r = \frac{c(u, \boldsymbol{p}_r)}{c(u, \iota)}, \tag{18}$$

$x_r = P_r Q_r$, $x = \Sigma_r x_r$ and $Q_r = \Sigma_i q_{ri}$. Substituting for x_r and P_r in (15) thus yields

$$\begin{aligned} q_{ri} &= g_{ri}[\boldsymbol{p}_r, P_r g_r(P_1, \cdots, P_n, x)] \\ &= g^*_{ri}(\boldsymbol{p}_1, \ldots\ldots, \boldsymbol{p}_n, x). \end{aligned} \tag{19}$$

Let us denote the *within group* expenditure elasticity for the ith good within the rth group of goods as $E_{(r)i}$, the *group* expenditure elasticity for the rth group of goods as $E_{(r)}$ and the *total* expenditure elasticity for the ith good within the rth group of goods as E_i, with an equivalent definition for the budget shares, w.

In a similar manner we can denote the within group price elasticity between the ith and j^{th} goods within the rth group of goods as $\mathrm{e}_{(r)ij}$, the group price elasticities as $\mathrm{e}_{(r)(s)}$ and the total price elasticities as e_{ij}. Note that the within group price elasticity assumes that group expenditure is unchanged in spite of the price change, whilst the total price elasticity allows for the relevant changes in group expenditure. Finally we can denote the equivalent compensated price elasticities as $\tilde{e}$.

Using the rules of calculus on (18) and (19) allows us to obtain the following results (see Edgerton (1992, 1993a)), where δ_{rs} denotes Kronecker's delta.

$$E_i = E_{(r)} E_{(r)i} \tag{20a}$$

$$e_{ij} = \delta_{rs} e_{(r)ij} + E_{(r)i} w_{(s)j} (\delta_{rs} + e_{(r)(s)}) \tag{20b}$$

$$= \delta_{rs} \tilde{e}_{(r)ij} + E_{(r)i} w_{(s)j} e_{(r)(s)} \tag{20c}$$

$$\tilde{e}_{ij} = \delta_{rs} \tilde{e}_{(r)ij} + E_{(r)i} w_{(s)j} \tilde{e}_{(r)(s)} . \tag{20d}$$

How should we interpret these results? Looking at (20b) for two goods within the same group, we can see that the total price elasticity is equal to a direct effect (the within group price elasticity) plus an indirect effect. The indirect effect measures how much a change in the prices of a single good affects the distribution between groups, and is a product of three factors. The first factor measures the relative change in the group price index, caused by a change in the price of the jth good (this equals $w_{(r)j}$), the second factor measures the effect a change in the price index has on the group expenditure $(1 + e_{(r)(s)})$, while the third factor measures the effect this change in within group expenditure has on the consumption of the ith good ($E_{(r)i}$).

If the own between group price elasticity $e_{(r)(r)} = -1$, then the group expenditure is unaffected by the price change and $e_{ij} = e_{(r)ij}$. If, on the other hand, $e_{(r)(r)} = 0$, then the price change produces a proportional effect on the group expenditure and $e_{ij} = \tilde{e}_{(r)ij}$. Note also that the difference between the within group price elasticity and the total price elasticity is small if the goods' within group budget shares or expenditure elasticities are small, or if $e_{(r)(r)}$ is close to -1. The group budget share has, however, no effect.

The above results can be extended to more general multi-stage budgeting without any conceptual difficulty.

4.3 ESTIMATION IN DEMAND SYSTEMS

4.3.1 Separable Demand Systems

Consider the AIDS/LAIDS model defined in (2) and (4), or the generalisations derived by assuming habit forming and/or structural change. These are defined in terms of complete systems, that is situations where *all* goods and services are to be explained. As discussed in Section 4.2.4 this is not the usual situation, we are nearly always forced to assume some form of separability to make the estimation process feasible.

If we have a two-stage budgeting process, where the first stage comprises of allocation between n groups of goods and the second stage comprises of allocation between m_r goods within each of the n groups, then the AIDS/LAIDS model can be written in stochastic form as

$$w_{(r)t} = \alpha_{(r)} + \sum_{(s)} \gamma_{(r)(s)} \ln p_{(s)t} + \beta_{(r)} (\ln x_t - \ln P_t) + \varepsilon_{(r)t} \tag{21a}$$

$$w_{(r)it} = \alpha_{(r)i} + \sum_j \gamma_{(r)ij} \ln p_{(r)jt} + \beta_{(r)i}(\ln x_{(r)t} - \ln P_{(r)t}) + \varepsilon_{(r)it}, \qquad (21b)$$

for $r = 1,...,n$, $i = 1,...,m_r$ and $t = 1,...,T$. Equation (21a) describes the allocation *between* groups, where $w_{(r)t}$ is the group budget share, $p_{(r)t}$ is a group price index, x_t is total expenditure in the system and P_t is the AIDS/LAIDS composite price index for the whole system. Equation (21b) describes allocation *within* the rth group, where $w_{(r)it}$ is the within group budget share, $p_{(r)jt}$ is the price (index) of the jth good, $x_{(r)t}$ is the total group expenditure and $P_{(r)t}$ the AIDS/LAIDS index for the rth group. The terms $\varepsilon_{(r)t}$ and $\varepsilon_{(r)it}$ represent the stochastic errors in these equations.

One of the inference problems that we must address is how much information shall we use when we estimate and analyse the system (21). Methods that utilise more information are, naturally enough, superior in the sense of having a higher precision *if* the information used is correct. They can, however, very well give a lower precision if the information is incorrect.

The information we use is basically of two sorts. Firstly, we have the information supplied in the assumptions used in specifying the model. It is well known that full information methods are more sensitive to misspecification than limited information methods. Secondly, we have the information supplied in the sample. In large samples this information will be precise and, given correct assumptions, full information methods will be more efficient. In small samples some of the information, for example that concerning the second moments of the error terms, can be very imprecise, in which case limited information methods may be preferable even in a correctly specified model.

In the context of the system (21), we can consider three levels of information. At the highest level (*system estimation*) we would estimate all $n + \Sigma_r m_r$ equations together. In this case we can utilise the (estimated) correlation structure between all the error terms. Note that weak separability is still being imposed through the large number of zero restrictions on the parameters.

At a middle level (*subsystem estimation*) we estimate the n equations in (21a) together and then separately estimate the n subsystems, each composed of m_r equations, in (21b). In this case we perform $n + 1$ independent estimations, in each of which we can only utilise the error correlation structure *within* each subsystem.

Finally, we can ignore all the relationships between the different equations, and perform $n + \Sigma_r m_r$ separate estimations (*single equation estimation*). No information on the error correlation structure can be utilised in this case.

A number of points can be noted. Firstly, the AIDS price index (2b) involves parameters from all the equations in a given subsystem, and thus single equation estimation is not possible. The same argument applies to the LAIDS model when there are cross equation restrictions (*e.g.* symmetry). The opposite is, in a sense, the case for LAIDS without cross equation restrictions. Since the regressors on the right-hand-side of (2a), (10a) and (13) are the same for all equations within the same subsystem, most subsystem estimation methods reduce to their single equation equivalents. Note, however, that testing subsystem hypotheses (such as homogeneity) requires information from the whole subsystem.

Finally, it is quite possible to make a compromise between system and subsystem estimation. We can, for example, estimate some but not all subsystems together. It is even quite possible, in the LAIDS case, to combine equations from different subsystems, something that can be useful when estimating the standard errors of the total elasticities described in (20). In this study we concentrate on subsystem (maximum likelihood) estimation for AIDS and single equation (ordinary least squares) estimation for LAIDS. In some cases various forms of system estimation are used.

4.3.2 Endogeneity and Exogeneity

The stochastic nature of the error terms in (21) is of vital importance when we make decisions concerning estimation and testing. The simplest methods demand restrictive assumptions on the stochastic properties of ε, whilst relaxing these assumptions requires the use of more complicated methods.

One of the basic assumptions, which is of primary importance when choosing estimation method, is that of exogeneity.[10] If all the explanatory variables are asymptotically uncorrelated with the error terms, then usual least squares or quasi-maximum likelihood methods will be consistent. If this is not so, then some form of instrumental variables method will be necessary.

There are three reasons why we can suspect lack of exogeneity in the system (21). Firstly, all demand systems are basically derived from simultaneous supply and demand models, which means that we can suspect that prices are endogenously determined. There are two reasons why we can hope that this nonexogeneity is of minor importance in this study, however. During the period of our study, most food goods in the Nordic countries have *either* had regulated prices (which if not exogenous should at least be predetermined in the sense of merely depending on previous years' supply) *or* have been determined in the world market (which has been affected very little by changes of demand in their own country).

The vast majority of all demand studies that to some extent disaggregate over goods, have ignored the problem of endogenous prices, either without comment or by appealing to similar arguments as the above. A few exceptions exist, notably Jorgenson *et al.* (1982) in their extensive translog modelling of U.S. demand, see also Wahl and Hayes (1990) for an analysis of meat demand using a LAIDS model. Both of these articles are also good examples of the problems involved with treating prices as endogenous, namely the need to find good instruments from the supply side.

The second form of presumptive endogeneity that occurs can be seen from an examination of (21a) or (2a). These equations can be rewritten in expenditure form,

---

[10] Many definitions of exogeneity exist, see for example Geweke (1984). Both *strict exogeneity* and *weak exogeneity* are sufficient, but not necessary, conditions to allow consistent estimation when treating the "exogenous" variable as nonstochastic.

by multiplying both sides of the equation by x_t. The left-hand-side variable is now the expenditure on the jth good, x_{jt}, while the right-hand-side contains the variable $z_t = \ln x_t$. Since $x_t = \Sigma_j x_{jt}$, we can see that z_t is a function of endogenous variables, and thus likely to be itself endogenous, see Pollak (1971, footnote 8), Attfield (1985) and Deaton (1986 pp. 1779-1780). Deaton, for example, shows that quite restrictive restrictions are needed on the error covariance matrix of a linear expenditure system if exogeneity is to be exact. If total expenditure is in fact endogenous to the system, then instruments will be needed to enable consistent estimation of the model. Assuming (i) the existence of collective wage bargaining, and (ii) that government's taxation decisions are, if not exogenous then at least merely dependent on consumers' expenditure at *earlier* time points, a possible instrument would be disposable income.

The third form of endogeneity arises in multi-stage budgeting processes. If we look at the complete system (21) we can see that the group expenditure $x_{(r)t}$ occurs on the right-hand-side of (21b). The group budget share $w_{(r)t}$ is, however, merely the ratio between the group expenditure and the total expenditure, that is

$$x_{(r)t} = w_{(r)t} x_t \; . \tag{22}$$

The group budget share is the explained variable in (21a), whilst substituting (22) into (21b) yields group budget shares as explanatory variables in the same system. This system is block recursive, and can thus be consistently estimated without the use of instrumental variable, if the variance-covariance matrix of the errors $\varepsilon_{(r)t}$ and $\varepsilon_{(r)it}$ is block diagonal.

Some authors, for example de Janvry *et al.* (1972), have argued that the errors in the different stages should be independent if separability is assumed. LaFrance (1991) has shown, however, that this is only possible under restrictive conditions on the covariance structure of the errors of the unconditional demand function.[11] He also shows that, under the assumptions he uses, the normal forms of instrumental variable estimates are also inconsistent. This latter result does not necessarily hold under other assumptions, however, see Edgerton (1993b).

Given the possibility of constructing consistent estimates (in general, that is having reasonable instruments available), we can always use Hausman tests to judge whether a departure from exogeneity is significant. Due to the availability of viable instruments, we only analyse the possible endogeneity of expenditure, and not prices, in this study.

---

[11] The unconditional demand function is simply the function found by substituting (21a) into (21b) through (22), see LaFrance's equation (19). The conditions needed for the consistency of least-squares methods are, for systems that are linear in expenditure, quite similar to those given by Deaton, and are related to Theil's (1971) "rational random errors hypothesis". For systems nonlinear in expenditure the situation is more complicated. See also Blackorby *et al* (1978 p. 279).

4.3.3 Choice of Estimation Method

In this section we shall briefly consider some aspects of estimation theory as applied to the allocation models of the type given in (21). The basic properties of the methods mentioned here can be found in the usual econometric textbooks, for example Amemiya (1985), Greene (1993), Harvey (1990), Judge *et al.* (1985) or Maddala (1992).

Let us quite generally consider the (sub)system of demand equations given by

$$w_{it} = f_i(\boldsymbol{Z}_t;\boldsymbol{\theta})+\varepsilon_{it}, \tag{23}$$

where f is a (possibly) nonlinear function, $\boldsymbol{Z}_t$ is the vector of explanatory variables and $\boldsymbol{\theta}$ is a vector of parameters. Letting $\boldsymbol{\varepsilon}_t$ be the $(n\times 1)$ vector of contemporous errors, we shall begin by making the following assumptions

$E(\boldsymbol{\varepsilon}_t)=\boldsymbol{0}$	Correct functional specification,[12]	(24a)
$E(\boldsymbol{\varepsilon}_t\boldsymbol{\varepsilon}_s')=\boldsymbol{0}$	Serial noncorrelation ($t\neq s$),	(24b)
$E(\boldsymbol{\varepsilon}_t\boldsymbol{\varepsilon}_t')=\boldsymbol{\Sigma}$	Homoscedasticity,	(24c)
$E(\boldsymbol{\varepsilon}_t \mid \boldsymbol{H}_s)=\boldsymbol{0}$	Instrumental variables ($t\geq s$),	(24d)
$\boldsymbol{\varepsilon}_t \sim N(\boldsymbol{0},\boldsymbol{\Sigma})$	Normality,	(24e)

where $\boldsymbol{H}_t$ is the instrument set that contains all the predetermined variables in $\boldsymbol{Z}_t$ plus enough other variables to allow estimation. If none of the explanatory variables are endogenous, we can set $\boldsymbol{H}_t=\boldsymbol{Z}_t$. In addition a number of regularity conditions are necessary concerning f and its first two derivatives w.r.t. $\boldsymbol{\theta}$. Note that the assumption of normality is only necessary when performing tests and for ensuring the asymptotic efficiency of the estimates.

In allocation models the fact that the budget shares sum to one implies that the covariance matrix of the errors, $\boldsymbol{\Sigma}$, must be singular. There are a number of ways of dealing with this, the usual procedure being to drop an equation, although using generalised inverses is in many ways preferable, see Bewley (1986), Dhrymes and Schwarz (1987) and Edgerton (1995) for discussion. In what follows we assume that one equation has been dropped.

Denoting the estimated system as

$$w_{it} = f_i(\boldsymbol{Z}_t;\hat{\boldsymbol{\theta}})+\hat{\varepsilon}_{it}, \tag{25}$$

we can describe the following methods:

[12] If the true function is g then ε in (23) will equal $g-f+$(*true errors*). This will in general have an expected value that does not equal zero.

Single Equation Methods:	
Ordinary Least Squares (OLS)	Minimise $\hat{\varepsilon}_i'\hat{\varepsilon}_i$
Ordinary Two Stage Least Squares(2SLS)	Minimise $\hat{\varepsilon}_i'\boldsymbol{P}\hat{\varepsilon}_i$
Limited Information System Methods:	
Systemwise Least Squares (SLS)	Minimise $\mathrm{tr}\,\hat{\boldsymbol{E}}'\hat{\boldsymbol{E}}$
Systemwise Two Stage Least Squares (S2SLS)	Minimise $\mathrm{tr}\,\hat{\boldsymbol{E}}'\boldsymbol{P}\hat{\boldsymbol{E}}$
Full Information System Methods:	
Seemingly Unrelated Regressions (SUR)	Minimise $\mathrm{tr}\,\boldsymbol{S}^{-1}\hat{\boldsymbol{E}}'\hat{\boldsymbol{E}}$
Iterated Seemingly Unrelated Regressions (ISUR)	Minimise $\mathrm{tr}\,\hat{\boldsymbol{S}}^{-1}\hat{\boldsymbol{E}}'\hat{\boldsymbol{E}}$
Maximum Likelihood (ML)	Minimise $\det\hat{\boldsymbol{E}}'\hat{\boldsymbol{E}}$
Three Stage Least Squares (3SLS)	Minimise $\mathrm{tr}\,\boldsymbol{S}^{-1}\hat{\boldsymbol{E}}'\boldsymbol{P}\hat{\boldsymbol{E}}$
Iterated Three Stage Least Squares (I3SLS)	Minimise $\mathrm{tr}\,\hat{\boldsymbol{S}}^{-1}\hat{\boldsymbol{E}}'\boldsymbol{P}\hat{\boldsymbol{E}}$

where $\hat{\boldsymbol{E}}$ denotes the $(T\times(n-1))$ matrix of residuals, with i^{th} row $\hat{\varepsilon}_i'$, and where $\boldsymbol{P}=\boldsymbol{H}(\boldsymbol{H}'\boldsymbol{H})^{-1}\boldsymbol{H}'$ is a $(T\times T)$ projection matrix. We basically follow the definitions in Bowden and Turkington (1984), denoting as $\boldsymbol{S}$ the estimate of $\boldsymbol{\Sigma}$ formed from OLS/SLS, and as $\hat{\boldsymbol{S}}$ the estimate of $\boldsymbol{\Sigma}$ formed iteratively.

Note first of all that ISUR and ML lead to identical estimates since the Oberhofer-Kmenta conditions are satisfied (Greene (1993, p. 493)), but that I3SLS is not a maximum likelihood method. Note also that the single equation methods and the limited information system methods are identical if there are no cross equation restrictions.[13] For linear models OLS/SLS/SUR/ISUR/ML are identical if all equations have the same explanatory variables, as are 2SLS/S2SLS/3SLS/I3SLS.

The definitions of 2SLS and 3SLS given above are based on the presumption that the same instruments are used in all equations. This is not necessary, however. For 2SLS the adjustment is simple, but for 3SLS a variety of methods are available if we wish to use different instruments in different equations. Computationally, the estimation of 3SLS becomes much more complex in this situation, and this alternative has not been available in common econometric packages.[14]

The shortage of degrees of freedom in our studies has excluded the possibility of using all exogenous variables in the *whole system* as instruments. The only practical alternative for 3SLS has thus been to use only a subset of the exogenous variables (or their principal components) as instruments. This implies, however, that for at least some equations, we are not able to use the exogenous variables actually present in that equation as instruments. This is an obviously undesirable property,

---

[13] As previously shown, the single equation methods are not relevant for AIDS models.

[14] The most recent version of TSP (4.2) now allows a specification of the generalised method of moment (GMM) which is, in fact, 3SLS with varying instruments.

and we have thus not used 3SLS for systemwise estimation.

The use of 3SLS for *subsystem* estimation is quite feasible, however, since the explanatory variables are the same in each equation and the number of exogenous variables in the subsystem is thus limited. The method is thus sometimes used in the nonlinear AIDS model (as stated above, 3SLS reduces to 2SLS for the linear LAIDS model in these circumstances).

Choice of Instrument Set and Instruments

The two and three stage methods defined earlier work by taking a certain instrument set (here denoted by $\boldsymbol{H}$) and then using the orthogonal projection of the explanatory variables on this set ($\boldsymbol{PZ}$) as instruments. For models that are linear in both the variables and the parameters this is a straightforward approach, but for nonlinear models several generalisations exist.

Let us start by assuming that prices and total expenditure are predetermined. Consider now the LAIDS model (21), which is linear in the parameters but nonlinear in the variables, since the right-hand-side of (21b) contains the variable

$$\ln\left(\frac{x_{(r)t}}{P_t}\right) = \ln\left(\frac{x_t w_{(r)t}}{P_t}\right) \tag{26}$$

and where $w_{(r)t}$ is the endogenous variable explained in (21a). The most obvious generalisation of 2/3SLS is to include the functions (26) amongst the explanatory variables Z_t and to include either x_t, x_t/P_t or $\ln(x_t/P_t)$ in the instrument set. We call this the method of *external instruments*.[15] It seems obvious that $\ln(x_t/P_t)$ should have a higher explanatory power for the function (26) than x_t or x_t/P_t, and we therefore use this variable when applying the method of external instruments in this book, see also Kelejian (1971).

Another generalisation is to obtain $\hat{w}_{(r)t}$ as the projection of $w_{(r)t}$ on $\boldsymbol{H}_t$, which in this case is the OLS predictions from (21a). The variable $I_t = \ln(x_t\hat{w}_{(r)}/P_t)$ can then be used as an instrument instead of the projection of (26) on $\boldsymbol{H}_t$. This is called the method of *restricted internal instruments* by Bowden and Turkington (1984).

An alternative method suggested by the same authors is to augment the original instrument set with I_t, which we call the method of *augmented internal instruments*. Yet a third approach is to replace $\ln(x_t/P_t)$ by I_t in the instrument set, which we call *substituted internal instruments*. This method reduces the problem of col-

[15] Bowden and Turkington (1981) call this method *strict* 2SLS/3SLS, but in their later book (Bowden and Turkington (1984)) define the method as an (unnamed) alternative to the method of *internal instruments*. Consistency has been established by Kelejian (1971) and Edgerton (1972), whilst Edgerton (1973) and Amemiya (1974) give the asymptotic standard errors. The latter is unfortunately misprinted in Bowden and Turkington's book. It is the method of external instruments that is to be found in the TSP and SAS program packages.

linearity amongst the instruments and is also computationally simple. For these reasons we use the substituted method when applying internal instruments in this study.

What shall we do if we consider x_t endogenous? In this case we can simply replace x_t with the (*per capita*) disposable income, y_t, in the instrument set. We now obtain $\hat{w}_{(r)t}$ as the predictions from the 2SLS estimation of (21a).

An examination of the asymptotic results given by Amemiya (1974) and Bowden and Turkington (1981,1984) for the external and internal instrument methods show that substituting or augmenting $\hat{w}$ to the instrument set and using standard (external instrument) nonlinear 2SLS programs will yield the correct asymptotic standard errors.

The application of 2SLS to AIDS models, that are nonlinear in both variables and parameters, is somewhat more complex. The methods of internal and external instruments carry through here in principle. One of the problems is to find instruments that are sufficiently highly correlated with the derivatives of the nonlinear functions f. Following the same motivation as prompted the use of LAIDS, we use Stone's price index when defining the variables $\ln(x_t/P_t)$ or I_t that are used in the instrument set.[16] The application of nonlinear 3SLS offers an even greater variety of choice, one possibility being to use the same instruments in every equation and the same definitions as above.

4.3.4 Estimation of Elasticities

The AIDS elasticities given in (5) - (7) are derived from the nonstochastic model (2). If, however, we have a stochastic model then we must distinguish between the budget share, w, and its conditional expectation, $E(w)$. Are the model elasticities now defined in terms of the stochastic w or the nonstochastic $E(w)$? In either case w should be replaced by $E(w)$ in the elasticity formulae, but if we are using a definition based on a stochastic w then terms depending on the derivatives of ε w.r.t. p and x (which may be nonzero) should also be included. For the sake of conceptual simplicity we shall therefore define our model elasticities in terms of $E(w)$.

We have introduced a stochastic component into the demand model through the simple use of an additive error term in (23), which can be seen as a linear approximation to a (probably) complex optimisation problem subject to uncertainty. In this simplified case $E(w)=f$, which for the AIDS/LAIDS model is given by the right hand side of (2a). The elasticities (5) - (9), with their dynamic and switching regressions generalisations, are thus estimated by replacing all parameters *and* budget shares by their estimated values.

Note that the elasticities are now nonlinear functions of the parameters α, ρ and γ. We calculate the standard errors of the AIDS elasticities by utilising linearisation techniques, which are quick and readily accessible in TSP. This method has been

[16] The AIDS definition of P_t, given by (2b), is of course used in the model.

shown by Green *et al.* (1987) and Krinsky and Robb (1986, 1990, 1991) to be quite effective. For the LAIDS model we sometimes follow Chalfant's suggestion, and calculate the standard errors of the elasticities by assuming $\hat{w}$ *to be nonstochastic.* This is obviously incorrect, but reduces the elasticities to linear combinations of the parameters, and our calculations have shown this to be a good approximation to the more exact method of linearisation.[17]

4.4 THE EVALUATION OF DEMAND SYSTEMS

4.4.1 The Problem of Misspecification

The assumptions given in (24) must naturally be tested before we can rely on any estimation results. If the assumptions are violated, then we must take appropriate measures *either* in the formulation of the model *or* in the method of estimation used. Such tests (misspecification tests) are characterised by having the common null hypothesis that (24a-e) *all* hold and alternative hypothesis that a given *specific* assumption does not hold. An effective misspecification test will thus have high power against one alternative hypothesis and low power against other hypotheses.

Misspecification testing is a vast area of statistical and econometric methodology, and we shall only give a brief motivation to the methods used in this study. Details can be found in the textbooks cited earlier. We will, however, discuss more thoroughly the problems associated with system misspecification testing and small sample approximations, since these topics are often only briefly mentioned (if at all) in standard textbooks.

Testing for Autocorrelation

The methodology used for misspecification testing in this study follows the ideas described in Godfrey (1988). We apply his line of reasoning to the problem of serial correlation, and then generalise to other forms of misspecification.

The basic method used by us to test for autocorrelation is the Breusch-Godfrey (BG) test. This has the advantages of (i) being applicable in the presence of lagged endogenous variables, (ii) being applicable for testing higher order autocorrelation, (iii) being asymptotically equivalent to the Lagrange Multiplier (LM) test and (iv) being computationally simple. For a single equation linear model $y_t = \mathbf{x}_t'\boldsymbol{\beta} + \varepsilon_t$, with k explanatory variables, the Breusch-Godfrey test against autoregressive errors of the gth order is defined as a test of $\alpha_1 = \alpha_2 = \cdots = \alpha_g = 0$ in

[17] We in fact replace $\hat{w}$ by the actual budget share w in many of our calculations of LAIDS standard errors. The difference is usually negligible, see Chapter 6.4.4.

$$y_t = x_t'\beta + \alpha_1\hat{\varepsilon}_{t-1} + \alpha_2\hat{\varepsilon}_{t-2} + \cdots + \alpha_g\hat{\varepsilon}_{t-g} + v_t. \tag{27}$$

The most usual way of performing this test is to use the result that TR^2 is asymptotically χ_g^2 distributed, where R^2 is non-centred. An alternative, however, is to use the F-statistic for the null hypothesis in (27), which is asymptotically $F_{g,T-k-g}$ distributed. Kiviet (1986) has shown that the F-test is in general a safer procedure.[18]

For nonlinear models Godfrey (1988) shows that $x_t'\beta$ can be replaced by $f(x_t,\beta)$ or by a first order Taylor series approximation. In our case neither of these approaches is appealing since the cross-equation restrictions in $\ln P$ imply re-estimating the whole system. This is not desirable in a diagnostic test, and we therefore use the simple approximation obtained by replacing $\ln P$ by $\ln \hat{P}$ in the AIDS formula. This is a satisfactory approximation if prices are reasonably collinear.

The above test is only strictly relevant if we are merely testing a single equation. The usual practice of performing such tests separately for all n (alternatively $n-1$) equations in a demand system, and then intuitively combining the results, can be misleading due to mass significance and dependent test statistics. System testing is quite simple, however, if we use Godfrey's (1988) theory of "local equivalent alternatives" (LEA).

Let us consider in the general nonlinear model $y_t = f(x_t, \theta_1, \theta_2) + \varepsilon_t$, which can *either* be a single equation, *or* a system of equations in stacked form. Typically θ_1 consists of regression parameters and θ_2 of distribution parameters of ε. Godfrey shows that an asymptotic equivalent to the LM test of the hypothesis $H_0: \theta_2 = \theta_2^0$ can be obtained by testing $H_0': \delta = 0$ in the model

$$y_t = f(x_t, \theta_1, \theta_2^0) + \left[\left. \frac{\partial \varepsilon_t(\hat{\theta}_1, \theta_2)}{\partial \theta_2} \right|_{\theta_2 = \theta_2^0} \right]' \delta + v_t \tag{28}$$

where $\hat{\theta}_1$ is the conditional maximum likelihood estimate obtained by estimating the model under H_0, and where

$$\varepsilon_t(\theta_1, \theta_2) = y_t - f(x_t, \theta_1, \theta_2). \tag{29}$$

Letting $\hat{\varepsilon}_t$ denote the residuals from the restricted model, we can transform (28) to

$$\hat{\varepsilon}_t = \left[f(x_t, \theta_1, \theta_2^0) - f(x_t, \hat{\theta}_1, \theta_2^0) \right] + \left[\left. \frac{\partial \varepsilon_t(\hat{\theta}_1, \theta_2)}{\partial \theta_2} \right|_{\theta_2 = \theta_2^0} \right]' \delta + v_t \tag{30}$$

[18] Note that y_t can be replaced by the OLS residuals as regressand in (27), since the difference between them is an exact linear combination of x_t. The test statistics are therefore not altered.

which, for nonlinear models, can be approximated as follows

$$\hat{\varepsilon}_t = \left[\frac{\partial f(\boldsymbol{\theta}_1, \boldsymbol{\theta}_2^0)}{\partial \boldsymbol{\theta}_1} \bigg|_{\boldsymbol{\theta}_1 = \hat{\boldsymbol{\theta}}_1} \right]' \boldsymbol{\beta}_* + \left[\frac{\partial \varepsilon_t(\hat{\boldsymbol{\theta}}_1, \boldsymbol{\theta}_2)}{\partial \boldsymbol{\theta}_2} \bigg|_{\boldsymbol{\theta}_2 = \boldsymbol{\theta}_2^0} \right]' \boldsymbol{\delta} + v_t, \tag{31}$$

where $\boldsymbol{\beta}_* = (\boldsymbol{\theta}_1 - \hat{\boldsymbol{\theta}}_1)$. For linear models (30) and (31) are exactly equivalent, since the first derivative then equals $\boldsymbol{x}_t$. For nonlinear models the two approaches are asymptotically equivalent. The hypothesis $\boldsymbol{\delta} = \mathbf{0}$ can now be tested using usual LRT, LM or Wald tests, or by asymptotically equivalent F-tests.

The alternative hypothesis considered in a systemwise Breusch-Godfrey test is

$$\boldsymbol{\varepsilon}_t = \boldsymbol{P}_1 \boldsymbol{\varepsilon}_{t-1} + \boldsymbol{P}_2 \boldsymbol{\varepsilon}_{t-2} + \cdots + \boldsymbol{P}_g \boldsymbol{\varepsilon}_{t-g} + \boldsymbol{v}_t, \tag{32}$$

where the stacked vectors are now reformulated into matrices, and where $\boldsymbol{P}_k$ is the partial correlation matrix between $\boldsymbol{\varepsilon}_t$ and $\boldsymbol{\varepsilon}_{t-k}$. Using (28) this implies testing the hypothesis $\boldsymbol{A}_1 = \boldsymbol{A}_2 = \cdots = \boldsymbol{A}_g = 0$ in the regression system

$$\boldsymbol{y}_t = \boldsymbol{f}(\boldsymbol{x}_t, \boldsymbol{\theta}) + \boldsymbol{A}_1 \hat{\boldsymbol{\varepsilon}}_{t-1} + \cdots + \boldsymbol{A}_g \hat{\boldsymbol{\varepsilon}}_{t-g} + \boldsymbol{v}_t. \tag{33}$$

Using (31) leads to a system with the primary residuals as second stage regressand, and using the first derivative of f instead of the function itself. Note that adding up implies that the column sums of the $\boldsymbol{P}$ matrices should be constant for each matrix. (If, for example, $\boldsymbol{P}_1$ is diagonal, then these diagonal elements should be equal). We are, however, mainly interested here in detecting if $\boldsymbol{P}$ differs from zero, not in determining the possible "correct" structure of $\boldsymbol{P}$.

It is debatable if a greater power is obtained by (a) using a low value of g and full $\boldsymbol{P}(\boldsymbol{A})$ matrices, or (b) using a larger value of g but merely diagonal $\boldsymbol{P}$ matrices (see Judge *et al.* (1985)). One disadvantage of using diagonal matrices in singular systems is that small sample tests are not invariant to which equation is dropped. Another disadvantage is that estimating (33) with ML does not reduce to OLS because of the cross-equation restrictions. In this study we therefore only report tests using full matrices, and due to the restricted degrees of freedom we only apply first order tests.

As previously noted when discussing single equation tests, we do not wish to estimate a lot of nonlinear regressions merely to perform a diagnostic test. The version of the systemwise Breusch-Godfrey test we use is thus a test of the hypothesis that $\alpha_{ij} = 0 \; \forall \, i,j$ in the following regression system

$$\hat{\varepsilon}_{it} = f_i(\boldsymbol{x}_t, \boldsymbol{\theta}) + \sum_{j=1}^{n-1} \alpha_{ij} \hat{\varepsilon}_{j,t-1} + v_{it}, \quad \text{for } i = 1, \ldots, n, \tag{34}$$

where $\ln P$ is replaced by $\ln \hat{P}$ in the AIDS function. After this replacement f is linear in the parameters, and it thus numerically irrelevant whether the the primary regressand or the residuals are chosen as regressand in (34). Note also that the singularity of the AIDS model, implied by adding up, means that only $n-1$ residuals can be used as dependent or independent variables. This is not a general result; LEA tests of other hypotheses can use squared residuals, which are not linearly dependent.

A final question is which test statistic should we use? A number of Monte Carlo studies have shown the usual asymptotic chi-squared tests to be severely biased if the number of equations in the system is at all large, see Bewley (1986) for a thorough discussion. In linear models with one or two identical restrictions in each equation, exact small sample adjustments to the Likelihood Ratio test (LRT) statistic are available, however. These adjusted LRT's can also be shown to be special cases of an approximation given in Rao (1973),[19] which can also be used in nonlinear models and for any number of different restrictions per equation. In the case of linear models with one identical restriction in each equation, the same numerical result can also be obtained by adjusting the Wald statistic.

We introduce Rao's test by first denoting as m_1 the number of restrictions per equation to be tested, as m_2 the number of estimated equations in the system and as k the number of parameters per equation in the unrestricted system. For our BG test we have $m_1 = m_2 = n-1$. We will also denote the error covariance matrix under the null hypothesis as Σ_R and under the alternative hypothesis as Σ_U. The Likelihood Ratio statistic, U, defined as twice the difference between the logarithms of the unrestricted and restricted likelihoods, is given by

$$U = T\left(\ln\det\hat{\Sigma}_R - \ln\det\hat{\Sigma}_U\right), \tag{35}$$

which is asymptotically distributed as $\chi_{m_1 m_2}$ under the null hypothesis. The small sample properties of this statistic are untractable, but as previously noted some advances have been made in investigating the distribution of the transformation

$$\Lambda = e^{-U/T} = \det\hat{\Sigma}_R / \det\hat{\Sigma}_U\,, \tag{36}$$

when either m_1 or m_2 are not greater than 2. A number of approximations are available for the more general case, the best of which is probably that given by Rao (1973 p. 556). The test statistic is now be given by

$$\Lambda^* = \left(\frac{hs-r}{m_1 m_2}\right)\left(\frac{1-\Lambda^{1/s}}{\Lambda^{1/s}}\right), \text{ where} \tag{37a}$$

[19] We would like to thank Lars Otto for bringing this result to our attention; it is surprising that it is not more widely used in econometrics. We shall denote these small-sample tests as "Exact", although this is only strictly true in linear models with one or two identical restrictions in each equation.

$$s = \sqrt{\frac{(m_1 m_2)^2 - 4}{m_1^2 + m_2^2 - 5}}, \tag{37b}$$

$$h = T - k - \tfrac{1}{2}(m_2 - m_1 + 1), \text{ and} \tag{37c}$$

$$r = \tfrac{1}{2} m_1 m_2 - 1. \tag{37d}$$

Λ^* is approximately $F_{m_1 m_2, hs-r}$ distributed under the null hypothesis. As previously reported, the use of F distributions usually yields better small sample approximations than the use of chi-squared distributions. Edgerton and Shukur (1995) have performed a large scale Monte Carlo experiment on the systemwise Breusch-Godfrey test, which shows that Rao's F-test is superior to all other statistics. This superiority grows with the number of equations, but even the Rao test performs poorly if $m_2 \geq 5$, rejecting a true null hypothesis far too often.

Three possible approaches are available if autocorrelation is discovered. The procedure we use is to try and find a better dynamic specification, which eliminates the problem. An alternative approach is to model the form of residual autocorrelation. This method has been described by Berndt and Savin (1975), but is fraught with difficulties due to the interrelations that exist between the autoregressive structure assumed for the errors and the adding up conditions. The third approach is to accept the loss of efficiency caused by autocorrelation, but to obtain consistent estimates of the standard errors of the parameters, see Newey and West (1987) and Andrews (1991). Such an approach is valid for both nonlinear and instrumental variables models, and can also be extended with improved efficiency to the generalised method of moments (GMM).

LEA Tests of Other Forms of Misspecification

According to Chavas and Segerson (1987), *heteroscedasticity* is always present in allocation models. The problem may, however, be of negligible order of importance, and should therefore be tested. The commonly applied White test uses a regression of squared residuals on all products and cross-products of the explanatory variable, which is not feasible in our case due to lack of degrees of freedom. The Breusch-Pagan (BP) test implies finding reasonable explanatory variables, an unspecified function of which models the possible heteroscedasticity. Following Bickel (1978), a plausible LEA approach is to regress the squared residuals from the restricted model on powers of the predictions from the same model. Since budget shares are always positive, we use the first order Bickel's form of the BP-test in this study.

A similar methodology is available if significant heteroscedasticity is discovered as was the case for autocorrelation. We can either adapt the basic demand system or try to model the form of changing error variability, both of which can be quite difficult without any *a priori* information. The third approach is to accept the heteroscedasticity, but use robust estimates of the standard errors, see White (1980). We use this method as the standard in our study, though it should also be noted that the approach does not correct for the bias in other misspecification tests caused by heteroscedasticity.[20] If we are willing to use GMM, then we can correct for autocorrelation and heteroscedasticity simultaneously.

Another alternative hypothesis is that of *Autoregressive Conditional Heteroscedasticity* (Arch), which can also be tested in LEA form. Such a test involves the regression of the squared residuals on lags of the squared residuals. Arch models can be estimated in modern computer programmes, and the GMM adjustment for autocorrelation and heteroscedasticity can usually be applied.

A number of tests are available when testing for *functional misspecification*. A commonly used test, which follows the ideas used above, is Ramsey's Reset. In linear allocation models this involves regressing budget shares on the original explanatory variables and powers (squares and higher) of the predicted budget shares. In the nonlinear AIDS model we propose the same solution here as for the autocorrelation test.[21] Note that Ramsey's test, as for other such general tests, is sensitive to many forms of misspecification, for example omitted variables, incorrect functional form, endogeneity in the explanatory variables *etc.* A rejection of the hypothesis of no functional misspecification should thus lead to an attempt to improve the model.

A test that has more specific power against *endogeneity* is the Hausman-Wu (HW) test. Consider testing the endogeneity of a subset $\boldsymbol{X}_1$ of the explanatory variables, where $\boldsymbol{X}_2$ is the set of explanatory variables considered *a priori* exogenous and $\boldsymbol{Z}_1$ is a set of instruments for $\boldsymbol{X}_1$. One form of the Hausman-Wu test is to regress $\boldsymbol{X}_1$ on $\boldsymbol{X}_2$ and $\boldsymbol{Z}_1$ and obtain predicted values $\hat{\boldsymbol{X}}_1$. The budget shares are then regressed on $\boldsymbol{X}_1$, $\boldsymbol{X}_2$ and $\hat{\boldsymbol{X}}$ and the significance of the prediction terms is tested.

In a model that is nonlinear in the variables there is a problem in deciding whether to use the method of external or internal instruments in the first regression. If the model is also nonlinear in the parameters, then there is also the same problem as earlier in deciding if, and in that case how, to make a linearisation approximation. Since we are merely performing a diagnostic test, we have chosen the simplest methods here, that is we use external instruments and approximate P by its AIDS estimate $\hat{P}$. More specifically we regress $\ln(x/\hat{P})$ on $\ln(z/\hat{P})$ and the "exogenous" variables in the first regression, where x is the group expenditure and z is either total private consumption or disposable income. The predictions from

[20] In the case of SLS and S2SLS (which make the unreasonable assumption that all equations have the same residual variance) the estimates will not be affected, but the standard errors will. It is not difficult to adjust for this, but the robust standard error estimates of the adjusted model are identical to the robust error estimates of the unadjusted model.

[21] The approximated $\hat{f}_t$ will not be perfectly collinear to $\hat{y}_t$, and the latter could thus be included in the regression LEA regressions. The degree of multicollinearity will be large, however, if our approximation is valid.

this regression are then used in the second regression, together with $\ln(x/\hat{P})$ and the exogenous variables.[22] Various forms of instrumental variables methods are sometimes used when the exogeneity hypothesis is rejected.

The results from the last two subsections are summarised in Table 1. In this table H_1 indicates the equation that does *not* hold under the alternative hypothesis. For each test the left-hand-side (LHS) and right-hand-side (RHS) variables are given, where the prefix "U" indicates those RHS variables that are untested and "T" those that are tested. The variable m_1 tells how many equations are included in the LEA system, while m_2 tells us how many variables are tested in each equation.

Table 1. Full Systemwise First Order LEA Misspecification Tests

Test	H_1	LHS	U-RHS	T-RHS	m_1	m_2
BG	Autocorrelation	$\hat{\varepsilon}_{it}$	f	$\hat{\varepsilon}_{j,t-1}$	$n-1$	$n-1$
BP	Heteroscedasticity	$\hat{\varepsilon}_{it}^2$	c	$\hat{w}_{jt}$	n	$n-1$
Arch	Arch	$\hat{\varepsilon}_{it}^2$	c	$\hat{\varepsilon}_{j,t-1}^2$	n	n
HW	Endogeneity	w_{it}	f	$\hat{x}$	$n-1$	1
Reset	Functional Misspecification	w_{it}	f	$\hat{w}_{jt}^2$	$n-1$	n

f represents the explanatory variables in the original AIDS system (using $\ln \hat{P}$), c represents the constant term and $\hat{x}$ the first stage predictions described above. The LHS of the BG test can be replaced by w without changing the test statistic.

Testing for Non-normality

For allocation models we know that ε cannot be normally distributed, since w is bounded between zero and one. Woodland (1979) has developed a method for taking this into explicit account, but empirical results showed negligible differences compared to the usual methods. A common test of normality is the Jarque-Bera (JB) Lagrange Multiplier test, which for a residual calculated with $\tau=T-k$ degrees of freedom, can be written

$$\lambda = \tau\left[\tfrac{1}{6}\hat{b}_1^2 + \tfrac{1}{24}(\hat{b}_2 - 3)^2\right], \tag{38}$$

where $b_1 = \mu_3/\mu_2^{3/2}$ is the measure of skewness and $b_2 = \mu_4/\mu_2^2$ the measure of kurtosis, and where the sample moments $\hat{\mu}_i$ are used to estimate b_i. Under the null hypothesis of normality (24e), λ is asymptotically distributed as χ_2^2, but Jarque and Bera (1987) have shown this approximation to be poor for small samples. Using

[22] A numerically identical procedure, when we have the same number of instruments as variables to test, is to replace $\hat{X}$ by the instruments (in this case $\ln(z/\hat{P})$).

Monte Carlo methods they enumerate tables of critical values for finite samples, which should be entered using τ as the number of observations.

An alternative method, which is the one we use, is to apply the small sample approximation proposed in Kendall and Stuart (1963 pp. 281-297), namely

$$\lambda = \frac{(\tau-1)^2}{\tau-2}\left[\frac{\hat{b}_1^2}{6} + \frac{(\tau-1)(\tau+1)}{24\tau(\tau-3)}\left(\hat{b}_2 - 3\frac{\tau-1}{\tau+1}\right)^2\right]. \tag{39}$$

This gives very similar results to the exact test, but the advantage of using (39) is that we obtain *P*-values. Note that we perform the Jarque-Bera test using ML residuals in (39) which leads to a further source of approximation; an alternative, at least for LAIDS models, would be to use recursive residuals. Although tests of multivariate normality do exist (*e.g.* see Spanos (1986 p. 596) or Barnett (1992)), it is not apparent how (39) can be generalised to small sample systemwise tests.[23] Only single equation JB tests are thus reported in this study.

Testing for Parameter Instability

The usual methods of testing for parameter constancy are either based on Chow tests (which assume that the point of structural change is known) or on Cusum or Cusumsq tests using recursive residuals. As previously stated, the use of nonlinear models makes the use of recursive residuals more difficult, and the exact distributional properties no longer apply.

An alternative approach is to base Cusum and Cusumsq tests on OLS residuals, see Ploberger and Krämer (1992) or McCabe and Harrison (1980), where the latter method leads to constructing a bounds test in a similar manner as for the familiar Durbin-Watson test. The authors suggest using the lower bound, however, which has approximately the same critical values as the recursive residual form of the test. We therefore use the following Cusumsq statistic, based on the ML residuals,

$$C = \max_{k+1\le s\le T}\left|\frac{1}{\hat{\sigma}^2 T}\sum_{t=1}^{s}\hat{\varepsilon}_t^2 - \frac{s-k}{T-k}\right|, \tag{40}$$

where critical values can be found, for example, in Johnston (1984 p. 560). Edgerton and Wells (1993, 1994) have extended these tables and also given an algorithm for calculating the *P*-values of the Cusumsq test.

The presence of structural change caused us to estimate the gradually switching regressions model given by (12-13). This model is estimated as follows. For given τ_1 and τ_2 the AIDS model is estimated by ML and the likelihood calculated. This is

---

[23] At the time of going to press it was brought to our attention that the omnibus test proposed by Mardia and Foster (1983) provides an appropriate small sample test of multivariate normality.

repeated for all pairs of τ_1 and τ_2 ($\tau_1 < \tau_2$), and the estimates that maximise the likelihood is chosen. This maximised likelihood can then be used in a likelihood ratio test, but note that the this does *not* have the usual asymptotic χ^2 distribution under the null hypothesis, since the statistic is only defined for integral time points. Note also that testing if $\boldsymbol{\beta}^*$ is zero in (13) only tests for structural change *at the given* time points τ_1 and τ_2.

Testing for Non-separability

The assumption of separability can be tested in a variety of ways. Swoffard and Whitney (1988) use nonparametric methods and Varian's Generalised Axiom of Revealed Preferences (GARP). This method has been criticised by Barnett and Choi (1989), who write "That (Varian's) approach checks sufficient but not necessary conditions for the data to satisfy a separable structure. Those sufficient conditions are so restrictive that the test is strongly biased towards rejection". They compare the performance of the GARP-test and various parametric tests, an approach that is followed up by Moschini (1992). In a recent paper Moschini *et al.* (1994) develop another parametric test, which can be used to test a variety of separability assumptions (local or global and homothetic of non-homothetic). A disadvantage with all these parametric methods is that they use Wald or Likelihood Ratio tests that demand the estimation of the unrestricted model, that is the model without assuming separability. In our case this is empirically impossible due to lack of degrees of freedom.

A parametric approach, more in the line with the research in this book, has been used by Alston and Chalfant (1987), who use non-nested testing to compare LAIDS models with different price and expenditure definitions. The spirit of this approach is to test separability by including *per capita* total real expenditure as an extra variable in the model. If the separability assumption is correct, this variable ought to have no effect.

It is apparent from footnote 22, however, that the Alston-Chalfant test procedure is essentially the same as the Hausman-Wu test of endogeneity of group expenditure. In fact, although LaFrance (1991) has shown that separability does not ensure exogeneity of group expenditure, it is certainly true that non-separability results in omitted variables with possible endogeneity problems.

We have therefore not been able to perform any explicit separability tests in this study. If, however, our results for the Reset and Hausman-Wu tests indicate no problems with either omitted variables or endogeneity of group expenditure, this can be taken as evidence in support of our separability assumption.

Interpretation of Test Results

The results of the tests discussed in this section can be interpreted in various ways.

A formal significance test is performed by first choosing a significance level and then comparing the relevant test statistic with its critical value at that level. A procedure that we and many other authors consider more informative is to calculate the statistic's P-value, which is the probability, under the null hypothesis, of by chance obtaining a more extreme test statistic then that actually obtained. The P-value measures the degree of credibility in the null hypothesis (small P-values imply low credibility), and can be used in a formal significance test by comparing with the significance level.

If we use a formal significance test we are faced with the problem of choosing an appropriate significance level. The use of P-values as descriptive measures does not eliminate such a choice, however, since ultimately we must still decide whether the null hypothesis' credibility is so low as to make it no longer viable. Traditionally, statisticians and economists have tended to use a 5 percent level, mainly no doubt because of the availability of tables in pre-computer days, but it is by no means certain that this is the most suitable level.

Maddala (1992, p. 32) argues that a higher significance level than the customary 5 percent (maybe as high as 25 percent to 50 percent!) should be used in "pretesting", since the benefits of treating misspecification when it occurs outweigh the drawbacks of unnecessary treatment when it does not. Maddala also refers to several authors who argue for higher significance levels than 5 percent for *all* tests in small samples, due to the relationship between significance level, power and sample size.[24]

In the above discussion we have only considered *single* tests. In multiple tests, however, the problem of mass significance arrises; *i.e.*, if q independent tests each use an individual significance level of α, then the probability under the null of rejecting at least one is $1-(1-\alpha)^q$, which tends to 1 as q increases whatever the value of α. Now in practice different test statistics are not independent but often highly correlated, which reduces the above effect, but MacKinnon (1992) still recommends significance levels of 0.1 percent to 1 percent (instead of 5 percent) when performing ten misspecification tests.

Various ways of reducing the problem of mass significance are available. For example the use of system tests, as described earlier in this section, eliminates the problem for any given test. Lack of degrees of freedom, however, restricts us to applying these tests separately to each of the six subsystems we estimate, and not to the whole system. An additional problem is that a test for one form of misspecification is also sensitive to other forms of misspecification. An obvious extension is to combine the BG, Reset and HW tests into one regression and the BP and Arch tests into another (see, for example, McGuirk *et al.* (1993, 1995)), but again lack of degrees of freedom does not allowed us to do this.

The effects of pretesting and small sample size thus indicate using higher significance levels than is customary so as to increase the chance of rejection,

---

[24] Note that the use of asymptotic results in small samples will increase the chance of rejecting the null. We consistently use small sample distributions in this study, however.

whilst mass significance indicates the opposite. Since we have reduced the problem of mass significance by using (sub)system tests, we use a 10 percent significance level as the benchmark for our misspecification tests.

4.4.2 Goodness-of-Fit Measures

The usual R^2 measure is only truly appropriate in a single equation context. For system estimation a number of alternatives have been suggested, see Judge *et al.* (1985 pp. 477-478). An easily applied generalisation is McElroy's R_*^2 measure

$$R_*^2 = 1 - \frac{\operatorname{tr} \boldsymbol{S}^{-1} \hat{\boldsymbol{\Sigma}}_e}{\operatorname{tr} \boldsymbol{S}^{-1} \hat{\boldsymbol{\Sigma}}_y} \tag{41}$$

where $\hat{\boldsymbol{\Sigma}}_e$ is the estimated residual covariance matrix, and $\hat{\boldsymbol{\Sigma}}_y$ is the estimated covariance matrix of the dependent variables. This measure reduces to the usual R^2 statistic in the single equation case, but also has the intuitive appeal of reducing to a weighted arithmetic mean of the equation-by-equation R^2 measures if the variables are orthogonal. Greene (1993, p. 490) suggests, however, that systemwise measures should only complement, but not replace, the single equation R^2.

The $\boldsymbol{S}$ matrix takes on different values depending on the estimation method. For systemwise least squares $\boldsymbol{S} = \boldsymbol{I}$, for seemingly unrelated regressions $\boldsymbol{S}$ is the initial covariance matrix estimate while for maximum likelihood $\boldsymbol{S} = \hat{\boldsymbol{\Sigma}}_e$. Letting m denote the number of estimated equations we can thus write the ML measure as

$$R_*^2 = 1 - \frac{m}{\operatorname{tr} \hat{\boldsymbol{\Sigma}}_e^{-1} \hat{\boldsymbol{\Sigma}}_y}. \tag{42}$$

Another generalisation has been suggested by Berndt (1991, p. 468), namely replacing the trace function in (42) by the determinant. This has the disadvantage of reducing to a weighted product when the variables are orthogonal, and not a weighted average. Berndt's measure is, however, easily modified so that it still reduces to the usual R^2 in the single equation case, but where it reduces to a weighted geometric mean when the variables are orthogonal. This modification, which we use in this study, can be written

$$\tilde{R}^2 = 1 - \sqrt[m]{\frac{\det \hat{\boldsymbol{\Sigma}}_e}{\det \hat{\boldsymbol{\Sigma}}_y}}. \tag{43}$$

Note that the system R^2:s can be adjusted for degrees of freedom in a similar manner to the single equation versions. Note also that is often useful to compare nested models by showing the relative improvement of one model over a less parameterised version. If, for example, R_S^2 is the goodness-of-fit from a static model, and R_D^2 the goodness-of-fit from a dynamic habit forming model, then the relative improvement can be expressed as

$$R_{D:S}^2 = \frac{R_D^2 - R_S^2}{1 - R_S^2}, \tag{44}$$

which we call the R^2 for the dynamic model *adjusted for the static model.* This adjustment can be applied for both single equation and system measures.

4.4.3 Testing Economic Hypotheses

There are a number of hypotheses of economic interest that we wish to test, if the model can be considered correctly specified. Homogeneity and symmetry are two examples, but hypotheses concerning elasticities are also of interest.

Let us first consider hypotheses that directly imply (linear) restrictions on the parameters. The usual methodologies of Likelihood Ratio (LRT), Wald and Lagrange Multiplier (LM) testing are available if we are using maximum likelihood methods. In fact LRT and Wald tests follow almost directly from the maximisation process (LRT) and the Taylor series technique used for finding standard errors (Wald).

These tests only have an asymptotic justification, however, and as previously remarked, a number of studies have shown that especially the Wald test has a considerable bias towards rejection in small samples if the number of equations is large. Several authors have proposed small sample corrections, the most common of which is to multiply the LRT (U) or Wald (W) statistics by $C=(T-k)/T$, where k is the average number of parameters per equation, see Bewley (1986) for a thorough discussion. If q is the number of restrictions being tested, then U, W, CU and CW are all distributed asymptotically as χ_q^2 under the null hypothesis.

Rao's "exact" LRT can be used here for both the homogeneity and the symmetry hypotheses. For homogeneity $m_1 = 1$, $m_2 = m = n-1$ and k is the average number of parameters per equation, whilst a test of symmetry (which also implies homogeneity) has $m_1 = n/2$ and the other parameters unchanged.

The homogeneity test, which is exact for linear models, can be simplified to

$$\Lambda^* = \left(\frac{T-k-m+1}{m}\right)\left(\frac{1-\Lambda}{\Lambda}\right). \tag{45a}$$

which is $F_{m,T-k-m+1}$ distributed under the null hypothesis. Bewley (1986) has shown that the adjusted Wald test,

$$W^* = \left(\frac{T-k-m+1}{mT}\right)W, \tag{45b}$$

is numerically equal to Λ^* in linear models. For the symmetry test no approximation to an exact Wald test is available, while (37) has to be applied directly for the Likelihood Ratio test.[25]

The tests considered so far assume homoscedasticity. It is easy to adapt the Wald tests to the heteroscedastic case, however, by simply using White's robust standard errors. Note that the "exact" LAIDS test (45b) is now merely asymptotic. As far as the authors know, no such methods are available for Likelihood Ratio or Lagrange Multiplier tests when non-specific heteroscedasticity is present.

Another complication occurs when estimating with non-ML methods. An alternative test, which is especially useful when using instrumental variables methods, is the Quasi Likelihood Ratio (QLR) test of Gallant and Jorgenson (1979). This is in fact a generalised sums-of-squares test, and can utilise the same small sample correction as given above.[26]

Utility maximisation also implies that the matrices given in (3d) shall be negative semidefinite. This can only be feasibly tested for a given time point (for example the base year) or for mean values, but cannot be globally imposed or tested within the AIDS framework. One possibility is to simply inspect all the estimated $\boldsymbol{K}_t$ matrices to see if they are negative semidefinite. This is quite time consuming, and we use instead a necessary condition, namely that these matrices have negative diagonal terms. This last condition is equivalent to simply checking if all compensated own-price elasticities are negative.

Another problem is how to test hypotheses concerning the AIDS/LAIDS elasticities. In these situations the alternative hypothesis is often unclear, and only Wald tests, or equivalently the use of confidence intervals, are really viable in such cases.

The assumptions of adding up[27], homogeneity, symmetry and negativity all follow from the budget constraint and utility maximisation. If now these assumptions are rejected, does this imply that we are rejecting the basic laws of demand? The answer to this is not apparent. Our tests also require a large number of other assumptions, including of course a correctly specified functional form. One aspect of this assumption is that aggregation over households occurs without undue bias, which in the AIDS case means that we are using a correct measure of population size, where account is taken of taste variations between households. If our model assumes a strong similarity of tastes across households (as ours does), and this is not correct, then it is quite possible that the microeconomic assumptions (3) will be rejected when using macro data, even though the macro AIDS model might still be an adequate approximation of the macro demand function. An interesting discussion concerning these questions is to be found in Keuzenkamp and Barten (1995).

---

[25] Evaluating P-values for fractional degrees of freedom has been solved by linear interpolation.

[26] It is important to use the same metric (estimate of Σ) for both the restricted and unrestricted models when estimating with non-ML methods. The test statistics can otherwise become nonsensical in small samples, see Engle (1984).

[27] The problems concerned with testing for adding up are discussed in Chapter 11.

5

A COMMON DYNAMIC AIDS MODEL FOR THE NORDIC COUNTRIES*

5.1 INTRODUCTION

5.1.1 Derivation of the Common Model

In the previous two chapters we discussed the economic and econometric pre-requisites that are necessary if we are to be able to obtain good estimates of a demand system. As we have seen, the choice of functional form is only partially determined by economic theory, that is we require that the demand system should be derived from an expenditure function (or equivalently, a utility function) with certain desirable properties, at least at the micro-level. A broad class of functions satisfy these conditions, amongst them such flexible functional forms as the Translog functions and Deaton and Muellbauer's (1980b) Almost Ideal Demand System (AIDS).

In this chapter we discuss the application of the dynamic AIDS model given by (4.10) to the Nordic countries. We will use the three stage budgeting process defined by the utility tree in Figure 2.1, and the resulting system is called the *Common Model.* The reason for choosing the AIDS functional form is quite straightforward: it is easy to apply, theoretically just as flexible as the translog and empirically there is little difference between the models (see, for example Lewbel (1989)). The choice of dynamic form needs some more explanation, however.

The static form of the AIDS system, (4.2), has been estimated in numerous applications, and has regularly been shown to exhibit significant autocorrelation in the residuals. This can be taken as an indication of dynamic misspecification, and several authors have addressed the problem of developing a dynamic version of the AIDS model. Two crucial problems concerning consistency with economic theory appear in their work. Firstly, the dynamic system should be derived from a proper expenditure function, and secondly, the adding-up property should be applicable.

One way of attacking the above problem is to use the method of translating, suggested by Pollak and Wales (1981) in the context of introducing demographic variation. The use of translating in connection with dynamic AIDS was first employed by Blanciforti and Green (1983), who proposed the following specification

* This chapter, which is the shared responsibility of all the authors, has been written by Bengt Assarsson and David Edgerton.

$$\alpha_i = \alpha_i^* + \alpha_i^{**} q_{i,t-1}, \tag{1}$$

which does not meet the adding-up requirement, however. Another proposal, suggested by Ray (1985), is to simply add the term $\sum_k \alpha_k^{**} q_{k,t-1}$ to the expenditure function (4.1). This will only change the form of the price index (4.2b), however. The method we use is that suggested by Alessie and Kapteyn (1991) and Assarsson (1991), namely to let

$$\alpha_i = \alpha_i^* + \sum_j \theta_{kj} w_{j,t-1}, \tag{2}$$

where $\sum_j \theta_{ij} = 0\ \forall_i$, or some other suitable restriction, is imposed for identification. The translating mechanisms suggested above can be interpreted as the way subsistence expenditures vary according to previous consumption patterns, since α_i represents the budget share for the ith good when expenditures are at subsistence level. Substituting (2) into (4.1) yields the expenditure function for this model, and the term

$$\sum_k \sum_j \theta_{kj} w_{j,t-1} \ln p_{kt} \tag{3}$$

can be interpreted as the cost of habits, which we expect to be positive. The relevant demand function obtained from this expenditure function is given in (4.10), and as previously stated this can also be seen as a special case of the interrelated partial adjustment model given by Anderson and Blundell (1983).

5.1.2 Analysing the Common Model

In the rest of this chapter we present and analyse the results of our estimation of the common model using Danish, Finnish, Norwegian and Swedish data.[1] This is done in three stages. Firstly, we discuss the statistical specification of the estimated model, that is we examine the data generating process given by (4.10) to see if it is statistically relevant. This is mainly done by considering the results of the diagnostic tests described in Chapter 4.4.1, but we also consider goodness-of-fit. Secondly, we test a number of economic hypotheses, such as homogeneity and symmetry. We also consider certain parameters (such as the constant term) and compensated elasticities, whose sign is indicated by economic theory, as well as the importance of habit forming. Finally, we consider the numerical values of the estimated parameters and elasticities.

At all stages of our analysis we look separately at the different countries, but we also compare these results and try to draw some general conclusions. The numerical results are mainly presented in the tables found in the appendix to this chapter, although some excerpts from these tables can be found in the main text where

[1] See chapter 2 for a discussion of the sources of our data

appropriate. In general, however, we concentrate on summarising the results when presenting them in the main text.

5.2 STATISTICAL EVALUATION

5.2.1 Introduction

In this section we mainly analyse the common model to see if it passes the diagnostic tests presented in Chapter 4. These tests can be roughly divided into two broad classes, which are not completely exclusive. Firstly we have tests that are related to the functional form of the model and the variables included therein, namely Ramsey's Reset test for omitted variables, the Hausman-Wu tests for endogeneity of total and group expenditure and the Cusumsq test for parameter instability. The other group of tests are concerned with properties of the error terms, *i.e.* the Breusch-Godfrey test of autocorrelation, the Breusch-Pagan test of heteroscedasticity, Engle's Arch test and the Jarque-Bera test of non-normality.

The above division can be useful when analysing our results, but it must be remembered that it is somewhat arbitrary. We know, for example, that tests for autocorrelated errors are also powerful against the alternative of (autocorrelated) omitted variables, and that the Cusumsq test is powerful against certain forms of heteroscedasticity.

The main thrust of our analysis is the use of systemwise tests, as described in Table 4.1, which are all first-order tests using cross components from all equations in the system. We evaluate *P*-values using the *F*-distribution associated with the appropriate "exact" likelihood ration test (ELRT). We also consider single equation tests for each equation, however, which are evaluated as usual *F*-tests *without* any cross components. Note that the *P*-values of the systemwise tests need not be an average of the single equation results, since the tests use different regressors, the regressands in the systemwise test can be correlated and we have the problem of mass significance. Significance of a systemwise test, where all the single equation tests are non-significant, indicates the presence of cross-equation effects. Rejection of the single equation tests, without rejection of the systemwise test, can be due to mass significance or to loss of power in the systemwise test in the absence of cross-equation effects.

The strategy we use differs somewhat from that which is customary. A cursory inspection of papers concerning the analysis of demand systems in the *American Journal of Agricultural Economics* between volumes 72 and 76:2, reveals only one example of systemwise tests, namely Alston and Chalfant (1991b) who consider an asymptotic systemwise Chow test. In fact very few of the articles in this period use more than at most one or two single equation diagnostic tests, usually only quoting a few Durbin-Watson statistics. A notable exception to this is the paper by McGuirk *et al.* (1993), who consider in detail the effects of multiple diagnostic testing in a single equation environment and even mention the need for systemwise tests.

Another difference to the usual approach is the use of a 10 percent significance level as the benchmark. The reasons for doing this were discussed in detail in Chapter 4.4.1, but it must be remembered that we are applying a more strict criterion than is usual, and we are thus more likely to reject the null hypotheses. We must also remember that a barely significant result for merely one or two of the single equation tests can be illusory, due to mass significance.

When judging the results of our diagnostic tests we look at tables of *P*-values for systemwise and single equation tests. As pointed out above, these tests have greater power against different alternative hypotheses, and it therefore makes sense to look at both sets of tests. To enable us to summarise the results we want to consider both how many of the different tests are significant and the strength of the significance; many very significant results obviously lead us to reject the null with some confidence while a few barely significant results are not very indicative. In Tables 1a-1c we attempt to provide a (somewhat arbitrary) taxonomy of significance, which is used in our further analysis.

Table 1a. Categorisation of Number of Significant Results

Mark	Test *with* system variant		Test *without* system variant	
	4 equations	3 equations	4 equations	3 equations
xxx	SYS & 3+	SYS & 2+	4	3
xx	SYS & 1 or 2 4	SYS & 1 3	3	2
x	SYS & 0 3	SYS & 0 2	2	1*

The entries in the table state the number of significant (10% level) results necessary to qualify for the given mark. SYS is the abbreviation for the systemwise test while the numbers indicate how many significant single equation tests are required. * = see Table 1b.

Table 1b. Categorisation of Size of P-Values

Font Style of Mark	Bold Upper Case	Bold Lower Case	Italic Lower Case
Size of *P*-value	SYS ≤ 1%, or at least 2 singles ≤ 1%	SYS ≤ 5%, or at least 2 singles ≤ 5%	SYS > 5%, and at most 1 single ≤ 5%S

* = only one *P*-value needs to be ≤ 1% or 5% to qualify for bold type in this cell of Table 1a.

Table 1c. Summary Categorisation of Strength of Significance

Strength	Abbreviation	Marks
Strong Significance	S	**XXX** or **XX** or **xxx**
Medium Significance	M	**X** or **xx** or *xxx*
Weak Significance	W	**x** or *xx* or *x*

A typical entry in Table 1a, for example "SYS & 1 or 2" in the third cell of the second column, indicates that a four equation system, where the systemwise test and one or two of the single equation tests are significant at the 10 percent level, is categorised with "xx". In a similar manner, the entry "4" in the same cell indicates that if all of the four single equation tests are significant, but not the systemwise test, then this is also marked "xx".

Using the same example as before, we can see from Table 1b that if the systemwise test or two of the single equation tests are significant at the 1 percent level then this is categorised "**XX**". If the same applies at the 5 percent level we use "**xx**", while otherwise we use "*xx*". Finally Table 1c tells us whether the result is considered to have strong, medium or weak significance. Hopefully this taxonomy allows us to distinguish between those cases with obvious significance, those with probable significance and those with doubtful significance.

Before looking at the results for the different countries, we must give a word of warning concerning interpretation. The results of the Finnish, Norwegian and Swedish estimations are based on roughly the same time span and number of observations. The Danish estimates are based on roughly 25 percent more observations, however, which has two implications. Firstly, the economies in the fifties might be considerably different from the rest of the time period, which would show itself in the Danish results but not in the others. A difference between Denmark and the other countries could then be due to this effect, rather than to any intrinsic difference.

The other effect is purely statistical. The greater number of observations in the Danish case leads to a greater precision in those estimates, and therefore to a greater chance of rejecting *any* null-hypothesis. This is, of course, well known, but it is surprising how often the concepts of *significance* and *importance* are still confused. For a large sample size we can, in other words, be *very* certain that a hypothesis is not *exactly* true, without the deviation from the hypothesis necessarily being of any great importance.

When analysing our model, we consider the six different subsystems defined by Figure 2.1, that is *Private Consumption*, *Food-at-Home*, *Animalia*, *Beverages*, *Vegetablia* and *Miscellaneous*. The results for the systemwise tests for all countries at this level are given in Table 2. Note that for the Jarque-Bera and Cusumsq tests, which only exist as single equation tests, we give the *average* P-value for each system. This is *not* a statistically correct procedure, and these averages can only be taken as a descriptive measure of confidence in the relevant null hypotheses. Table 2 also contains two goodness-of-fit measures, namely the systemwise R^2 adjusted for degrees of freedom, and the relative improvement in R^2 caused by fitting a dynamic instead of a static model (see Chapter 4.4.4).

In many ways it would seem more natural to apply our diagnostic tests, *etc.* to the complete system comprising of all estimated equations. This involves problems of the type discussed in footnote 3 on page 107, however, *i.e.* that maximum likelihood estimation is not possible due to singularity in the estimated Hessian matrix. For this reason we only consider the different subsystems independently. See

Table 2. Systemwise Diagnostic Tests (P-values) and Measures of Goodness-of-Fit

Land		Systemwise *P*-values						Average *P*-value		Adjusted R^2	
		BG	BP	Arch	Reset	HW(tx)	HW(di)	JB	Cusumsq	df	D:S
	PC	.583	.692	.786	**.021**		**.043**	.687	.294	.932	.441
	FAH	.520	.720	**.065**	.971	**.060**	.909	.588	.205	.753	.286
Den-	A	.774	.934	.849	**.020**	.139	.105	.544	**.034**	.837	.516
mark	B	**.002**	**.001**	.573	.247	.346	**.068**	.683	**.000**	.874	.308
	V	.451	.519	.549	**.086**	.512	**.065**	.771	.155	.807	.211
	M	.825	.726	.613	.108	**.001**	**.000**	.680	**.098**	.921	.483
	PC	.281	.369	.393	.162		**.048**	.735	**.070**	.939	.160
	FAH	**.086**	.304	.148	.515	.138	**.073**	.834	.190	.896	.233
Fin-	A	.767	**.001**	.360	.802	.663	.419	.211	.255	.773	.027
land	B	.628	.486	.809	.340	.811	.616	.598	.108	.906	.101
	V	.787	.660	.844	.199	**.001**	**.001**	.850	.112	.870	.296
	M	**.000**	.659	.266	.248	**.000**	**.000**	.330	.389	.875	.358
	PC	**.010**	**.056**	.373	**.078**		**.034**	.714	.254	.910	.320
	FAH	.913	.598	.502	.282	.284	.479	.645	.131	.880	.120
Nor	A	.659	.329	.277	**.042**	.578	.492	.557	.131	.920	.450
-way	B	.187	.144	.447	.462	.848	.743	.631	.367	.840	.260
	V	.155	**.034**	**.000**	.287	**.029**	**.002**	.329	**.017**	.940	.060
	M	**.013**	.194	**.000**	.179	**.000**	**.000**	.236	**.057**	.950	.290
	PC	**.034**	.430	.553	**.001**		**.001**	.265	.246	.943	.211
	FAH	.319	.525	.597	**.078**	.291	.505	.801	.199	.826	.416
Swe-	A	.236	**.032**	.684	.259	.327	.294	.704	.280	.824	–.066
den	B	.955	.257	.834	**.061**	.677	.498	.894	.380	.923	.433
	V	.399	.487	.724	.506	.242	.334	.910	.380	.884	.002
	M	.602	.727	.705	.489	.840	.949	.786	.255	.932	.545

The following abbreviations are used: Private consumption (PC), Food-at-home (FAH), Animalia (A), Beverages (B), Vegetablia (V), Miscellaneous (M), Breusch-Godfrey (BG), Breusch-Pagan (BP), Hausman-Wu (HW) and Jarque-Bera (JB). The HW instruments are disposable income (di) or total expenditure (tx). Figures in bold face indicate *P*-values of less than 10%. The R^2 measures have been adjusted for degrees of freedom (df) and for both improvement over the static model and for degrees of freedom (D:S).

Chapter 6 for a further discussion of this type of problem.

5.2.2 Analyses for the Different Countries

Denmark

The results of the systemwise diagnostic tests are given for all countries in Table 2, while the single equation results can be found in Table A3 in the appendix to this chapter. Using the taxonomy described in Tables 1a-c, we summarise the Danish results as follows.

Table 3. Summary of Diagnostic Tests for Denmark

	BG	BP	Arch	Reset	HW(tx)	HW(di)	JB	Cusumsq
PC				xx	–	xx		
FAH			*xx*		xx			
A				xx			*x*	xxx
B	XX	XXX	*x*	x		XXX		XXX
V				*xx*		*xx*		xx
M					XXX	XXX		*xx*

The same abbreviations are used as in Table 2.

Looking at Table 3 we can see that the *beverages* subsystem is quite severely misspecified, both regarding functional form and error structure. No subsystem is free from misspecification, but it is the third stage of the budget process that seems most questionable. Note that it is the tests connected with the functional form that seem to be most in doubt (Reset, Hausman-Wu and Cusumsq), as apart from *beverages* the error structure seems to be reasonably well specified.

The long time span covered by the Danish data leads to a greater chance of rejection, as indicated earlier. Preferences may change over a forty year period, which will quite reasonably be indicated in a Cusumsq test. Note that, except for *beverages*, the homoscedasticity hypothesis is not rejected (either with Breusch-Pagan or Arch), which seems to indicate that the Cusumsq results are due to parameter instability, not "normal" heteroscedasticity.

Problems with possible endogeneity of both total and group expenditures are common. These can be due to the actual structure of conditional demand systems (see Deaton (1986), LaFrance (1991) and Edgerton (1993b)), but the simultaneous significance of the Reset tests seems to indicate problems with the separability structure.

Another aspect of the statistical evaluation is goodness-of-fit. From Tables 1 and A2 we can see that all systemwise adjusted R^2 :s are greater than 0.75, which is a satisfactory, if not outstanding, result. The single equation values are all over 0.50, with the exception of the *animalia* equation in the second stage, which is only 0.37, and the *potatoes* equation at the third stage (0.47).

A total of 19 of the 47 cells in Table 3 show a significant result, though only 7 of these are strongly significant in the sense we defined earlier. Quite a lot of work seems still to be necessary on the Danish model, however. It seems unlikely that preferences have been stable under the whole period, and some sort of switching regressions model might be appropriate. The functional form and separability assumption might also be investigated, especially for the third stage (concentrating on the *beverages* subsystem), and some form of IV estimation might be appropriate. Work along these lines might also improve the goodness-of-fit for those systems and equations where this is poor.

Table 4. Summary of Diagnostic Tests for Finland

	BG	BP	Arch	Reset	HW(tx)	HW(di)	JB	Cusumsq
PC					–	xx		
FAH	*x*					*xx*		
A		X						X
B								*x*
V				*x*	XXX	XXX		*xx*
M	X				XXX	XXX		

The same abbreviations are used as in Table 2.

Finland

The summary for the Finnish tests is given in Table 4. Firstly we can see that the no pattern seems to be discernible for the tests of the error structure. A few significant results can be seen, but none are strongly significant and the general impression seems to be that these results are fairly satisfactory.

The tests of functional form, *etc.*, are, however, more problematic, especially for the *vegetablia* and *miscellaneous* subsystems. These subsystems have significant results for the endogeneity tests, and also weak significance (for *vegetablia*) for Reset and Cusumsq. Adjustments to the separability structure seem to be required most of all, although use of IV methods might also be appropriate. Total and group expenditures seem also to exhibit endogeneity in the first two stages of the process, reinforcing the suggestion of using disposable income as an instrument.

Regarding goodness-of-fit, we can see that all systemwise adjusted R^2:s are greater than 0.75, which is again satisfactory. The single equation values are also all over 0.50, with the exception of the fish equation at the third stage, which is only 0.32.

The Finnish model seems on the whole to work quite well. Only 19 of 47 cells are significant, with only 4 of these being strongly significant. Some work seems to be necessary on the *vegetablia* and *miscellaneous* subsystems, however, and the possible use of IV methods might be advisable.

Norway

Looking at Table 5 we can see that the Norwegian model seems to suffer from a fair amount of misspecification. A total of 23 cells exhibit some significance, but it should be noted that only 6 results are strongly significant.

The *vegetablia* and *miscellaneous* subsystems are both badly misspecified, with strong significance being registered for various aspects of both error and model structure. *Private consumption* also exhibits a considerable number of significant results, none of them strongly significant, however. Furthermore, the *food-at-home*

Table 5. Summary of Diagnostic Tests for Norway

	BG	BP	Arch	Reset	HW(tx)	HW(di)	JB	Cusumsq
PC	xx	*xx*		*xx*	–	xx		
FAH								x
A				*xx*				*x*
B		x					X	X
V		x	X		xx	XXX	xx	xxx
M	xxx	x	XX		XXX	XXX	xx	xx

The same abbreviations are used as in Table 2.

equation, which the rest of the model is based upon, passes all of the single equation tests at the 5 percent level.

Two of the subsystems also exhibit autocorrelation in the residuals, which might indicate that an adjustment to the dynamic structure could be useful, and the use of IV estimates might help reduce the effect of endogeneity. In many subsystems significant Cusumsq statistics are accompanied by significant heteroscedasticity, suggesting that it may be the error variances that vary over time, and not the structural parameters.

The goodness-of-fit measures are quite good for the Norwegian model, being over 0.80 for both the systemwise and the single equation statistics.

Sweden

The results for the Swedish model are summarised in Table 6. The general impression is that the model is fairly well specified, only 10 cells are significant with merely 3 being strongly significant. This is particularly so for the third stage subsystems, where the *vegetablia* and *miscellaneous* subsystems pass all the diagnostic tests.

The only real exception to the above is the first stage, which is severely misspecified. A more detailed study of Table A3 in the appendix reveals that the *food-at-home* equation passes all the single equation tests, however. It is mainly the *restaurants* equation that is badly misspecified. This is important, since the rest of

Table 6. Summary of Diagnostic Tests for Sweden

	BG	BP	Arch	Reset	HW(tx)	HW(di)	JB	Cusumsq
PC	xx			XX	–	XX	x	*x*
FAH				*xx*				
A	x	xxx						*x*
B				*xx*				
V								
M								

The same abbreviations are used as in Table 2.

the model is built upon divisions of the *food-at-home* category.

Some evidence exists that adjusting the functional form might bring some improvement, since three of the subsystems have significant Reset results. Otherwise the Swedish results seem to indicate a satisfactory application of the common model. This is reinforced by looking at the goodness-of-fit statistics, which are all over 0.80 for the systemwise measures and over 0.60 in the single equation cases.

5.2.3 Comparisons and Conclusions

A summary of the significance of the various misspecification tests for the different countries is given in Table 7. Using this table and the results presented for the individual countries, we can arrive at a number of general conclusions.

1. The first stage is misspecified for all countries with regards to endogeneity of total expenditure and omitted variables.
2. Group expenditures are endogenous in at least some parts of stage two and three for all countries except Sweden.
3. Parameter instability is widespread for Denmark and Norway. The two countries have a somewhat different profile, however. In Denmark it seems to be the structural parameters that are unstable, whilst in Norway it can well be the error variances. Some evidence of this can also be seen in Finland.
4. The *vegetablia* and *miscellaneous* subsystems are misspecified for all countries except Sweden.
5. The general result seems to be that the Swedish and Finnish models pass the diagnostic tests reasonably well, while the Danish and Norwegian models perform less satisfactorily. This is especially true for the *vegetablia* and *miscellaneous* subsystems for Norway.

A number of measures can be taken to remedy some of the problems cited above. Some evidence seems to be present for changing the dynamic structure of the first stage, at least for Norway and Sweden. A switching regressions model may also be relevant for Denmark and Norway. Changes in the separability structure of the model may also help.

Another approach is to adjust the estimation method. Instrumental variable estimation (probably using disposable income as an instrument) can be tried, for

Table 7. Number of Significant Results for Misspecification Tests

	Strong	Medium	Weak	All
Denmark	7	5	7	19
Finland	4	4	5	13
Norway	6	10	7	23
Sweden	3	2	5	10

The maximum number of significant results is 47.

example, if endogeneity problems remain after adjusting the model. The occasional presence of heteroscedasticity does not seem to warrant sophisticated modelling, but our use of White's robust standard errors seems to be wise.

5.3 TESTING ECONOMIC HYPOTHESES

5.3.1 Introduction

In the previous section we discussed the statistical evaluation of the common model, treated as a data generating process. In this section we consider some economic implications of the model. This strategy is reasonable for those countries (Sweden and Finland) that passed the diagnostic tests reasonably well, but may be more doubtful for Denmark and Norway. Since the common model is quite misspecified for these countries, it is an open question as to how informative any tests of economic hypotheses can be. For the sake of completeness all countries and commodity groups are included in the discussion in this section, but the results for the more misspecified (sub)systems must be treated with some caution.

The economic hypotheses consider here are of two types. Firstly we have those which are associated with the model we are using. Looking at equation (4.10), which defines the common model, we expect all the constant terms (α_i:s) to lie between zero and one, since they represent budget shares at subsistence expenditure. We can also consider the relevance of the dynamic model by looking at the relative increase of the degrees of freedom adjusted R^2 when moving from the static to the dynamic model (see equation (4.44)) and by looking at the sign of the own lags (θ_{ii}:s), which can be expected to be positive. Testing the separability structure is a further hypothesis of this type, although this was also considered in the previous section.

The other types of hypothesis we consider are those connected with the laws of demand. Homogeneity and symmetry can be tested using LR or Wald tests. Negativity is more difficult to test within the AIDS framework, since the matrix we are looking at varies from observation to observation. A necessary condition, however, is that the compensated own-price elasticities ($\tilde{e}_{ii}$:s) should always be negative. Finally, tests of adding up are considered in Chapter 11.

The tables to be presented in the rest of this section are based upon Tables A1, A2, A4, A7 and A10 in the appendix. We denote with "**X**" those cases where the one-sided 90 percent confidence intervals do not include values with the correct sign, for at least one of the α_i:s, θ_{ii}:s and $\tilde{e}_{ii}$:s respectively in the system being studied.[2] For the elasticities this must hold when evaluated at both the mean and last values, if it only holds for one of these we denote it with "*x*". The results for the

---

[2] This has been performed in practice by seeing if the estimated parameter/elasticity lies more than 1.3 times the robust standard error from values with the correct sign. The critical value for a one sided 10% significance test from a normal distribution is 1.282.

formal tests of *homogeneity*, *homogeneity and symmetry* and *statics* (*no dynamics*) are also marked with "**X**" if both the "exact" LRT and the robust Wald test are significant at the 10 percent level, while "*x*" is used if only one is. Note that for the Wald tests, only the test of homogeneity is an "exact" F-test. Both LRT and Wald tests are used since they capture different aspects of the testing situation, the Wald test is (asymptotically) robust against heteroscedasticity while the LRT is "exact" in the meaning described in Chapter 4.4.3.

Finally, the results for the separability hypothesis are based on the simultaneous rejection of both the Reset and Hausman-Wu tests presented in the previous section. In this case we mark those cells where the Reset test and at least one of the endogeneity tests are significant, an "**X**" being used to denote the significance combinations SS or SM, an "**x**" for the combinations MM or SW and an "*x*" for the combinations MW and WW, (see Table 1c for an explanation of these abbreviations).

5.3.2 Analyses for the Different Countries

Denmark

The most obvious conclusion from Table 8 is that the static model is rejected for all subsystems. This can also be seen by looking at the goodness-of-fit measures, where the system relative improvement of dynamic over static is always greater than 20 percent. Note, however, that in two cases we have statistically significant negative own lags. The simultaneous significance rejection of the Reset and Hausman-Wu tests indicate that the separability structure seems somewhat doubtful.

As noted in the previous section, the Danish model did not perform that well as a data generating process. The homogeneity and symmetry hypotheses are also often rejected, the exceptions being for *animalia* and *miscellaneous*. Nearly all compensated own-price elasticities are negative, however, which agrees with the negativity hypothesis. We can also see that some of the constant terms are negative in the *beverages* subsystem, which is the most poorly specified in the model.

Table 8. Summary of Tests of Restrictions for Denmark

	$0 \le \alpha_i \le 1$	$\theta_{ii} \ge 0$	Separability	Static	Homogeneity	Hom/Sym	$\tilde{e}_{ii} \le 0$
PC	**X**	**X**	**x**	**X**	*x*		
FAH				**X**		**X**	
A				**X**			
B	**X**		**x**	**X**	**X**	**X**	*x*
V			*x*	**X**	**X**	**X**	
M		**X**		**X**			

The same abbreviations are used as in Table 2, plus that Hom/Sym is the abbreviation for homogeneity and symmetry. The marks indicate rejection of the null hypotheses given in the column headings.

Finland

The hypothesis of a static system is not rejected for the *animalia* subsystem in the Finnish case. In fact the effect of dynamics is considerably less than for Denmark, the systemwise goodness-of-fit increases being less than 20 percent for *private consumption*, *animalia* and *beverages*, and the single equation increases are less than 10 percent for the *miscellaneous* system within *food-at-home*, for all of the *animalia* equations, for *soft drinks* and for *sugar*. A negative own lag can also be found in the *beverages* subsystem. The separability structure seems to be quite satisfactory, however.

The laws of demand are also rejected firmly in the Finnish case, the exceptions being *vegetablia* and *miscellaneous* that are the two subsystems that exhibit the greatest statistical misspecification! As in the Danish case, however, nearly all compensated own-price elasticities are negative, and for Finland none of the constant terms are significantly negative.

Table 9. Summary of Tests of Restrictions for Finland

	$0 \le \alpha_i \le 1$	$\theta_{ii} \ge 0$	Separability	Static	Homogeneity	Hom/Sym	$\tilde{e}_{ii} \le 0$
PC				X	X	X	
FAH				X	X	X	
A					X	X	
B		X		X	X	X	*x*
V			x	X			
M				X		X	

The same abbreviations and notes apply as in Table 8.

Table 10. Summary of Tests of Restrictions for Norway

	$0 \le \alpha_i \le 1$	$\theta_{ii} \ge 0$	Separability	Static	Homogeneity	Hom/Sym	$\tilde{e}_{ii} \le 0$
PC	X		*x*	X		*x*	
FAH	X	X		X	X	X	
A				X	X	X	
B	X			X	X	X	
V				*x*	X	X	
M				X			

The same abbreviations and notes apply as in Table 8.

Norway

The static model is soundly rejected for Norway, although in two cases (*food-at-home* and *vegetablia*) the dynamic model's gain in goodness-of-fit is less than 20 percent. The laws of demand are also rejected in all cases except *miscellaneous* and (maybe) *private consumption*. Once again these two systems are statistically misspecified. Although the negativity hypothesis does not seem to be in question, we can see that we have unreasonable constant terms in half of the commodity groups.

Sweden

Even in the Swedish model we reject the static hypothesis in general. The *animalia* and *vegetablia* subsystems are exceptions, and in these cases the systemwise improvement of goodness-of-fit is also less than 20 percent. The single equation measures are less than 10 percent for all the components of the above subsystems, as is also the case for the *services* equation. Separability seems to be a problem in the first stage, but does not seem to be troublesome in the rest of the model.

The hypotheses of homogeneity, and homogeneity and symmetry, are both rejected, except for the *miscellaneous* subsystem. In this case the negativity hypothesis is soundly rejected, however, with a very large positive compensated own-price elasticity for sugar (0.78 at the mean and 2.00 in 1989!). Positive compensated own-price elasticities are actually observed in four different equations, which is peculiar to Sweden. No significantly negative constant terms or own lags are observed, however.

Table 11. Summary of Tests of Restrictions for Sweden

	$0 \leq \alpha_i \leq 1$	$\theta_{ii} \geq 0$	Separability	Static	Homogeneity	Hom/Sym	$\tilde{e}_{ii} \leq 0$
PC			**X**	**X**	**X**	**X**	
FAH				**X**	*x*	**X**	
A					**X**	**X**	**X**
B				**X**	**X**	**X**	*x*
V					**X**	**X**	*x*
M				**X**			**X**

The same abbreviations and notes apply as in Table 8.

5.3.3 Comparisons and Conclusions

We can see that the *homogeneity* and *homogeneity and symmetry* hypotheses are always rejected whenever any of the subsystems is correctly specified statistically. In those cases where the laws of demand are not rejected, then the equations seem to be misspecified statistically. This should not be taken as indicating that the laws of demand are actually incorrect at the micro-level, however, but rather that the system is misspecified in some way, see also the discussion in Chapter 4. When the statistical specification is "correct", then the main source of error can well be due to aggregation over individuals and households, see Deaton and Muellbauer (1980a) and Keuzenkamp and Barten (1991). If the AIDS model is correct this could be due to an incorrect measure of population size, but it is more likely that the basic assumptions of the PIGLOG expenditure function are violated. Remember that the rejection of the hypotheses is not likely to be due to incorrect asymptotics, since our "exact" tests are designed to correct for the systemwise effect of many equations.

One general conclusion is thus that the aggregate time-series demand functions for the Nordic countries do not satisfy the laws of demand as specified at the micro-level. This does not mean that these functions are useless, if they are correctly statistically specified they can still be used to estimate the macro-parameters and elasticities. This seems to be the case in Sweden and Finland, but may be somewhat more doubtfully in the other two countries due to the greater degree of misspecification in their data generating processes. Another conclusion is that habit-forming is important for all countries and in nearly all systems. There does not seem to be any obvious pattern to tell us where the static model could be accepted.

A further question that arises is how to proceed if a hypothesis concerning some set of restrictions is not rejected. Two strategies are common here. The first is to impose the restrictions exactly and "save" degrees of freedom. Actually this is a chimera, in such two-stage estimation data snooping is causing the true variances of the estimates to increase anyway. The other strategy is to not impose the restrictions. Since the only difference between these strategies occurs when the null hypothesis is not rejected, and in this case the parameter values in general are quite close to the hypothesised, then the practical effect on the estimates is usually quite small. The main effect is on the precision, which is probably greater in the two-stage strategy *but* will be incorrectly estimated. The results presented in this book usually follow the strategy of never imposing the restrictions, and thus maintaining correctly estimated standard errors. The only exception is in the Norwegian case where restrictions are imposed when they are not rejected at the 5 percent level, *i.e.* homogeneity is imposed in the first stage and homogeneity and symmetry in the *miscellaneous* subsystem.

5.4 ANALYSIS OF ELASTICITY ESTIMATES

5.4.1 Introduction

In this section we examine more closely the signs and values of the elasticities. We investigate how different food groups can be classified as luxuries/necessities and price elastic/inelastic, both regarding within their group and totally. The possibility of observing so called inferior goods (negative expenditure elasticity) or Giffen goods (positive own-price elasticity) is also considered, but it can already be noted that we tend to interpret such results as a sign of misspecification rather than an actual occurrence of what are rather rare economic phenomena. We also study certain cross-price elasticities.

Note that we do not make any formal tests of the hypothesis that all parameters or elasticities are identical for the different countries, partly due to econometric problems[3], but mainly due to the obvious dissimilarities between our results.

[3] Testing this hypothesis entails simultaneously estimating all the parameters for the different countries.

It should also be remembered that we are using expenditure data in our estimation, which has been obtained from the national accounts' series on private consumption. Most international food demand studies use disappearance data, which measures physical quantities for both the private and public sectors. The choice of expenditure or disappearance data is thus important when judging the effect of quality changes such as shifts from low to high processed foodstuffs. Expenditure data allow for the possibility that an increasing proportion of a good is highly processed and thereby may increase the expenditure, although the consumption of the good may actually decrease when measured in physical terms. This has implications on the interpretation of our elasticity estimates, especially when comparing them with other international results.

5.4.2 Within Group Elasticities

In many ways it is not particularly interesting to see whether a good is a *within group* luxury or necessity, it is rather the *total* elasticities that are of interest. Although the total elasticities have been estimated, and are also given in the tables in the appendix, we have in general not been able to calculate their standard errors since this would entail estimating the whole system simultaneously, something that is not possible when using maximum likelihood. We are thus forced to take a somewhat more indirect approach when analysing total elasticities, a point we shall return to later.[4] We therefore begin this section with an analysis of the within group characteristics.

When possible we would like to study the different effects through their parameter values, since we then merely have to look at one set of estimates and standard errors. When we look at elasticities directly, however, we must also take account of the variation over time. In the following tables we will therefore be judging the within group division of expenditure elasticities by looking at the β_i:s. In all other situations, however, we must look at the elasticities directly, and in these cases we only examine values at the mean and last year.

In Table 12 we examine the within group divisions into luxuries, necessities and inferior goods (expenditure elasticities), and into elastic, inelastic and Giffen goods (own-price elasticities). Only results that significantly differ from the boundaries of the divisions[5] are shown. Results given in brackets for the own-price elasticities, indicate that only one of the values at the mean and at the last year are significant.

What are the main impressions we can get from Table 12? Firstly, looking at the first stage, we can see that *food-at-home* is a significant necessity for all coun-

---

[4] As pointed out by a reviewer, an alternative approach would have been to use the bootstrap, or other Monte Carlo simulation method, to estimate the standard errors of the total elasticities.

[5] We have used ±2 standard errors as the critical values. The boundaries are $\beta_i = 0$ for luxury/necessity, $E_i = 0$ for necessity/inferior, $e_{ii} = -1$ for elastic/inelastic and $e_{ii} = 0$ for inelastic/Giffen.

Table 12. Classification of Within Group Elasticities. Significant Results

	Expenditure Elasticities			Own-Price Elasticities		
	Luxury	Necessity	Inferior	Elastic	Inelastic	Giffen
Food–at–home		D N S			D F N S	
Restaurants	F S					
Nondurables	D N S				F N S	
Services					D N S	
Animalia		F			D F N S	
Beverages	F N				F	
Vegetablia		N			D F N S	
Miscellaneous		D N			F N S	
Meat	F N S				D S	
Fish		S			F S	
Milk, Cheese and Eggs		D F N			D N S	(S)
Soft Drinks		S		F	S	
Hot Drinks		D F N S			D F N S	(D) (F) (S)
Alcoholic Drinks	D F N S			N	D	
Bread and Cereals	S	D F			D F N	
Fruit and Vegetables	D F	S			S	
Potatoes		S			D F N S	S
Fats and Oils	S	N			D F N S	
Sugar	N	S	S		D (F) N S	S
Confectionery *etc*					N S	

D = Denmark, F = Finland, N = Norway and S = Sweden.

tries except Finland. This is as expected, though the Finnish result is not just insignificant but has the "wrong" sign, something that has implications on the total elasticities to be discussed later on. Similarly the *restaurants* category is as expected a luxury in Finland and Sweden.

In all stages the own-price elasticities are rarely significantly elastic, and for the first stage they are mostly significantly inelastic. It is only *restaurants* that has insignificant results for more than one country. It can be seen from Table A1(a) that the own-price parameter is insignificant for *restaurants* in all countries, and this is not mainly due to low precision but rather to very small parameter estimates.

Looking at the other stages, we can see that the results are quite similar for the different countries in the second stage, and for *animalia* and *beverages* in the third. At the second stage few expenditure elasticities are significantly "luxuries" or "necessities", where our use of inverted commas in the text signifies that this classification is within *food-at-home*. At the third stage we can see that *meat* is in general a luxury and *milk, cheese and eggs* a necessity within *animalia*, whilst *alcoholic drinks* is a luxury and *hot drinks* a necessity within *beverages*. It is also in the *beverages* group that the only examples of goods being (within group) price-elastic can be noted, namely for Finnish *soft drinks* and Norwegian *alcoholic drinks*. In the case of *hot drinks* the own-price elasticities are significantly positive for three of the countries for the last year, something that actually also holds for the compensated elasticities.

The results for *vegetablia* and *miscellaneous* groups are more mixed. The Swedish estimates give *bread and cereals* as a within group luxury and *fruit and vegetables* as a within group necessity, while the opposite is true for Denmark and Finland. Only Sweden has *potatoes* as a within group necessity, but it is only the Swedish within group own-price elasticity that is significantly positive. A similar sort of dichotomy can be observed between Sweden and Norway regarding *fats and oils* and *sugar*, where again the Swedish necessity for sugar is accompanied by a positive own-price elasticity.

5.4.3 Total Elasticities

As previously noted, the standard errors of the total elasticities are not available from ML estimation of the common model. Anticipating the results of the next chapter, the dynamic Swedish model has also been estimated in LAIDS form using SUR. In particular we have estimated the model under the assumption of independent subsystems, which leads to the usual OLS estimates, but where standard errors of total elasticities can also be calculated. The results of these estimations are given in the appendix to Chapter 6 (Tables 6.A5 and 6.A6), where we can see that the AIDS and LAIDS elasticities differ only minutely. The standard errors given for the OLS estimates in the LAIDS model can thus be used as a reasonable approximation to the AIDS standard errors in the Swedish case.

Problems arise for the other countries, which have not been estimated using systemwise LAIDS. Looking at the results for Sweden we can see that the standard errors are much more similar for the total expenditure elasticities than for the within group elasticities, and in particular the very small within group standard error for *alcoholic drinks* and the large one for *potatoes* have disappeared. The results for the own-price standard errors are very similar both within group and totally. The length of the Swedish confidence intervals for the total elasticities is thus very similar for all foodstuffs.

Since we are now moving into the realm of supposition, a simple rule-of-thumb is to be desired. We therefore indicate a result outside the interval ±0.4 as "large" for the total expenditure elasticities, while we use ±0.3 for the total own-price elasticities. The term "large" is approximately equivalent to "significant at the 5 percent level" for Sweden, if maybe a little conservative. A comparison of the within group standard errors for the different countries (in Tables A5-A10) reveals that these are similar to the Swedish results, and thus the above intervals should perform reasonably well for all countries and goods. The only really obvious exceptions are for the total expenditures of Finnish *potatoes*, *fats and oils* and

Table 13. Classification of Total Elasticities. "Large" Results

	Luxury	Necessity	Inferior	Elastic	Inelastic	Giffen
Meat		(S)			D F N S	
Fish		F N S			F S	
Milk, Cheese and Eggs		D F N S			D F N S	
Soft Drinks	F	(D) S			(N) S	
Hot Drinks		D F N S	(F) (N)		D F N S	
Alcoholic Drinks	F N	S			D F	
Bread and Cereals		D F N S			D F N	
Fruit and Vegetables	F	N S			D F N S	
Potatoes	F	D N S			D F N S	
Fats and Oils		D (F) N S			D F N S	
Sugar		D S	(S)		D F N S	S
Confectionery *etc*	(F)	D N S			F N S	

D = Denmark, F = Finland, N = Norway and S = Sweden.

confectionery, where the within group values are twice as large as the other countries'. In these cases we have, in a rather *ad hoc* manner, doubled the length of the confidence interval. These "large" results are given in Table 13.

The results of this analysis are much more uniform than for the within group analysis. The majority of all foodstuffs are necessities, the main exceptions being for Finland where *soft drinks*, *alcoholic drinks*, *fruit and vegetables*, *potatoes* and (maybe) *confectionery* are luxuries. As previously noted, the reason for this is that *food-at-home* is a luxury in the Finnish case, albeit non-significant at that level. Note that the disaggregated results for Finland are, with the exception of *potatoes*, not completely contradictory to intuition. Other results concerning the total expenditure elasticities are that the *alcoholic drinks* group is also a luxury in Norway, though it is a necessity in Sweden. In a couple of cases we can observe inferior goods at the end of the period, namely for *hot drinks* in Finland and Norway, and for *sugar* in Sweden. These results are not so apparent at the mean value, however.

The own-price elasticities reveal that nearly all goods are inelastic, while none are "significantly" elastic. In only one case (Swedish *sugar*) is the own-price elasticity significantly positive, however. This "Giffen" case should probably be interpreted as a change from direct consumption of sugar to the use of prefabricated foodstuffs. As shown in Table 1.1, the total consumption of sugar has not fallen in Sweden during the estimation period.

Using Tables A11 and A13, we collect some results concerning total cross-price elasticities in Table 14. In this case, however, we have an even worse situation than in Table 13 as far as judging the stochastic error is concerned. We have not systematically analysed the standard errors of the LAIDS cross-price elasticities, neither have we made a systematic comparison between these LAIDS and AIDS elasticities. The results have been calculated, however, and a summary inspection

Table 14. Classification of Total Cross-Price Elasticities. "Large" Results

Price Change in	Effect on	≥ 20%	≤ –20%
Meat	Fish	D F N S	
	Milk, Cheese and Eggs		F S
	Soft Drinks	(D) F	
	Alcoholic Drinks	(D) F	(N)
	Fruit and Vegetables	N	(F)
	Potatoes		F
	Sugar	(N)	F
	Confectionery *etc*		F
Fish			
Milk, Cheese and Eggs	Meat		S
	Fish		F
	Soft Drinks	F	
	Alcoholic Drinks	F	
	Potatoes		(F)
	Sugar		F
	Confectionery *etc*		F
Soft Drinks	Hot Drinks	D	
	Sugar		(N)
Hot Drinks	Soft Drinks		(S)
Alcoholic Drinks	Soft Drinks	D F N S	
	Hot Drinks	N	D (F) S
	Fruit and Vegetables	F	
	Potatoes	F	
	Sugar	(F)	N (S)
	Confectionery *etc*	D (F)	N
Bread and Cereals	Potatoes	N	
	Sugar		N
Fruit and Vegetables	Alcoholic Drinks	(N)	
	Potatoes	D	N
	Sugar		N
	Confectionery *etc*		N
Potatoes			
Fats and Oils	Sugar	S	D F (N)
	Confectionery *etc*	F	
Sugar	Fats and Oils		S
Confectionery *etc*	Meat	D	
	Fish	D	
	Milk, Cheese and Eggs	(D)	
	Alcoholic Drinks	S	
	Fats and Oils	(F)	
	Sugar	D F (N)	S

D = Denmark, F = Finland, N = Norway and S = Sweden.

shows the AIDS/LAIDS estimates to be very similar, while the standard errors lie between 0.04 and 0.20. The predominant value of the standard errors is about 0.10, and rather than make further unwarranted assumptions we have decided to simply present those cross-price elasticities that are greater than 0.20 in absolute value. We have called this results for "large" in the table, but no great emphasis should be placed on their statistical properties.

An examination of Table 14 reveals no substantial evidence for similarity between the countries. Looking at the cross-elasticities formed between goods in the same group we do find that the *number* of large elasticities is roughly the same, between seven and nine for all countries. The cross-elasticities between goods in different groups varies considerably from country to country, however, being more than double so many in Finland than in Sweden.

Only two results are unequivocal. An increase in meat prices seems to cause an increase in the consumption of fish, and an increase in alcohol prices seems to cause an increase in the consumption of soft drinks. *Meat* and *fish* thus appear to be substitutes, as are also *alcoholic drinks* and *soft drinks*.[6] This seems to be intuitively plausible. Another tendency is that certain groups affect general consumption patterns in a more profound way. For example, we can see that *meat, milk, cheese and eggs*, *alcoholic drinks* and *confectionery* have large effects on many groups for at least some countries, whilst *fish* and *potatoes* do not have any such effects.

5.4.4 Joint Classification of Expenditure and Own-Price Elasticities.

In the earlier part of this section we have mainly been looking at the classification of goods as luxuries, necessities, *etc*. Here we shall consider a categorisation with regard to the joint numerical values of both the total expenditure and own-price elasticities. This is naturally going to be a somewhat *ad hoc* procedure, and to be interesting a schematic representation must be able to distinguish different commodity patterns for the different countries.

We concentrate on distinguishing between small, medium and large elasticities. A cursory inspection of the total elasticities evaluated at the mean suggests that the following division (after rounding to one decimal place) yields a convenient taxonomy,

Expenditure elasticities: ≤ 0.4 ; $(0.5, 0.9)$; ≥ 1.0

Own-Price elasticities: ≥ -0.2 ; $(-0.3, -0.5)$; $(-0.6, -0.8)$; ≤ -0.9 .

Note that we have divided the own-price elasticities into four groups to provide a

[6] The strict definition of *substitutes* and *complements* applies to the compensated price elasticities. Since the total budget shares of the different foodstuffs are quite small, we expect income effects to also be small. This is confirmed by an examination of Tables A11-A15, which shows very small differences between the total price elasticities and compensated price elasticities.

Table 15. Elasticity Classification for Denmark

		Total Own-Price Elasticities			
		≥ –0.2	(–0.3, –0.5)	(–0.6, –0.8)	≤ –0.9
Total	≤ 0.4		Bread/Cereals Potatoes	Fats and Oils Sugar	
Expenditure	(0.5, 0.9)	Hot Drinks	Meat Milk, Cheese and Eggs Alcoholic Drinks	Confectionery	Fish Soft Drinks
Elasticities	≥ 1.0		Fruit and Vegetables		

Table 16. Elasticity Classification for Finland

		Total Own-Price Elasticities			
		≥ –0.2	(–0.3, –0.5)	(–0.6, –0.8)	≤ –0.9
Total	≤ 0.4	Milk, Cheese and Eggs Bread/Cereals	Potatoes Fats and Oils		
Expenditure	(0.5, 0.9)	Hot Drinks	Fish Fruit and Vegetables		
Elasticities	≥ 1.0	Meat	Sugar Confectionery	Alcoholic Drinks	Soft Drinks

Table 17. Elasticity Classification for Norway

		Total Own-Price Elasticities			
		≥ –0.2	(–0.3, –0.5)	(–0.6, –0.8)	≤ –0.9
Total	≤ 0.4	Fats and Oils	Hot Drinks Bread/Cereals Potatoes		
Expenditure	(0.5, 0.9)	Milk, Cheese and Eggs Sugar Confectionery	Fruit and Vegetables	Fish Meat	
Elasticities	≥ 1.0			Soft Drinks	Alcoholic Drinks

Table 18. Elasticity Classification for Sweden

		Total Own-Price Elasticities			
		≥ –0.2	(–0.3, –0.5)	(–0.6, –0.8)	≤ –0.9
Total	≤ 0.4	Hot Drinks Potatoes Sugar	Fish Confectionery	Soft Drinks Fruit and Vegetables	
Expenditure	(0.5, 0.9)	Milk, Cheese and Eggs	Meat Fats and Oils	Bread/Cereals	Alcoholic Drinks
Elasticities	≥ 1.0				

slightly more detailed picture. It is naturally of interest to even consider a more qualified categorisation, where values of the elasticities evaluated at other time points are also taken into account. For the sake of simplicity we only present a summary at the mean value here, although we will return to the question of how elasticities vary over time in the next chapter.

Looking at Tables 15-18, the first impression is that Finland has food commodities with larger expenditure elastcities and smaller (absolute) price elasticities than the other Nordic countries. In particular Denmark has only one commodity group with very small price elasticities (*hot drinks*) while Sweden has no commoditries in the upper range of the expenditure elasticities. In the following list we look more closely at the different commodity groups. We will only comment if a specific pattern is discernible.

Meat. Medium/high expenditure elasticities

Milk, Cheese and Eggs. Low price elasticities and (usually) medium expenditure elasticities. Finland has low expenditure elasticity

Soft Drinks. Usually high price and/or expenditure elasticities. Sweden has low expenditure elasticity

Hot Drinks. Low price elasticities and medium/low expenditure elasticities.

Alcoholic Drinks. High price elasticities (except for Denmark) and medium/high expenditure elasticities.

Bread and Cereals. Low price elasticities and low/medium expenditure elasticities except for Sweden.

Fruit and Vegetables. Medium price elasticities.

Potatoes. Low/medium price elasticities and low expenditure elasticities.

Fats and Oils. Low expenditure elasticities, except for Sweden.

In general these findings concur with what is generally thought to apply to foodstuffs, that is the consumption of basics like dairy products, bread and potatoes is not very sensitive to changes in price and income. The results also agree with the usual preconceptions concerning the Nordic counties, such as the low sensitivity of coffee consumption and the high sensitivity of alcohol (except for Denmark, which also agrees with commonly held ideas).

Table 19. Elasticities from the Michalek and Keyzer (MK) and Nordic Studies
(a) Total Expenditure Elasticities

MK	Year	Meat	Fish	MCE	Hot drk	Br/Crls	Fr/Veg	Potato	Fats	Sugar	Other
H	85	0.07	0.00	0.14	0.12	0.37	0.13	0.00	0.12	0.00	0.10
B/L	85	0.30	0.42	0.52	0.13	0.10	0.25	0.36	0.04	0.76	0.60
D	85	0.33	0.34	0.80	0.03	0.03	0.43	0.47	0.03	0.64	0.24
G	85	0.24	0.02	0.13	0.36	0.06	0.26	0.05	0.33	0.11	0.30
UK	85	0.01	0.03	0.01	0.02	0.02	0.01	0.02	0.01	0.02	0.11
Ir	85	0.36	1.97	0.21	1.17	1.11	0.78	0.28	0.67	0.39	0.42
It	85	0.87	0.58	0.93	0.50	0.08	0.48	0.41	0.21	0.27	0.18
Fr	85	0.65	0.15	0.96	0.52	0.23	0.00	0.37	0.48	0.84	1.03
Nordic	Year	Meat	Fish	MCE	Hot drk	Br/Crls	Fr/Veg	Potato	Fats	Sugar	Confect
D	$\overline{72}$	0.87	0.87	0.59	0.46	0.32	1.10	0.33	0.34	0.35	0.51
F	$\overline{76}$	1.14	0.51	0.27	0.53	0.43	1.73	2.02	0.60	1.21	1.52
N	$\overline{76}$	0.95	0.48	0.52	0.15	0.40	0.59	0.10	0.24	0.82	0.47
S	$\overline{77}$	0.64	0.18	0.47	0.21	0.61	0.34	–0.10	0.53	–0.24	0.37

(b) Total Uncompensated Own-Price Elasticities

MK	Year	Meat	Fish	MCE	Hot drk	Br/Crls	Fr/Veg	Potato	Fats	Sugar	Other
H	85	-0.32	0.00	-0.60	–0.55	-1.50	–0.58	0.00	-0.52	0.00	–0.48
B/L	85	–0.36	–0.59	–0.67	–0.19	–0.15	–0.35	–0.51	–0.06	–1.09	–0.80
D	85	–0.58	–0.62	–1.38	–0.06	–0.05	–0.77	–0.85	–0.06	–1.17	–0.45
G	85	–0.56	–0.06	–0.31	–0.83	–0.14	–0.60	–0.12	–0.78	–0.26	–0.70
UK	85	–0.12	–0.64	–0.18	–0.40	–0.34	–0.28	–0.45	–0.32	–0.36	–1.24
Ir	85	–0.19	–0.84	–0.22	–0.43	–0.61	–0.30	–0.11	–0.26	–0.14	–0.17
It	85	–0.38	–0.27	–0.41	–0.23	–0.04	–0.23	–0.19	–0.10	–0.12	–0.09
Fr	85	–0.29	–0.08	–0.44	–0.26	–0.12	–0.00	–0.19	–0.24	–0.43	–0.49
Nordic	Year	Meat	Fish	MCE	Hot drk	Br/Crls	Fr/Veg	Potato	Fats	Sugar	Confect
D	$\overline{72}$	–0.51	–0.90	–0.37	–0.23	–0.36	–0.50	–0.54	–0.64	–0.67	–0.84
F	$\overline{76}$	–0.23	–0.32	0.10	–0.22	–0.12	–0.29	–0.53	–0.34	–0.29	–0.37
N	$\overline{76}$	–0.66	–0.79	–0.21	–0.27	–0.43	–0.55	–0.48	–0.18	–0.24	–0.13
S	$\overline{77}$	–0.35	–0.26	0.00	–0.07	–0.71	–0.57	0.14	–0.34	0.81	–0.43

The following abbreviations have been used in Table 19. Michalek and Keyzer (MK), Holland (H), Belgium/Luxembourg (B/L), Denmark (D), West Germany (G), United Kingdom (UK), Ireland (Ir), Italy (It), France (Fr), Finland (F), Norway (N), Sweden (S), Milk, Cheese and Eggs (MCE), Hot Drinks (Hot drk), Bread and Cereals (Br/Crls), Fruit and Vegetables (Fr/Veg), Confectionery *etc.* (Confect). A bar over the year number indicates that a mean value result has been quoted.

5.4.5 International Comparisons

One way of judging the reliability of our results is to compare them with those found in other, similar, studies. Although there exist a vast number of papers that have estimated some sort of elasticities for food products, most of these are not strictly relevant here. A large group of articles are those concerned with very disaggregated commodities (often meat or dairy products), while most others are very aggregated (*food* being treated as a single commodity).

The paper that bears the most resemblance to our work is undoubtedly that of Michalek and Keyzer (1992). For each of eight EEC countries the elasticities for ten commodity groups (that are essentially the same as ours) are calculated using a two-stage AIDS/LES system. Total elasticities have been derived as a special case of our (4.20). Michalek and Keyzer (MK) only use a static model, however, which may partly be due to the very small sample they are using (yearly data from 1970 - 1985).

Another recent study is Huang (1993), who uses a static Rotterdam-like differential model for 39 U.S. foodstuffs divided into seven groups. These groups correspond very poorly with ours, however, and for this reason we do not present Huang's results here.

A comparison between the total elasticities from MK and our studies is given in Table 19. Before examining these results it is important to remember the differences between the two models being used. Firstly, the static nature of the MK model almost certainly gives rise to misspecification, even though the inclusion of time trends could alleviate this problem. Secondly, the AIDS/LES functional form is much more restrictive than our model, and has been estimated by MK in such a way as to ensure that the laws of demand are imposed. The only chance of judging the model's adequacy could therefore have come through misspecification testing, which was unfortunately not reported.

Looking at the Danish results in Table 19 we can see that the own-price elasticities do not differ too greatly between the studies, except for one or two commodities. The expenditure elasticities differ quite considerably, however. The general impression is actually quite confusing, both studies reveal considerable differences between countries, and if some tendency at all is to be seen it is that the MK paper seems to report elasticities that usually are closer to zero than the ones given in our study.

Since we have found that the dynamic model is to be preferred to the static model in the Nordic countries, it is probably more reasonable to mainly restrict our comparisons to those studies that allow for dynamic effects in some manner. Our use of flexible functional forms makes comparisons with very restrictive demand systems (such as the pure linear expenditure system) also seem less relevant.

Using the extended bibliography (supplied in the files described in Appendix 2) we have found six international papers that can be compared with our's as regards the elasticities for either the *food-at-home* group in the first stage or the *animalia* group in the second stage. These are described in Table 20. Note that the dynamic LAIDS model used by Blanciforti and Green (1983) and Mergos and Donatos (1989) does not satisfy adding up, and that the price elasticity formula they use is not (4.8), but instead one shown by Buse (1994) to be inappropriate.

Table 20. Some International Studies of Food Demand

Paper (with abbreviation)		Model	Country	Data period
Manser (1976)	(M)	D-ITL	USA	1948-1972
Klevmarken (1979)	(K)	ITL (AR)	Sweden	1950-1970
Deaton and Muellbauer (1980b)	(DM)	Δ-AIDS	UK	1954-1974
Anderson and Blundell (1983)	(AB)	D-AIDS	Canada	1947-1979
Blanciforti and Green (1983)	(BG)	D-LAIDS	USA	1948-1978
Mergos and Donatos (1989)	(MD)	D-LAIDS	Greece	1960-1986
Michalek and Keyzer (1992)	(MK)	AIDS/LES	EEC	1970-1985

The following new abbreviations are used: ITL = Indirect Translog, D = Dynamic model, Δ = First difference model, AR = Static model with autoregressive errors, LES = Linear Expenditure System

Consider first the elasticities for *food*. All the above papers, except Manser's, include such a commodity group, but the definitions are somewhat different. Some articles use food, beverages and tobacco (FBT) as their definition, whilst others use food excluding alcohol (F).[7] In our study we define the commodity group as food and beverages (FB). In Table 21 we compare the results for these international studies with the common model for the Nordic countries. Note that the year quoted for each paper is now the year used to calculate the elasticities.

We can see that the British studies are exceptional, although this may in part be due to the choice of models. The Nordic countries fit fairly well into the pattern given by the other studies, althought he expenditure elasticities, with the exception of the Swedish, are somewhat large, however.

Table 21. Total Expenditure and Uncompensated Own-Price Elasticities for Food

Country	Author	Year	Commodity	Model	Equations	E_i	e_{ii}
Sweden	K	60	FBT	ITL (AR)	4	0.61	–0.19
USA	BG	$\overline{63}$	F	D-LAIDS	11	0.37	–0.32
UK	DM	$\overline{64}$	F	Δ-AIDS	8	0.04	0.22
Canada	AB	71	FBT	D-AIDS	5	0.23	–0.54
Greece	MD	$\overline{73}$	FBT	D-LAIDS	7	0.62	–0.40
UK	MK	85	F	AIDS	3	0.02	–0.37
Germany	MK	85	F	AIDS	3	0.23	–0.87
Denmark	MK	85	F	AIDS	3	0.33	–0.77
Denmark	Nordic	$\overline{72}$	FB	D-AIDS	4	0.69	–0.39
Finland	Nordic	$\overline{76}$	FB	D-AIDS	4	1.09	–0.43
Norway	Nordic	$\overline{76}$	FB	D-AIDS	4	0.78	–0.34
Sweden	Nordic	$\overline{77}$	FB	D-AIDS	4	0.47	–0.58

The same abbreviations are used as in Table 19 while the use of an over bar indicates that the value at the mean year was calculated. The own-price elasticity in the first row has been calculated from the compensated price elasticity, using data found in Klevmarken (1979, 1981).

[7] It is not always apparent whether non-alcoholic beverages (such as soft drinks and coffee) are included in this group or not. It is also unclear in some studies how restaurant meals are treated.

Table 22. Expenditure and Own-Price Elasticities for Animalia Within Food

Country	Author	Year	Commodity	Model	Equations	E_i	e_{ii}
USA	M	59	F	D-ITL	4	1.11	–0.53
USA	BG	$\overline{63}$	F	D-LAIDS	4	1.15	–0.62
Denmark	Nordic	$\overline{72}$	FB	D-AIDS	4	1.11	–0.82
Finland	Nordic	$\overline{76}$	FB	D-AIDS	4	1.53	–0.44
Norway	Nordic	$\overline{76}$	FB	D-AIDS	4	1.29	–0.69
Sweden	Nordic	$\overline{77}$	FB	D-AIDS	4	1.24	–0.74

The same abbreviations are used as in Table 19 and the text.

Three of the international studies (M, K and BG) have a second stage that treats groups of food commodities. Unfortunately, these are not very compatible with the groupings used in our study. The same commodity groups are used by Manser and by Blanciforti and Green, and in the case of *animalia* we do have a correspondence to our study. Klevmarken's groupings also differ from ours in nearly all cases, the only exceptions being *fish* and *restaurants*. Both are nested within *food* in the second stage, however, and a comparison with our study would thus entail calculating total elasticities using estimates from two stages calculated from different data sources and using somewhat different definitions. We therefore merely consider the within food results for *animalia*.

We can see from Table 22 that the results for the Nordic countries seem to compare reasonably well with those from the USA, again the exception is maybe the Finnish expenditure elasticities that are somewhat high.

5.5 CONCLUSIONS

In this chapter we have applied the methodology laid out in the beginning of the book. In particular, our quite stringent approach to misspecification testing is in sharp contrast to many other studies of food demand, which often merely report Durbin-Watson statistics. The results of such studies cannot be trusted until further evidence concerning their reliability is available!

We discovered early on in our investigation that the static model gave very poor results regarding misspecification tests, and we therefore abandoned this model in favour of a dynamic AIDS specification (which we called the common model). The static model is nested inside this system, but was firmly rejected in nearly all instances. Since this confirms the results of a number of other studies, it is surprising that (untested) static models are still so popular in many food demand analyses.

Although the common model is evidently superior to the static model, it is not without its problems. The results of the misspecification tests are not completely satisfactory, in particular for Denmark and Norway. The first stage of our utility tree does not seem to be correctly specified, and in general the use of instrumental variable methods could be advantageous. The general separability pattern we

Table 23. Summary of Total Elasticities at Mean Values for the Nordic Countries

	Expenditure Elasticities				Own-Price Elasticities			
	D	F	N	S	D	F	N	S
Meat	0.9	1.1	1.0	0.6	–0.5	–0.2	–0.7	–0.4
Fish	0.9	0.5	0.5	0.2	–0.9	–0.3	–0.8	–0.3
Milk, Cheese and Eggs	0.6	0.3	0.5	0.5	–0.4	0.1	–0.2	0.0
Soft Drinks	0.7	1.7	1.1	0.3	–1.1	–1.2	–0.7	–0.6
Hot Drinks	**0.5**	**0.5**	**0.2**	0.2	**–0.2**	**–0.2**	–0.3	**–0.1**
Alcoholic Drinks	0.9	2.1	1.8	0.6	–0.5	–0.6	–0.9	–0.9
Bread and Cereals	0.3	0.4	0.4	0.6	–0.4	–0.1	–0.4	–0.7
Fruit and Vegetables	1.1	1.7	0.6	0.3	–0.5	–0.3	–0.6	–0.6
Potatoes	0.3	2.0	0.1	–0.1	–0.5	–0.5	**–0.5**	0.1
Fats and Oils	0.3	0.6	0.2	0.5	–0.6	–0.3	–0.2	–0.3
Sugar	0.3	1.2	0.8	**–0.2**	**–0.7**	**–0.3**	–0.2	**0.8**
Confectionery *etc*	0.5	1.5	0.5	0.4	–0.8	–0.4	–0.1	–0.4

Bold type indicates a difference of greater than ±0.3 in absolute value from elasticity at last value.
D = Denmark, F = Finland, N = Norway and S = Sweden.

assume does not seem to be a serious problem, however, although an investigation for one or more countries can be of interest.

Even though the results of this part of the analysis could be better, we believe that they do not invalidate the rest of our results. Our tests of economic hypotheses confirm the commonly found conclusion that the laws of demand do not aggregate very successfully from the micro-level to the macro-level. The elasticity estimates we obtain are therefore not measuring the behaviour of a *representative consumer*, but should rather be interpreted as the average (or total) effects of price and income changes on the market being modelled.

If we are prepared to accept the common model as at least an approximation to the true aggregate demand model, then we can use Table 23 as a summary, to one decimal place, of the total elasticities for the different countries. These are the elasticities calculated at the mean value of the variables, but we have indicated with bold type those cases where this value differs from the elasticity calculated at the last value by 0.3 or more. Reference to Tables A8 and A9 is necessary when this occurs.

In the rest of the book we shall address some of the problems raised in this chapter.

APPENDIX

Table A1. Parameter Values in the Common Model

(a) Private Consumption

		Parameters				*Robust Standard Errors*			
		D	F	N	S	*D*	*F*	*N*	*S*
Constant	1	0.60	0.19	–0.12	0.74	*0.10*	*0.13*	*0.07*	*0.09*
α_i	2	0.24	–0.02	0.18	–0.01	*0.04*	*0.06*	*0.04*	*0.08*
	3	–0.25	0.26	0.29	–0.06	*0.16*	*0.20*	*0.08*	*0.16*
	4	0.41	0.56	0.65	0.33	*0.09*	*0.25*	*0.10*	*0.11*
Expenditure	1	–0.10	0.03	–0.08	–0.17	*0.04*	*0.04*	*0.01*	*0.03*
β_i	2	–0.02	0.08	0.01	0.06	*0.02*	*0.02*	*0.01*	*0.03*
	3	0.16	0.00	0.09	0.12	*0.05*	*0.07*	*0.01*	*0.06*
	4	–0.04	–0.11	–0.02	–0.01	*0.03*	*0.08*	*0.02*	*0.03*
Own Price	1	0.16	0.21	0.23	0.04	*0.03*	*0.02*	*0.03*	*0.04*
γ_{ii}	2	0.03	–0.01	0.01	–0.04	*0.02*	*0.01*	*0.01*	*0.03*
	3	0.03	0.10	0.15	0.08	*0.01*	*0.04*	*0.03*	*0.03*
	4	0.09	0.12	0.07	0.15	*0.04*	*0.07*	*0.03*	*0.01*
Own Lag	1	–0.22	0.11	0.38	–0.05	*0.14*	*0.14*	*0.10*	*0.06*
θ_{ii}	2	0.63	0.21	0.44	0.17	*0.14*	*0.15*	*0.15*	*0.16*
	3	0.64	0.31	0.36	0.37	*0.10*	*0.18*	*0.07*	*0.08*
	4	0.44	0.30	–0.24	0.28	*0.13*	*0.25*	*0.20*	*0.14*
Durbin–Watson	1	1.82	1.71	1.97	2.53				
	2	2.04	1.57	1.96	2.48				
	3	1.62	1.45	2.52	2.37				
	4	2.11	1.02	2.15	1.40				

1 = Food-at-Home, 2 = Restaurants and Cafés, 3 = Other Nondurables, 4 = Other Services
D = Denmark, F = Finland, N = Norway, S = Sweden

Table A1. Parameter Values in the Common Model

(b) Food-at-Home

		Parameters				*Robust Standard Errors*			
		D	F	N	S	*D*	*F*	*N*	*S*
Constant	1	0.30	0.48	0.33	0.32	*0.03*	*0.06*	*0.12*	*0.07*
α_i	2	0.19	0.06	0.91	0.19	*0.04*	*0.08*	*0.17*	*0.09*
	3	0.25	0.32	−0.07	0.30	*0.02*	*0.06*	*0.16*	*0.06*
	4	0.25	0.14	−0.16	0.18	*0.02*	*0.06*	*0.06*	*0.05*
Expenditure	1	0.05	−0.12	−0.02	0.03	*0.04*	*0.04*	*0.03*	*0.05*
β_i	2	0.02	0.13	0.16	0.02	*0.04*	*0.05*	*0.04*	*0.12*
	3	−0.02	−0.01	−0.09	−0.02	*0.02*	*0.04*	*0.03*	*0.05*
	4	−0.06	0.00	−0.05	−0.03	*0.02*	*0.03*	*0.02*	*0.10*
Own Price	1	0.08	0.14	0.12	0.10	*0.02*	*0.02*	*0.03*	*0.02*
γ_{ii}	2	0.04	0.07	0.15	0.01	*0.03*	*0.02*	*0.06*	*0.03*
	3	0.11	0.15	0.08	0.08	*0.02*	*0.03*	*0.04*	*0.02*
	4	0.02	0.14	0.12	0.05	*0.02*	*0.03*	*0.01*	*0.02*
Own Lag	1	0.01	0.23	−0.14	0.33	*0.11*	*0.06*	*0.12*	*0.14*
θ_{ii}	2	0.58	0.22	0.29	0.48	*0.09*	*0.15*	*0.10*	*0.07*
	3	−0.03	0.27	0.32	0.17	*0.12*	*0.10*	*0.18*	*0.17*
	4	0.39	0.03	−0.10	0.08	*0.11*	*0.08*	*0.03*	*0.13*
Durbin–Watson	1	1.87	1.97	1.64	1.81				
	2	1.92	1.36	1.92	2.11				
	3	2.17	2.35	1.83	2.14				
	4	1.87	1.92	1.69	2.53				

1 = Animalia, 2 = Beverages, 3 = Vegetablia, 4 = Miscellaneous

Table A1. Parameter Values in the Common Model
(c) Animalia

		Parameters				*Robust Standard Errors*			
		D	F	N	S	*D*	*F*	*N*	*S*
Constant	1	0.31	−0.03	1.08	0.30	*0.09*	*0.07*	*0.27*	*0.11*
α_i	2	0.26	0.17	−0.03	0.25	*0.04*	*0.05*	*0.15*	*0.05*
	3	0.43	0.86	−0.06	0.44	*0.09*	*0.06*	*0.20*	*0.09*
Expenditure	1	0.07	0.28	0.15	0.12	*0.05*	*0.04*	*0.06*	*0.06*
β_i	2	0.01	−0.02	−0.05	−0.09	*0.02*	*0.02*	*0.04*	*0.03*
	3	−0.08	−0.26	−0.10	−0.03	*0.04*	*0.04*	*0.04*	*0.06*
Own Price	1	0.16	0.13	0.15	0.23	*0.05*	*0.06*	*0.10*	*0.04*
γ_{ii}	2	0.01	0.04	0.03	0.08	*0.01*	*0.01*	*0.03*	*0.01*
	3	0.14	0.20	0.21	0.30	*0.04*	*0.07*	*0.05*	*0.03*
Own Lag	1	0.46	0.18	0.52	0.06	*0.10*	*0.10*	*0.08*	*0.13*
θ_{ii}	2	0.53	0.21	0.35	0.03	*0.06*	*0.13*	*0.09*	*0.10*
	3	0.37	0.01	0.21	0.04	*0.08*	*0.09*	*0.08*	*0.09*
Durbin–Watson	1	2.14	1.98	1.95	1.13				
	2	2.08	1.88	2.24	1.90				
	3	2.17	1.80	2.04	1.03				

1 = Meat, 2 = Fish, 3 = Milk, Cheese and Eggs

(d) Beverages

		Parameters				*Robust Standard Errors*			
		D	F	N	S	*D*	*F*	*N*	*S*
Constant	1	0.28	0.11	0.09	0.39	*0.04*	*0.06*	*0.13*	*0.02*
α_i	2	0.34	0.19	−0.55	0.19	*0.12*	*0.14*	*0.15*	*0.02*
	3	0.38	0.70	1.46	0.42	*0.11*	*0.10*	*0.15*	*0.02*
Expenditure	1	−0.01	0.00	−0.04	−0.04	*0.01*	*0.01*	*0.03*	*0.02*
β_i	2	−0.09	−0.15	−0.18	−0.11	*0.03*	*0.03*	*0.04*	*0.03*
	3	0.10	0.15	0.22	0.15	*0.02*	*0.02*	*0.03*	*0.03*
Own Price	1	−0.01	−0.02	0.05	0.04	*0.02*	*0.01*	*0.05*	*0.01*
γ_{ii}	2	0.14	0.09	0.24	0.14	*0.01*	*0.01*	*0.06*	*0.02*
	3	0.21	0.04	0.24	0.10	*0.05*	*0.03*	*0.09*	*0.02*
Own Lag	1	0.48	0.08	0.53	0.60	*0.08*	*0.15*	*0.09*	*0.07*
θ_{ii}	2	0.26	0.40	0.08	0.12	*0.13*	*0.15*	*0.05*	*0.05*
	3	0.31	−0.45	0.06	0.10	*0.15*	*0.12*	*0.06*	*0.07*
Durbin–Watson	1	1.97	2.12	2.32	1.82				
	2	1.63	2.24	2.15	2.19				
	3	1.36	2.39	2.21	2.23				

1 = Hot Drinks, 2 = Soft Drinks, 3 = Alcoholic Drinks

Table A1. Parameter Values in the Common Model
(e) Vegetablia

		Parameters				*Robust Standard Errors*			
		D	F	N	S	*D*	*F*	*N*	*S*
Constant	1	0.76	1.02	0.08	0.14	*0.07*	*0.15*	*0.20*	*0.07*
α_i	2	0.09	0.01	0.81	0.67	*0.07*	*0.21*	*0.24*	*0.06*
	3	0.15	−0.03	0.10	0.19	*0.06*	*0.14*	*0.12*	*0.03*
Expenditure	1	−0.25	−0.32	−0.07	0.19	*0.06*	*0.09*	*0.05*	*0.06*
β_i	2	0.29	0.24	0.12	−0.10	*0.07*	*0.12*	*0.06*	*0.05*
	3	−0.05	0.08	−0.05	−0.09	*0.04*	*0.08*	*0.03*	*0.02*
Own Price	1	0.05	0.06	0.16	0.05	*0.02*	*0.05*	*0.05*	*0.05*
γ_{ii}	2	0.05	0.09	0.20	0.07	*0.02*	*0.06*	*0.11*	*0.03*
	3	0.03	0.03	0.03	0.07	*0.01*	*0.02*	*0.01*	*0.01*
Own Lag	1	0.27	0.15	0.18	0.25	*0.09*	*0.07*	*0.11*	*0.10*
θ_{ii}	2	0.27	0.49	0.25	−0.05	*0.09*	*0.06*	*0.20*	*0.10*
	3	0.00	0.06	−0.05	0.03	*0.09*	*0.11*	*0.15*	*0.03*
Durbin–Watson	1	1.95	1.76	2.18	2.06				
	2	2.01	1.87	1.76	2.11				
	3	1.64	2.00	1.46	1.37				

1 = Bread and Cereals, 2 = Fruit and Vegetables, 3 = Potatoes

(f) Miscellaneous

		Parameters				*Robust Standard Errors*			
		D	F	N	S	*D*	*F*	*N*	*S*
Constant	1	0.51	0.74	−0.04	0.43	*0.04*	*0.15*	*0.12*	*0.05*
α_i	2	0.29	0.12	0.49	0.25	*0.04*	*0.19*	*0.15*	*0.02*
	3	0.21	0.14	0.55	0.32	*0.05*	*0.28*	*0.22*	*0.05*
Expenditure	1	−0.06	−0.19	−0.10	0.12	*0.04*	*0.10*	*0.03*	*0.05*
β_i	2	−0.02	0.02	0.09	−0.12	*0.04*	*0.12*	*0.04*	*0.02*
	3	0.09	0.17	0.01	0.00	*0.06*	*0.17*	*0.06*	*0.05*
Own Price	1	0.06	0.04	0.16	0.15	*0.02*	*0.06*	*0.04*	*0.03*
γ_{ii}	2	0.03	0.09	0.11	0.11	*0.01*	*0.04*	*0.03*	*0.01*
	3	0.00	0.04	0.15	0.17	*0.04*	*0.07*	*0.03*	*0.04*
Own Lag	1	−0.01	0.36	0.35	−0.14	*0.08*	*0.10*	*0.05*	*0.13*
θ_{ii}	2	0.31	0.07	−0.03	0.03	*0.09*	*0.07*	*0.09*	*0.07*
	3	−0.68	0.47	0.43	0.56	*0.06*	*0.09*	*0.07*	*0.08*
Durbin–Watson	1	1.61	2.16	2.65	1.47				
	2	2.26	2.29	1.08	1.82				
	3	2.35	2.33	1.44	1.38				

1 = Fats and Oils, 2 = Sugar, 3 = Confectionery, *etc.*

Table A2. Measures of Goodness-of-Fit for the Common Model

	RSQ				ARSQ				ARSQ(static)				AKAIKE			
	D	F	N	S	D	F	N	S	D	F	N	S	D	F	N	S
Private Consumption	*0.947*	*0.956*	*0.940*	*0.961*	*0.932*	*0.939*	*0.910*	*0.943*	*0.441*	*0.160*	*0.320*	*0.211*	*–25.3*	*–26.0*	*–28.3*	*–27.4*
Food-at-home	0.996	0.994	0.990	0.996	0.995	0.992	0.990	0.994	0.135	0.206	0.480	0.228				
Restaurants and Cafés	0.784	0.996	0.910	0.860	0.720	0.994	0.880	0.794	0.426	0.307	0.510	0.321				
Nondurables	0.876	0.846	0.990	0.942	0.840	0.788	0.980	0.914	0.663	0.238	0.680	0.317				
Services	0.996	0.954	0.950	0.991	0.995	0.936	0.940	0.986	0.735	0.321	0.660	0.037				
Food-at-home	*0.810*	*0.925*	*0.910*	*0.882*	*0.753*	*0.896*	*0.880*	*0.826*	*0.286*	*0.233*	*0.120*	*0.416*	*–23.8*	*–23.3*	*–25.0*	*–24.8*
Animalia	0.517	0.946	0.880	0.882	0.374	0.926	0.830	0.826	0.150	0.410	0.120	0.445				
Beverages	0.861	0.954	0.900	0.938	0.819	0.936	0.860	0.909	0.505	0.137	0.190	0.683				
Vegetablia	0.729	0.950	0.920	0.731	0.649	0.931	0.880	0.604	–0.003	0.480	0.060	0.409				
Miscellaneous	0.961	0.968	0.960	0.950	0.949	0.956	0.940	0.926	0.574	0.081	0.130	0.518				
Animalia	*0.865*	*0.820*	*0.940*	*0.866*	*0.837*	*0.773*	*0.920*	*0.824*	*0.516*	*0.027*	*0.450*	*–0.066*	*–13.6*	*–13.8*	*–14.5*	*–14.6*
Meat	0.826	0.940	0.970	0.918	0.790	0.924	0.960	0.893	0.303	–0.025	0.630	–0.097				
Fish	0.865	0.461	0.850	0.839	0.837	0.320	0.810	0.788	0.646	0.096	0.640	–0.050				
Milk, Cheese & Eggs	0.904	0.938	0.980	0.894	0.884	0.922	0.980	0.860	0.371	–0.066	0.320	–0.072				
Beverages	*0.896*	*0.925*	*0.880*	*0.942*	*0.874*	*0.906*	*0.840*	*0.923*	*0.308*	*0.101*	*0.260*	*0.433*	*–13.3*	*–14.9*	*–12.7*	*–14.8*
Soft Drinks	0.925	0.922	0.880	0.915	0.910	0.902	0.840	0.888	0.367	0.019	0.450	0.705				
Hot Drinks	0.978	0.990	0.950	0.966	0.973	0.987	0.940	0.955	0.199	0.158	0.200	0.328				
Alcoholic Drinks	0.977	0.992	0.870	0.953	0.973	0.990	0.830	0.939	0.197	0.189	0.140	0.166				
Vegetablia	*0.840*	*0.897*	*0.960*	*0.912*	*0.807*	*0.870*	*0.940*	*0.884*	*0.211*	*0.296*	*0.060*	*0.002*	*–13.4*	*–12.5*	*–14.1*	*–16.0*
Bread and Cereals	0.935	0.976	0.930	0.878	0.921	0.970	0.910	0.840	0.409	0.376	0.190	0.095				
Fruit and Vegetables	0.938	0.953	0.930	0.845	0.925	0.941	0.920	0.796	0.320	0.550	0.170	0.097				
Potatoes	0.564	0.612	0.970	0.950	0.474	0.510	0.960	0.934	0.022	0.343	0.010	–0.038				
Miscellaneous	*0.934*	*0.901*	*0.960*	*0.948*	*0.921*	*0.875*	*0.950*	*0.932*	*0.483*	*0.358*	*0.290*	*0.545*	*–12.1*	*–10.4*	*–12.3*	*–14.7*
Fats and Oils	0.986	0.964	0.990	0.933	0.984	0.954	0.990	0.912	0.651	0.614	0.510	0.767				
Sugar	0.924	0.869	0.830	0.978	0.908	0.835	0.800	0.971	0.541	–0.005	0.260	0.401				
Confectionery *etc*	0.985	0.955	0.960	0.968	0.982	0.943	0.960	0.958	0.748	0.453	0.480	0.802				

ARSQ is the RSQ adjusted for degrees of freedom. ARSQ(static) measures the relative improvement comparing ARSQ in the dynamic and static models.
Text and numbers in italics refer to system statistics.

Table A3. Diagnostic Tests for the Common Model – P-Values

	(a) Breusch-Godfrey				(b) Breusch-Pagan				(c) ARCH				(d) RESET			
	D	F	N	S	D	F	N	S	D	F	N	S	D	F	N	S
Private Consumption	*0.583*	*0.281*	*0.010*	*0.034*	*0.692*	*0.369*	*0.056*	*0.430*	*0.786*	*0.393*	*0.373*	*0.553*	*0.021*	*0.162*	*0.078*	*0.001*
Food-at-home	0.580	0.433	0.905	0.284	0.979	0.462	0.156	0.254	0.372	0.373	0.383	0.905	0.926	0.337	**0.096**	0.103
Restaurants and Cafés	0.806	0.365	0.884	**0.071**	0.293	0.279	**0.002**	**0.084**	0.834	**0.088**	**0.034**	0.435	0.686	0.725	0.343	**0.069**
Nondurables	0.223	0.146	**0.057**	0.452	0.303	0.671	0.238	0.688	0.433	**0.071**	0.845	0.732	**0.022**	0.969	0.389	0.940
Services	0.773	**0.007**	0.470	0.107	0.901	0.582	0.456	0.563	0.430	0.735	0.745	0.428	**0.045**	**0.002**	0.114	**0.079**
Food-at-home	*0.520*	***0.086***	*0.913*	*0.319*	*0.720*	*0.304*	*0.598*	*0.525*	***0.065***	*0.148*	*0.502*	*0.597*	*0.971*	*0.515*	*0.282*	***0.078***
Animalia	0.718	0.937	0.432	0.598	0.287	0.800	0.490	0.213	0.321	**0.051**	0.690	0.947	0.200	0.225	0.104	0.120
Beverages	0.931	0.105	0.788	0.729	0.251	0.255	0.907	0.972	0.380	0.541	0.437	0.378	0.817	0.122	0.261	**0.097**
Vegetablia	0.531	0.319	0.436	0.826	0.787	0.202	0.238	0.909	0.610	0.812	0.543	0.644	0.767	0.565	0.109	0.181
Miscellaneous	0.695	0.903	0.452	0.218	0.272	**0.055**	0.509	0.644	**0.014**	0.161	0.239	0.664	0.917	0.554	**0.080**	**0.086**
Animalia	*0.774*	*0.767*	*0.659*	*0.236*	*0.934*	***0.001***	*0.329*	***0.032***	*0.849*	*0.360*	*0.277*	*0.684*	***0.020***	*0.802*	***0.042***	*0.259*
Meat	0.627	0.879	0.958	**0.021**	0.292	0.388	0.543	**0.025**	0.600	0.532	0.549	0.861	0.521	0.457	**0.070**	**0.044**
Fish	0.783	0.805	0.434	0.771	0.856	0.385	0.281	0.283	0.601	0.323	0.901	0.744	**0.012**	0.777	0.579	0.951
Milk, Cheese & Eggs	0.502	0.653	0.641	**0.039**	0.556	0.115	0.464	**0.056**	0.905	0.950	0.158	0.673	0.264	0.613	0.350	0.838
Beverages	***0.002***	*0.628*	*0.187*	*0.955*	***0.001***	*0.486*	*0.144*	*0.257*	*0.573*	*0.809*	*0.447*	*0.834*	*0.247*	*0.340*	*0.462*	***0.061***
Soft Drinks	0.792	0.547	0.210	0.709	**0.006**	0.410	0.287	0.571	0.961	0.556	0.525	0.432	0.225	0.897	0.530	0.254
Hot Drinks	0.284	0.426	0.597	0.701	**0.000**	0.976	**0.016**	**0.089**	**0.001**	0.305	0.967	0.187	**0.024**	0.941	0.429	**0.077**
Alcoholic Drinks	**0.063**	0.291	0.664	0.505	**0.003**	0.942	**0.024**	0.156	**0.072**	0.950	0.724	0.653	**0.006**	0.853	0.551	0.318
Vegetablia	*0.451*	*0.787*	*0.155*	*0.399*	*0.519*	*0.660*	***0.034***	*0.487*	*0.549*	*0.844*	***0.000***	*0.724*	***0.086***	*0.199*	*0.287*	*0.506*
Bread and Cereals	0.602	0.559	0.554	0.926	0.722	0.952	0.430	0.291	0.625	0.758	0.908	0.879	**0.002**	**0.096**	0.701	0.128
Fruit and Vegetables	0.543	0.871	0.533	0.989	0.740	0.654	0.427	0.380	0.423	0.785	0.412	0.717	0.116	**0.013**	0.577	0.719
Potatoes	0.226	0.924	**0.059**	0.169	0.218	0.139	0.164	**0.033**	0.368	0.340	0.371	0.925	0.691	0.259	**0.022**	**0.098**
Miscellaneous	*0.825*	***0.000***	***0.013***	*0.602*	*0.726*	*0.659*	*0.194*	*0.727*	*0.613*	*0.266*	***0.000***	*0.705*	*0.108*	*0.248*	*0.179*	*0.489*
Fats and Oils	0.180	0.460	**0.071**	0.234	0.292	0.231	0.355	0.880	0.904	0.718	0.259	0.378	0.111	0.556	0.132	0.344
Sugar	0.254	0.285	**0.005**	0.539	0.911	0.945	**0.008**	0.163	0.190	0.920	**0.040**	0.311	0.218	**0.010**	0.274	0.966
Confectionery *etc*	0.273	0.261	0.235	0.107	0.377	0.251	**0.038**	0.460	0.866	0.900	0.689	0.781	0.869	0.272	**0.049**	0.275

Text and numbers in italics refer to system tests. Numbers in bold face indicate **significance** at the 10% level

Table A3. Diagnostic Tests for the Common Model – P-Values (continued)

	(e) Hausman-Wu (tx)				(f) Hausman-Wu (di)				(g) Jarque-Bera				(h) Cusumsq			
	D	F	N	S	D	F	N	S	D	F	N	S	D	F	N	S
Private Consumption					***0.043***	***0.048***	***0.034***	***0.001***								
Food-at-home					0.659	**0.022**	**0.069**	0.369	0.466	0.618	0.535	0.580	**0.008**	0.021	0.177	0.650
Restaurants and Cafés					**0.005**	0.320	**0.018**	0.494	0.834	0.891	0.855	**0.000**	0.683	**0.009**	0.362	**0.000**
Nondurables					**0.015**	0.960	0.112	**0.091**	0.946	0.897	0.890	**0.021**	0.232	0.127	0.411	**0.054**
Services					0.175	0.111	0.112	**0.000**	0.503	0.534	0.574	0.459	0.250	0.125	**0.067**	0.282
Food-at-home	***0.060***	*0.138*	*0.284*	*0.291*	*0.909*	***0.073***	*0.479*	*0.505*								
Animalia	0.238	**0.034**	0.968	**0.099**	0.876	0.196	0.112	0.735	0.451	0.766	0.981	0.885	0.221	0.254	0.118	0.141
Beverages	**0.037**	0.942	0.401	**0.056**	0.601	0.173	0.313	0.711	0.524	0.863	0.548	0.918	0.336	0.202	**0.047**	**0.066**
Vegetablia	**0.044**	0.121	0.874	0.982	0.499	**0.014**	0.944	0.384	0.540	0.718	0.235	0.591	**0.029**	0.288	**0.000**	0.440
Miscellaneous	0.913	0.590	**0.078**	0.200	0.876	0.399	0.365	0.191	0.838	0.988	0.815	0.810	0.233	**0.017**	0.358	0.150
Animalia	*0.139*	*0.663*	*0.578*	*0.327*	*0.105*	*0.419*	*0.492*	*0.294*								
Meat	0.157	0.817	0.831	0.962	0.300	0.583	0.719	0.373	0.666	0.162	0.702	0.930	**0.031**	0.273	0.158	0.211
Fish	**0.056**	0.397	0.422	0.158	**0.032**	0.264	0.682	0.407	0.918	0.293	0.143	0.748	**0.061**	**0.000**	0.173	0.541
Milk, Cheese & Eggs	0.536	0.548	0.579	0.452	0.927	0.302	0.292	0.144	**0.047**	0.177	0.827	0.433	**0.009**	0.491	**0.062**	**0.088**
Beverages	0.346	0.811	0.848	0.677	**0.068**	0.616	0.743	0.498								
Soft Drinks	0.886	0.539	0.576	0.865	0.482	0.323	0.461	0.617	0.119	0.789	0.949	0.898	**0.001**	0.060	0.963	0.459
Hot Drinks	0.314	0.797	0.877	0.475	**0.031**	0.443	0.862	0.231	0.967	0.638	**0.000**	0.794	**0.000**	0.209	**0.000**	0.287
Alcoholic Drinks	0.189	0.976	0.680	0.380	**0.019**	0.621	0.565	0.426	0.962	0.367	0.944	0.992	**0.000**	**0.054**	0.138	0.395
Vegetablia	*0.512*	***0.001***	***0.029***	*0.242*	***0.065***	***0.001***	***0.002***	*0.334*								
Bread and Cereals	0.961	**0.023**	0.973	0.291	0.588	0.049	**0.025**	0.147	0.845	0.859	**0.023**	0.956	**0.016**	0.171	**0.015**	0.233
Fruit and Vegetables	0.441	**0.000**	0.327	0.453	0.333	**0.000**	**0.001**	0.183	0.820	0.830	**0.006**	0.784	**0.017**	**0.086**	**0.016**	0.237
Potatoes	0.299	**0.009**	**0.020**	**0.087**	**0.021**	**0.004**	**0.001**	0.226	0.649	0.861	0.957	0.991	0.433	**0.080**	**0.020**	0.671
Miscellaneous	***0.001***	***0.000***	***0.000***	*0.840*	***0.000***	***0.000***	***0.000***	*0.949*								
Fats and Oils	**0.001**	**0.000**	**0.015**	0.590	**0.000**	**0.000**	**0.004**	0.832	0.738	0.567	0.670	0.966	**0.021**	0.664	0.134	0.362
Sugar	**0.071**	**0.009**	**0.000**	0.784	**0.058**	**0.012**	**0.002**	0.806	0.723	0.129	**0.015**	0.540	0.205	0.352	**0.000**	0.107
Confectionery *etc*	**0.000**	**0.000**	**0.000**	0.686	**0.000**	**0.000**	**0.000**	0.772	0.580	0.295	**0.023**	0.853	**0.069**	0.152	**0.038**	0.298

Text and numbers in italics refer to system tests. Numbers in bold face indicate **significance** at the 10% level

Table A4. Tests of Restrictions for the Common Model – P-Values

	"Exact" Likelihood Ratio Test				Robust Wald Test			
	D	F	N	S	D	F	N	S
Private Consumpt.								
Homogeneity		0.004	**0.516**	0.002	0.092	0.001	**0.504**	0.000
Homog & Symmetry		0.004	**0.172**	0.002	**0.241**	0.000	0.000	0.000
Static		0.027	0.001	0.020	0.000	0.000	0.000	0.000
Food-at-home								
Homogeneity		0.046	0.005	0.101	**0.165**	0.040	0.000	0.080
Homog & Symmetry		0.046	0.001	0.024	0.000	0.009	0.000	0.017
Static		0.004	0.084	0.002	0.000	0.000	0.000	0.000
Animalia								
Homogeneity		0.032	0.018	0.002	**0.233**	0.002	0.004	0.000
Homog & Symmetry		0.027	0.038	0.006	**0.361**	0.000	0.000	0.000
Static		**0.290**	0.000	**0.857**	0.000	0.095	0.000	**0.402**
Beverages								
Homogeneity		0.021	0.042	0.028	0.010	0.010	0.029	0.037
Homog & Symmetry		0.043	0.024	0.002	0.000	0.008	0.002	0.000
Static		0.074	0.005	0.000	0.000	0.036	0.000	0.000
Vegetablia								
Homogeneity		**0.498**	0.000	0.002	0.000	**0.392**	0.000	0.000
Homog & Symmetry		**0.592**	0.000	0.004	0.000	**0.500**	0.000	0.000
Static		0.001	**0.177**	**0.438**	0.008	0.000	0.023	**0.172**
Miscellaneous								
Homogeneity		**0.101**	**0.126**	**0.805**	**0.138**	**0.143**	**0.211**	**0.765**
Homog & Symmetry		0.004	**0.241**	**0.132**	**0.215**	0.000	**0.255**	**0.132**
Static		0.000	0.001	0.000	0.000	0.000	0.000	0.000

P-Values for the Likelihood Ratio tests and the Wald homogeneity tests are "exact", and use the F distribution. The other Wald tests are corrected asymptotic, and use the Chi-squared distribution. The Wald tests are calculated using White's Robust covariance estimates. Exact LRT tests were not calculated for Denmark

Numbers in bold face indicate *non-significance* at the 10% level.

Table A5. Expenditure Elasticities – at Mean Value
Within Group Elasticities

	Elasticities				*Robust Standard Errors*			
	D	F	N	S	*D*	*F*	*N*	*S*
Food-at-home	0.69	1.09	0.78	0.47	*0.12*	*0.11*	*0.04*	*0.09*[*]
Restaurants	0.75	1.98	1.15	2.30	*0.24*	*0.22*	*0.18*	*0.72*
Nondurables	1.71	1.02	1.41	1.58	*0.19*	*0.34*	*0.06*	*0.30*
Services	0.89	0.70	0.96	0.97	*0.08*	*0.21*	*0.05*	*0.07*
Animalia	1.14	0.68	0.94	1.09	*0.11*	*0.10*	*0.06*	*0.14*
Beverages	1.09	1.56	1.73	1.07	*0.17*	*0.19*	*0.18*	*0.29*
Vegetablia	0.93	0.95	0.63	0.93	*0.08*	*0.16*	*0.15*	*0.16*
Miscellaneous	0.65	1.00	0.60	0.78	*0.10*	*0.21*	*0.11*	*0.27*
Meat	1.11	1.53	1.29	1.24	*0.08*	*0.07*	*0.12*	*0.13*
Fish	1.11	0.68	0.66	0.35	*0.20*	*0.26*	*0.25*	*0.21*
Milk, Cheese, Eggs	0.75	0.36	0.71	0.92	*0.14*	*0.09*	*0.13*	*0.15*
Soft Drinks	0.93	1.00	0.80	0.62	*0.12*	*0.11*	*0.16*	*0.25*
Hot Drinks	0.62	0.31	0.11	0.40	*0.12*	*0.14*	*0.17*	*0.14*
Alcoholic Drinks	1.16	1.22	1.36	1.21	*0.04*	*0.03*	*0.05*	*0.04*
Bread and Cereals	0.50	0.41	0.82	1.39	*0.11*	*0.16*	*0.13*	*0.12*
Fruit and Vegetables	1.73	1.67	1.20	0.78	*0.17*	*0.32*	*0.10*	*0.11*
Potatoes	0.51	1.95	0.21	–0.22	*0.44*	*0.84*	*0.47*	*0.33*
Fats and Oils	0.77	0.55	0.51	1.43	*0.15*	*0.23*	*0.16*	*0.18*
Sugar	0.78	1.11	1.75	–0.65	*0.34*	*0.80*	*0.29*	*0.23*
Confectionery *etc*	1.15	1.39	1.01	1.00	*0.10*	*0.40*	*0.08*	*0.08*

Total Elasticities

	Elasticities			
	D	F	N	S
Meat	0.87	1.14	0.95	0.64
Fish	0.87	0.51	0.48	0.18
Milk, Cheese, Eggs	0.59	0.27	0.52	0.47
Soft Drinks	0.69	1.70	1.08	0.31
Hot Drinks	0.46	0.53	0.15	0.21
Alcoholic Drinks	0.87	2.08	1.84	0.62
Bread and Cereals	0.32	0.43	0.40	0.61
Fruit and Vegetables	1.10	1.73	0.59	0.34
Potatoes	0.33	2.02	0.10	–0.10
Fats and Oils	0.34	0.60	0.24	0.53
Sugar	0.35	1.21	0.82	–0.24
Confectionery *etc*	0.51	1.52	0.47	0.37

Table A6. Uncompensated Own-Price Elasticities – at Mean Value

Within Group Elasticities

	Elasticities				*Robust Standard Errors*			
	D	F	N	S	*D*	*F*	*N*	*S*
Food-at-home	−0.39	−0.43	−0.34	−0.58	*0.09*	*0.07*	*0.08*	*0.08*
Restaurants	−0.50	−1.02	−0.78	−1.71	*0.37*	*0.14*	*0.14*	*0.48*
Nondurables	−0.94	−0.48	−0.52	−0.63	*0.05*	*0.16*	*0.09*	*0.11*
Services	−0.71	−0.52	−0.80	−0.63	*0.09*	*0.27*	*0.08*	*0.04*
Animalia	−0.82	−0.44	−0.69	−0.74	*0.08*	*0.11*	*0.07*	*0.07*
Beverages	−0.87	−0.74	−0.94	−0.98	*0.15*	*0.10*	*0.10*	*0.12*
Vegetablia	−0.50	−0.36	−0.69	−0.68	*0.09*	*0.15*	*0.14*	*0.12*
Miscellaneous	−0.82	−0.13	−0.10	−0.60	*0.11*	*0.17*	*0.05*	*0.11*
Meat	−0.80	−0.81	−1.05	−0.61	*0.09*	*0.12*	*0.12*	*0.09*
Fish	−0.94	−0.35	−0.85	−0.28	*0.13*	*0.13*	*0.16*	*0.15*
Milk, Cheese, Eggs	−0.47	0.00	−0.40	−0.14	*0.15*	*0.22*	*0.11*	*0.09*
Soft Drinks	−1.09	−1.25	−0.74	−0.57	*0.15*	*0.12*	*0.25*	*0.18*
Hot Drinks	−0.29	−0.24	−0.28	−0.08	*0.10*	*0.09*	*0.08*	*0.07*
Alcoholic Drinks	−0.74	−1.03	−1.14	−0.96	*0.08*	*0.04*	*0.05*	*0.03*
Bread and Cereals	−0.52	−0.29	−0.56	−1.00	*0.09*	*0.17*	*0.13*	*0.11*
Fruit and Vegetables	−0.94	−0.76	−0.84	−0.71	*0.05*	*0.14*	*0.14*	*0.06*
Potatoes	−0.57	−0.67	−0.48	0.15	*0.06*	*0.16*	*0.11*	*0.08*
Fats and Oils	−0.70	−0.56	−0.27	−0.52	*0.08*	*0.14*	*0.14*	*0.09*
Sugar	−0.70	−0.45	−0.44	0.83	*0.11*	*0.33*	*0.05*	*0.17*
Confectionery *etc*	−1.01	−0.96	−0.79	−0.73	*0.09*	*0.12*	*0.08*	*0.09*

Total Elasticities

	Elasticities			
	D	F	N	S
Meat	−0.51	−0.23	−0.66	−0.35
Fish	−0.90	−0.32	−0.79	−0.26
Milk, Cheese, Eggs	−0.37	0.10	−0.21	0.00
Soft Drinks	−1.07	−1.20	−0.69	−0.56
Hot Drinks	−0.23	−0.22	−0.27	−0.07
Alcoholic Drinks	−0.53	−0.60	−0.87	−0.85
Bread and Cereals	−0.36	−0.12	−0.43	−0.71
Fruit and Vegetables	−0.50	−0.29	−0.55	−0.57
Potatoes	−0.54	−0.53	−0.48	0.14
Fats and Oils	−0.64	−0.34	−0.18	−0.34
Sugar	−0.67	−0.29	−0.24	0.81
Confectionery *etc*	−0.84	−0.37	−0.13	−0.43

Table A7. Compensated Own-Price Elasticities – at Mean Value
Within Group Elasticities

	Elasticities				*Robust Standard Errors*			
	D	F	N	S	*D*	*F*	*N*	*S*
Food-at-home	−0.16	−0.05	−0.06	−0.43	*0.09*	*0.07*	*0.11*	*0.09*
Restaurants	−0.45	−0.87	−0.72	−1.60	*0.35*	*0.12*	*0.38*	*0.46*
Nondurables	−0.55	−0.28	−0.22	−0.30	*0.10*	*0.20*	*0.14*	*0.07*
Services	−0.39	−0.25	−0.44	−0.22	*0.09*	*0.22*	*0.14*	*0.03*
Animalia	−0.40	−0.19	−0.30	−0.35	*0.06*	*0.08*	*0.07*	*0.06*
Beverages	−0.59	−0.38	−0.56	−0.72	*0.12*	*0.11*	*0.11*	*0.13*
Vegetablia	−0.30	−0.13	−0.54	−0.44	*0.08*	*0.13*	*0.13*	*0.10*
Miscellaneous	−0.72	0.03	−0.02	−0.49	*0.12*	*0.18*	*0.06*	*0.11*
Meat	−0.13	0.00	−0.38	0.01	*0.08*	*0.13*	*0.11*	*0.09*
Fish	−0.84	−0.31	−0.75	−0.23	*0.13*	*0.12*	*0.15*	*0.12*
Milk, Cheese, Eggs	−0.23	0.15	−0.17	0.19	*0.12*	*0.20*	*0.10*	*0.08*
Soft Drinks	−1.00	−1.16	−0.60	−0.51	*0.15*	*0.13*	*0.24*	*0.16*
Hot Drinks	−0.11	−0.18	−0.25	−0.01	*0.07*	*0.06*	*0.05*	*0.07*
Alcoholic Drinks	−0.01	−0.18	−0.30	−0.10	*0.07*	*0.02*	*0.06*	*0.03*
Bread and Cereals	−0.27	−0.07	−0.26	−0.32	*0.04*	*0.09*	*0.10*	*0.06*
Fruit and Vegetables	−0.24	−0.15	−0.15	−0.37	*0.09*	*0.21*	*0.16*	*0.06*
Potatoes	−0.52	−0.50	−0.47	0.13	*0.06*	*0.10*	*0.10*	*0.07*
Fats and Oils	−0.46	−0.34	−0.17	−0.11	*0.07*	*0.07*	*0.44*	*0.11*
Sugar	−0.61	−0.28	−0.23	0.78	*0.10*	*0.23*	*0.33*	*0.16*
Confectionery *etc*	−0.33	−0.35	−0.10	−0.09	*0.06*	*0.11*	*0.14*	*0.07*

Total Elasticities

	Elasticities			
	D	F	N	S
Meat	−0.45	−0.16	−0.59	−0.31
Fish	−0.89	−0.31	−0.78	−0.26
Milk, Cheese, Eggs	−0.34	0.12	−0.20	0.02
Soft Drinks	−1.06	−1.19	−0.68	−0.56
Hot Drinks	−0.22	−0.21	−0.26	−0.07
Alcoholic Drinks	−0.48	−0.50	−0.78	−0.82
Bread and Cereals	−0.35	−0.10	−0.42	−0.69
Fruit and Vegetables	−0.47	−0.24	−0.53	−0.55
Potatoes	−0.54	−0.52	−0.48	0.14
Fats and Oils	−0.64	−0.33	−0.17	−0.33
Sugar	−0.67	−0.27	−0.23	0.81
Confectionery *etc*	−0.83	−0.34	−0.12	−0.42

Table A8. Expenditure Elasticities – at Last Value
Within Group Elasticities

	Elasticities				*Robust Standard Errors*			
	D	F	N	S	*D*	*F*	*N*	*S*
Food-at-home	0.57	1.12	0.75	0.41	*0.15*	*0.14*	*0.04*	*0.11*
Restaurants	0.77	1.78	1.13	2.13	*0.22*	*0.19*	*0.15*	*0.62*
Nondurables	1.85	1.02	1.40	1.65	*0.27*	*0.36*	*0.06*	*0.34*
Services	0.92	0.74	0.96	0.97	*0.06*	*0.17*	*0.05*	*0.06*
Animalia	1.13	0.68	0.95	1.09	*0.11*	*0.10*	*0.06*	*0.14*
Beverages	1.09	1.50	1.76	1.08	*0.17*	*0.18*	*0.19*	*0.33*
Vegetablia	0.93	0.95	0.61	0.93	*0.08*	*0.15*	*0.15*	*0.16*
Miscellaneous	0.64	1.00	0.62	0.80	*0.10*	*0.26*	*0.11*	*0.25*
Meat	1.11	1.50	1.31	1.26	*0.07*	*0.06*	*0.13*	*0.09*
Fish	1.16	0.66	0.73	0.40	*0.27*	*0.28*	*0.20*	*0.14*
Milk, Cheese, Eggs	0.76	0.31	0.72	0.92	*0.14*	*0.10*	*0.13*	*0.09*
Soft Drinks	0.95	1.00	0.84	0.71	*0.08*	*0.09*	*0.12*	*0.19*
Hot Drinks	0.17	−0.55	−0.31	0.20	*0.25*	*0.31*	*0.25*	*0.19*
Alcoholic Drinks	1.13	1.19	1.35	1.21	*0.03*	*0.03*	*0.05*	*0.04*
Bread and Cereals	0.42	0.41	0.84	1.38	*0.13*	*0.16*	*0.12*	*0.12*
Fruit and Vegetables	1.62	1.65	1.21	0.77	*0.14*	*0.33*	*0.11*	*0.11*
Potatoes	0.54	2.07	−0.29	−0.33	*0.42*	*0.97*	*0.74*	*0.36*
Fats and Oils	0.64	0.38	0.25	1.49	*0.23*	*0.30*	*0.24*	*0.20*
Sugar	0.50	1.17	2.06	−1.83	*0.86*	*1.25*	*0.46*	*0.40*
Confectionery *etc*	1.11	1.28	1.01	1.00	*0.08*	*0.29*	*0.07*	*0.07*

Total Elasticities

	Elasticities			
	D	F	N	S
Meat	0.72	1.13	0.93	0.56
Fish	0.75	0.50	0.52	0.18
Milk, Cheese, Eggs	0.49	0.24	0.51	0.41
Soft Drinks	0.59	1.67	1.11	0.31
Hot Drinks	0.11	−0.93	−0.41	0.09
Alcoholic Drinks	0.71	1.99	1.78	0.53
Bread and Cereals	0.22	0.44	0.38	0.52
Fruit and Vegetables	0.86	1.75	0.55	0.29
Potatoes	0.28	2.20	−0.13	−0.13
Fats and Oils	0.23	0.42	0.12	0.49
Sugar	0.18	1.31	0.96	−0.60
Confectionery *etc*	0.41	1.43	0.47	0.33

Table A9. Uncompensated Own-Price Elasticities – at Last Value
Within Group Elasticities

	Elasticities				*Robust Standard Errors*			
	D	F	N	S	*D*	*F*	*N*	*S*
Food-at-home	−0.19	−0.28	−0.27	−0.53	*0.11*	*0.08*	*0.09*	*0.08*
Restaurants	−0.54	−1.03	−0.82	−1.62	*0.33*	*0.11*	*0.12*	*0.41*
Nondurables	−0.87	−0.45	−0.52	−0.57	*0.09*	*0.18*	*0.09*	*0.12*
Services	−0.79	−0.57	−0.82	−0.67	*0.07*	*0.24*	*0.07*	*0.03*
Animalia	−0.83	−0.43	−0.70	−0.75	*0.08*	*0.11*	*0.07*	*0.07*
Beverages	−0.86	−0.77	−0.93	−0.97	*0.15*	*0.09*	*0.11*	*0.13*
Vegetablia	−0.51	−0.38	−0.68	−0.69	*0.09*	*0.14*	*0.15*	*0.12*
Miscellaneous	−0.82	0.09	−0.13	−0.63	*0.11*	*0.22*	*0.05*	*0.10*
Meat	−0.81	−0.82	−1.04	−0.58	*0.09*	*0.11*	*0.13*	*0.09*
Fish	−0.91	−0.31	−0.87	−0.33	*0.19*	*0.14*	*0.14*	*0.14*
Milk, Cheese, Eggs	−0.47	0.08	−0.42	−0.18	*0.16*	*0.24*	*0.11*	*0.09*
Soft Drinks	−1.06	−1.20	−0.79	−0.67	*0.11*	*0.10*	*0.19*	*0.14*
Hot Drinks	0.45	0.60	−0.06	0.20	*0.20*	*0.22*	*0.09*	*0.10*
Alcoholic Drinks	−0.80	−1.03	−1.15	−0.97	*0.06*	*0.03*	*0.05*	*0.02*
Bread and Cereals	−0.48	−0.30	−0.60	−1.00	*0.10*	*0.16*	*0.12*	*0.10*
Fruit and Vegetables	−0.98	−0.77	−0.83	−0.71	*0.04*	*0.14*	*0.15*	*0.06*
Potatoes	−0.59	−0.61	−0.16	0.25	*0.06*	*0.17*	*0.16*	*0.09*
Fats and Oils	−0.56	−0.47	0.07	−0.44	*0.12*	*0.16*	*0.20*	*0.10*
Sugar	−0.34	−0.13	−0.15	2.08	*0.34*	*0.45*	*0.11*	*0.32*
Confectionery *etc*	−1.03	−1.01	−0.82	−0.75	*0.07*	*0.12*	*0.07*	*0.08*

Total Elasticities

	Elasticities			
	D	F	N	S
Meat	−0.44	−0.19	−0.68	−0.33
Fish	−0.88	−0.28	−0.77	−0.30
Milk, Cheese, Eggs	−0.35	0.17	−0.27	−0.02
Soft Drinks	−1.02	−1.15	−0.73	−0.65
Hot Drinks	0.46	0.58	−0.07	0.21
Alcoholic Drinks	−0.49	−0.55	−0.87	−0.86
Bread and Cereals	−0.35	−0.12	−0.45	−0.71
Fruit and Vegetables	−0.48	−0.30	−0.55	−0.56
Potatoes	−0.55	−0.48	−0.17	0.24
Fats and Oils	−0.53	−0.33	0.10	−0.27
Sugar	−0.33	0.00	0.01	2.05
Confectionery *etc*	−0.81	−0.10	−0.09	−0.45

Table A10. Compensated Own-Price Elasticities – at Last Value
Within Group Elasticities

	Elasticities				*Robust Standard Errors*			
	D	F	N	S	*D*	*F*	*N*	*S*
Food-at-home	−0.06	0.03	−0.03	−0.42	*0.11*	*0.09*	*0.20*	*0.10*
Restaurants	−0.48	−0.85	−0.75	−1.50	*0.32*	*0.09*	*0.27*	*0.38*
Nondurables	−0.52	−0.26	−0.21	−0.27	*0.13*	*0.22*	*0.16*	*0.08*
Services	−0.33	−0.25	−0.43	−0.21	*0.07*	*0.19*	*0.17*	*0.03*
Animalia	−0.40	−0.18	−0.29	−0.35	*0.06*	*0.08*	*0.06*	*0.06*
Beverages	−0.60	−0.38	−0.56	−0.74	*0.12*	*0.11*	*0.12*	*0.14*
Vegetablia	−0.30	−0.14	−0.54	−0.44	*0.08*	*0.12*	*0.14*	*0.10*
Miscellaneous	−0.72	0.21	−0.05	−0.50	*0.12*	*0.24*	*0.05*	*0.10*
Meat	−0.12	0.02	−0.42	0.01	*0.08*	*0.13*	*0.13*	*0.09*
Fish	−0.84	−0.27	−0.73	−0.27	*0.18*	*0.13*	*0.12*	*0.11*
Milk, Cheese, Eggs	−0.23	0.20	−0.17	0.17	*0.13*	*0.22*	*0.09*	*0.08*
Soft Drinks	−0.93	−1.10	−0.60	−0.57	*0.11*	*0.11*	*0.18*	*0.12*
Hot Drinks	0.47	0.55	−0.10	0.23	*0.18*	*0.20*	*0.07*	*0.10*
Alcoholic Drinks	0.04	−0.08	−0.30	−0.09	*0.06*	*0.02*	*0.06*	*0.03*
Bread and Cereals	−0.29	−0.07	−0.25	−0.31	*0.05*	*0.09*	*0.09*	*0.06*
Fruit and Vegetables	−0.21	−0.16	−0.16	−0.37	*0.08*	*0.20*	*0.17*	*0.06*
Potatoes	−0.53	−0.45	−0.18	0.23	*0.06*	*0.13*	*0.15*	*0.08*
Fats and Oils	−0.45	−0.35	0.10	−0.06	*0.10*	*0.10*	*1.44*	*0.12*
Sugar	−0.32	−0.02	0.02	2.00	*0.33*	*0.37*	*0.89*	*0.31*
Confectionery *etc*	−0.16	−0.24	−0.03	−0.05	*0.05*	*0.08*	*0.16*	*0.06*

Total Elasticities

	Elasticities			
	D	F	N	S
Meat	−0.40	−0.13	−0.62	−0.30
Fish	−0.87	−0.28	−0.76	−0.30
Milk, Cheese, Eggs	−0.33	0.18	−0.25	0.00
Soft Drinks	−1.01	−1.14	−0.71	−0.65
Hot Drinks	0.46	0.57	−0.08	0.21
Alcoholic Drinks	−0.46	−0.44	−0.79	−0.83
Bread and Cereals	−0.35	−0.10	−0.44	−0.69
Fruit and Vegetables	−0.45	−0.25	−0.53	−0.55
Potatoes	−0.55	−0.47	−0.17	0.24
Fats and Oils	−0.53	−0.33	0.10	−0.26
Sugar	−0.33	0.01	0.01	2.05
Confectionery *etc*	−0.79	−0.07	−0.07	−0.44

Table A11. Total Uncompensated Cross-Price Elasticities – at Mean Values

DENMARK	M	F	MCE	SD	HD	AD	BC	FV	P	FO	S	CO
Meat	–0.51	0.02	–0.09	0.01	0.04	0.08	–0.16	–0.13	–0.03	0.11	0.04	0.20
Fish	0.30	–0.90	–0.10	0.01	0.04	0.08	–0.16	–0.13	–0.03	0.11	0.04	0.20
Milk, Cheese & Eggs	–0.19	0.05	–0.37	0.01	0.02	0.06	–0.11	–0.09	–0.02	0.07	0.03	0.14
Soft Drinks	0.14	0.02	0.07	–1.07	–0.17	0.77	0.10	0.08	0.02	–0.05	–0.02	–0.10
Hot Drinks	0.09	0.01	0.05	0.28	–0.23	–0.76	0.07	0.05	0.01	–0.04	–0.01	–0.07
Alcohol	0.17	0.02	0.09	–0.06	–0.15	–0.53	0.12	0.10	0.02	–0.07	–0.02	–0.13
Bread and Cereals	–0.02	0.00	–0.01	0.00	0.01	0.03	–0.36	0.04	0.03	0.00	0.00	–0.01
Fruit & Vegetables	–0.08	–0.01	–0.04	0.01	0.04	0.09	–0.04	–0.50	0.00	–0.02	–0.01	–0.03
Potatoes	–0.02	0.00	–0.01	0.00	0.01	0.03	0.10	0.31	–0.54	0.00	0.00	–0.01
Fats and Oils	0.05	0.01	0.03	0.02	0.06	0.14	0.11	0.09	0.02	–0.64	–0.06	0.06
Sugar	0.05	0.01	0.03	0.02	0.06	0.14	0.11	0.09	0.02	–0.28	–0.67	0.30
Confectionery *etc*	0.08	0.01	0.04	0.03	0.09	0.20	0.17	0.13	0.03	–0.01	0.02	–0.84
FINLAND	**M**	**F**	**MCE**	**SD**	**HD**	**AD**	**BC**	**FV**	**P**	**FO**	**S**	**CO**
Meat	–0.23	–0.05	–0.21	0.00	0.00	0.00	–0.02	–0.02	0.00	0.03	0.01	0.03
Fish	1.16	–0.32	–0.93	0.00	0.00	0.00	–0.01	–0.01	0.00	0.01	0.01	0.01
Milk, Cheese & Eggs	–0.25	0.07	0.10	0.00	0.00	0.00	–0.01	0.00	0.00	0.01	0.00	0.01
Soft Drinks	0.24	0.03	0.20	–1.20	0.01	0.79	–0.15	–0.09	–0.02	–0.11	–0.04	–0.11
Hot Drinks	0.07	0.01	0.06	0.04	–0.22	0.03	–0.05	–0.03	–0.01	–0.04	–0.01	–0.03
Alcohol	0.29	0.04	0.25	0.07	–0.13	–0.60	–0.18	–0.11	–0.02	–0.14	–0.05	–0.13
Bread and Cereals	–0.06	–0.01	–0.05	0.01	0.02	0.05	–0.12	0.02	–0.01	–0.01	0.00	–0.01
Fruit & Vegetables	–0.22	–0.03	–0.19	0.03	0.08	0.20	–0.18	–0.29	0.10	–0.05	–0.02	–0.05
Potatoes	–0.26	–0.03	–0.22	0.03	0.10	0.24	0.02	0.16	–0.53	–0.06	–0.02	–0.06
Fats and Oils	–0.18	–0.02	–0.15	0.01	0.03	0.06	0.05	0.03	0.01	–0.34	0.18	0.14
Sugar	–0.35	–0.05	–0.30	0.02	0.05	0.13	0.11	0.07	0.01	–0.53	–0.29	0.58
Confectionery *etc*	–0.44	–0.06	–0.38	0.02	0.06	0.16	0.13	0.08	0.02	0.48	–0.08	–0.37
NORWAY	**M**	**F**	**MCE**	**SD**	**HD**	**AD**	**BC**	**FV**	**P**	**FO**	**S**	**CO**
Meat	–0.66	0.09	0.07	0.02	0.03	0.08	0.07	0.11	0.01	–0.03	–0.02	–0.10
Fish	0.88	–0.79	–0.18	0.01	0.02	0.04	0.04	0.06	0.01	–0.02	–0.01	–0.05
Milk, Cheese & Eggs	–0.03	0.02	–0.21	0.01	0.02	0.04	0.04	0.06	0.01	–0.02	–0.01	–0.05
Soft Drinks	–0.13	–0.04	–0.04	–0.69	–0.01	0.26	0.07	0.11	0.01	0.01	0.00	0.03
Hot Drinks	–0.02	–0.01	–0.01	–0.12	–0.27	0.34	0.01	0.02	0.00	0.00	0.00	0.00
Alcohol	–0.22	–0.06	–0.06	0.05	–0.16	–0.87	0.12	0.19	0.02	0.01	0.01	0.05
Bread and Cereals	0.15	0.04	0.04	0.01	0.01	0.03	–0.43	0.10	–0.11	0.00	0.00	–0.01
Fruit & Vegetables	0.22	0.06	0.06	0.01	0.01	0.04	–0.16	–0.55	0.05	0.00	0.00	–0.02
Potatoes	0.04	0.01	0.01	0.00	0.00	0.01	0.55	–0.91	–0.48	0.00	0.00	0.00
Fats and Oils	0.05	0.01	0.01	–0.04	–0.05	–0.14	–0.08	–0.13	–0.02	–0.18	–0.02	0.17
Sugar	0.17	0.05	0.05	–0.14	–0.18	–0.48	–0.29	–0.46	–0.06	–0.05	–0.24	0.20
Confectionery *etc*	0.10	0.03	0.03	–0.08	–0.10	–0.28	–0.17	–0.26	–0.03	0.04	0.04	–0.13
SWEDEN	**M**	**F**	**MCE**	**SD**	**HD**	**AD**	**BC**	**FV**	**P**	**FO**	**S**	**CO**
Meat	–0.35	–0.06	–0.39	0.02	0.04	0.15	–0.06	–0.05	–0.01	–0.04	–0.01	–0.09
Fish	0.31	–0.26	–0.14	0.01	0.01	0.04	–0.02	–0.01	0.00	–0.01	0.00	–0.03
Milk, Cheese & Eggs	–0.43	–0.03	0.00	0.02	0.03	0.11	–0.04	–0.04	–0.01	–0.03	–0.01	–0.07
Soft Drinks	–0.03	–0.01	–0.02	–0.56	–0.22	0.38	0.01	0.01	0.00	0.05	0.01	0.11
Hot Drinks	–0.02	–0.01	–0.02	–0.07	–0.07	–0.27	0.01	0.01	0.00	0.03	0.01	0.07
Alcohol	–0.07	–0.02	–0.05	–0.03	–0.18	–0.85	0.02	0.02	0.00	0.10	0.03	0.21
Bread and Cereals	0.16	0.04	0.11	–0.01	–0.02	–0.09	–0.71	0.00	–0.15	–0.04	–0.01	–0.09
Fruit & Vegetables	0.09	0.02	0.06	–0.01	–0.01	–0.05	0.12	–0.57	0.05	–0.02	–0.01	–0.05
Potatoes	–0.02	–0.01	–0.02	0.00	0.00	0.01	0.16	–0.07	0.14	0.01	0.00	0.01
Fats and Oils	–0.16	–0.04	–0.12	0.03	0.05	0.18	0.12	0.11	0.02	–0.34	–0.40	–0.05
Sugar	0.07	0.02	0.05	–0.01	–0.02	–0.08	–0.05	–0.05	–0.01	0.26	0.81	–0.74
Confectionery *etc*	–0.11	–0.03	–0.08	0.02	0.03	0.12	0.08	0.07	0.01	–0.13	0.01	–0.43

Table A12. Total Compensated Cross-Price Elasticities – at Mean Values

DENMARK	M	F	MCE	SD	HD	AD	BC	FV	P	FO	S	CO
Meat	–0.45	0.03	–0.06	0.02	0.06	0.13	–0.12	–0.10	–0.02	0.12	0.04	0.23
Fish	0.37	–0.89	–0.06	0.02	0.06	0.13	–0.12	–0.10	–0.02	0.12	0.04	0.23
Milk, Cheese & Eggs	–0.14	0.06	–0.34	0.01	0.04	0.09	–0.08	–0.07	–0.02	0.08	0.03	0.16
Soft Drinks	0.19	0.03	0.10	–1.06	–0.15	0.81	0.12	0.10	0.02	–0.04	–0.02	–0.08
Hot Drinks	0.12	0.02	0.07	0.29	–0.22	–0.74	0.08	0.07	0.02	–0.03	–0.01	–0.05
Alcohol	0.23	0.03	0.12	–0.05	–0.13	–0.48	0.16	0.13	0.03	–0.05	–0.02	–0.10
Bread and Cereals	0.00	0.00	0.00	0.01	0.02	0.04	–0.35	0.05	0.04	0.00	0.00	0.00
Fruit & Vegetables	0.01	0.00	0.00	0.02	0.06	0.15	0.00	–0.47	0.00	0.00	0.00	0.01
Potatoes	0.00	0.00	0.00	0.01	0.02	0.04	0.12	0.32	–0.54	0.00	0.00	0.00
Fats and Oils	0.08	0.01	0.04	0.02	0.07	0.15	0.12	0.10	0.02	–0.64	–0.06	0.07
Sugar	0.08	0.01	0.04	0.02	0.07	0.16	0.13	0.10	0.02	–0.27	–0.67	0.31
Confectionery *etc*	0.12	0.02	0.06	0.04	0.10	0.23	0.18	0.15	0.04	0.00	0.02	–0.83
FINLAND	**M**	**F**	**MCE**	**SD**	**HD**	**AD**	**BC**	**FV**	**P**	**FO**	**S**	**CO**
Meat	–0.16	–0.04	–0.15	0.01	0.02	0.05	0.03	0.02	0.00	0.06	0.02	0.06
Fish	1.19	–0.31	–0.90	0.00	0.01	0.02	0.01	0.01	0.00	0.03	0.01	0.03
Milk, Cheese & Eggs	–0.23	0.07	0.12	0.00	0.01	0.01	0.01	0.00	0.00	0.01	0.01	0.01
Soft Drinks	0.35	0.04	0.30	–1.19	0.05	0.88	–0.07	–0.04	–0.01	–0.07	–0.03	–0.07
Hot Drinks	0.11	0.01	0.09	0.04	–0.21	0.06	–0.02	–0.01	0.00	–0.02	–0.01	–0.02
Alcohol	0.43	0.05	0.37	0.09	–0.09	–0.50	–0.09	–0.05	–0.01	–0.09	–0.03	–0.09
Bread and Cereals	–0.03	0.00	–0.02	0.01	0.03	0.07	–0.10	0.03	–0.01	0.00	0.00	0.00
Fruit & Vegetables	–0.11	–0.01	–0.09	0.04	0.12	0.29	–0.10	–0.24	0.11	–0.01	0.00	–0.01
Potatoes	–0.13	–0.02	–0.11	0.04	0.14	0.34	0.11	0.22	–0.52	–0.01	–0.01	–0.01
Fats and Oils	–0.14	–0.02	–0.12	0.01	0.04	0.09	0.08	0.05	0.01	–0.33	0.18	0.16
Sugar	–0.27	–0.03	–0.23	0.02	0.08	0.19	0.16	0.10	0.02	–0.51	–0.27	0.61
Confectionery *etc*	–0.34	–0.04	–0.29	0.03	0.09	0.24	0.21	0.13	0.03	0.52	–0.07	–0.34
NORWAY	**M**	**F**	**MCE**	**SD**	**HD**	**AD**	**BC**	**FV**	**P**	**FO**	**S**	**CO**
Meat	–0.59	0.11	0.09	0.04	0.05	0.12	0.10	0.16	0.02	–0.02	–0.01	–0.07
Fish	0.92	–0.78	–0.17	0.02	0.02	0.07	0.05	0.09	0.01	–0.01	–0.01	–0.04
Milk, Cheese & Eggs	0.01	0.04	–0.20	0.02	0.02	0.07	0.06	0.09	0.01	–0.01	–0.01	–0.04
Soft Drinks	–0.05	–0.01	–0.01	–0.68	0.01	0.31	0.11	0.17	0.02	0.02	0.01	0.06
Hot Drinks	–0.01	0.00	0.00	–0.12	–0.26	0.35	0.01	0.02	0.00	0.00	0.00	0.01
Alcohol	–0.09	–0.02	–0.02	0.07	–0.13	–0.78	0.18	0.28	0.03	0.03	0.02	0.11
Bread and Cereals	0.18	0.05	0.05	0.01	0.02	0.05	–0.42	0.12	–0.11	0.00	0.00	0.00
Fruit & Vegetables	0.27	0.08	0.07	0.02	0.02	0.07	–0.14	–0.53	0.05	0.00	0.00	0.00
Potatoes	0.05	0.01	0.01	0.00	0.00	0.01	0.55	–0.91	–0.48	0.00	0.00	0.00
Fats and Oils	0.07	0.02	0.02	–0.04	–0.05	–0.13	–0.08	–0.12	–0.01	–0.17	–0.02	0.18
Sugar	0.23	0.07	0.06	–0.13	–0.16	–0.44	–0.26	–0.42	–0.05	–0.04	–0.23	0.23
Confectionery *etc*	0.13	0.04	0.04	–0.07	–0.09	–0.26	–0.15	–0.24	–0.03	0.04	0.05	–0.12
SWEDEN	**M**	**F**	**MCE**	**SD**	**HD**	**AD**	**BC**	**FV**	**P**	**FO**	**S**	**CO**
Meat	–0.31	–0.05	–0.36	0.03	0.05	0.19	–0.03	–0.03	0.00	–0.03	–0.01	–0.08
Fish	0.32	–0.26	–0.13	0.01	0.01	0.05	–0.01	–0.01	0.00	–0.01	0.00	–0.02
Milk, Cheese & Eggs	–0.40	–0.02	0.02	0.02	0.04	0.14	–0.02	–0.02	0.00	–0.03	–0.01	–0.06
Soft Drinks	–0.02	0.00	–0.01	–0.56	–0.22	0.40	0.02	0.02	0.00	0.05	0.02	0.12
Hot Drinks	–0.01	0.00	–0.01	–0.07	–0.07	–0.26	0.02	0.01	0.00	0.03	0.01	0.08
Alcohol	–0.03	–0.01	–0.02	–0.02	–0.17	–0.82	0.05	0.04	0.01	0.10	0.03	0.23
Bread and Cereals	0.19	0.05	0.14	–0.01	–0.01	–0.05	–0.69	0.02	–0.15	–0.04	–0.01	–0.08
Fruit & Vegetables	0.11	0.03	0.08	0.00	–0.01	–0.03	0.14	–0.55	0.05	–0.02	–0.01	–0.04
Potatoes	–0.03	–0.01	–0.02	0.00	0.00	0.01	0.15	–0.07	0.14	0.01	0.00	0.01
Fats and Oils	–0.13	–0.04	–0.09	0.03	0.05	0.21	0.14	0.12	0.02	–0.33	–0.40	–0.03
Sugar	0.06	0.02	0.04	–0.01	–0.02	–0.09	–0.06	–0.06	–0.01	0.26	0.81	–0.75
Confectionery *etc*	–0.09	–0.02	–0.07	0.02	0.04	0.14	0.10	0.09	0.01	–0.12	0.01	–0.42

Table A13. Total Uncompensated Cross-Price Elasticities – at Last Values

DENMARK	M	F	MCE	SD	HD	AD	BC	FV	P	FO	S	CO
Meat	–0.44	0.01	–0.05	0.03	0.02	0.14	–0.10	–0.12	–0.03	0.06	0.01	0.29
Fish	0.40	–0.88	–0.16	0.03	0.02	0.15	–0.11	–0.12	–0.03	0.07	0.01	0.31
Milk, Cheese & Eggs	–0.13	0.04	–0.35	0.02	0.02	0.10	–0.07	–0.08	–0.02	0.04	0.01	0.20
Soft Drinks	0.20	0.02	0.10	–1.02	–0.14	0.67	0.10	0.12	0.03	–0.03	–0.01	–0.13
Hot Drinks	0.03	0.00	0.02	0.60	0.46	–1.75	0.02	0.02	0.00	0.00	0.00	–0.02
Alcohol	0.23	0.02	0.12	–0.02	–0.15	–0.49	0.12	0.14	0.03	–0.03	–0.01	–0.16
Bread and Cereals	0.00	0.00	0.00	0.01	0.01	0.04	–0.35	0.06	0.03	0.00	0.00	0.00
Fruit & Vegetables	0.01	0.00	0.00	0.03	0.02	0.15	0.00	–0.48	0.01	0.00	0.00	0.00
Potatoes	0.00	0.00	0.00	0.01	0.01	0.05	0.07	0.36	–0.55	0.00	0.00	0.00
Fats and Oils	0.07	0.01	0.03	0.03	0.03	0.15	0.08	0.10	0.02	–0.53	–0.14	0.10
Sugar	0.05	0.01	0.03	0.02	0.02	0.12	0.07	0.08	0.02	–0.79	–0.33	0.62
Confectionery *etc*	0.11	0.01	0.06	0.05	0.04	0.26	0.15	0.17	0.04	0.00	0.02	–0.81
FINLAND	**M**	**F**	**MCE**	**SD**	**HD**	**AD**	**BC**	**FV**	**P**	**FO**	**S**	**CO**
Meat	–0.19	–0.04	–0.18	0.00	0.00	0.04	0.00	0.00	0.00	0.02	0.01	0.04
Fish	1.24	–0.28	–1.01	0.00	0.00	0.02	0.00	0.00	0.00	0.01	0.00	0.02
Milk, Cheese & Eggs	–0.28	0.07	0.17	0.00	0.00	0.01	0.00	0.00	0.00	0.00	0.00	0.01
Soft Drinks	0.29	0.03	0.20	–1.15	–0.01	0.77	–0.09	–0.07	–0.01	–0.06	–0.02	–0.13
Hot Drinks	–0.16	–0.02	–0.11	0.04	0.58	–0.33	0.05	0.04	0.01	0.03	0.01	0.07
Alcohol	0.35	0.04	0.24	0.08	–0.13	–0.55	–0.11	–0.08	–0.01	–0.07	–0.03	–0.16
Bread and Cereals	–0.05	0.00	–0.03	0.01	0.01	0.08	–0.12	0.03	–0.02	–0.01	0.00	–0.02
Fruit & Vegetables	–0.18	–0.02	–0.13	0.04	0.04	0.30	–0.14	–0.30	0.10	–0.03	–0.01	–0.07
Potatoes	–0.23	–0.02	–0.16	0.05	0.05	0.38	0.00	0.14	–0.48	–0.04	–0.01	–0.09
Fats and Oils	–0.16	–0.02	–0.11	0.01	0.01	0.06	0.04	0.03	0.01	–0.33	0.15	0.24
Sugar	–0.51	–0.05	–0.36	0.03	0.03	0.20	0.14	0.10	0.02	–1.09	0.00	0.99
Confectionery *etc*	–0.55	–0.06	–0.39	0.03	0.03	0.22	0.15	0.11	0.02	0.43	–0.04	–0.10
NORWAY	**M**	**F**	**MCE**	**SD**	**HD**	**AD**	**BC**	**FV**	**P**	**FO**	**S**	**CO**
Meat	–0.68	0.13	–0.04	0.03	0.02	0.08	0.09	0.12	0.01	–0.02	–0.01	–0.09
Fish	0.74	–0.77	–0.14	0.02	0.01	0.05	0.05	0.07	0.00	–0.01	–0.01	–0.05
Milk, Cheese & Eggs	–0.04	0.07	–0.27	0.02	0.01	0.05	0.05	0.06	0.00	–0.01	–0.01	–0.05
Soft Drinks	–0.12	–0.04	–0.08	–0.73	–0.02	0.26	0.09	0.13	0.01	0.01	0.01	0.05
Hot Drinks	0.04	0.01	0.03	–0.15	–0.07	0.47	–0.03	–0.05	0.00	0.00	0.00	–0.02
Alcohol	–0.19	–0.06	–0.13	0.05	–0.13	–0.87	0.15	0.20	0.01	0.01	0.01	0.08
Bread and Cereals	0.16	0.05	0.12	0.01	0.00	0.02	–0.45	0.11	–0.11	0.00	0.00	–0.01
Fruit & Vegetables	0.24	0.07	0.17	0.01	0.01	0.03	–0.15	–0.55	0.06	0.00	0.00	–0.01
Potatoes	–0.06	–0.02	–0.04	0.00	0.00	–0.01	0.86	–1.68	–0.17	0.00	0.00	0.00
Fats and Oils	0.03	0.01	0.02	–0.02	–0.01	–0.07	–0.04	–0.06	0.00	0.10	–0.13	0.02
Sugar	0.23	0.07	0.16	–0.20	–0.12	–0.56	–0.36	–0.49	–0.03	–0.22	0.01	0.08
Confectionery *etc*	0.11	0.03	0.08	–0.10	–0.06	–0.27	–0.18	–0.24	–0.02	0.00	0.01	–0.09
SWEDEN	**M**	**F**	**MCE**	**SD**	**HD**	**AD**	**BC**	**FV**	**P**	**FO**	**S**	**CO**
Meat	–0.33	–0.06	–0.40	0.03	0.03	0.15	–0.05	–0.04	–0.01	–0.03	–0.01	–0.09
Fish	0.29	–0.30	–0.11	0.01	0.01	0.05	–0.01	–0.01	0.00	–0.01	0.00	–0.03
Milk, Cheese & Eggs	–0.41	–0.02	–0.02	0.02	0.02	0.11	–0.03	–0.03	0.00	–0.02	0.00	–0.07
Soft Drinks	–0.04	–0.01	–0.03	–0.65	–0.18	0.32	0.02	0.01	0.00	0.06	0.01	0.16
Hot Drinks	–0.01	0.00	–0.01	–0.08	0.21	–0.39	0.00	0.00	0.00	0.02	0.00	0.04
Alcohol	–0.07	–0.02	–0.05	–0.02	–0.17	–0.86	0.03	0.02	0.00	0.09	0.02	0.27
Bread and Cereals	0.16	0.05	0.13	–0.02	–0.02	–0.09	–0.71	0.01	–0.15	–0.03	–0.01	–0.09
Fruit & Vegetables	0.09	0.03	0.07	–0.01	–0.01	–0.05	0.13	–0.56	0.04	–0.02	0.00	–0.05
Potatoes	–0.04	–0.01	–0.03	0.00	0.00	0.02	0.15	–0.09	0.24	0.01	0.00	0.02
Fats and Oils	–0.12	–0.04	–0.09	0.04	0.04	0.21	0.13	0.11	0.02	–0.27	–0.46	–0.12
Sugar	0.15	0.05	0.12	–0.05	–0.05	–0.26	–0.16	–0.14	–0.02	0.24	2.05	–1.30
Confectionery *etc*	–0.08	–0.03	–0.06	0.03	0.03	0.14	0.09	0.07	0.01	–0.12	0.00	–0.45

Table A14. Total Compensated Cross-Price Elasticities – at Last Values

DENMARK	**M**	**F**	**MCE**	**SD**	**HD**	**AD**	**BC**	**FV**	**P**	**FO**	**S**	**CO**
Meat	−0.40	0.02	−0.03	0.03	0.03	0.17	−0.09	−0.10	−0.02	0.07	0.01	0.32
Fish	0.44	−0.87	−0.14	0.03	0.03	0.18	−0.09	−0.10	−0.02	0.07	0.02	0.33
Milk, Cheese & Eggs	−0.11	0.04	−0.33	0.02	0.02	0.12	−0.06	−0.07	−0.01	0.05	0.01	0.22
Soft Drinks	0.23	0.02	0.12	−1.01	−0.13	0.69	0.12	0.13	0.03	−0.02	−0.01	−0.11
Hot Drinks	0.04	0.00	0.02	0.60	0.46	−1.74	0.02	0.02	0.01	0.00	0.00	−0.02
Alcohol	0.27	0.03	0.14	−0.02	−0.15	−0.46	0.14	0.16	0.04	−0.03	−0.01	−0.13
Bread and Cereals	0.01	0.00	0.01	0.01	0.01	0.05	−0.35	0.07	0.03	0.00	0.00	0.01
Fruit & Vegetables	0.06	0.01	0.03	0.04	0.03	0.18	0.02	−0.45	0.01	0.00	0.00	0.02
Potatoes	0.02	0.00	0.01	0.01	0.01	0.06	0.08	0.36	−0.55	0.00	0.00	0.01
Fats and Oils	0.08	0.01	0.04	0.03	0.03	0.16	0.09	0.10	0.02	−0.53	−0.14	0.11
Sugar	0.06	0.01	0.03	0.02	0.02	0.13	0.07	0.08	0.02	−0.78	−0.33	0.63
Confectionery *etc*	0.14	0.01	0.07	0.05	0.05	0.28	0.16	0.18	0.04	0.01	0.02	−0.79
FINLAND	**M**	**F**	**MCE**	**SD**	**HD**	**AD**	**BC**	**FV**	**P**	**FO**	**S**	**CO**
Meat	−0.13	−0.04	−0.14	0.01	0.01	0.10	0.04	0.03	0.01	0.03	0.01	0.06
Fish	1.26	−0.28	−0.99	0.01	0.01	0.04	0.02	0.01	0.00	0.01	0.00	0.03
Milk, Cheese & Eggs	−0.27	0.07	0.18	0.00	0.00	0.02	0.01	0.01	0.00	0.01	0.00	0.01
Soft Drinks	0.38	0.04	0.27	−1.14	0.00	0.87	−0.03	−0.02	0.00	−0.04	−0.02	−0.10
Hot Drinks	−0.21	−0.02	−0.15	0.04	0.57	−0.38	0.02	0.01	0.00	0.02	0.01	0.05
Alcohol	0.46	0.05	0.32	0.10	−0.12	−0.44	−0.03	−0.02	0.00	−0.05	−0.02	−0.12
Bread and Cereals	−0.02	0.00	−0.01	0.01	0.01	0.10	−0.10	0.04	−0.02	0.00	0.00	−0.01
Fruit & Vegetables	−0.08	−0.01	−0.06	0.05	0.05	0.40	−0.07	−0.25	0.10	−0.01	−0.01	−0.03
Potatoes	−0.11	−0.01	−0.07	0.06	0.07	0.51	0.09	0.20	−0.47	−0.02	−0.01	−0.04
Fats and Oils	−0.14	−0.01	−0.10	0.01	0.01	0.09	0.06	0.04	0.01	−0.33	0.15	0.25
Sugar	−0.44	−0.05	−0.30	0.03	0.04	0.27	0.19	0.13	0.02	−1.08	0.01	1.02
Confectionery *etc*	−0.47	−0.05	−0.33	0.04	0.04	0.30	0.20	0.15	0.03	0.44	−0.04	−0.07
NORWAY	**M**	**F**	**MCE**	**SD**	**HD**	**AD**	**BC**	**FV**	**P**	**FO**	**S**	**CO**
Meat	−0.62	0.15	0.00	0.05	0.03	0.13	0.11	0.16	0.01	−0.01	−0.01	−0.06
Fish	0.77	−0.76	−0.12	0.03	0.02	0.07	0.06	0.09	0.01	−0.01	0.00	−0.04
Milk, Cheese & Eggs	−0.01	0.08	−0.25	0.03	0.02	0.07	0.06	0.09	0.01	−0.01	0.00	−0.04
Soft Drinks	−0.05	−0.01	−0.03	−0.71	−0.01	0.31	0.13	0.17	0.01	0.02	0.01	0.09
Hot Drinks	0.02	0.01	0.01	−0.16	−0.08	0.45	−0.05	−0.06	0.00	−0.01	0.00	−0.03
Alcohol	−0.08	−0.02	−0.05	0.08	−0.11	−0.79	0.20	0.28	0.02	0.02	0.02	0.14
Bread and Cereals	0.19	0.06	0.13	0.01	0.01	0.04	−0.44	0.12	−0.11	0.00	0.00	0.00
Fruit & Vegetables	0.27	0.08	0.19	0.02	0.01	0.06	−0.14	−0.53	0.06	0.00	0.00	0.01
Potatoes	−0.07	−0.02	−0.05	−0.01	0.00	−0.01	0.85	−1.68	−0.17	0.00	0.00	0.00
Fats and Oils	0.04	0.01	0.02	−0.02	−0.01	−0.06	−0.04	−0.06	0.00	0.10	−0.13	0.02
Sugar	0.29	0.09	0.20	−0.19	−0.11	−0.51	−0.33	−0.45	−0.03	−0.21	0.01	0.11
Confectionery *etc*	0.14	0.04	0.10	−0.09	−0.06	−0.25	−0.16	−0.22	−0.01	0.00	0.01	−0.07
SWEDEN	**M**	**F**	**MCE**	**SD**	**HD**	**AD**	**BC**	**FV**	**P**	**FO**	**S**	**CO**
Meat	−0.30	−0.06	−0.38	0.03	0.03	0.18	−0.02	−0.02	0.00	−0.03	0.00	−0.08
Fish	0.30	−0.30	−0.10	0.01	0.01	0.06	−0.01	−0.01	0.00	−0.01	0.00	−0.02
Milk, Cheese & Eggs	−0.39	−0.02	0.00	0.02	0.03	0.13	−0.02	−0.02	0.00	−0.02	0.00	−0.06
Soft Drinks	−0.03	−0.01	−0.02	−0.65	−0.18	0.33	0.03	0.02	0.00	0.06	0.01	0.17
Hot Drinks	−0.01	0.00	−0.01	−0.08	0.21	−0.39	0.01	0.01	0.00	0.02	0.00	0.05
Alcohol	−0.04	−0.01	−0.03	−0.02	−0.17	−0.83	0.05	0.04	0.01	0.10	0.02	0.29
Bread and Cereals	0.19	0.06	0.15	−0.01	−0.01	−0.07	−0.69	0.02	−0.15	−0.03	0.00	−0.07
Fruit & Vegetables	0.11	0.03	0.08	−0.01	−0.01	−0.04	0.14	−0.55	0.05	−0.01	0.00	−0.04
Potatoes	−0.05	−0.01	−0.03	0.00	0.00	0.02	0.15	−0.10	0.24	0.01	0.00	0.02
Fats and Oils	−0.10	−0.03	−0.08	0.04	0.04	0.23	0.15	0.13	0.02	−0.26	−0.46	−0.10
Sugar	0.12	0.04	0.09	−0.05	−0.06	−0.29	−0.18	−0.16	−0.03	0.24	2.05	−1.32
Confectionery *etc*	−0.07	−0.02	−0.05	0.03	0.03	0.16	0.10	0.09	0.01	−0.11	0.00	−0.44

Part II

SPECIAL STUDIES

6

EXTENSIONS TO THE COMMON MODEL

by David Edgerton*

6.1 INTRODUCTION

The common model that has been used in this book is the dynamic AIDS model given by (4.10), which has been applied to the three-stage budgeting process described in Figure 2.1. Even though we have tried to motivate this decision using theoretical and intuitive arguments, it is obvious that a good deal of arbitrariness has been involved in our choices concerning model and estimation method. In Chapter 5 we presented the results obtained from estimation of this common model. The estimated models for the different countries were subjected to a battery of diagnostic tests, which they passed with varying success. The power of these tests can be quite low against specific forms of misspecification, however, and small changes in model specification can thus lead to quite large changes in our inferences.

In this chapter we present the results of a number of sensitivity analyses. As regards choice of model, we study variations in the separability structure using Norwegian data. Different choices of functional form and dynamic structure are analysed for Denmark[1], whilst a comparison of different forms of the AIDS/LAIDS models is performed for Sweden. The effect of different assumptions regarding endogeneity/exogeneity is investigated using Swedish data. Finally, we analyse the problems connected with parameter instability, using Danish, Finnish and Swedish data to estimate the gradually switching regressions model (4.11 - 4.13).

Swedish data is also used for the analysis of a number of problems concerning estimation. The differences between various forms of system and subsystem estimation are discussed, as is the choice of estimator (*i.e.*, instrumental variables, maximum likelihood or seemingly unrelated regressions). A few special problems are also treated, such as whether to use heteroscedasticity robust standard errors and the effect of the choice between actual and predicted budget shares when estimating elasticities.

In some instance the questions raised in this chapter can be answered by using formal significance tests. In many cases, however, an informal sensitivity analysis is more appropriate. Since one of the main aims of the project behind this book is to

---

* Kyrre Rickertsen has written the sixth section of this chapter, which is concerned with Norwegian data. Anders Hummelmose and Ilkka Laurila have performed the computations using Danish and Finnish data.

[1] An analysis of Swedish data using an error correction model is to be found in Chapter 7.

obtain reliable elasticity measures for disaggregate foodstuffs, an investigation of the variation of these elasticities thus constitutes an important element of our sensitivity analyses.

Note that much of the information used in our analysis is collected in the tables that are to be found in the Appendix to this chapter. A number of other tables are given directly in the text, however.

6.2 THE METHODOLOGY OF THE CHAPTER

6.2.1 The Common Model

The analysis in this chapter is based upon deviations from the common model described in the previous two chapters. To recapitulate, the estimated form of the common model has the following characteristics:[2]

1. A demand function with
   Habit formation dynamics [D],
   Nonlinear AIDS (with fixed α_0) functional form [AIDS(fix)].
2. Inferences formed using
   ISUR (=ML) as estimation method [ML],
   Subsystem estimation structure [SS],
   Estimated budget shares in elasticities [$\hat{w}$].
   White's robust standard errors [R],
3. Separability structure as in Figure 2.1.

Note that the estimated within group elasticities in the common model use estimated budget shares, but for computational reasons actual budget shares are used when estimating total elasticities.

A complete sensitivity analysis would demand that the parameters describing all the seven points above, be allowed to vary simultaneously. Such a design would, however, lead to a very large experiment[3] and an unwieldy number of comparisons. We therefore merely allow one or two parameters to vary at a time, holding the remaining terms fixed. The generality of our conclusions will, of course, be weakened because of this, but it seems to be the only tractable approach.

6.2.2 Alternative Demand Functions

The common model is a dynamic AIDS system, to which there are a large number of alternatives. Consider first the dynamic part of the structure (4.10a), which in

[2] The notation in square brackets indicates the abbreviations used in the rest of this chapter.

[3] The terms *experiment* and *experimental design* are used here to describe our sensitivity analysis, not the collection of the original data (which was, of course, non-experimental).

matrix terms can be written $w_t = \Theta w_{t-1}$. The static model $\Theta = 0$, the diagonal dynamic model $\Theta = \theta I$ and the first difference model $\Theta = I$ are three such alternatives; another is replacing the lagged budget shares w_{t-1} by the lagged expenditures q_{t-1}. The static model has, of course, been investigated for all the countries in this study, and has been found wanting regarding both predictive power and diagnostic checks. The other alternatives have also been considered, but are only compared systematically using Danish data. A further possibility is to perform a cointegration analysis using an error correction model, and such a study is reported for Swedish data in Chapter 7. In this chapter we also report the results of a comparison between the common model and the gradually switching regressions AIDS model (4.13) for Danish, Finnish and Swedish data.

Another question concerns the functional form to be used. Again, there are a large number of demand functions that have been used in different studies, such as the linear expenditure system (LES), the Rotterdam model and the translog system. Some of these alternatives are considered using Danish data for a part of the utility tree. In this chapter we also consider the application of various modifications to the standard AIDS model, using Swedish data. In their seminal article, Deaton and Muellbauer (1980b) effectively described three different systems: (i) the full non-linear AIDS system where the parameter α_0 is estimated (AIDS(free)), (ii) non-linear AIDS where α_0 is fixed *a priori* using the arguments described in Chapter 4.2.1 (AIDS(fix)) and (iii) the linear version of the system using Stone's price index (LAIDS). Their reason for not using AIDS(free) was due to problems with the empirical identification of α_0, that is the likelihood was very flat for this parameter. Both the other alternatives avoid this difficulty, though in different ways.

The benchmark model in our application of the AIDS system is to fix α_0. This raises the problem of how to determine the "real subsistence expenditure", which theoretically should be the *a priori* value.[4] The rather subjective nature of this choice is probably one of the reasons why most empirical work is based on the LAIDS model, which avoids the parameter α_0 completely.

A number of studies treat problems that concern the theoretical validity of the LAIDS model. Alston *et al.* (1994) and Buse (1994), for example, consider how to best approximate the AIDS elasticities using the LAIDS estimates, and it is the results of these studies that have lead us to use (4.8) in our empirical analysis. Only a few other published examples exist, however, that compare AIDS and LAIDS.[5] Regarding the AIDS(free) method, the only published results we have found that use this method are Lewbel (1989) and Michalek and Keyzer (1992), who do not compare it with the other models.[6]

---

[4] This is illustrated by the fact that the Danish, Finnish and Swedish estimation of AIDS(fix) have used one third of the minimum observed real total expenditure, while the Norwegian estimates are based on one half. The flatness of the likelihood means, however, that this difference has almost no effect on the results.

[5] The papers by Blanciforti and Green (1983b), Blanciforti *et al* (1986) and Georgantelis *et al* (1987) do make comparisons, but they all use LAIDS elasticity formulae shown by Buse (1994) to be inaccurate. Teklu *et al* (1992, p. 53) refer to an unpublished paper showing that the two models yield similar results

[6] Michalek and Keyzer (1992) are also somewhat vague as to how α_0 has been estimated.

6.2.3 Alternative Estimation Methods

We concentrate here on two aspects of estimation methodology: (i) whether or not to take account of the theoretical endogeneity of group and total expenditure, and (ii) what balance should be struck between full and limited information methods. Swedish data is used to perform these studies using the LAIDS functional form.[7]

There are two reasons why the LAIDS model is used in this section. Firstly, and somewhat begging the question discussed in the previous section, the numerical differences between AIDS(fix) and LAIDS turned out to be very small. Secondly, the computational savings are sizeable for full information methods, especially regarding the standard errors of the total elasticities. The same line of reasoning has meant that we use actual budget shares (which are also assumed nonstochastic) when estimating elasticities and their standard errors.

To investigate the first point we use instrumental variables methods. As discussed in Chapter 4, this raises questions concerning what instruments to use and how to use them. If we assume that total expenditure (TX) is exogenous, then this variable can be used in the instrument set in the second and third budget levels. If total expenditure is assumed endogenous, then we use disposable income (DI) in the instrument set at all budget levels. As regards how to use the instruments, we employ the methods of *external instruments* (EIV) and *substituted internal instruments* (IIV) described in Chapter 4.3.3. The first method is the "classic" IV method usually available in computer programme packets, whilst the second seems intuitively to better utilise the information available in the nonlinearities between the variables.

The second methodological question concerns how much system information to use. At the bottom rung of the ladder we have the subsystem methods, denoted SUR(SS) and ML(SS). These both reduce to ordinary least squares, OLS(SS), in the LAIDS model without cross equation restrictions. These methods involve no estimation of error covariance matrices, and to be able to estimate standard errors of the total elasticities one has to assume that there are no error correlations between budget levels.

To illustrate the next level of complexity, assume that we are interested in the total elasticities for *meat*. These formulae involve the three equations of the *animalia* subsystem at the third budget level, the *animalia* equation at the second budget level and the *food-at-home* equation at the first budget level - a total of five equations. Estimation of these five equations together, using SUR or ISUR (ML), now uses correlations between different budget stages. These estimates differ from both OLS and from each other, and are are denoted SUR(5) and ML(5). Note that this method is not possible when using nonlinear AIDS, since we then cannot estimate a single equation from a subsystem.

A somewhat more elaborate method is to estimate the complete first stage, the

---

[7] All the Swedish results given in this book are based on data from 1963-1989. The LAIDS model has also been estimated using data from 1963-1990, and these results can be found in, for example, Edgerton (1993a).

complete subsystem for *food-at-home* at the second stage and the *animalia* subsystem at the third stage. This involves a total of eleven equations, and the estimators SUR(11) and ML(11) are also usable in nonlinear AIDS. This covariance structure seems more plausible, allowing correlations between several equations at different levels. A disadvantage of both this method and the five-equation system, however, is that the estimates of the first two stages will be different depending upon which subsystem is used in the third stage. To be more explicit, the *food-at-home* price and expenditure elasticities are not the same when the *animalia* equations are estimated as when the *beverages* equations are estimated.

A system method that avoids this last problem is the twenty-equation system that simultaneously estimates all the subsystems in Figure 2.1. The methods SUR(20) and ML(20) utilise not only the covariances between the different budget stages, but even the covariances between different subsystems in the third stage.

A number of practical details should be mentioned at this point. Whenever a complete system or subsystem is estimated, the resulting error covariance matrix will be singular. The usual method of solving this is to delete one equation, which is the procedure used here. The actual number of equations estimated in, for example, SUR(5), SUR(11) and SUR(20) are thus four, eight and fourteen respec-

Table 1. Alternative Specifications of the AIDS Model Used in this Chapter

Alternative	Dynamics	Model	Estimation	Shares	S.e.
Common	D	AIDS(fix)	ML(SS)	$\hat{w}$	R
Switching	SwD	AIDS(fix)	ML(SS)	$\hat{w}$	R
AIDS-	D	AIDS(free)	ML(SS)	$\hat{w}$	R
type	D	LAIDS	OLS(SS)	$\hat{w}$	R
	D	LAIDS	EIV-DI	$\hat{w}$	R
IV-	D	LAIDS	EIV-TX	$\hat{w}$	R
method	D	LAIDS	IIV-DI	$\hat{w}$	R
	D	LAIDS	IIV-TX	$\hat{w}$	R
	D	LAIDS	ML(5)	w	R
Estimation	D	LAIDS	ML(11)	w	R
and	D	LAIDS	SUR(5)	w	R
Structure	D	LAIDS	SUR(11)	w	R
	D	LAIDS	SUR(20)	w	R
Shares-type	D	LAIDS	OLS(SS)	w	R
	D	LAIDS	OLS(SS)	w	NR
Nonrobust	D	LAIDS	ML(5)	w	NR
standard	D	LAIDS	ML(11)	w	NR
errors	D	LAIDS	SUR(5)	w	NR
	D	LAIDS	SUR(11)	w	NR
	D	LAIDS	SUR(20)	w	NR

The abbreviations used are those given in sections 6.2.1 - 6.2.3.

tively. A second point is that ML breaks down, due to singularity in the estimated Hessian matrix, if the number of linearly independent variables in the estimated LAIDS system is greater than the number of observations. The equivalent restriction for SUR is merely that the number of independent variables in *each equation* must be less than the number of observations to allow estimation. The number of variables used in ML(5) and ML(11) is 23 and for ML(20) it is 41, which means that ML(20) is not estimable since there are only 26 observations in the Swedish data. The fact that 26×20 ($T \times m$) is much larger than 41 does not help us here, since the matrix to be inverted is still singular (which will soon be apparent if estimation is attempted). This point has been made, *e.g.*, by Deaton (1986, p. 1785), and is analogous to the "undersized sample" problem in the FIML estimation of simultaneous equation systems.

Two final points in our LAIDS analysis of the Swedish data are that (i) we compare the usual nonrobust (NR) formula for standard errors with White's robust formula, and (ii) we compare elasticities calculated using estimated and actual budget shares. In Table 1 we find a specification of all the alternatives used in this part of the study.

6.3 GRADUALLY SWITCHING DYNAMIC AIDS MODELS

6.3.1 Analysis of Swedish Data

In this section we compare the common model to the gradually switching dynamic AIDS model (4.13), which is estimated using maximum likelihood applied to every subsystem separately (ML(SS)). As explained in Chapter 4, we are using a simplified form of the switching model in our study, due to lack of degrees of freedom. We are not proposing this model as a "true" picture of possible changes in aggregate preferences, but rather using it as a more powerful method of testing parameter constancy in the common model.

Goodness-of-fit

Although not reported directly in this book, the static AIDS model (denoted S) produces fairly good results regarding in-sample predictions. In the previous chapter we saw that goodness-of-fit is further improved when the dynamic habit forming form (D) is used, and in addition the error process now more closely resembles white noise. A necessary condition for the dynamic switching regressions model (SwD) to be considered a useful yardstick, is that an additional improvement in goodness of fit should be obtained.

In Table 2 we report some goodness-of-fit measures, where we use Akaike's information criterion and the systemwise R^2 given by (4.43) - adjusted for degrees

Table 2. Goodness-of-Fit in the Swedish Gradually Switching Regressions Model

	Break	Adjusted Systemwise R^2					Akaike		P-value ELRT	
	Years	D	swd	swd:S	swd:sws	swd:D	D	swd	swd:sws	swd:D
PC	70, 82	0.943	0.963	0.485	0.253	0.346	–27.4	–28.6	0.010	0.000
FAH	75, 79	0.826	0.901	0.608	0.341	0.429	–24.8	–26.4	0.001	0.000
A	68, 84	0.824	0.922	0.529	0.058	0.558	–14.6	–16.2	0.240	0.000
B	84, 88	0.923	0.960	0.706	0.046	0.481	–14.8	–16.1	0.254	0.000
V	75, 85	0.884	0.941	0.491	–0.090	0.490	–16.0	–17.3	0.953	0.000
M	73, 84	0.932	0.964	0.760	0.342	0.472	–14.7	–16.0	0.001	0.000

The following abbreviations are used: Private Consumption (PC), Food-at-home (FAH), Animalia (A), Beverages (B), Vegetablia (V), Miscellaneous (M), Static (S), Dynamic (D), Switching (sw) and "Exact" Likelihood Ratio Test (ELRT). The notation swd:D denotes the comparison between models sws and D.

of freedom. We also report certain comparisons between the switching regressions model and some nested models, using the R^2 measure of relative improvement (4.44) and the P-value of Rao's "exact likelihood ratio test" (4.37) of the hypothesis of no difference between models. Note that distribution of the ELRT is not strictly correct in this case, due to the discontinuities introduced by the break years.

We can see that according to the ELRT the switching regression model does indeed lead to a significant improvement in goodness-of-fit, and between 35 percent and 55 percent of the variation remaining in the common model is explained by the introduction of the switching parameters. Note, however, that in three cases - *animalia*, *beverages* and *vegetablia* - there is no significant difference between the switching dynamic and the switching static models. Since in two of these instances there is also no difference between the ordinary static and dynamic models, we can maybe draw the conclusion that in some situations the dynamic structure of our data can be better explained by parameter non-constancy than by habit forming.

We can also see that the break years found by the maximum likelihood procedure vary considerably in the different subsystems, which complicates any economic interpretation. It should also be noted that these break points probably have a large standard error; the breaks that gave "next maximum" likelihood are sometimes quite different from the ML estimates. Small changes in data or model could thus lead to varying results.

Diagnostic Tests

One of the main reasons for abandoning the static model was the high degree of residual autocorrelation we found. If we are to leave the relatively successful common model, we would want our alternative to perform as least as well regarding diagnostic checking. In Tables 3a and 3b we give the results of the misspecification tests discussed in Chapter 4.4.1, where for the sake of comparison the results for both the common model and the gradually switching regressions model are given. The system results use the F-distributions of the exact likelihood ratio tests,

Table 3. P-Values for the Swedish Common and Switching Models

(a) System Tests

	BG	BP	Arch	Reset	HW(di)	HW(tx)	H	HS
PC	0.024	0.341	0.711	0.071	0.058		0.019	0.012
	0.034	*0.430*	*0.553*	*0.001*	*0.001*		*0.002*	*0.002*
FAH	0.100	0.370	0.716	0.007	0.540	0.994	0.051	0.014
	0.289	*0.525*	*0.597*	*0.078*	*0.505*	*0.291*	*0.101*	*0.024*
A	0.954	0.105	0.193	0.060	0.190	0.016	0.001	0.002
	0.236	*0.032*	*0.743*	*0.259*	*0.294*	*0.327*	*0.002*	*0.006*
B	0.476	0.406	0.310	0.037	0.193	0.671	0.105	0.205
	0.955	*0.257*	*0.684*	*0.061*	*0.498*	*0.677*	*0.028*	*0.002*
V	0.052	0.034	0.868	0.424	0.557	0.295	0.000	0.000
	0.399	*0.487*	*0.671*	*0.506*	*0.334*	*0.242*	*0.002*	*0.004*
M	0.857	0.450	0.923	0.956	0.940	0.988	0.000	0.000
	0.602	*0.727*	*0.672*	*0.489*	*0.949*	*0.840*	*0.805*	*0.132*

(b) Single Equation Tests

	Jarque-Bera				Cusumsq			
	1	2	3	4	1	2	3	4
PC	0.564	0.103	0.008	0.849	0.592	0.000	0.003	0.131
	0.580	*0.000*	*0.021*	*0.459*	*0.650*	*0.000*	*0.054*	*0.282*
FAH	0.858	0.424	0.980	0.528	0.299	0.232	0.193	0.037
	0.885	*0.918*	*0.591*	*0.810*	*0.141*	*0.066*	*0.440*	*0.150*
A	0.994	0.791	0.796		0.266	0.870	0.055	
	0.930	*0.748*	*0.433*		*0.211*	*0.541*	*0.088*	
B	0.886	0.971	0.981		0.018	0.159	0.169	
	0.898	*0.794*	*0.992*		*0.459*	*0.287*	*0.395*	
V	0.109	0.046	0.498		0.128	0.297	0.467	
	0.956	*0.784*	*0.991*		*0.233*	*0.237*	*0.671*	
M	0.061	0.668	0.315		0.245	0.081	0.246	
	0.966	*0.540*	*0.853*		*0.362*	*0.107*	*0.298*	

Figures in plain text are for the gradually switching AIDS model. Figures in *italics* are for the common model. The same abbreviations are used as in Table 2 plus the following for tests: Breusch-Godfrey (BG), Breusch-Pagan (BP), Hausman-Wu (HW), Homogeneity (H) and Symmetry (S). The instruments in the HW tests are Disposable Income (di) or Total eXpenditure (tx).

the Jarque-Bera values come from the χ^2-distribution of approximation (4.39) while the results of Edgerton and Wells (1993, 1994) are used for the Cusumsq test.

For the common model we can see that the results for the second and third stages show very few signs of misspecification (although it is important to remember that the lack of degrees of freedom implies a low power). There is some indication of heteroscedasticity in the *animalia* subsystem, and the Reset test is somewhat significant for the *food-at-home* and *beverages* subsystems. The group expenditures do not seem to be endogenous, however, which indicates that the separability structure may not be too incorrectly specified.

The first stage (*private consumption*) is severely misspecified. One or more omitted variables, which vary significantly over time and are autocorrelated, could explain these test results. The *food-at-home* equation is, however, the least misspecified in this subsystem.[8] This is important to us, since it is the calculation of expenditure and own-price elasticities for this group that necessitates the estimation of the first stage.

Unfortunately it seems that the gradually switching regressions model does not help to remove any misspecification. Rather, the reverse seems to be true. The first stage is still very misspecified (even if a slight improvement can be detected). The second and third stages are also beginning to be seriously misspecified, however. If, for example, we use a 20 percent significance level as indicating misspecification, then there are eleven such cases for the system tests of the second and third stages of the gradually switching AIDS model, compared to only three for the common model. The same increase can also be seen for the single equation normality and Cusumsq tests. The latter is maybe the most surprising, since the *raison d'être* behind the switching regressions model is to account for structural change!

Finally, we can see that both homogeneity and symmetry are nearly always rejected for the common model as well as the alternative.

Elasticities

When comparing elasticities from different models, an intuitive point of departure would be to look at their values at mean prices and expenditures. Looking at Tables A5-A6 in the appendix to this chapter, we can see that the differences between the common model and the gradually switching AIDS model are greater than 0.2 for *milk etc.*, *alcohol*, *bread and cereals*, *fruit and vegetables*, *potatoes*, *fats and oils* and *sugar* regarding total expenditure elasticities. For total own-price elasticity the equivalent list is *alcohol*, *bread and cereals*, *fruit and vegetables*, *sugar* and (almost) *confectionery*. The choice of model does not, therefore, seem irrelevant.

Negative total expenditure elasticities and positive total own uncompensated price elasticities were obtained in the common model for *sugar* and (marginally) *potatoes*. These "unreasonable" values disappear for *potatoes* in the gradually switching model, and become less marked for *sugar*. In this sense the alternative model seems to be an improvement over the common model.

Life is, however, a little more complicated. What a policy maker usually demands from the econometrician is a single point estimate of an elasticity. The

---

[8] These results are not all given in the tables, but the worst result for this equation is a P-value of 0.103 for the Reset test

econometrician, on the other hand, knows that, in general, this wish cannot be fulfilled. The estimated elasticities he can deliver will, for a number of reasons, both vary and be imprecise. In particular, the following causes of variation can be expected:

1. Variation due to changes in prices and incomes (model consistent variation),
2. Imprecision due to random error (stochastic variation), and
3. Imprecision due to specification error (structural variation)

The first two sources of variation can, for a given model, be measured by calculating the *range* (or variance) and the *standard errors* of the estimated elasticities. The third source of variation, which includes such factors as omitted variables and changes in preferences, will be greater the less robust the elasticities are to changes in model specification. In this case it can thus be appropriate to study the variation of the average elasticities for different models.

The range over time of the expenditure and own-price elasticities for the common and gradually switching AIDS models are given in Tables A1-A2, while their standard errors are found in Tables A3-A6. Before analysing these tables in more detail, two points should be noted. Firstly, the nonlinearities in the elasticity formulae (4.5) to (4.9) imply that the mean elasticities are not the same as the elasticities evaluated at the mean values of prices and expenditures. This explains the difference between Tables A1-A2 and A3-A6. Secondly, we do not evaluate the standard errors of the total elasticities when using the AIDS models, since this would involve estimating a fourteen-equation nonlinear model (admittedly with block diagonal error covariance matrix). We will, however, somewhat beg the questions raised in later sections of this chapter, and observe from Tables A3-A4 that the standard errors of the within group elasticities of the common model (denoted AIDS-D(ML)) are almost identical with those of alternative model B1 (LAIDS-D(OLS)). We thus use the standard errors of the total elasticities for this LAIDS model as proxies for those of the common model in some of our later analyses.

Let us first look at the variation of the elasticities over the estimation period 1964-1989. Table 4 tells us how many of the expenditure and own-price elasticities, for the different goods, that have ranges (*i.e.*, differences betwen maximum and minimum values) lying within given intervals. This is done for both the common model (D) and the gradually switching AIDS model (SwD), and for both the 12 total elasticities for foodstuffs and the 20 within group elasticities. We can see, for example, that for seven foodstuffs the difference between the largest and smallest total expenditure elasticities in the common model lies between 0.1 and 0.2.

From Table 4 we can see that some elasticities vary quite considerably over the estimation period, as is expected since budget shares vary over time. In particular this is true for the troublesome sugar equation. Note also that the common model has a significantly larger proportion of elasticities with small ranges, even if the largest range (sugar) is also greater for the common model.

When comparing the two models, we can see from Table A1-A2 that for about

Table 4. The Number of Swedish Elasticities that Lie in Given Range Intervals

Range	Total Elasticities				Within Group Elasticities			
	Expenditure		Own-Price		Expenditure		Own-price	
	D	SwD	D	SwD	D	SwD	D	SwD
< 0.1	1	2	5	2	11	4	11	6
0.1 – 0.2	7	3	4	4	5	5	5	8
0.2 – 0.3	2	2	0	3	0	3	1	2
0.3 – 0.5	1	5	1	2	2	5	1	3
0.5 – 1.0	1	0	1	0	1	2	1	0
>1.0	0	0	1	1	1	1	1	1

The same abbreviations are used as in Table 2.

half of the elasticities the ranges do not overlap. This would seem to indicate considerable differences between the models, although for this deduction to be valid, we must eliminate stochastic variation as the cause. A study of Tables A3-A6 shows, however, that there is considerable stochastic variation.

The robust standard errors of the total expenditure elasticities (using, as explained earlier, the LAIDS' result as a proxy for the common model) lie in the interval 0.1 to a little over 0.2, with a somewhat lower result for the equivalent own-price elasticities. Usual approximate 95 percent confidence intervals of ±2 standard errors thus cover, in the worst case, a range of 0.85. In fact it is only for *sugar* that both expenditure and own-price total elasticities have ranges that are not covered by a 95 percent confidence interval, although *hot drinks* and *potatoes* do have total own-price elasticities that satisfy this criterion. In fact, relaxing the interval to ±1 standard error (with a confidence of roughly two thirds) only adds the total expenditure elasticities for *hot drinks* and *potatoes* to those with ranges inside the given interval. All other goods have a stochastic error for the total elasticities far in excess of the model consistent variation.

As previously noted, the hypotheses of no difference between the common and gradually switching AIDS models are soundly rejected using likelihood ratio tests. This need not necessarily apply to all goods, however, and from Tables A5-A6 we can see that the total expenditure and own-price elasticities for *meat*, *fish*, *soft drinks*, *hot drinks* and *confectionery etc.* exhibit a variation between these models that is lower than ±1 standard error (using the common model's standard error). It should be noted, however, that the standard errors of the total elasticities are not estimated (or proxied) for the gradually switching AIDS model.

Finally, we can compare the differences between the total and the within group elasticities. These differences are considerable for the expenditure elasticities, which is not surprising since the first stage expenditure elasticity of *food-at-home* is not near unity, being merely 0.5. The differences are less for the own-price elasticities, which is also partly due to the low *food-at-home* expenditure elasticity, see (4.20b). More unexpected, maybe, are the large differences between the standard errors of the within group and total elasticities, which could lead to severe misinterpretation of the stochastic variation. For example, in the common model *alcohol* has a standard error for the group expenditure elasticity of only 0.04, whilst the figure for the total expenditure elasticity is 0.21.

Conclusions

The first point to be made is that the choice between models does lead to statistically significant effects. The elasticities do differ from model to model, although in many cases these differences fall within the usual bounds set by stochastic variation. These differences are clearly in excess of the model consistent variation, however, for nearly all goods. It is thus important to decide which model is to be preferred.

There are two factors that speak in favour of the switching regressions model: it has a better goodness-of-fit and fewer "unreasonable" elasticities. The arguments against seem to be more convincing, however. The diagnostic tests certainly indicate a greater degree of misspecification in this model, where the results concerning parameter stability seem to be especially difficult to explain. That we are only allowing some of the parameters to vary over time (compare (4.13) with (4.11)) is a theoretical weakness that may account for this problem, but in the practical choice between models we are faced with balancing a significant (but hardly dramatic) improvement in fit against a clear deterioration in specification properties.

If one considers avoidance of misspecification as a prerequisite for good economic modelling, then the common model is certainly to be preferred. Even the principle of parsimony seems to lead to the same choice. This does not imply that we are fully satisfied with the common model. The stochastic variation of the elasticity estimates is large, which basically is a function of the sample size that is difficult to amend. The model is also obviously theoretically deficient for some goods, notably *sugar*. In this case it is not the time-series properties that are the problem (this equation seems to be admirably specified) but rather a long term change in preferences that runs contrary to falling prices and increasing income.[9]

In this subsection we have merely considered the effect that choice of dynamic structure has on our results. More general conclusions, concerning the values of the elasticities, will be addressed in section five, where we also take other sensitivity analyses into account.

6.3.2 Analysis of Finnish Data

A comparison of the Finnish and Swedish results for the switching regressions model shows a considerable degree of similarity. Starting with the goodness-of-fit

[9] Health aspects can be one factor the plays a role, but the increased use of processed foods is probably more important. The *total* consumption of sugar has not declined despite the large decrease in *direct* consumption.

Table 5. Goodness-of-Fit in the Finnish Gradually Switching Regressions Model

	Break	Adjusted Systemwise R^2					Akaike		*P*-value ELRT	
	Years	D	swd	swd:S	swd:sws	swd:D	D	swd	swd:sws	swd:D
PC	75, 84	0.939	0.964	0.500	0.163	0.405	−26.0	−27.5	0.030	0.000
FAH	70, 82	0.896	0.917	0.388	0.316	0.202	−23.3	−24.0	0.000	0.002
A	63, 64	0.773	0.856	0.383	0.014	0.366	−13.8	−14.7	0.360	0.000
B	64, 70	0.906	0.924	0.275	0.176	0.194	−14.9	−15.3	0.017	0.004
V	78, 85	0.870	0.914	0.537	−0.055	0.342	−12.5	−13.3	0.835	0.000
M	61, 87	0.875	0.927	0.628	0.304	0.420	−10.4	−11.4	0.001	0.000

The same abbreviations are used as in Table 2.

measures we can see from Table 5 that the improvement over the common model is 20 percent to 40 percent for the Finnish case, only slightly less than for Sweden. In two cases there is no significant difference between the switching dynamic and switching static models - *animalia* and *vegetablia*. These are two of the cases where this also applies to the Swedish data! Especially for *vegetablia* the dynamic properties seem to be quite weak, which may be a result of how data is collected (the figures for home production, which is considerable for potatoes and fruit, is approximated heavily). Note also that the estimation of the break years is quite different for Finland and Sweden, although no pattern is apparent either within countries or between them. As noted earlier, the standard errors of the break points tend to be large, however.

Turning to the diagnostic tests, these are given in Tables 6a and 6b. In Chapter 5 we saw that the common model performed relatively well for Finland and Sweden as regards misspecification. The Swedish results were somewhat better than the Finnish, with the exception of the first stage which was quite well specified for Finland but not for Sweden. These results carry over, more or less, to the switching model. The most noticeable difference is that the switching model satisfies the misspecification tests better than the common model in Finland, which is not true for Sweden. In four cases system results that were significant at the 10 percent level for the common model become insignificant in the switching alternative, and for several others the degree of significance becomes weaker. The exception to this is the Cusumsq test, where significance is worsened in five cases, and only improved in two.

The two main misspecification problems in the Finnish case seem to be the endogeneity of expenditures, which affects all three stages, and lack of parameter stability. Note that the Reset test is not significant, which seems to indicate that no strong bias due to misspecified separability or functional form seems to be present. Finally we can see that homogeneity and symmetry are rejected in nearly all cases.

A selection of results concerning the elasticity estimates is given in Tables A7 and A8. Looking first at the difference between the switching regressions model and the common model, we can see that total expenditure elasticities differ by more than 0.2 at the mean for *fish*, *soft drinks*, *fruit and vegetables*, *sugar* and *confec-*

Table 6. P-Values for the Finnish Common and Switching Models

(a) System Tests

	BG	BP	Arch	Reset	HW(di)	HW(tx)	H	HS
PC	0.789	0.609	0.761	0.529	0.268		0.032	0.002
	0.281	*0.369*	*0.393*	*0.162*	*0.048*		*0.004*	*0.004*
FAH	0.263	0.596	0.239	0.560	0.148	0.328	0.000	0.001
	0.086	*0.304*	*0.148*	*0.515*	*0.073*	*0.138*	*0.046*	*0.046*
A	0.580	0.073	0.711	0.508	0.142	0.372	0.006	0.012
	0.767	*0.001*	*0.360*	*0.802*	*0.419*	*0.663*	*0.032*	*0.027*
B	0.270	0.417	0.664	0.132	0.592	0.626	0.038	0.078
	0.628	*0.486*	*0.809*	*0.340*	*0.616*	*0.811*	*0.021*	*0.043*
V	0.517	0.175	0.810	0.641	0.039	0.027	0.001	0.003
	0.787	*0.660*	*0.844*	*0.199*	*0.001*	*0.001*	*0.592*	*0.001*
M	0.312	0.419	0.107	0.152	0.002	0.002	0.000	0.000
	0.000	*0.659*	*0.266*	*0.248*	*0.000*	*0.000*	*0.101*	*0.004*

(b) Single Equation Tests

	Jarque-Bera				Cusumsq			
	1	2	3	4	1	2	3	4
PC	0.279	0.972	0.942	0.895	0.008	0.008	0.006	0.012
	0.618	*0.891*	*0.897*	*0.534*	*0.021*	*0.009*	*0.127*	*0.125*
FAH	0.821	0.618	0.990	0.883	0.173	0.181	0.828	0.014
	0.766	*0.863*	*0.718*	*0.988*	*0.254*	*0.202*	*0.788*	*0.017*
A	0.085	0.949	0.185		0.332	0.000	0.381	
	0.162	*0.293*	*0.177*		*0.273*	*0.000*	*0.491*	
B	0.862	0.714	0.317		0.283	0.132	0.055	
	0.789	*0.638*	*0.367*		*0.060*	*0.209*	*0.054*	
V	0.873	0.829	0.901		0.010	0.001	0.267	
	0.859	*0.830*	*0.861*		*0.178*	*0.086*	*0.080*	
M	0.918	0.825	0.783		0.475	0.409	0.428	
	0.567	*0.129*	*0.295*		*0.664*	*0.352*	*0.152*	

Figures in plain text are for the gradually switching AIDS model. Figures in *italics* are for the common model. The same abbreviations are used as in Table 2 and 3.

tionery. Applying the same criterion to the total own-price elasticities shows differences for *soft drinks*, *fats and oils*, *sugar* and *confectionery*.

The elasticities in general exhibit the "correct" sign for Finland. The total own-price elasticity is positive for *potatoes*, but the standard error (albeit of the within group elasticity) is twice as large. For *hot drinks* the elasticities have the expected sign at the mean, but show large "incorrect" signs in 1990. The differences between the mean value of the elasticities and the values in 1990 are also great for *potatoes*, *fats and oils*, *sugar* and *confectionery*.

The difference between the switching dynamic and the common model is somewhat smaller in Finland than in Sweden, and doesn't always affect the same commodities. The goods in the *miscellaneous* group seem to be the most unstable, which is a similar conclusion to that reached for Sweden. Note that the difference between the mean and the 1990 elasticities are also great for these goods, especially for the troublesome *sugar* equation. In Finland even *hot drinks* exhibits a high degree of variability.

The differences between the total and the within group own-price elasticities are in general greater in Finland than in Sweden. This is mainly due to the fact that the *food-at-home* expenditure elasticity is twice as large here, having a value of about one. This also has the effect of making the total expenditure elasticities be more like the within group elasticities than in Sweden.

6.3.3 Analysis of Danish Data

An analysis of the difference between the switching regressions model and the common model, using Danish data, reveals a number of similarities with the Finnish and Swedish results. The Danish goodness-of-fit measures in Table 7 show that the improvement of the switching regressions model over the common model is 25 percent to 45 percent, which lies between the Swedish and Finnish results. Although no formal tests are made between the switching dynamic and switching static models for Denmark, it can be seen from the R^2 values that in two subsystems - *food-at-home* and *vegetablia* - the dynamic model offers no improvement over the static model. For *vegetablia* this reinforces the comments made in the previous subsection, *i.e.*, the dynamic properties seem to be quite weak for this group.

Turning to the diagnostic tests, these are given in Tables 8a and 8b. In Chapter 5 we saw that the common model performed less well for Denmark than for Finland and Sweden as regards misspecification. This was particularly so for the *beverages* group and for the tests regarding the functional form (Reset, Hausman-Wu and Cusumsq).

Table 7. Goodness-of-Fit in the Danish Gradually Switching Regressions Model

	Break	Adjusted Systemwise R^2					Akaike		*P*-value C-Wald	
	Years	D	swd	swd:S	swd:sws	swd:D	D	swd	swd:sws	swd:D
PC	71, 89	0.932	0.953		0.204	0.312	–25.3	–26.4		0.000
FAH	75, 90	0.753	0.850		0.059	0.391	–23.8	–25.2		0.032
A	63, 73	0.837	0.880		0.413	0.263	–13.6	–14.1		0.000
B	58, 60	0.874	0.930		0.292	0.440	–13.3	–14.3		0.000
V	85, 89	0.807	0.868		–0.062	0.315	–13.4	–14.1		0.952
M	66, 87	0.921	0.941		0.521	0.258	–12.1	–12.7		0.000

The same abbreviations are used as in Table 2. C-Wald is the corrected Wald test.

Table 8. P-Values for the Danish Common and Switching Models

(a) System Tests

	BG	BP	Arch	Reset	HW(di)	HW(tx)	H	HS
PC	0.669	0.765	0.626	0.160	0.001		.202	0.190
	0.583	*0.707*	*0.786*	*0.021*	*0.043*		*.092*	*0.241*
FAH	0.005	0.854	0.850	0.280	0.738	0.440	.000	0.000
	0.520	*0.720*	*0.065*	*0.971*	*0.909*	*0.060*	*.165*	*0.000*
A	0.327	0.088	0.588	0.178	0.091	0.386	.071	0.015
	0.774	*0.934*	*0.849*	*0.020*	*0.105*	*0.139*	*.233*	*0.361*
B	0.803	0.032	0.758	0.326	0.945	0.953	.225	0.000
	0.002	*0.001*	*0.573*	*0.247*	*0.068*	*0.346*	*.010*	*0.000*
V	0.108	0.042	0.742	0.365	0.053	0.384	.000	0.000
	0.451	*0.519*	*0.549*	*0.086*	*0.065*	*0.512*	*.000*	*0.000*
M	0.713	0.306	0.715	0.631	0.003	0.015	.000	0.000
	0.825	*0.726*	*0.613*	*0.108*	*0.000*	*0.001*	*.138*	*0.215*

(b) Single Equation Tests

	Jarque-Bera				Cusumsq			
	1	2	3	4	1	2	3	4
PC	0.797	0.639	0.935	0.266	0.015	0.214	0.024	0.288
	0.466	*0.834*	*0.946*	*0.250*	*0.008*	*0.683*	*0.232*	*0.250*
FAH	0.818	0.345	0.382	0.812	0.100	0.031	0.001	0.396
	0.451	*0.524*	*0.540*	*0.838*	*0.221*	*0.336*	*0.029*	*0.233*
A	0.810	0.897	0.727		0.708	0.106	0.078	
	0.666	*0.918*	*0.047*		*0.013*	*0.061*	*0.009*	
B	0.216	0.782	0.824		0.004	0.019	0.380	
	0.119	*0.967*	*0.962*		*0.001*	*0.000*	*0.000*	
V	0.318	0.900	0.720		0.003	0.007	0.394	
	0.845	*0.820*	*0.649*		*0.016*	*0.017*	*0.433*	
M	0.946	0.813	0.879		0.011	0.077	0.031	
	0.738	*0.723*	*0.580*		*0.021*	*0.206*	*0.069*	

Figures in plain text are for the gradually switching AIDS model. Figures in *italics* are for the common model. The same abbreviations are used as in Tables 2 and 3

A number of differences can be seen, however, when we consider the switching models. This satisfies the misspecification tests better than the common model in Denmark and Finland, but not for Sweden. In four cases system results that were significant at the 10 percent level for the common model become insignificant in the switching alternative, and for several others the degree of significance becomes weaker. The results of the single equation Cusumsq tests are somewhat ambiguous, however, improving for *animalia* and *beverages*, but becoming worse for *food-at-*

home. In general these results seem to be quite like the Finnish, but different from those for Sweden.

As in Finland, the main misspecification problems in the Danish case seem to be the endogeneity of total expenditure and lack of parameter stability. In the common model there are also some problems with the Reset test, but these disappear in the dynamic switching model. On the other hand, heteroscedasticity begins to appear, although the significance of this is not very strong. Note that the *beverages* subsystem seems to be fairly well specified in the switching model.

The tests of homogeneity and symmetry lead to rejection in most cases. In fact the switching model rejects these hypotheses more often than the common model, in particular for *animalia* and *miscellaneous*. Homogeneity is no longer rejected for the *beverages* subsystem, however.

Turning to the elasticity estimates, a selection of results is given in Tables A9 and A10. The differences between the total elasticities in the switching regressions model and the common model are much less for Denmark than for Sweden and Finland. The total expenditure elasticities differ by more than 0.2 at the mean only for *soft drinks* and *alcoholic drinks*, while the total own-price elasticities show such differences only for *soft drinks*. The elasticities also exhibit the "correct" sign in nearly all cases for Denmark, the only incorrect sign is a positive total own-price elasticity for *hot drinks* in 1990.

The differences between the mean and the 1990 elasticities are also quite small for Denmark, except for *hot drinks* and *sugar*. These were unstable even for Finland, and in the case of *sugar* for Sweden as well. The differences between the total and the within group elasticities lie in-between the Finnish and Swedish results, which is to be expected since the Danish *food-at-home* expenditure elasticity also lies in-between the values for Finland and Sweden.

6.3.4 General Conclusions Concerning the Switching Model

A number of general conclusions can be drawn from our analysis of the switching dynamic AIDS models. Firstly these lead to a significant improvement in goodness-of-fit, compared with the common model, for all the countries investigated. In some situations the switching static model performed just as well, however, indicating that the switching process is somewhat confounded with the dynamics of the model. A second conclusion is that the switching model did not always lead to an improvement in the misspecification tests, in the Swedish case the reverse being true. In particular the Cusumsq tests, which we would most of all have expected to improve since we are now modelling parameter change, in fact becomes worse for both Sweden and Finland, and are ambiguous for Denmark. Thirdly, it also becomes apparent that the choice between models is of varying importance, the Danish switching model leading to elasticities that are fairly similar to those from the common model, while the differences are much larger for Sweden and Finland.

It can also be noted that the same equations crop up as problematic in both the common and switching models and for all countries. In particular *sugar* and *hot drinks* seem to suffer from quality and preference changes, while poor data hampers the estimation of *potatoes*. The dynamic properties of the first stage also seem hard to capture.

6.4 OTHER ANALYSES FOR SWEDEN

6.4.1 Comparison of Different AIDS Functional Forms

The common model uses the nonlinear dynamic AIDS system (4.10), with an *a priori* chosen value of α_0. The second of our "experiments" is to compare this model with the commonly used linear approximation (in our case, dynamic LAIDS) and with the more general model where α_0 is chosen by the data. The common model can thus be thought of as an approximation to the "true" AIDS model, while LAIDS is an approximation to both of the nonlinear models.

Comparison Between Free and Fixed α_0

To compare two models we must first estimate them. This is not always a simple matter for the model with free α_0, since the likelihood is usually very flat with respect to this parameter around the maximum. Since we encountered no difficulties when estimating the common model, we have chosen a grid search method for estimating the AIDS(free) model. In practice this is done in three stages. Firstly, the likelihood is calculated for a fixed value of α_0, and then this fixed value is increased (or decreased) by steps in the direction that increases the likelihood. This is continued until the likelihood starts to decrease, which gives an approximate ML solution. In the second stage the approximation is improved by calculating the likelihood at sufficiently small steps inside the interval given by the first stage. Finally, to enable us to obtain standard errors, the system is re-estimated with all parameters free, using the ML values as starting values. We have met no difficulties when estimating four of the subsystems, but in the other two cases (*food-at-home* and *animalia*) slightly different estimates have been obtained using different starting values. In these cases we have chosen the values that maximise the likelihood. For the *food-at-home* system, singularities have prevented the calculation of the standard errors of all elasticities.

In Table 9 we compare the results for the models with fix and free common intercept, giving parameter values and results for tests of the hypothesis of no difference between the two models. The standard errors (and Wald tests) use White's robust formula, whereas the likelihood ratio test assumes homoscedasticity. Note that we use a simple degrees-of-freedom correction to the usual LRT and Wald tests, since Rao's exact LRT can break down when the number of restrictions

Table 9. Comparison of Swedish Dynamic AIDS Models with Fix and Free α_0

		Fix α_0		Free α_0				*P*-Value	
	dfcor	α_0	ln *L*	α_0	exp(α_0)	ln *L*	se(α_0)	CLRT	CWLD
PC	0.654	2.251	383.24	106	∞	383.78	114	0.401	0.461
FAH	0.654	1.194	348.80	−720	0	351.33	773	0.069	0.450
A	0.731	0.182	203.82	1010	∞	205.25	1194	0.148	0.470
B	0.731	−0.357	206.43	−129	0	212.77	59	0.002	0.062
V	0.731	−0.105	222.35	−21	0	222.77	25	0.433	0.464
M	0.731	−0.693	205.63	154	∞	206.23	110	0.346	0.229

The same abbreviations are used as in Table 2 plus the following: Degrees of Freedom Correction (dfcor), Likelihood (L), Standard Error (se), Corrected Likelihood Ratio Test (CLRT), Corrected Wald Test (CWLD).

is less than the number of equations.

We can see from this table that the estimated α_0 parameters have very large absolute values. Taking exponentials, which should lead to an interpretation as subsistence level group consumption, yields the unreasonable values of zero or infinity. In the same manner, only one of the twenty intercepts α_i lies between zero and one, which is the interval to be expected since these parameter values can be interpreted as budget shares. Note, however, that the likelihood is indeed very flat, and that the standard errors of α_0 are very large. Only in one case, for *beverages*, is the hypothesis of no difference between models clearly rejected.

If we study Tables A3-A6 we can see that there is a considerable difference between the total expenditure elasticities given by the fix (AIDS-D(ML)) and free (AIDS-D-A0(ML)) models. The differences are much smaller for the total own-price elasticities, and smaller again for most of the within group elasticities. The main exception to the last statement is for the first stage elasticities, and in particular the *food-at-home* expenditure elasticity, and it is this difference that causes the total elasticities to differ so much.

To summarise, there does not seem to be any compelling reason for using the model with free α_0. The AIDS interpretations of the intercept terms are usually lost, the model is in general not statistically distinguishable from the common model, the computational problems are not inconsiderable and improvement in goodness-of-fit is minimal.

Comparison between AIDS and LAIDS

An examination of Tables A3-A6 shows that the differences between the AIDS and LAIDS forms of the common model[10] are quite small. Looking at the expenditure

[10] The two models to compare are AIDS-D-ML* and LAIDS-D-OLS*, where the asterisk indicates that the estimated budget shares have been used to form the within group elasticities.

elasticities (evaluated at the mean) we can see that the absolute value of the difference between the models never exceeds 0.057 for the total elasticities and 0.053 for the within group values, and is in most cases much smaller. For the own-price elasticities the corresponding figures are 0.030 and 0.034. An examination of the various goods shows that the differences between the models are, with very few exceptions, *much* smaller than both the standard errors and the range over time.

As previously noted, for practical computational reasons we have only calculated the standard errors of the within group elasticities for the common model. If we compare these with the standard errors for the LAIDS model we can see that the differences are small. The largest absolute difference in standard errors is less than 10 percent of the common model's value, and for most goods considerably less. The LAIDS values do tend to underestimate those of the common model, however.

The findings in this section support one of the results found by Green and Alston (1990) and Alston *et al.* (1994), namely that the Chalfant formula for the LAIDS elasticities gives a good approximation to the AIDS elasticities.

6.4.2 Comparing Maximum Likelihood and Instrumental Variables

The Hausman-Wu tests for the common model, presented for example in Table 3a, give no indication of exogeneity when using total expenditure as an instrument, and are only significant in the first stage when using disposable income as instrument. This seems to indicate that the recursive manner in which the group expenditures appear in the system does not lead to any serious misspecification. Total expenditure may not be exogenous in the first stage, but the fact that no evidence of exogeneity is to be seen in the other stages, plus the fact that the Reset test is also highly significant in the first stage, seems to indicate a more general problem of misspecification in the first stage rather than a specific problem with endogeneity. It should be noted that the *food-at-home* equation does not exhibit significant Hausman-Wu or Reset values, it is rather the *restaurants and cafés* and (especially) the *services* equations that are problematical.

The Hausman-Wu tests presented above are calculated using the method of external instruments (see Chapters 4.3.3 and 4.4.4). This yields simple tests, but the method of internal instruments, which utilises the functional form of the non-linearities, is intuitively more appealing. We therefore calculate both external and (substituted) internal IV estimates, using both disposable income and total expenditure as instruments; a total of four different IV estimates applied to the LAIDS version of the common model. The choice of which instruments to use depends on what assumptions are made concerning endogeneity. The choice between external and internal instruments can be made using efficiency arguments, however, since both methods have the same consistency properties whatever the assumptions.

Looking at Tables A3-A4, we can see that the differences between the EIV-DI and OLS within group elasticities are in general less than one of the EIV-DI standard errors, with the exception of the *services* equation. This agrees the findings of the Hausman-Wu test. Note, however, that the standard errors are very large in the *vegetablia* equations of the third stage.

Comparing the internal and external IV methods[11], we can see that the standard errors of the internal IV elasticities are usually smaller than for the external IV elasticities when using total expenditure as an instrument. The comparison is not so consistent when using disposable income, but the extremely large standard errors mentioned above become considerably smaller when using internal IV in this case. It thus seems sensible to prefer the IIV method to EIV for both sets of instruments, and in what follows we will only consider the method of internal instruments.

Turning now to Tables A5-A6, we can see that the total elasticities do not differ very greatly between OLS and IIV-TX, that is the use of total expenditure as an instrument for group expenditures does not make very much difference. The standard errors of the within group elasticities (from Tables A3-A4) also seem to indicate no significant differences, with the exception of the *bread and cereals* and *fruit and vegetables* equations, where the IV methods have considerably larger standard errors.

The differences between OLS and IIV-DI are greater than those given above. To some extent this is due to the larger standard errors encountered here, a common problem when using IV methods. The possible reduction in asymptotic bias has to be weighed against a certain decrease in small sample precision. A direct adoption of the IIV-DI results does not seem very attractive, one possibility being to use these estimates only in the first stage. Such a strategy would certainly agree with the results of the Hausman-Wu tests, but ignores the possibility (probability) that the poor performance of the diagnostic tests depends on a more general form of misspecification. If we did indeed merely use IIV-DI in the first stage, then the total expenditure elasticities would be reduced by about 20 percent, with a much smaller effect on the price elasticities.

Summing up, the practical consequences of group expenditure endogeneity do not seem to be very great, and can probably be ignored with impunity. Total expenditure ought possibly to be treated as endogenous in the first stage, but the misspecification of these equations can equally well be a function of other problems, such as incorrect separability assumptions. Using disposable income as an instrument for total expenditure does not seem to work very well, and a possible alternative that may be worth trying is to use lagged total expenditure.

6.4.3 Comparing Single Equation, Subsystem and System Estimation

When estimating a multi-stage LAIDS model with OLS, we are ignoring any information that can exist in the covariances *between* the errors in the different stages. We are not necessarily assuming that the *within group* error covariances are

[11] In the first stage, the IIV-di estimates are the same as the EIV-di estimates, whilst both IIV-tx and EIV-tx reduce to OLS. This explains the blank columns in Tables A2a/b.

zero, but information about these latter covariances does not increase the asymptotic efficiency of our estimates if the between group error covariances are zero.

If, on the other hand, we do not assume that all the between group error covariances are zero, then we can increase the asymptotic efficiency of our estimates by applying SUR jointly to those stages/groups whose between group error covariances are not assumed zero. These estimates are not numerically equivalent to OLS, since the regressors in different groups are not the same. Iterating the SUR regressions leads, as usual, to ML estimates.

As described in Section 6.2.3, we have used five different system estimation methods. SUR(20) estimates the utility tree given by Figure 2.1 without assuming any zero covariances, SUR(11) allows for non-zero covariances between the different stages, but assumes zero covariances between the different groups in the third stage while SUR(5) in addition assumes zero covariances within the equations of the first and second stages. ML(11) and ML(5) are the equivalent iterated estimates, whereas noted earlier we do not have enough observations to estimate ML(20).

The assumption of weak separability does not imply that the error covariances between groups/stages should be zero, but intuitively we would expect that the "more" separable our goods are, the smaller such covariances should be. The assumption that only certain within group covariances are zero, which is used when applying SUR(5)/ML(5), seems rather counter intuitive, however.

A couple of theoretical points should be made before considering the results of our analysis. Firstly, there is never any asymptotic efficiency to be gained by iterating SUR estimates. Secondly, there is no guarantee that the asymptotic increase in precision for SUR over OLS (and of SUR(20) over SUR(11)) will be reflected in small sample efficiency. There is an obvious trade off between degrees of freedom and efficiency; the fewer observations available, the more uncertain our covariance estimates become and the less likely we are to obtain better estimates using the more complicated methods.

Total elasticities for the different methods can be found in Tables A5-A6. The first points to be noted are that the standard errors are fairly steadily decreasing as the size of the estimated system increases, and that they are smaller for ML than SUR. The possible exceptions to both these points are SUR(5) and ML(5). It should be remembered, however, that these decreasing results are to a large part due to the mechanics of least squares, and do not reflect the increasing imprecision in the variance estimates.[12]

When studying the actual elasticity estimates, we can see that in quite a few situations ML(5) deviates considerably from the other methods and yields estimates with unreasonable values. Otherwise, the difference between the methods is not extreme, even though, as is to be expected, they increase the more dissimilar the

---

[12] The error sum of squares is automatically reduced when more parameters are estimated. Since we are using the asymptotic formula $s^2 = SSE/T$, which is not corrected for degrees-of-freedom, a tendency towards decreasing standard errors is to be expected.

assumptions are. The SUR methods lie only occasionally more than one standard error from the OLS estimates, whilst the ML(11) estimates diverge somewhat more. It should be noted, however, that the number of linearly independent variables in the ML(11) system is 23, while the number of observations is 26. This means that this method is very close to breaking down.

Consider now the three methods which are not making peculiar covariance assumptions nor on the verge of becoming singular; OLS, SUR(11) and SUR(20). The difference between their elasticity estimates seems to be quite minor, and the theoretical gain in asymptotic efficiency of the system methods does not seem to translate here into any radical small sample gains.

6.4.4 Other Comparisons

Comparing Elasticities Calculated Using Actual or Estimated Budget Shares

In Chapter 4.4.3 the we discussed two different approaches to the estimation of elasticities within the sample period; the formulae (4.5-4.9, 4.20) can either be used with the observed or the estimated budget shares.[13] If we use actual budget shares, then it becomes necessary to use Chalfant's approximation (*i.e.,* considering them to be nonstochastic) when calculating the standard errors of the elasticities. It is also possible to employ Chalfant's approximation when using estimated budget shares, but this method has not been systematically investigated in this study.

The two procedures reported in Tables A3-A6, regarding the use of budget shares, are as follows. For the within group elasticities, to be found in Tables A3-A4, we either use estimated budget shares (assumed *stochastic* for the calculation of standard errors) or actual budget shares (assumed *nonstochastic* for the calculation of standard errors). Methods using the first approach are denoted with an asterisk, while those using the second approach have no asterisk. For the total elasticities, given in Tables A5-A6, the methods using the second approach (no asterisk) are as above. The methods denoted by an asterisk use estimated budget shares in formulae (4.5-4.9), but, for computational simplicity, actual budget shares in formula (4.20). No standard errors are calculated for these last methods.

Comparing now the LAIDS-D(OLS) within group elasticities, calculated using the two approaches given above, we can see from Tables A3-A4 that the results are very similar. Both the actual estimates and (especially) the standard errors are very close, except for the *sugar* equation and, to a lesser extent, the *potatoes* equation. It should be remembered, however, that the means of the estimated and actual budget shares are identical. The difference between a mean actual budget share and the estimated budget share evaluated at the mean of the prices and expenditures, will thus usually be small. We expect the difference between the two methods of calcu-

[13] It is obviously not possible to use actual budget shares when predicting elasticities for new values of prices and expenditures.

lating elasticities to be greater when looking at individual time points, and although this has not been systematically investigated there is some indication that this is the case. The differences are still quite small, however, and the estimated standard errors continue to be close. Looking at the total elasticities given in Tables A5-A6, we can see that similar conclusions to the above can still be reached. The differences for *sugar* and *potatoes* have now become smaller, however.

Although a more systematic study is probably necessary to remove all sources of doubt, it does seem reasonable to assume that the differences caused by using actual or estimated budget shares are of minor importance when calculating elasticities.

Comparing Robust and Non-Robust Standard Errors

White's robust formula gives consistent standard error estimates in the presence of unspecified heteroscedasticity. Theoretically, we know that allocation models tend to lead to non-constant error variances, see Chavas and Segerson (1987), and this prompted us to use White's formula as standard in this study. The results of our diagnostic tests (see Table 3a) seem to indicate, however, that heteroscedasticity is not a serious problem.

Tables A5-A6 compare White's robust with the classic non-robust results for the LAIDS version of the common model, estimated using OLS, SUR and ML. These results show that the robust errors are in general 10-20 percent *smaller* than the equivalent non-robust estimates. This result is a little surprising, since one expects robust estimates also to be conservative. The usual text book argument for why we expect heteroscedasticity to cause the classic formula to underestimate the standard errors is, however, based on the assumption that the error variances are positively correlated with the regressors. This can be a reasonable assumption if the regressand and the regressors are all positively correlated, which is common in economic time-series. In our case the regressors do indeed tend to increase with time, but the regressand is a budget share, which can both increase or decrease with time. There is thus no *a priori* reason to expect either under or overestimation.

The above result, that the robust standard errors are smaller than the classic ones, is also found for the other countries in this study. This implies that we obtain narrower confidence intervals, but also reject Wald tests more often, than would otherwise be the case when using robust standard errors.

6.5 CONCLUSIONS FROM THE SWEDISH STUDY

The results of the sensitivity analysis presented in this chapter, seem to indicate no compelling reason for abandoning the common model. A number of approaches are shown to be unreasonable (*e.g.* AIDS(free) and ML(5)) or inferior to other alternatives (external instruments). Furthermore, it is shown that the variability caused by

Table 10. Summary of Swedish Elasticities at Mean Values

(a) Total Expenditure Elasticities

	AIDS		DYNAMIC LAIDS								AIDS	
	SwD ML	D ML	OLS	SUR 11	SUR 20	ML 11	IIV DI	IIV TX	2 x *s.e.* OLS	2 x *s.e.* ML11	D-ML Range	D-ML 1989
M	0.7	0.6	0.7	0.7	0.7	0.7	0.3	0.7	0.4	0.2	0.2	0.6
F	0.2	0.2	0.2	0.1	0.1	0.1	0.0	0.1	0.3	0.1	0.1	0.2
MCE	0.2	0.5	0.5	0.5	0.4	0.6	0.4	0.5	0.2	0.1	0.2	0.4
SD	0.2	0.3	0.3	0.3	0.3	0.2	0.3	0.3	0.4	0.2	0.2	0.3
HD	0.3	0.2	0.2	0.2	0.3	0.1	0.3	0.2	0.2	0.1	0.2	0.1
AD	0.9	0.6	0.7	0.6	0.8	0.4	0.9	0.6	0.4	0.3	0.2	0.5
BC	0.4	0.6	0.7	0.7	0.6	0.7	0.1	0.9	0.3	0.2	0.2	0.5
FV	0.7	0.3	0.4	0.3	0.3	0.1	0.4	0.1	0.2	0.1	0.1	0.3
P	0.2	−0.1	−0.1	0.0	−0.1	−0.1	0.1	0.0	0.3	0.1	0.3	−0.1
FO	0.0	0.5	0.6	0.6	0.6	0.5	0.6	0.7	0.4	0.3	0.1	0.5
S	0.0	−0.2	−0.2	−0.3	−0.3	−0.3	−0.4	−0.4	0.2	0.2	0.6	−0.6
CO	0.4	0.4	0.4	0.4	0.5	0.3	0.5	0.4	0.3	0.2	0.1	0.3

(b) Total Uncompensated Own-price Elasticities

	AIDS		DYNAMIC LAIDS								AIDS	
	SwD ML	D ML	OLS	SUR 11	SUR 20	ML 11	IIV DI	IIV TX	2 x *s.e.* OLS	2 x *s.e.* ML11	D-ML Range	D-ML 1989
M	−0.4	−0.4	−0.4	−0.3	−0.2	−0.9	−0.4	−0.3	0.2	0.1	0.1	−0.3
F	−0.3	−0.3	−0.2	−0.2	−0.2	−0.4	−0.1	−0.1	0.3	0.1	0.1	−0.3
MCE	0.0	0.0	0.0	0.1	0.1	−0.3	−0.2	0.0	0.2	0.1	0.1	0.0
SD	−0.5	−0.6	−0.5	−0.6	−0.5	−0.4	−0.5	−0.5	0.3	0.3	0.2	−0.7
HD	−0.1	−0.1	−0.1	−0.1	−0.1	−0.1	−0.1	0.0	0.2	0.1	0.5	0.2
AD	−0.5	−0.9	−0.9	−0.9	−0.9	−0.7	−0.9	−0.9	0.2	0.2	0.0	−0.9
BC	−0.4	−0.7	−0.7	−0.8	−0.7	−0.9	−0.1	−1.0	0.2	0.1	0.0	−0.7
FV	−0.3	−0.6	−0.6	−0.5	−0.5	−0.5	−0.5	−0.5	0.1	0.1	0.0	−0.6
P	0.0	0.1	0.1	0.1	0.2	0.1	0.1	0.1	0.1	0.0	0.5	0.2
FO	−0.2	−0.3	−0.3	−0.4	−0.4	−0.5	−0.4	−0.3	0.2	0.1	0.2	−0.3
S	0.6	0.8	0.6	0.6	0.6	0.4	0.9	0.9	0.3	0.2	2.0	2.0
CO	−0.2	−0.4	−0.4	−0.5	−0.5	−0.5	−0.5	−0.4	0.2	0.1	0.0	−0.5

The following abbreviations are used: Meats (M), Fish (F), Milk, Cheese and Eggs (MCE), Soft Drinks (SD), Hot Drinks (HD), Alcoholic Drinks (HD), Bread and Cereals (BC), Fruit and Vegetables (FV), Potatoes (P), Fats and Oils (FO), Sugar (S) and COnfectionery *etc.* (CO). Other abbreviations follow from the text or earlier tables.

model consistent and stochastic variation, makes it unreasonable to quote elasticity results to more than, at the most, one decimal place.

In Table 10 we present the total elasticities at the mean for the "reasonable" methods. We also present the standard errors (actually, twice the standard errors) for the two methods that usually have the largest and smallest values. Lastly, for the common model we give the range over time (the difference between the maximum and minimum values of the elasticities for different years) and the 1989 values. The final column has not been presented previously in this chapter, but represents the latest elasticity estimates that can be given by the common model.

Our results can be summarised as follows for Sweden:

1. None of our groups of foods are luxuries and all are price inelastic.
2. The *sugar* equation is too poorly specified to be useful.
3. *Fish, hot drinks* and *potatoes* have expenditure elasticities that are approximately equal to zero.
4. *Milk, cheese and eggs, hot drinks* and *potatoes* have own-price elasticities that are approximately equal to zero
5. An interval of ±0.25 is the *minimum* level of uncertainty that can be given with regards to stochastic and model consistent variation.
6. In most cases variability between different structures also falls within the interval given above.

Due to the sources of uncertainty discussed in this chapter, it would probably be unwise of us to try and give inferences that are too precise. The points given above concerning total elasticities for different food groups will thus be presented in the following schematic table. Note that we choose a somewhat different classification here to that presented in Table 5.18, since in Chapter 5 we were mainly concerned with comparing the results of the common model for the different Nordic countries, while in this chapter we wish to present the most appropriate results for Sweden.

Table 11. Elasticity Classification for Sweden

		Total Own-Price Elasticities			
		≥–0.2	(–0.3, –0.4)	(–0.5, –0.6)	≤ –0.7
Total	≤ 0.2	Hot Drinks Potatoes	Fish		
Expenditure	(0.3, 0.4)	Milk, Cheese and Eggs		Fruit and Vegetables Confectionery	Soft Drinks
Elasticities	≥0.5		Meat Fats and Oils		Alcoholic Drinks Bread/Cereals

6.6 A SEPARABILITY ANALYSIS FOR NORWAY
by Kyrre Rickertsen

6.6.1 Weak Separability and Commodity Partitions

The specification of goods in the common model, presented in Chapters 4 and 5, was given by the utility tree in Figure 2.1. This specification was based on the availability of data for all the Nordic countries and some prior beliefs regarding separability among various groups of foods.

The separability structure may, in principle, be tested by parametric or non-parametric methods. In practice parametric tests are impossible in the common model, due to lack of degrees-of freedom as discussed in Chapter 4.4.1. Non-parametric tests are possible, however. The data can be tested for consistency with the chosen structure by, for example, checking for violations of Varian's (1982) generalised axiom of revealed preferences (GARP). If the data violates GARP, one interpretation is that the data are not consistent with the proposed separability structure. Unfortunately a violation of GARP can also be given several other equally plausible interpretations, *e.g.*, structural change in demand, inadequacy of the representative consumer approach or measurement errors. The nonparametric approach is therefore not pursed further here.

It is, however, of intrinsic interest to estimate demand elasticities for a commodity partition that is more detailed than the one used in the common model. The sensitivity of the numerical values of the estimated elasticities to changes in the separability structure will also be investigated. Finally the results of the diagnostic tests suggested severe misspecification in the *vegetablia* and *miscellaneous* sub-systems for the Norwegian data, see Table 5.5. No alternative and intuitively appealing partition of the *miscellaneous* group is evident, but another specification of the *vegetablia* group does seem possible.

To study these questions, an alternative partitioning of the goods is specified. This grouping is estimated using Norwegian data and the dynamic almost ideal model described in Chapter 4. The original Nordic partitioning and the new Alternative partitioning are denoted "N" and "A" in Figure 1. Stage one is identical for both specifications and is excluded from the figure. At stage two, *milk and cream* (8 percent of the expenditure for *food-at-home*) belongs to the group *animalia* in the Nordic specification, but to the group *beverages* in the Alternative specification. The groups *vegetablia* and *miscellaneous* remain unchanged.

The major differences are at the third stage, and these differences are indicated by the light lines in the figure. Finally, a fourth stage concentrating on the demand for *meat* is added. Disappearance data published by the Agricultural Budget Commission, and prices of representative meats published by the Central Bureau of Statistics, are used for estimating this stage. Unfortunately, it is impossible to construct a consistent data series for the consumer price of poultry, which is therefore excluded from this stage. Poultry accounted, on average, for only three percent

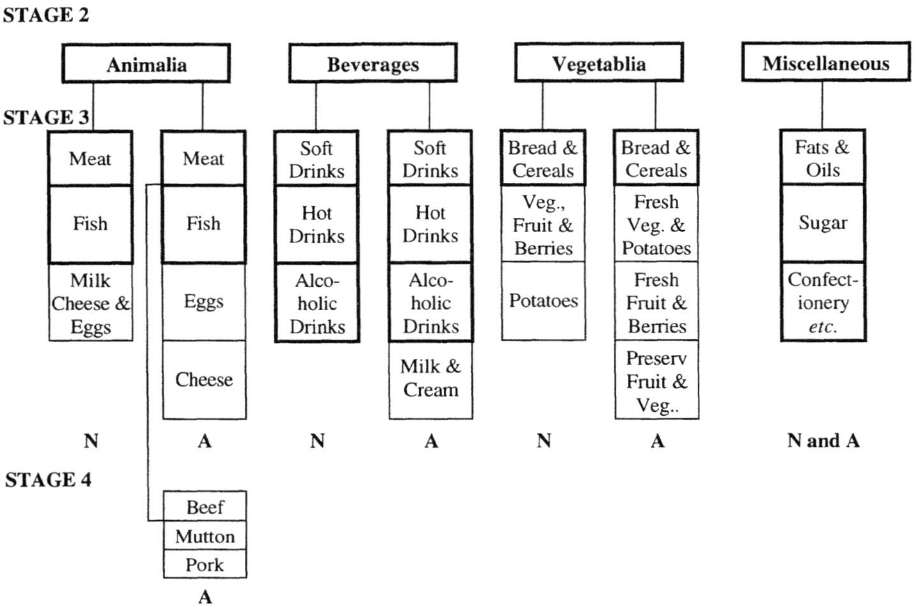

Figure 1. Utility Tree in the Nordic and the Alternative Specification

of meat expenditure during the estimation period.[14]

6.6.2 Results of Specification and Misspecification Tests

The *P*-values of Rao's "exact" Likelihood Ratio test for various restrictions are shown in the Table 12. Neither symmetry nor homogeneity are rejected at the five percent level for *animalia* and *meat*, and the restrictions are imposed for these groups. The hypothesis of no dynamics is not rejected for *food-at-home* and *meat*, although this hypothesis *conditional* on symmetry is strongly rejected for *meat* when using a corrected Wald test. The dynamic model is used, however, even for *food-at-home* for the sake of theoretical consistency, since elasticities are interpreted somewhat differently in static and dynamic models.

About 43 percent of the estimated parameters are significant at the second and third stages above. This is somewhat less than in the Nordic specification where about half the parameters were significant at the corresponding stages. However, this reduction is not surprisingly given that the number of parameters has increased from 112 to 160 at these stages.

Results regarding various economic hypotheses in the Alternative and Nordic

[14] All the Norwegian results given in this book are based on data from 1960-1988. The models have also been estimated using data from 1960-1991, and these results can be found in Rickertsen (1994).

Table 12. Tests of Restrictions in the Norwegian Alternative Specification

	P-values of "Exact" Likelihood Ratio Tests		
	Homogeneity	Symmetry	No Dynamics
Food-at-home	0.003	0.001	0.144
Animalia	0.468	0.231	0.000
Beverages	0.001	0.000	0.026
Vegetablia	0.006	0.025	0.004
Meat	0.217	0.300	0.155*

* The *P*-value for the corrected Wald test of the hypothesis "No dynamics conditional on symmetry" is 0.002.

Table 13. Summary of Tests of Restrictions for Norway

	$0 \leq \alpha_i \leq 1$	$\theta_{ii} \geq 0$	Static	Homogeneity	Hom/Sym	$\tilde{e}_{ii} \leq 0$
Food-at-Home	N/A	N/A	N/*a*	N/A	N/A	
Animalia			N/A	N/*a*	N/*a*	
Beverages	N/A		N/A	N/A	N/A	
Vegetablia			*n*/A	N/A	N/A	
Meat			*a*	*a*		

partitionings are compared in Table 13. The table is specified according to the rules given in Section 5.3.1. However, "N" and "A", denoting rejection of the hypotheses in the Nordic and Alternative specifications respectively, replace the "X" used in Chapter 5.

The Alternative partitioning improves the specification results for the group *animalia*. Both homogeneity and symmetry are accepted according to the Likelihood Ratio test but rejected according to the Wald test for this group. For the *meat* group, only the Wald test of homogeneity leads to rejection at the 10 percent level.

Results of various diagnostic tests and goodness of fit measures are presented in Table 14, where the various tests at equation and system level are described in Chapter 4. Several results are worth noting. Firstly, parameter stability is a major problem. The Cusumsq test indicates that there is a problem with parameter constancy in 10 of the 19 equations. Except for this, the single equations seem reasonably well specified.

Secondly, the system tests suggest misspecification in several cases where misspecification is rejected by the conventionally used single equation tests. This is the case for autocorrelation (*animalia* and *vegetablia*) and functional form misspecification (*food-at-home* and *animalia*). These results show the importance of applying systemwise tests in addition to single equation tests. Finally, the separability assumption for *food-at-home* is questionable according to our Reset and Hausman-Wu tests at the system level.

The goodness of fit is generally high, with R^2 values below 0.9 in only six of the equations. Only the *meat* group exhibits relatively poor goodness-of-fit. The R^2(st) values show how much of the residual variation from the static model, adjusted for the degrees-of-freedom, that is explained by the dynamic model. There are quite

Table 14. Goodness-of-Fit and Diagnostic Tests for Alternative Specification

				Small sample *P*-Values						
Equation	*w*	R^2	R^2(st)	BG	BP	Arch	Reset	HW(tx)	JB	Cusumsq
FAH		*0.91*	*0.10*	*0.351*	*0.177*	*0.623*	***0.067***	***0.014***		
Animalia	0.33	0.91	0.35	0.338	0.645	0.237	0.365	0.649	0.943	**0.043**
Beverages	0.30	0.75	0.32	0.742	0.400	0.931	0.756	0.214	0.965	0.217
Vegetablia	0.24	0.97	−0.12	**0.067**	0.237	0.877	0.308	0.481	0.250	0.502
Miscellan.	0.13	0.95	0.15	0.665	0.633	0.207	0.288	**0.001**	0.981	0.115
Animalia		*0.90*	*0.43*	***0.001***	*0.498*	*0.571*	***0.071***	*0.724*		
Meat	0.64	0.95	0.85	0.503	0.460	0.353	0.254	0.534	0.617	0.115
Fish	0.18	0.90	0.76	0.944	**0.075**	0.724	0.179	0.674	0.398	**0.010**
Cheese	0.11	0.81	0.47	0.267	0.654	0.453	0.323	0.871	0.532	0.428
Eggs	0.07	0.98	0.40	0.502	**0.060**	0.584	0.571	0.267	0.942	**0.003**
Beverages		*0.95*	*0.20*	*0.247*	*0.448*	*0.846*	*0.253*	*0.957*		
Soft drinks	0.13	0.90	0.19	0.288	0.269	0.326	0.480	0.929	0.939	0.832
Hot drinks	0.16	0.96	0.12	0.692	**0.056**	0.972	0.484	0.971	**0.028**	**0.000**
Alcohol	0.44	0.96	−0.11	0.400	0.859	0.523	0.655	0.759	0.939	0.124
Milk/cream	0.27	0.99	0.42	**0.081**	0.694	0.196	0.368	0.571	0.785	**0.037**
Vegetablia		*0.89*	*0.28*	***0.091***	*0.806*	*0.957*	*0.892*	*0.312*		
Bread	0.36	0.93	0.15	0.226	0.179	0.637	0.716	0.993	0.778	**0.002**
Fresh veg.	0.17	0.96	0.41	0.855	0.350	0.905	0.308	0.162	0.752	**0.002**
Fresh fruit	0.29	0.83	0.14	0.664	0.968	0.611	0.933	0.648	0.815	**0.002**
Presv frt/veg	0.18	0.95	0.30	0.414	0.134	0.456	0.774	**0.093**	0.254	**0.001**
Meat		*0.70*	*0.07*	*0.507*	***0.003***	*0.237*	*0.351*	*0.718*		
Beef	0.41	0.59	−0.01	**0.090**	0.102	0.815	0.562	0.755	0.709	0.313
Mutton	0.13	0.78	0.14	0.947	**0.060**	0.656	0.994	0.442	0.623	0.581
Pork	0.47	0.62	−0.02	**0.074**	0.299	0.717	0.459	0.964	0.806	**0.073**

The abbreviations are the same as those used in Table 3. In addition *w* is the within group budget share, the R^2 measures are all adjusted for degrees-of-freedom and R^2(st) measures the relative improvement of the dynamic over the static model. *Italic* text refers to system tests and measures, **bold face** numbers indicate significance at the 10% level.

large variations among the various subsystems, but the dynamic model nevertheless represents an improvement for 15 of the 19 equations and for each subsystem.

Misspecification test results for the two partitionings are compared in Table 15, where we follow the rules given in Chapter 5.2.1 and the "N" and "A" notation from Table 13. The severe misspecification in the *vegetablia* group is substantially reduced in the Alternative partitioning. Misspecification in the form of heteroscedasticity, Arch, endogeneity of group expenditures (using total expenditure as instrument) and non-normal errors is removed. Serial independence is not rejected at the 10 percent level for all of the systems. Parameter instability and endogeneity of total expenditure (using disposable income as instrument) persist, however

The movement of *milk* from the *animalia* to the *beverages* group seems to cause

Table 15. Summary of Diagnostic Tests for Norway

	BG	BP	Arch	Reset	HW(tx)	HW(di)	JB	Cusumsq
FAH				*a*	**aa**	**aa**		**n**
A	A			*nn/a*				*n*/**A**
B		**n**					N	**N/a**
V	*a*	**n**	N		**nn**	NNN/AAA	**nn**	**nnn/AAA**
Meat	*a*	AA						*a*

The same abbreviations are used as in Table 3.

misspecification for *food-at-home* and the group *animalia*. On the other hand, misspecification in the *beverages* subsystem is reduced. Finally, the meat group seems merely to have problems with heteroscedasticity.

6.6.3 Analysis of Elasticity Estimates

The short-run uncompensated own-price and expenditure elasticities, calculated at mean values of the input variables, are presented in Table 16. Both estimated within group and total elasticities, calculated according to the correction formulae in Chapter 4, are given. Goods and commodity groups that are identical across the two specifications are printed in bold type.

Given the differences in commodity grouping for the two specifications, differences for the estimated within group elasticities are to be expected. Furthermore, we have to remember the stochastic variation in the numerical values of the elasticities. If we look at usual 95 percent confidence intervals of ± two standard errors, we find that the own-price elasticity of the group *miscellaneous* and the expenditure elasticities of *meat*, *fish* and *alcoholic drinks* are more than two (Nordic) standard errors apart. This highlights the point that choice among *a priori* reasonable commodity partitions may have large effects for the values of the within group elasticities.

The main interest is related to the total elasticities, however. The absolute deviation of the own-price elasticities between the two specifications is quite small for many goods, being less than 0.1 for all the identical goods at the third stage. The largest variation is 0.18 for the group *vegetablia*. The variation in expenditure elasticities is below 0.2 for all goods and groups other than *fish,* where it is as much as 0.58. The elasticities for *beef, mutton*, *pork*, *eggs*, *cheese*, *milk*, *potatoes and fresh vegetables*, *fresh fruit and berries* and *preserved vegetablia* have not been estimated previously. These elasticities are all of reasonable magnitudes. The total own-price elasticities show inelastic demand for all the goods in both specifications, while the total expenditure elasticities are inelastic except for *pork*, *fish*, *alcoholic drinks* and *soft drinks*.

In conclusion, it is evident that the choice between a priori reasonable commodity partitionings does lead to statistically significant effects for some goods.

Table 16. Norwegian Elasticities for the Nordic and Alternative Specifications

	Nordic				Alternative			
	Within group		Total		Within group		Total	
	Price	Exp	Price	Exp	Price	Exp	Price	Exp
Animalia	−0.69	0.94	−0.43	0.74	−0.93	1.15	−0.67	0.90
	0.07	*0.06*			*0.14*	*0.22*		
Beverages	−0.94	1.73	−0.69	1.35	−0.92	1.39	−0.64	1.08
	0.10	*0.18*			*0.12*	*0.20*		
Vegetablia	**−0.69**	**0.63**	**−0.59**	**0.49**	**−0.85**	**0.51**	**−0.77**	**0.40**
	0.14	*0.15*			*0.07*	*0.11*		
Miscellaneous	**−0.10**	**0.60**	**−0.05**	**0.47**	**−0.21**	**0.60**	**−0.16**	**0.47**
	0.05	*0.11*			*0.06*	*0.21*		
Meat	**−1.05**	**1.29**	**−0.66**	**0.95**	**−0.88**	**0.97**	**−0.68**	**0.87**
	0.12	*0.12*			*0.08*	*0.08*		
Beef					−0.64	0.90	−0.59	0.83
					0.12	*0.10*		
Mutton					−0.52	0.74	−0.51	0.68
					0.16	*0.13*		
Pork					−0.80	1.15	−0.71	1.06
					0.09	*0.09*		
Fish	**−0.85**	**0.66**	**−0.79**	**0.48**	**−0.93**	**1.18**	**−0.85**	**1.06**
	0.16	*0.25*			*0.08*	*0.21*		
Milk,cheese and eggs	−0.40	0.71	−0.27	0.52				
	0.11	*0.13*						
Eggs					−0.35	0.85	−0.34	0.77
					0.17	*0.18*		
Cheese					−0.81	0.96	−0.76	0.86
					0.11	*0.28*		
Milk					−0.30	0.54	−0.25	0.59
					0.06	*0.09*		
Soft drinks	**−0.74**	**0.80**	**−0.69**	**1.08**	**−0.78**	**1.09**	**−0.73**	**1.18**
	0.25	*0.16*			*0.23*	*0.31*		
Hot drinks	**−0.28**	**0.11**	**−0.27**	**0.15**	**−0.22**	**−0.03**	**−0.22**	**−0.03**
	0.08	*0.17*			*0.07*	*0.27*		
Alcoholic drinks	**−1.14**	**1.36**	**−0.87**	**1.84**	**−1.08**	**1.59**	**−0.81**	**1.72**
	0.05	*0.05*			*0.06*	*0.08*		
Bread and cereals	**−0.56**	**0.82**	**−0.43**	**0.40**	**−0.53**	**0.82**	**−0.46**	**0.33**
	0.13	*0.13*			*0.20*	*0.20*		
Veg., fruit and berries	−0.84	1.20	−0.55	0.59				
	0.14	*0.10*						
Potatoes	−0.48	0.21	−0.48	0.10				
	0.11	*0.47*						
Potatoes/fresh veg.					−0.61	0.74	−0.59	0.29
					0.10	*0.22*		
Fresh fruit and berry					−0.95	1.46	−0.85	0.58
					0.11	*0.18*		
Presv. veg. and fruit					−0.48	0.84	−0.44	0.33
					0.14	*0.27*		

Short-run uncompensated own-price and expenditure elasticities. Robust standard errors in *italic* type.

Although the choice of partitioning is of minor importance for the elasticities of most goods in our case, it greatly affects the total expenditure elasticity of *fish*.

There are only minor improvements regarding specification test results in the Alternative partitioning. However, misspecification is substantially reduced in the *vegetablia* subsystem, indicating that the alternative separability structure may be more in accordance with the Norwegian data than the structure of the common model.

6.7 DIFFERENT FUNCTIONAL FORMS FOR DENMARK

6.7.1 The Models that Have Been Analysed

The models analysed in this book are restricted, in the main, to various types of the "Almost Ideal" specification. The common model described in Chapter 5 is a dynamic AIDS model, while in this chapter we also look at switching regressions and linearised forms. It is by no means obvious, however, that this family of models is the most appropriate, and the purpose of this section is to compare it to other commonly used functional forms such as the tranlog model proposed by Christensen *et al.* (1975). At the same time we will also analyse a number of specific alternatives within the AIDS family, some of which we have not considered earlier.

The reason we have chosen the almost ideal model as the basis for our study is that it has a flexible functional form that can be obtained from utility maximisation and that, under certain restrictions, it allows for aggregation over households. These points should therefore be analysed when comparing different models, and we have thus chosen a number of different alternatives in this chapter.

Firstly, we estimate two so called benchmark models that are simply statistical data generating processes without any economic justification, namely a *simple linear trend* and a *first order autoregressive* (*AR1*) model. Secondly we look at a traditional econometric model; the *constant elasticity of demand system* (*CEDS*), which cannot globally satisfy adding up. Finally we look at three models that can satisfy utility maximisation; the *linear expenditure system* (*LES*), the *translog model* (*TLM*) and the *almost ideal demand system* (*AIDS*). Note that all of our models are expressed with budget shares as the dependent variables.

Two variants of the translog model are considered; the *indirect translog* (*ITLM*) and the *direct translog* (*DTLM*), based on Taylor expansions of the indirect and the direct utility functions respectively. The translog model and the AIDS model, which is based on a Taylor expansion of the expenditure function, thus have so called flexible functional forms, while the LES model is based on the more restrictive Stone-Geary utility function. Two versions of the almost ideal model are also considered; the standard model and the *gradually switching almost ideal system* (*S/AIDS*).

The CEDS, LES, ITLM, AIDS and S/AIDS models are all estimated in both

Table 17. The Models Used in the Danish Comparative Study

BENCHMARK MODELS	
Trend	$w_{it} = \alpha_i + \beta_i t + \varepsilon_{it}$
AR1	$w_{it} = \alpha_i + \beta_i w_{i,t-1} + \varepsilon_{it}$
STATIC MODELS	
CEDS	$\ln w_{it} = \alpha_i + (E_i - 1)\ln x_t + (e_{ii} + 1)\ln p_{it} + \varepsilon_{it}$
LES	$w_{it} = \gamma_i\left(\frac{p_{it}}{x_t}\right) + \beta_i\left(1 - \sum_j \gamma_j\left(\frac{p_{jt}}{x_t}\right)\right) + \varepsilon_{it}$
ITLM	$w_{it} = \dfrac{\alpha_i + \sum_j \gamma_{ij} \ln\left(\frac{p_{jt}}{x_t}\right)}{-1 + \sum_k \sum_j \gamma_{kj} \ln\left(\frac{p_{jt}}{x_t}\right)} + \varepsilon_{it}$
DTLM	$w_{it} = \dfrac{\alpha_i + \sum_j \gamma_{ij} \ln q_{jt}}{-1 + \sum_k \sum_j \gamma_{kj} \ln q_{jt}} + \varepsilon_{it}$
AIDS	(4.2)
S/AIDS	(4.11) with $\alpha_i^* = \theta_{ij} = \theta_{ij}^* = 0$
DYNAMIC MODELS	
CEDS-*w*	$\alpha_{it} = \alpha_i^* + \theta_i w_{i,t-1}$
LES-*q*	$\gamma_{it} = \gamma_i^* + \theta_i q_{i,t-1}$
ITLM-*w*	$\alpha_{it} = \alpha_i^* + \sum_j \theta_{ij} w_{j,t-1}$ with $\sum_j \theta_{ij} = 0$
AIDS-*w*	(4.10)
AIDS-*q*	$\alpha_{it} = \alpha_i^* + \sum_j \psi_{ij} \ln q_{j,t-1}$
S/AIDS-*w*	(4.11) with $\alpha_i^* = \theta_{ij}^* = 0$
S/AIDS-*q*	$\alpha_{it} = \alpha_i^* + \sum_j \psi_{ij} \ln q_{j,t-1}$

The abbreviations are explained in the text.

static and dynamic form, whilst the DTLM model is only estimated in static form.

In the dynamic models we must decide how the passage of time should affect the decision process, or, to be more explicit, how the habit forming mechanism is to appear in the demand function. In the common model we allow this to happen by including lagged budget shares (denoted *w*) amongst the regressors, but an equally plausible alternative is to allow lagged quantities (denoted *q*) to appear. We estimate CEDS, ITLM, AIDS and S/AIDS in *w*-dynamic systems, and LES, AIDS and

S/AIDS in q-dynamic systems.

The basic forms of all of these models are described in standard text books on demand theory, such as Deaton and Muellbauer (1980a). A summary of the models we use, with relevant formulae for the demand functions, is to be found in Table 17. Note that the switching regressions models allows both the price and expenditure parameters to vary, as opposed to the analysis in the third section of this chapter where merely the expenditure parameters varied. The difference is due to the fact that we only use Danish data in this section, which allows estimation of more parameters due to the greater number of observations. The results for this model are thus not directly comparable with those given in 6.3.3.

Data

The functional forms described in Table 17 are applied to the second stage of the utility tree given in Figure 2.1, *i.e.*, to the decomposition of *food-at-home* into the groups *animalia*, *beverages*, *vegetablia* and *miscellaneous*. This provides us with comparative information on the different model without making the calculations too extensive. We use the Danish data from 1953-1990, as in the analysis of the common model. A total of 38 observations is thus available for the static models, but since only 37 of these are available for the dynamic models we use, for the sake of compatibility, merely the period 1954-1990 in all our estimations.[15]

6.7.2 A Comparison of the Models

Misspecification Tests

The models under study are evaluated using some of the misspecification tests discussed earlier. In particular we calculate the LM statistics to detect first order autocorrelation (Breusch-Godfrey), first order heteroscedasticity (Breusch-Pagan) and non-normality (Jarque-Bera), as well as the Cusumsq test for parameter stability. These results are presented in Table 18, while some additional tests (including second order variants) are given in the appendix, Table A11.[16]

Looking at the Breusch-Godfrey test in Table 18, we can see that the dynamic flexible functional form models (TLM and AIDS) and the AR1 model in general exhibit no problems with autocorrelation. The other models show significant autocorrelation, especially for the *beverages* and *miscellaneous* groups. These results are supported by the figures for the other autocorrelation tests in Table A11.

The Breusch-Pagan and Jarque-Bera tests are only significant in a few cases,

[15] Most of the results given in this section can be found in more detail in Hummelmose (1992).

[16] The calculations presented in this section were actually performed quite early on in the project, and the test statistics we were using at that time were merely the traditional single equation large sample LM tests.

Table 18. P-Values of Single Equation Tests Using Danish Data

	(a) Breusch-Godfrey; First Order				(b) Breusch-Pagan; First Order			
Models	Anim	Bev	Veg	Misc	Anim	Bev	Veg	Misc
trend	0.22	**0.00**	**0.00**	**0.00**				
AR1	0.60	0.89	0.41	0.73				
CEDS	0.13	**0.00**	**0.02**	**0.00**	0.31	0.23	0.51	0.14
LES	0.33	0.23	0.29	**0.00**	**0.08**	0.26	0.18	**0.02**
ITLM	**0.03**	0.25	0.62	**0.00**	**0.05**	0.30	0.32	0.92
DTLM	0.47	**0.01**	**0.06**	**0.00**	0.15	0.15	0.25	0.49
AIDS	0.26	**0.04**	0.86	**0.00**	0.44	1.00	0.41	0.25
S/AIDS	0.75	**0.08**	0.37	0.49	0.76	0.73	0.36	0.41
CEDS-*w*	0.26	**0.05**	0.92	**0.00**	0.45	0.92	0.39	0.29
LES-*q*	0.38	**0.00**	0.84	**0.02**	1.00	0.32	**0.08**	0.68
ITLM-*w*	0.32	0.73	0.60	0.23	0.73	0.25	0.24	0.79
AIDS-*w*	0.46	0.46	0.38	0.32	0.58	0.65	0.89	1.00
AIDS-*q*	0.62	0.27	0.89	0.22	0.48	0.48	0.48	0.58
S/AIDS-*w*	0.92	0.23	0.14	0.71	0.65	0.81	0.39	0.63
S/AIDS-*q*	0.17	0.45	0.43	0.69	0.30	0.52	0.46	0.92
	(c) Jarque-Bera				(d) Cusumsq			
Models	Anim	Bev	Veg	Misc	Anim	Bev	Veg	Misc
trend	0.53	0.77	0.64	0.50				
AR1	0.81	0.98	0.91	0.90				
CEDS	0.60	0.17	0.93	0.70	0.33	**0.00**	0.51	**0.07**
LES	0.98	0.27	0.48	0.64	**0.02**	**0.03**	**0.01**	0.19
ITLM	0.79	**0.05**	0.86	0.38	**0.04**	0.26	**0.03**	0.22
DTLM	0.90	0.13	0.93	0.54	**0.08**	0.22	**0.02**	0.70
AIDS	0.81	0.98	0.96	0.53	0.49	0.31	**0.04**	0.63
S/AIDS	0.67	0.59	0.56	0.83	**0.00**	0.15	**0.00**	0.43
CEDS-*w*	0.81	0.97	0.95	0.55	0.46	0.40	**0.02**	0.68
LES-*q*	0.39	0.40	0.99	0.57	**0.03**	0.28	**0.00**	**0.00**
ITLM-*w*	0.79	0.61	0.82	0.91	0.12	0.45	**0.01**	0.15
AIDS-*w*	0.96	0.70	0.86	0.65	0.35	**0.05**	**0.03**	0.22
AIDS-*q*	0.92	0.93	0.99	0.72	**0.04**	**0.07**	**0.00**	0.20
S/AIDS-*w*	0.33	**0.01**	**0.10**	0.50	**0.02**	0.22	**0.00**	0.12
S/AIDS-*q*	0.43	0.34	0.89	0.38	**0.00**	**0.00**	**0.00**	**0.01**

The abbreviations for the models are those given in the text. The Breusch-Godfrey, Breusch-Pagan and Jarque-Bera tests are all large sample LM tests, with *P*-values evaluated using the χ^2 distribution. Figures in bold face type indicate significance at the 10% level.

showing that all the models handle heteroscedasticity and non-normality satisfactorily. The only surprising result, maybe, is that the S/AIDS-*w* model has two significant results when testing for non-normality. The Cusumsq test, however, reveals a great number of significant results, especially for the *vegetablia* group, but even to a somewhat lesser extent for *animalia* and *beverages*. The AIDS, CEDS-*w* and ITLM-*w* models are those that show the best results here, with only *vegetablia* being significant, although the AIDS-*w* is only slightly worse. The difference between the Cusumsq and Breusch-Pagan tests also reveal that it is probably the regression parameters and not the variances that are unstable.

The conclusion we can draw from the misspecification tests is that the dynamic indirect translog, using lagged budget shares, seems to perform quite well, and that the equivalent dynamic AIDS is only slightly worse. The other models seem to perform less well, at least for some of the tests.

Goodness-of-Fit

A summary of some goodness-of-fit measures (R^2 adjusted for degrees-of-freedom, the relative improvement in the adjusted R^2 between different models and the Akaike measure) are presented in Table 19.

Looking first of all at the basic R^2 measure, we can see that it is the *animalia* equation that exhibits the worst goodness-of-fit. The other equations show quite reasonable results for most models, but it is only some of the AIDS models that have satisfactory goodness-of-fit for *animalia*. The trend model performs poorly for all equations, while the AR1 model is poor for *animalia*, but satisfactory for the other equations.

In the light of the comments in the previous paragraph, we have chosen AR1 to be the benchmark model with which to compare the other models. The results of this comparison are given in the second part of the Table 19. Here we can see that it is only the dynamic flexible functional form models plus the static switching AIDS model that outperform AR1 for all equations. In fact, it is only the switching models that give a real improvement for *miscellaneous*.

The results in the other parts of the table show that the dynamic models consistently give considerable improvements over their static counterparts, with the possible exceptions of the switching models (especially the dynamic-*w* model). The switching models, on the other hand, are consistently better than the non-switching models. The results can also be used to compare the AIDS and translog models. In this case we find that the AIDS-*w* and ITLM-*q* models perform almost identically. A comparison between the AIDS-*q* and AIDS-*w* dynamic models shows, however, that the models using lagged quantities seem to perform better, especially in the *animalia* and *beverages* equations.

To summarise, the model that gives the best goodness-of-fit, even when we adjust for degrees-of-freedom, is one of the most heavily parametrised models, namely S/AIDS-*q*. The other dynamic switching model is no better than the static switching model, however, and this static model would be the second choice using the goodness-of-fit criterion. Of the non-switching models, the AIDS model with lagged quantities performs best, while no difference can be detected between the dynamic translog and AIDS models using lagged budget shares.

Table 19. Goodness-of-Fit Measures for Different Models Using Danish Data

	ARSQ					Improvement in ARSQ over AR1					Akaike
Model	Anim	Bev	Veg	Misc	SYS	Anim	Bev	Veg	Misc	SYS	
trend	0.16	0.35	0.55	0.42							
AR1	0.05	0.79	0.69	0.83							
CEDS	0.12	0.45	0.80	0.68		0.07	−1.68	0.35	−0.82		
LES	−0.02	0.53	0.75	0.57	0.29	−0.08	−1.30	0.20	−1.47		−21.02
ITLM	0.18	0.80	0.78	0.81	0.56	0.13	0.02	0.27	−0.09		−22.20
DTLM	0.22	0.74	0.73	0.78	0.51	0.18	−0.26	0.13	−0.29		−22.51
AIDS	0.36	0.74	0.84	0.74	0.56	0.33	−0.24	0.47	−0.46		−22.75
S/AIDS	0.64	0.94	0.89	0.92	0.81	0.62	0.73	0.64	0.52		−24.87
CEDS-*w*	0.40	0.77	0.85	0.76		0.37	−0.11	0.51	−0.37		
LES-*q*	0.41	0.89	0.75	0.75	0.57	0.37	0.49	0.18	−0.45		−22.53
ITLM-*w*	0.27	0.84	0.83	0.86	0.64	0.23	0.22	0.44	0.22		−22.57
AIDS-*w*	0.37	0.82	0.85	0.86	0.64	0.33	0.13	0.50	0.19		−22.58
AIDS-*q*	0.63	0.96	0.85	0.83	0.77	0.61	0.81	0.52	0.01		−23.87
S/AIDS-*w*	0.58	0.94	0.89	0.91	0.81	0.55	0.70	0.64	0.46		−24.83
S/AIDS-*q*	0.77	0.98	0.89	0.90	0.85	0.76	0.92	0.63	0.44		−25.58
	Improvement in ARSQ over static model					Improvement in ARSQ over non-switching					
Model	Anim	Bev	Veg	Misc	SYS	Anim	Bev	Veg	Misc	SYS	
S/AIDS						0.44	0.78	0.32	0.67	0.56	
CEDS-*w*	0.32	0.58	0.24	0.24							
LES-*q*	0.42	0.78	−0.03	0.41	0.39						
ITLM-*w*	0.11	0.20	0.23	0.29	0.18						
AIDS-*w*	0.01	0.30	0.05	0.45	0.18						
AIDS-*q*	0.42	0.84	0.10	0.32	0.49						
S/AIDS-*w*	−0.17	−0.13	0.01	−0.13	0.03	0.33	0.65	0.29	0.34	0.48	
S/AIDS-*q*	0.36	0.70	−0.03	−0.18	0.24	0.39	0.59	0.22	0.43	0.35	

The same abbreviations are used as in Table 18. ARSQ is the R^2 measure adjusted for degrees of freedom, SYS denotes the system statistic given by (4.43) and the "improvement over" statistics are given by (4.44).

Non-nested Tests

In our discussion on goodness-of-fit in the previous section, we only looked at which models gave the best fit. In this section we try to see if the differences between models are statistically significant, and in particular we compare the AIDS and translog models. It should be noted that significance tests of the hypotheses of "no dynamics" and "no switching" have already been presented in the AIDS framework in Chapters 5.3 and 6.3.

There is, however, a problem concerned with testing the AIDS and translog models, namely that neither is nested within the other. The static model is nested within the dynamic model, and the non-switching model is nested within the switching, which means that standard testing procedures apply (ignoring the fact that the breakpoints are determined stochastically in the switching model, as pointed out in 6.3.1).

One method of testing two non-nested hypotheses is to build a joint model that combines both the original models, and then simply to perform nested tests of the two hypotheses against this joint model. This methodology has been used by Lewbel (1989) in testing between static AIDS and translog models, but is not really viable in this study (at least for the dynamic models) due to lack of degrees-of-freedom. We have instead decided to use the *J*-test proposed by Davidson and MacKinnon (1981), see also Maddala (1992) and Greene (1993). For a test of the hypothesis H_f: $E(y|x)=f(\boldsymbol{x},\boldsymbol{\beta})$ against H_g: $E(y|x)=g(\boldsymbol{x},\boldsymbol{\gamma})$, this test is based on the following strategy in a single equation environment.

(i) Estimate $\boldsymbol{\beta}$ and $\boldsymbol{\gamma}$ from the two models, and form the predictions $\hat{y}_f$ and $\hat{y}_g$.

(ii) Estimate the models $E(y|x)=f(\boldsymbol{x},\boldsymbol{\beta})+\alpha_f\hat{y}_g$ and $E(y|x)=g(\boldsymbol{x},\boldsymbol{\gamma})+\alpha_g\hat{y}_f$.

(iii) Test $\alpha_f=0$ and $\alpha_g=0$ in the two models in (ii).

If $\alpha_f=0$ then $f(\boldsymbol{x},\boldsymbol{\beta})$ is sufficient to explain y, while $\alpha_g=0$ implies that $g(\boldsymbol{x},\boldsymbol{\gamma})$ is sufficient. The testing procedure can, however, also lead to the result that both hypotheses are rejected or that neither are rejected. The various decision rules are therefore summarised in Table 20.

Table 20. Different Alternatives in the Davidson-MacKinnon J-Test

Hypothesis $\alpha_f=0$	Hypothesis $\alpha_g=0$	
	Not Rejected	Rejected
Not Rejected	Either model can explain the data	$E(y|x)=g(\boldsymbol{x},\boldsymbol{\gamma})$ sufficient to explain the data
Rejected	$E(y|x)=f(\boldsymbol{x},\boldsymbol{\beta})$ sufficient to explain the data	Neither model can explain the data

The above strategy is based on a single equation model. If we have a system of n equations of rank $n-1$, then the models that are estimated at stage (ii) include predictions for all the endogenous variables, and the tests of restrictions in stage (iii) have $n-1$ degrees-of-freedom in each equation, or $(n-1)^2$ for the whole system.

In Table 21 we present the results of a comparison of the static ITLM and AIDS models, and the ITLM-*w*, AIDS-*w*, and AIDS-*q* models. In both cases we use asymptotic Wald tests to calculate the *P*-values. For the static models we can see that AIDS is significantly better than ITLM for *animalia*, while the reverse is true for *beverages* and (maybe) *miscellaneous*. For *vegetablia* and the system as a whole it is evident that neither model is sufficient by itself, a result that agrees with

Table 21. P-Values of the J-Test Using Danish Data

Null Model	Predictions	Animalia	Beverages	Vegetablia	Miscellaneous	System
ITLM	AIDS	0.00	0.37	0.01	0.07	0.00
AIDS	ITLM	0.97	0.01	0.03	0.00	0.00
ITLM-*w*	AIDS-*w*	0.55	0.36	0.78	0.87	0.06
AIDS-*w*	ITLM-*w*	0.86	0.18	0.74	0.41	0.30
ITLM-*w*	AIDS-*q*	0.00	0.00	0.06	0.28	0.00
AIDS-*q*	ITLM-*w*	0.32	0.07	0.38	0.10	0.03
AIDS-*w*	AIDS-*q*	0.00	0.00	0.37	0.07	0.00
AIDS-*q*	AIDS-*w*	0.96	0.21	0.12	0.00	0.04

the findings of Lewbel (1989).

For the dynamic models it seems that the ITLM-*w* and AIDS-*w* models work equally well in the sense that neither gives any additional information to the other model. This is certainly true when looking at each equation own its own, although for the system as a whole the AIDS-*w* model gives significant extra information at the 10 percent level (but not at the 5 percent level). The AIDS-*q* model gives significant extra information to both the other models. The reverse is also true, but for fewer single equations and with less strength for the system as a whole.

To summarise, it seems that neither the translog nor the AIDS models are sufficient to explain the data by themselves. All models seem to give extra information to all other models. The only exception to this is the ITLM-*w*/AIDS-*w* model pair, for which neither gives any extra information to the other. Nonetheless there seems to be some evidence, which is not completely conclusive, that the AIDS-*q* model is the preferred dynamic model in this set of data.

Comparison of Elasticities

The estimated second stage elasticities for the different models, calculated at mean values, are to be found in Table A12 in the appendix to this chapter. Since within group elasticities at this level of aggregation are of little importance in themselves, it is rather the comparison between different models that is of interest.

The first impression is that there is very little pattern in the results. One obvious observation is that all the compensated own-price elasticities are negative, which agrees with the Slutsky conditions. In addition to this it can be seen that the switching models have large group expenditure elasticities for *beverages*, that the static CEDS and LES models have own-price elasticities that are large in absolute value for most goods, that AIDS-*q* and the switching models have small (in absolute value) own-price elasticities, and that the S/AIDS-*w* model has large standard errors for the price elasticities.

6.7.3 Conclusion

The flexible functional form models clearly outperform the benchmark and non-flexible models. This is the most important conclusion from this section, and is unequivocal. The choice between the different flexible models is more difficult, however.

The superior goodness-of-fit of the switching models is offset by their inferior misspecification. The switching model that best passes the diagnostic tests is in fact the static model, which has only slightly lower R^2. The dynamic non-switching models clearly outperform their static equivalents, but the choice between them is not easy. The ITLM-*w* and AIDS-*w* are difficult to distinguish using any criterion, while the AIDS-*q* model is slightly better than the others regarding goodness-of-fit and the non-nested tests, but slightly worse regarding the diagnostic tests. On balance the AIDS-*q* model is probably to be preferred, but this choice is not clear cut and the common model (AIDS-*w*) cannot be discarded.

It is obvious that some sort or time effect, due to habit forming and/or to changing preferences, is at work. It is quite difficult to distinguish between these two effects, however. None of the models we have estimated exhibit sufficient parameter constancy to be satisfactory, which shows that the true temporal effects have not been modelled correctly. This conjecture is also supported by the non-nested tests, and it is along these lines that further work ought to be applied.

APPENDIX

Table A1. Variations over Time in Swedish Expenditure Elasticities

(a) Within Group Expenditure Elasticities

	AIDS-SwD				AIDS-D			
	Max	Min	Range	Mean	Max	Min	Range	Mean
Food-at-home	0.59	0.45	0.14	0.52	0.56	0.41	0.16	0.49
Restaurants	2.74	2.04	0.69	2.39	2.44	2.13	0.31	2.27
Nondurables	1.58	1.39	0.19	1.48	1.66	1.55	0.12	1.61
Services	1.04	0.94	0.10	0.99	0.97	0.97	0.01	0.97
Animalia	0.93	0.85	0.07	0.89	1.09	1.08	0.01	1.09
Beverage	1.49	1.33	0.16	1.40	1.08	1.06	0.02	1.07
Vegetablia	1.03	1.00	0.03	1.01	0.93	0.92	0.01	0.93
Miscellaneous	0.64	0.46	0.17	0.55	0.80	0.75	0.05	0.78
Meat	1.64	1.43	0.21	1.52	1.26	1.23	0.03	1.24
Fish	0.47	0.38	0.09	0.43	0.40	0.25	0.15	0.34
Milk, Cheese, Eggs	0.69	0.25	0.44	0.49	0.92	0.91	0.02	0.92
Soft Drinks	0.67	0.13	0.54	0.33	0.71	0.52	0.19	0.61
Hot Drinks	0.61	0.21	0.39	0.45	0.54	0.20	0.35	0.38
Alcoholic Drinks	1.25	1.21	0.04	1.23	1.23	1.20	0.03	1.21
Bread and Cereals	0.88	0.63	0.24	0.74	1.42	1.37	0.05	1.39
Fruit & Vegetables	1.49	1.25	0.24	1.39	0.79	0.76	0.02	0.78
Potatoes	0.61	0.25	0.36	0.45	0.06	−0.52	0.58	−0.21
Fats and Oils	0.49	0.01	0.49	0.25	1.49	1.35	0.14	1.44
Sugar	0.45	−0.99	1.43	−0.04	0.07	−1.83	1.90	−0.58
Confectionery	1.66	1.32	0.34	1.47	1.00	1.00	0.00	1.00

(b) Total Expenditure Elasticities

	AIDS-SwD				AIDS-D			
	Max	Min	Range	Mean	Max	Min	Range	Mean
Meat	0.83	0.59	0.24	0.71	0.75	0.56	0.19	0.66
Fish	0.22	0.18	0.04	0.20	0.21	0.15	0.06	0.18
Milk, Cheese, Eggs	0.31	0.12	0.19	0.22	0.56	0.41	0.15	0.49
Soft Drinks	0.41	0.08	0.33	0.24	0.41	0.25	0.15	0.32
Hot Drinks	0.50	0.13	0.37	0.33	0.30	0.09	0.22	0.20
Alcoholic Drinks	1.10	0.75	0.35	0.90	0.75	0.53	0.21	0.63
Bread and Cereals	0.42	0.35	0.07	0.38	0.72	0.52	0.19	0.63
Fruit, Vegtables	0.90	0.56	0.34	0.73	0.40	0.29	0.11	0.35
Potatoes	0.33	0.11	0.22	0.24	0.03	−0.27	0.30	−0.10
Fats and Oils	0.15	0.00	0.15	0.07	0.60	0.49	0.12	0.54
Sugar	0.14	−0.28	0.42	−0.01	0.03	−0.60	0.63	−0.21
Confectionery	0.53	0.37	0.16	0.42	0.44	0.33	0.12	0.38

Table A2. Variations over Time in Swedish Own-Price Elasticities

(a) Within Group Uncompensated Own-Price Elasticities

	AIDS-SwD				AIDS-D			
	Max	Min	Range	Mean	Max	Min	Range	Mean
Food-at-home	−0.53	−0.64	0.11	−0.59	−0.53	−0.65	0.11	−0.59
Restaurants	−1.64	−1.84	0.19	−1.72	−1.62	−1.79	0.17	−1.70
Nondurables	−0.41	−0.53	0.12	−0.47	−0.57	−0.66	0.09	−0.61
Services	−0.56	−0.68	0.12	−0.61	−0.60	−0.67	0.08	−0.63
Animalia	−0.61	−0.67	0.06	−0.65	−0.72	−0.76	0.03	−0.74
Beverage	−0.56	−0.68	0.13	−0.62	−0.97	−0.98	0.01	−0.98
Vegetablia	−0.70	−0.72	0.03	−0.71	−0.66	−0.69	0.03	−0.68
Miscellaneous	−0.29	−0.44	0.15	−0.37	−0.55	−0.63	0.08	−0.59
Meat	−0.77	−0.84	0.07	−0.81	−0.57	−0.64	0.06	−0.61
Fish	−0.19	−0.33	0.14	−0.27	−0.18	−0.33	0.15	−0.27
Milk, Cheese, Eggs	0.13	−0.25	0.38	−0.07	−0.05	−0.20	0.15	−0.13
Soft Drinks	−0.42	−0.67	0.25	−0.53	−0.47	−0.67	0.20	−0.56
Hot Drinks	0.18	−0.30	0.48	−0.09	0.20	−0.27	0.48	−0.05
Alcoholic Drinks	−0.95	−0.97	0.02	−0.96	−0.95	−0.97	0.02	−0.96
Bread and Cereals	−0.48	−0.66	0.17	−0.56	−0.99	−1.00	0.01	−1.00
Fruit & Vegetables	−0.54	−0.62	0.08	−0.59	−0.70	−0.72	0.03	−0.71
Potatoes	0.25	−0.22	0.47	−0.01	0.42	−0.09	0.52	0.15
Fats and Oils	−0.17	−0.46	0.29	−0.32	−0.44	−0.64	0.21	−0.52
Sugar	1.79	−0.04	1.83	0.60	2.08	0.06	2.02	0.75
Confectionery	−0.82	−0.90	0.08	−0.88	−0.67	−0.75	0.09	−0.72

(b) Total Uncompensated Own-Price Elasticities

	AIDS-SwD				AIDS-D			
	Max	Min	Range	Mean	Max	Min	Range	Mean
Meat	−0.42	−0.46	0.04	−0.44	−0.32	−0.39	0.07	−0.35
Fish	−0.17	−0.29	0.13	−0.24	−0.17	−0.30	0.14	−0.25
Milk, Cheese, Eggs	0.17	−0.11	0.29	0.02	0.08	−0.04	0.11	0.01
Soft Drinks	−0.41	−0.62	0.21	−0.51	−0.47	−0.65	0.19	−0.56
Hot Drinks	0.20	−0.23	0.43	−0.04	0.21	−0.25	0.46	−0.04
Alcoholic Drinks	−0.44	−0.56	0.12	−0.50	−0.83	−0.88	0.04	−0.85
Bread and Cereals	−0.37	−0.48	0.11	−0.42	−0.70	−0.73	0.03	−0.72
Fruit, Vegtables	−0.32	−0.36	0.05	−0.35	−0.56	−0.58	0.02	−0.57
Potatoes	0.26	−0.20	0.46	0.00	0.41	−0.09	0.50	0.14
Fats and Oils	−0.17	−0.38	0.21	−0.28	−0.27	−0.44	0.17	−0.33
Sugar	1.76	0.00	1.76	0.61	2.05	0.06	1.98	0.73
Confectionery	−0.19	−0.33	0.14	−0.26	−0.41	−0.46	0.05	−0.44

In Tables A1 and A2, AIDS-D is the common model and AIDS-SwD is the gradually switching regressions nonlinear AIDS model

Table A3. Swedish Within Group Expenditure Elasticities at Mean Values (with Robust Standard Errors)

	AIDS			LAIDS						*AIDS - S.E.*			*LAIDS - S.E.*					
	SwD	D	D-α_0							*SwD*	*D*	*D-α_0*						
	ML*	ML*	ML*	OLS*	OLS	EIV-di*	EIV-tx*	IIV-di*	IIV-tx*	*ML**	*ML**	*ML**	*OLS**	*OLS*	*EIV-di**	*EIV-tx**	*IIV-di**	*IIV-tx**
FAH	0.51	0.47	0.66	0.51	0.53	0.41				*0.09*	*0.09*	*0.10*	*0.08*	*0.08*	*0.13*			
RC	2.27	2.30	2.34	2.27	2.24	1.99				*0.50*	*0.72*	*0.43*	*0.67*	*0.64*	*0.84*			
ND	1.44	1.58	1.21	1.57	1.60	1.18				*0.33*	*0.30*	*0.21*	*0.29*	*0.30*	*0.38*			
SV	1.00	0.97	1.01	0.95	0.95	1.26				*0.07*	*0.07*	*0.06*	*0.07*	*0.07*	*0.13*			
A	0.89	1.09	1.22	1.09	1.01	1.15	1.31	0.74	1.11	*0.09*	*0.14*	–	*0.14*	*0.14*	*0.19*	*0.17*	*0.34*	*0.15*
B	1.39	1.07	0.95	1.07	1.07	0.94	0.59	1.81	0.97	*0.22*	*0.29*	*0.12*	*0.29*	*0.29*	*0.31*	*0.30*	*0.69*	*0.21*
V	1.01	0.93	1.06	0.92	0.92	0.75	0.92	0.52	0.91	*0.19*	*0.16*	*0.11*	*0.16*	*0.16*	*0.14*	*0.15*	*0.35*	*0.13*
M	0.56	0.78	0.45	0.81	0.80	1.18	1.08	1.14	0.92	*0.20*	*0.27*	*0.23*	*0.27*	*0.28*	*0.35*	*0.31*	*0.55*	*0.28*
M	1.51	1.24	1.11	1.24	1.24	1.12	1.25	0.96	1.29	*0.07*	*0.13*	*0.07*	*0.13*	*0.13*	*0.18*	*0.16*	*0.27*	*0.15*
F	0.44	0.35	0.39	0.34	0.33	0.12	0.07	0.00	0.10	*0.24*	*0.21*	*0.86*	*0.21*	*0.21*	*0.37*	*0.28*	*0.54*	*0.26*
MCE	0.47	0.92	1.08	0.92	0.92	1.17	1.02	1.43	0.95	*0.10*	*0.15*	*0.07*	*0.15*	*0.16*	*0.21*	*0.20*	*0.34*	*0.17*
SD	0.32	0.62	0.73	0.56	0.57	0.36	0.55	0.47	0.56	*0.14*	*0.25*	*0.17*	*0.24*	*0.24*	*0.35*	*0.34*	*0.28*	*0.26*
HD	0.48	0.40	0.39	0.43	0.42	0.70	0.61	0.41	0.31	*0.14*	*0.14*	*0.09*	*0.14*	*0.14*	*0.21*	*0.23*	*0.18*	*0.19*
AD	1.23	1.21	1.21	1.21	1.21	1.17	1.17	1.23	1.25	*0.03*	*0.04*	*0.04*	*0.04*	*0.04*	*0.06*	*0.06*	*0.04*	*0.04*
BC	0.73	1.39	1.39	1.41	1.41	–17.04	0.99	0.30	1.90	*0.10*	*0.12*	*0.11*	*0.12*	*0.12*	*175.67*	*0.35*	*1.08*	*0.36*
FV	1.37	0.78	0.78	0.75	0.75	20.94	1.04	1.87	0.19	*0.08*	*0.11*	*0.09*	*0.11*	*0.11*	*240.75*	*0.33*	*1.11*	*0.34*
P	0.46	–0.22	–0.19	–0.20	–0.18	30.80	0.85	0.52	–0.04	*0.38*	*0.33*	*0.31*	*0.31*	*0.30*	*382.90*	*0.52*	*1.02*	*0.46*
FO	0.14	1.43	1.21	1.43	1.42	1.26	1.54	1.39	1.59	*0.18*	*0.18*	*0.13*	*0.18*	*0.18*	*0.58*	*0.27*	*0.25*	*0.17*
S	–0.01	–0.65	–0.60	–0.65	–0.49	–0.75	–0.70	–0.98	–0.83	*0.39*	*0.23*	*0.28*	*0.23*	*0.20*	*0.79*	*0.36*	*0.44*	*0.23*
CO	1.44	1.00	1.09	1.00	1.00	1.09	0.96	1.05	0.95	*0.09*	*0.08*	*0.06*	*0.08*	*0.08*	*0.26*	*0.13*	*0.12*	*0.08*

All columns *with* * have elasticities and standard errors calculated using estimated budget shares calculated at the mean of prices and expenditures. Columns *without* * use mean actual budget shares, assumed to be nonstochastic when evaluating standard errors. LAIDS elasticities use Chalfant's approximate formula.

The following abbreviations are used in Tables A3 - A6: Meats (M), Fish (F), Milk, Cheese and Eggs (MCE), Soft Drinks (SD), Hot Drinks (HD), Alcoholic Drinks (AD), Bread and Cereals (BC), Fruit and Vegetables (FV), Potatoes (P), Fats and Oils (FO), Sugar (S) and COnfectionery *etc* (CO). Also used are External and Internal Instrumental Variables (EIV and IIV), Disposable Income (di) and Total eXpenditure (tx). AIDS-D-α_0 represents nonlinear AIDS with free α_0 parameter.

Table A4.Swedish Within Group Own-Price Elasticities at Mean Values (with Robust Standard Errors)

	AIDS			LAIDS						*AIDS - S.E.*			*LAIDS - S.E.*					
	SwD	D	D-α_0							*SwD*	*D*	*D-α_0*						
	ML*	ML*	ML*	OLS*	OLS	EIV-di*	EIV-tx*	IIV-di*	IIV-tx*	*ML**	*ML**	*ML**	*OLS**	*OLS*	*EIV-di**	*EIV-tx**	*IIV-di**	*IIV-tx**
FAH	−0.58	−0.58	−0.65	−0.60	−0.61	−0.62				*0.08*	*0.08*	*0.16*	*0.08*	*0.07*	*0.07*			
RC	−1.65	−1.71	−2.05	−1.74	−1.73	−1.59				*0.35*	*0.48*	*0.48*	*0.49*	*0.47*	*0.58*			
ND	−0.51	−0.63	−0.54	−0.64	−0.62	−0.52				*0.20*	*0.11*	*0.17*	*0.11*	*0.12*	*0.16*			
SV	−0.61	−0.63	−0.64	−0.63	−0.62	−0.71				*0.04*	*0.04*	*0.03*	*0.04*	*0.04*	*0.06*			
A	−0.64	−0.74	−0.80	−0.74	−0.74	−0.76	−0.80	−0.64	−0.75	*0.03*	*0.07*	–	*0.07*	*0.07*	*0.08*	*0.08*	*0.11*	*0.07*
B	−0.63	−0.98	−0.96	−0.98	−0.98	−0.97	−0.93	−1.06	−0.97	*0.09*	*0.12*	*0.14*	*0.12*	*0.12*	*0.13*	*0.13*	*0.16*	*0.12*
V	−0.71	−0.68	−0.73	−0.67	−0.67	−0.59	−0.67	−0.48	−0.67	*0.14*	*0.12*	*0.07*	*0.12*	*0.12*	*0.10*	*0.11*	*0.19*	*0.11*
M	−0.37	−0.60	−0.58	−0.60	−0.60	−0.67	−0.65	−0.66	−0.62	*0.07*	*0.11*	*0.30*	*0.11*	*0.11*	*0.11*	*0.11*	*0.13*	*0.11*
M	−0.81	−0.61	−0.64	−0.60	−0.61	−0.61	−0.60	−0.61	−0.60	*0.05*	*0.09*	*0.06*	*0.09*	*0.08*	*0.09*	*0.08*	*0.10*	*0.09*
F	−0.29	−0.28	−0.22	−0.28	−0.26	−0.14	−0.11	−0.07	−0.13	*0.14*	*0.15*	*0.98*	*0.15*	*0.15*	*0.21*	*0.16*	*0.31*	*0.16*
MCE	−0.03	−0.14	−0.20	−0.15	−0.14	−0.28	−0.19	−0.41	−0.16	*0.06*	*0.09*	*0.23*	*0.10*	*0.10*	*0.14*	*0.12*	*0.24*	*0.12*
SD	−0.52	−0.57	−0.60	−0.54	−0.54	−0.40	−0.53	−0.48	−0.54	*0.10*	*0.18*	*0.17*	*0.18*	*0.18*	*0.23*	*0.23*	*0.18*	*0.17*
HD	−0.13	−0.08	0.01	−0.08	−0.06	−0.13	−0.11	−0.07	−0.06	*0.08*	*0.07*	*0.04*	*0.08*	*0.08*	*0.09*	*0.09*	*0.08*	*0.08*
AD	−0.96	−0.96	−0.90	−0.96	−0.96	−0.95	−0.95	−0.97	−0.97	*0.03*	*0.03*	*0.02*	*0.03*	*0.03*	*0.03*	*0.03*	*0.03*	*0.03*
BC	−0.55	−1.00	−1.00	−1.01	−1.01	13.59	−0.70	−0.19	−1.37	*0.07*	*0.11*	*0.10*	*0.11*	*0.11*	*150.35*	*0.25*	*0.79*	*0.27*
FV	−0.60	−0.71	−0.72	−0.70	−0.70	−4.72	−0.77	−0.97	−0.56	*0.03*	*0.06*	*0.06*	*0.06*	*0.06*	*37.85*	*0.09*	*0.30*	*0.10*
P	−0.04	0.15	0.15	0.13	−0.11	−0.10	0.11	0.12	0.13	*0.10*	*0.08*	*0.08*	*0.07*	*0.07*	*1.57*	*0.11*	*0.10*	*0.08*
FO	−0.24	−0.52	−0.47	−0.52	−0.52	−0.49	−0.53	−0.51	−0.54	*0.08*	*0.09*	*0.09*	*0.09*	*0.09*	*0.09*	*0.10*	*0.08*	*0.10*
S	0.58	0.83	0.82	0.81	0.64	0.85	0.83	0.94	0.88	*0.22*	*0.17*	*0.25*	*0.17*	*0.15*	*0.36*	*0.20*	*0.23*	*0.17*
CO	−0.89	−0.73	−0.79	−0.73	−0.73	−0.78	−0.70	−0.76	−0.70	*0.06*	*0.09*	*0.08*	*0.09*	*0.09*	*0.15*	*0.11*	*0.09*	*0.09*

All columns *with* * have elasticities and standard errors calculated using estimated budget shares calculated at the mean of prices and expenditures. Columns *without* * use mean actual budget shares, assumed to be nonstochastic when evaluating standard errors. LAIDS elasticities use Chalfant's approximate formula. For abbreviations, see Table A3.

Table A5. Swedish Total Expenditure Elasticities at Mean Values

	AIDS			DYNAMIC LAIDS										
	SwD	D	D-α_0											
	ML*	ML*	ML*	OLS*	OLS	SUR5	SUR11	SUR20	ML5	ML11	EIV-di*	EIV-tx*	IIV-di*	IIV-tx*
Meat	0.68	0.64	0.89	0.70	0.71	0.70	0.70	0.69	0.66	0.72	0.52	0.84	0.29	0.74
Fish	0.20	0.18	0.31	0.19	0.19	0.15	0.12	0.10	0.06	0.14	0.06	0.05	0.00	0.06
Milk, Cheese, Eggs	0.21	0.47	0.86	0.52	0.53	0.51	0.47	0.37	0.54	0.57	0.55	0.68	0.43	0.54
Soft Drinks	0.23	0.31	0.46	0.31	0.32	0.30	0.35	0.29	–0.03	0.17	0.14	0.16	0.34	0.28
Hot Drinks	0.34	0.21	0.24	0.24	0.24	0.17	0.19	0.30	–0.17	0.08	0.26	0.18	0.30	0.15
Alcoholic Drinks	0.87	0.62	0.75	0.66	0.68	0.58	0.65	0.78	0.01	0.35	0.45	0.35	0.90	0.62
Bread and Cereals	0.37	0.61	0.96	0.67	0.69	0.63	0.69	0.61	0.42	0.67	-5.19	0.47	0.06	0.89
Fruit and Vegetables	0.70	0.34	0.54	0.36	0.37	0.24	0.28	0.29	0.10	0.11	6.38	0.49	0.39	0.09
Potatoes	0.24	–0.10	–0.13	–0.10	–0.09	–0.04	–0.03	–0.07	–0.04	–0.11	9.39	0.40	0.11	–0.02
Fats and Oils	0.04	0.53	0.36	0.59	0.60	0.60	0.62	0.60	–1.40	0.48	0.60	0.85	0.64	0.75
Sugar	0.00	–0.24	–0.18	–0.27	–0.21	–0.22	–0.27	–0.33	0.27	–0.32	–0.36	–0.39	–0.45	–0.39
Confectionery etc	0.41	0.37	0.32	0.41	0.43	0.40	0.45	0.45	–0.09	0.32	0.52	0.53	0.48	0.45

Standard Errors

	DYNAMIC LAIDS											
	Non-robust						Robust					
	OLS	SUR5	SUR11	SUR20	ML5	ML11	OLS	SUR5	SUR11	SUR20	ML5	ML11
Meat	0.19	0.18	0.18	0.15	0.13	0.10	0.18	0.17	0.17	0.15	0.11	0.09
Fish	0.16	0.14	0.13	0.10	0.11	0.08	0.13	0.12	0.11	0.09	0.09	0.05
Milk, Cheese, Eggs	0.16	0.16	0.14	0.10	0.12	0.08	0.12	0.12	0.10	0.09	0.10	0.07
Soft Drinks	0.17	0.16	0.17	0.14	0.14	0.09	0.21	0.18	0.19	0.13	0.16	0.10
Hot Drinks	0.13	0.10	0.10	0.11	0.10	0.05	0.11	0.09	0.08	0.09	0.09	0.04
Alcoholic Drinks	0.24	0.22	0.23	0.21	0.20	0.15	0.21	0.20	0.21	0.20	0.19	0.14
Bread and Cereals	0.21	0.18	0.19	0.15	0.13	0.15	0.16	0.16	0.16	0.12	0.14	0.12
Fruit, Vegetables	0.14	0.10	0.11	0.10	0.05	0.05	0.10	0.08	0.08	0.07	0.05	0.04
Potatoes	0.15	0.12	0.13	0.10	0.07	0.05	0.15	0.12	0.13	0.08	0.07	0.04
Fats and Oils	0.25	0.24	0.23	0.20	0.29	0.16	0.22	0.19	0.18	0.18	0.32	0.13
Sugar	0.14	0.13	0.14	0.14	0.12	0.11	0.11	0.10	0.10	0.10	0.10	0.08
Confectionery etc	0.17	0.16	0.16	0.15	0.05	0.10	0.16	0.14	0.14	0.12	0.06	0.08

Table A6. Swedish Total Own-Price Elasticities at Mean Values

	AIDS			DYNAMIC LAIDS										
	SwD ML*	D ML*	D-α_0 ML*	OLS*	OLS	SUR5	SUR11	SUR20	ML5	ML11	EIV-di*	EIV-tx*	IIV-di*	IIV-tx*
Meat	−0.43	−0.35	−0.45	−0.35	−0.35	−0.35	−0.29	−0.21	−0.73	−0.89	−0.39	−0.37	−0.40	−0.34
Fish	−0.26	−0.26	−0.20	−0.26	−0.25	−0.21	−0.22	−0.17	−0.24	−0.44	−0.13	−0.11	−0.07	−0.12
Milk, Cheese, Eggs	0.04	0.00	−0.06	−0.01	0.00	−0.03	0.06	0.13	−0.30	−0.33	−0.10	−0.05	−0.16	−0.01
Soft Drinks	−0.51	−0.56	−0.59	−0.53	−0.54	−0.59	−0.60	−0.53	−0.38	−0.44	−0.40	−0.52	−0.47	−0.53
Hot Drinks	−0.08	−0.07	0.02	−0.07	−0.05	−0.07	−0.12	−0.13	−0.02	−0.09	−0.11	−0.09	−0.06	−0.05
Alcoholic Drinks	−0.50	−0.85	−0.80	−0.85	−0.86	−0.83	−0.88	−0.85	−0.06	−0.68	−0.85	−0.85	−0.87	−0.86
Bread and Cereals	−0.42	−0.71	−0.76	−0.73	−0.73	−0.75	−0.79	−0.74	−0.73	−0.92	8.63	−0.50	−0.11	−0.98
Fruit and Vegetables	−0.34	−0.57	−0.59	−0.56	−0.56	−0.53	−0.55	−0.54	−0.46	−0.53	-1.22	−0.58	−0.50	−0.53
Potatoes	−0.03	0.14	0.15	0.12	0.11	0.12	0.12	0.15	0.11	0.15	0.64	0.14	0.14	0.13
Fats and Oils	−0.22	−0.34	−0.32	−0.34	−0.34	−0.38	−0.40	−0.35	0.15	−0.55	−0.35	−0.36	−0.36	−0.35
Sugar	0.58	0.81	0.80	0.78	0.62	0.57	0.60	0.61	0.62	0.39	0.83	0.81	0.92	0.86
Confectionery etc	−0.24	−0.43	−0.47	−0.45	−0.44	−0.45	−0.49	−0.49	0.22	−0.54	−0.50	−0.45	−0.48	−0.43

Standard Errors

	DYNAMIC LAIDS											
	Non-robust						Robust					
	OLS	SUR5	SUR11	SUR20	ML5	ML11	OLS	SUR5	SUR11	SUR20	ML5	ML11
Meat	0.12	0.12	0.11	0.10	0.10	0.06	0.09	0.09	0.08	0.07	0.08	0.07
Fish	0.17	0.16	0.15	0.13	0.12	0.05	0.14	0.14	0.13	0.12	0.09	0.04
Milk, Cheese, Eggs	0.14	0.14	0.14	0.12	0.13	0.08	0.09	0.09	0.08	0.07	0.09	0.07
Soft Drinks	0.20	0.19	0.18	0.16	0.16	0.15	0.17	0.16	0.16	0.13	0.16	0.13
Hot Drinks	0.06	0.05	0.05	0.04	0.05	0.03	0.08	0.07	0.05	0.04	0.06	0.03
Alcoholic Drinks	0.11	0.11	0.11	0.07	0.11	0.09	0.10	0.10	0.10	0.09	0.11	0.08
Bread and Cereals	0.14	0.14	0.13	0.12	0.11	0.08	0.12	0.12	0.10	0.08	0.13	0.07
Fruit, Vegetables	0.06	0.06	0.06	0.06	0.05	0.04	0.05	0.05	0.05	0.05	0.06	0.03
Potatoes	0.06	0.06	0.06	0.05	0.06	0.02	0.07	0.07	0.07	0.03	0.07	0.02
Fats and Oils	0.13	0.13	0.12	0.09	0.15	0.06	0.12	0.12	0.12	0.08	0.21	0.05
Sugar	0.17	0.17	0.15	0.12	0.17	0.11	0.15	0.16	0.14	0.10	0.14	0.12
Confectionery etc	0.10	0.10	0.10	0.08	0.07	0.07	0.12	0.12	0.11	0.07	0.07	0.06

Table A7. AIDS Expenditure Elasticities for Finland (with Robust Standard Errors)

	Mean				1990				*Within Group – S.E.*			
	Within Group		Total		Within Group		Total		*Mean*		*1990*	
	SwD	D	SwD	D	SwD	D	SwD	D	*SwD*	*D*	*SwD*	*D*
Food-at-home	1.15	1.09			1.17	1.12			*0.10*	*0.11*	*0.12*	*0.14*
Restaurants	1.91	1.98			1.72	1.78			*0.20*	*0.22*	*0.18*	*0.19*
Nondurables	1.26	1.02			1.23	1.02			*0.15*	*0.34*	*0.18*	*0.36*
Services	0.50	0.70			0.63	0.74			*0.09*	*0.21*	*0.07*	*0.17*
Animalia	0.69	0.68			0.71	0.68			*0.10*	*0.10*	*0.10*	*0.10*
Beverages	1.47	1.56			1.33	1.50			*0.14*	*0.19*	*0.13*	*0.18*
Vegetablia	0.96	0.95			1.00	0.95			*0.15*	*0.16*	*0.14*	*0.15*
Miscellaneous	1.04	1.00			1.15	1.00			*0.21*	*0.21*	*0.26*	*0.26*
Meat	1.49	1.53	1.20	1.14	1.47	1.50	1.22	1.13	*0.06*	*0.07*	*0.06*	*0.06*
Fish	1.04	0.68	0.83	0.51	1.02	0.66	0.85	0.50	*0.21*	*0.26*	*0.22*	*0.28*
Milk, Cheese,& Eggs	0.36	0.36	0.29	0.27	0.31	0.31	0.26	0.24	*0.09*	*0.09*	*0.10*	*0.10*
Soft Drinks	0.60	1.00	1.02	1.70	0.74	1.00	1.15	1.67	*0.20*	*0.11*	*0.13*	*0.09*
Hot Drinks	0.37	0.31	0.63	0.53	–0.43	–0.55	–0.67	–0.93	*0.23*	*0.14*	*0.47*	*0.31*
Alcoholic Drinks	1.24	1.22	2.10	2.08	1.21	1.19	1.88	1.99	*0.05*	*0.03*	*0.04*	*0.03*
Bread and Cereals	0.28	0.41	0.31	0.43	0.33	0.41	0.38	0.44	*0.14*	*0.16*	*0.13*	*0.16*
Fruit, & Vegetables	1.85	1.67	2.04	1.73	1.75	1.65	2.03	1.75	*0.18*	*0.32*	*0.19*	*0.33*
Potatoes	1.79	1.95	1.98	2.02	2.13	2.07	2.48	2.20	*0.77*	*0.84*	*0.84*	*0.97*
Fats and Oils	0.52	0.55	0.62	0.60	0.12	0.38	0.16	0.42	*0.17*	*0.23*	*0.20*	*0.30*
Sugar	2.41	1.11	2.88	1.21	2.64	1.17	3.55	1.31	*0.19*	*0.80*	*0.42*	*1.25*
Confectionery *etc*	0.77	1.39	0.92	1.52	1.19	1.28	1.60	1.43	*0.25*	*0.40*	*0.12*	*0.29*

Table A8. AIDS Uncompensated Own-Price Elasticities for Finland (*with Robust Standard Errors*)

	Mean				1990				*Within Group – S.E.*			
	Within Group		Total		Within Group		Total		*Mean*		*1990*	
	SwD	D	SwD	D	SwD	D	SwD	D	*SwD*	*D*	*SwD*	*D*
Food-at-home	–0.32	–0.43			–0.12	–0.28			*0.06*	*0.07*	*0.08*	*0.08*
Restaurants	–0.99	–1.02			–1.00	–1.03			*0.14*	*0.14*	*0.11*	*0.11*
Nondurables	–0.33	–0.48			–0.22	–0.45			*0.10*	*0.16*	*0.12*	*0.18*
Services	–0.02	–0.52			–0.20	–0.57			*0.13*	*0.27*	*0.10*	*0.24*
Animalia	–0.44	–0.44			–0.45	–0.43			*0.11*	*0.11*	*0.10*	*0.11*
Beverages	–0.74	–0.74			–0.75	–0.77			*0.09*	*0.10*	*0.09*	*0.09*
Vegetablia	–0.36	–0.36			–0.40	–0.38			*0.14*	*0.15*	*0.13*	*0.14*
Miscellaneous	–0.24	–0.13			–0.10	0.09			*0.15*	*0.17*	*0.20*	*0.22*
Meat	–0.73	–0.81	–0.15	–0.23	–0.75	–0.82	–0.11	–0.19	*0.13*	*0.12*	*0.12*	*0.11*
Fish	–0.41	–0.35	–0.37	–0.32	–0.38	–0.31	–0.33	–0.28	*0.10*	*0.13*	*0.11*	*0.14*
Milk, Cheese,& Eggs	0.00	0.00	0.10	0.10	0.07	0.08	0.17	0.17	*0.23*	*0.22*	*0.25*	*0.24*
Soft Drinks	–1.00	–1.25	–0.98	–1.20	–1.00	–1.20	–0.96	–1.15	*0.12*	*0.12*	*0.10*	*0.10*
Hot Drinks	–0.25	–0.24	–0.22	–0.22	0.60	0.60	0.58	0.58	*0.10*	*0.09*	*0.22*	*0.22*
Alcoholic Drinks	–1.03	–1.03	–0.55	–0.60	–1.04	–1.03	–0.50	–0.55	*0.04*	*0.04*	*0.03*	*0.03*
Bread and Cereals	–0.24	–0.29	–0.13	–0.12	–0.31	–0.30	–0.17	–0.12	*0.14*	*0.17*	*0.12*	*0.16*
Fruit, & Vegetables	–0.81	–0.76	–0.22	–0.29	–0.84	–0.77	–0.29	–0.30	*0.10*	*0.14*	*0.10*	*0.14*
Potatoes	–0.55	–0.67	–0.45	–0.53	–0.50	–0.61	–0.37	–0.48	*0.13*	*0.16*	*0.12*	*0.17*
Fats and Oils	–0.29	–0.56	–0.09	–0.34	0.11	–0.47	0.15	–0.33	*0.12*	*0.14*	*0.19*	*0.16*
Sugar	–1.02	–0.45	–0.57	–0.29	–1.48	–0.13	–1.21	0.00	*0.12*	*0.33*	*0.40*	*0.45*
Confectionery *etc*	–0.63	–0.96	–0.40	–0.37	–0.91	–1.01	–0.19	–0.10	*0.06*	*0.12*	*0.08*	*0.12*

Table A9. AIDS Expenditure Elasticities for Denmark (with Robust Standard Errors)

	Mean				1990				*Within Group – S.E.*			
	Within Group		Total		Within Group		Total		*Mean*		*1990*	
	SwD	D	SwD	D	SwD	D	SwD	D	*SwD*	*D*	*SwD*	*D*
Food-at-home	0.77	0.69			0.73	0.57			*0.13*	*0.12*	*0.18*	*0.15*
Restaurants	1.35	0.75			1.55	0.77			*0.16*	*0.24*	*0.18*	*0.22*
Nondurables	1.21	1.71			0.98	1.85			*0.12*	*0.19*	*0.17*	*0.27*
Services	1.01	0.89			1.05	0.92			*0.07*	*0.08*	*0.06*	*0.06*
Animalia	1.07	1.14			1.15	1.13			*0.10*	*0.11*	*0.09*	*0.11*
Beverages	1.28	1.09			1.02	1.09			*0.08*	*0.17*	*0.10*	*0.17*
Vegetablia	0.86	0.93			0.95	0.93			*0.08*	*0.08*	*0.07*	*0.08*
Miscellaneous	0.59	0.65			0.68	0.64			*0.09*	*0.10*	*0.09*	*0.10*
Meat	1.17	1.11	0.96	0.87	1.27	1.11	1.07	0.72	*0.05*	*0.08*	*0.05*	*0.07*
Fish	1.01	1.11	0.83	0.87	0.80	1.16	0.68	0.75	*0.20*	*0.20*	*0.37*	*0.27*
Milk, Cheese,& Eggs	0.65	0.75	0.53	0.59	0.52	0.76	0.44	0.49	*0.10*	*0.14*	*0.12*	*0.14*
Soft Drinks	0.92	0.93	0.91	0.69	0.97	0.95	0.73	0.59	*0.11*	*0.12*	*0.08*	*0.08*
Hot Drinks	0.60	0.62	0.59	0.46	0.07	0.17	0.05	0.11	*0.08*	*0.12*	*0.18*	*0.25*
Alcoholic Drinks	1.14	1.16	1.12	0.87	1.16	1.13	0.86	0.71	*0.02*	*0.04*	*0.02*	*0.03*
Bread and Cereals	0.41	0.50	0.27	0.32	0.20	0.42	0.14	0.22	*0.06*	*0.11*	*0.08*	*0.13*
Fruit, & Vegetables	1.84	1.73	1.21	1.10	1.78	1.62	1.24	0.86	*0.12*	*0.17*	*0.10*	*0.14*
Potatoes	0.52	0.51	0.34	0.33	0.59	0.54	0.42	0.28	*0.41*	*0.44*	*0.38*	*0.42*
Fats and Oils	0.79	0.77	0.36	0.34	1.08	0.64	0.53	0.23	*0.11*	*0.15*	*0.16*	*0.23*
Sugar	0.88	0.78	0.40	0.35	0.06	0.50	0.03	0.18	*0.31*	*0.34*	*0.90*	*0.86*
Confectionery *etc*	1.15	1.15	0.52	0.51	1.04	1.11	0.52	0.41	*0.08*	*0.10*	*0.07*	*0.08*

Table A10. AIDS Uncompensated Own-Price Elasticities for Denmark (with Robust Standard Errors)

	Mean				1990				*Within Group – S.E.*			
	Within Group		Total		Within Group		Total		*Mean*		*1990*	
	SwD	D	SwD	D	SwD	D	SwD	D	*SwD*	*D*	*SwD*	*D*
Food-at-home	–0.41	–0.39			–0.23	–0.19			*0.09*	*0.09*	*0.11*	*0.11*
Restaurants	–0.78	–0.50			–0.80	–0.54			*0.16*	*0.37*	*0.14*	*0.33*
Nondurables	–0.59	–0.94			–0.27	–0.87			*0.06*	*0.05*	*0.08*	*0.09*
Services	–0.69	–0.71			–0.80	–0.79			*0.08*	*0.09*	*0.07*	*0.07*
Animalia	–0.72	–0.82			–0.76	–0.83			*0.05*	*0.08*	*0.05*	*0.08*
Beverages	–0.65	–0.87			–0.56	–0.86			*0.08*	*0.15*	*0.10*	*0.15*
Vegetablia	–0.48	–0.50			–0.52	–0.51			*0.07*	*0.09*	*0.07*	*0.09*
Miscellaneous	–0.87	–0.82			–0.89	–0.82			*0.09*	*0.11*	*0.09*	*0.11*
Meat	–0.95	–0.80	–0.59	–0.51	–1.00	–0.81	–0.53	–0.44	*0.08*	*0.09*	*0.07*	*0.09*
Fish	–0.78	–0.94	–0.74	–0.90	–0.68	–0.91	–0.66	–0.88	*0.10*	*0.13*	*0.16*	*0.19*
Milk, Cheese,& Eggs	–0.60	–0.47	–0.48	–0.37	–0.52	–0.47	–0.43	–0.35	*0.10*	*0.15*	*0.12*	*0.16*
Soft Drinks	–0.97	–1.09	–0.92	–1.07	–0.98	–1.06	–0.90	–1.02	*0.17*	*0.15*	*0.12*	*0.11*
Hot Drinks	–0.32	–0.29	–0.21	–0.23	0.36	0.45	0.36	0.46	*0.05*	*0.10*	*0.11*	*0.20*
Alcoholic Drinks	–0.99	–0.74	–0.60	–0.53	–1.02	–0.80	–0.49	–0.49	*0.05*	*0.08*	*0.05*	*0.06*
Bread and Cereals	–0.46	–0.52	–0.33	–0.36	–0.29	–0.48	–0.24	–0.35	*0.06*	*0.09*	*0.07*	*0.10*
Fruit, & Vegetables	–0.95	–0.94	–0.49	–0.50	–0.97	–0.98	–0.43	–0.48	*0.04*	*0.05*	*0.04*	*0.04*
Potatoes	–0.56	–0.57	–0.53	–0.54	–0.59	–0.59	–0.55	–0.55	*0.06*	*0.06*	*0.06*	*0.06*
Fats and Oils	–0.58	–0.70	–0.55	–0.64	–0.49	–0.56	–0.45	–0.53	*0.08*	*0.08*	*0.10*	*0.12*
Sugar	–0.76	–0.70	–0.73	–0.67	–0.40	–0.34	–0.40	–0.33	*0.10*	*0.11*	*0.33*	*0.34*
Confectionery *etc*	–0.83	–1.01	–0.71	–0.84	–0.86	–1.03	–0.71	–0.81	*0.11*	*0.09*	*0.12*	*0.07*

Table A11. P-Values of Further Single Equation Tests Using Danish Data

	(a) Durbin-Watson (Statistic)				(b) Ljung-Box			
Models	Anim	Bev	Veg	Misc	Anim	Bev	Veg	Misc
Trend	1.55	0.32	0.72	0.30	0.44	**0.00**	**0.00**	**0.00**
AR1	1.77	2.00	2.21	1.83	0.73	0.69	0.16	0.78
CEDS	1.45	0.58	1.17	0.42	0.51	**0.00**	**0.01**	**0.00**
LES	1.60	0.70	0.86	0.38	0.38	**0.02**	**0.00**	**0.00**
ITLM	1.66	1.55	2.23	1.26	0.16	0.86	0.88	**0.01**
DTLM	1.71	1.07	1.40	0.82	0.22	**0.04**	0.41	**0.00**
AIDS	1.60	1.17	1.89	0.77	0.11	0.92	0.81	**0.00**
S/AIDS	1.97	1.22	2.30	1.74	0.67	0.60	0.78	0.64
CEDS-*w*	1.61	1.21	1.96	0.77	0.11	0.94	0.83	**0.00**
LES-*q*	1.69	0.68	2.04	1.19	0.62	**0.00**	0.72	**0.01**
ITLM-*w*	1.64	1.85	2.13	1.54	0.21	0.75	0.73	0.59
AIDS-*w*	1.70	1.72	2.27	1.61	0.16	0.90	0.94	0.89
AIDS-*q*	1.83	1.62	1.92	1.57	0.42	0.32	0.39	**0.03**
S/AIDS-*w*	1.87	1.39	2.50	2.10	0.76	0.71	0.82	0.95
S/AIDS-*q*	2.46	2.19	2.25	2.08	0.63	0.33	0.75	**0.04**

	(c) Breusch-Godfrey; Second Order				(d) Breusch-Pagan; Second Order			
Models	Anim	Bev	Veg	Misc	Anim	Bev	Veg	Misc
Trend	**0.09**	**0.00**	**0.00**	**0.00**				
AR1	0.28	0.55	0.17	0.84				
CEDS	**0.10**	**0.00**	**0.04**	**0.00**	0.49	0.47	0.33	**0.09**
LES	**0.07**	**0.00**	**0.00**	**0.00**	0.15	0.53	**0.01**	**0.02**
ITLM	**0.06**	0.47	0.77	**0.00**	**0.03**	0.28	0.60	0.98
DTLM	**0.04**	**0.01**	**0.09**	**0.00**	**0.06**	0.35	0.11	0.75
AIDS	0.23	**0.07**	0.86	**0.00**	0.67	0.48	0.58	0.51
S/AIDS	0.18	**0.02**	0.13	0.51	0.92	0.87	0.59	0.71
CEDS-*w*	0.22	**0.09**	0.91	**0.00**	0.68	0.68	0.82	0.40
LES-*q*	0.59	**0.00**	0.34	**0.05**	0.75	0.60	**0.03**	0.90
ITLM-*w*	0.42	0.77	0.43	0.18	0.68	0.50	0.43	0.71
AIDS-*w*	0.53	0.67	0.43	0.62	0.85	0.83	0.85	0.65
AIDS-*q*	0.67	0.43	0.65	0.40	0.51	0.77	0.30	0.54
S/AIDS-*w*	0.42	0.12	**0.06**	0.52	0.90	0.97	0.62	0.41
S/AIDS-*q*	0.11	0.28	0.11	0.84	0.58	0.35	0.45	0.99

The abbreviations for the models are those given in section 6.7. The Breusch-Godfrey, Breusch-Pagan and Ljung-Box tests are all large sample tests, with *P*-values evaluated using the c^2 distribution. Figures in bold face type indicating significance at the 10% level. The Durbin-Watson figures are the usual statistics.

Table A12. Danish Within Group Elasticities Calculated at Mean Values

	Anim	Bev	Veg	Misc	*Anim*	*Bev*	*Veg*	*Misc*
	Group Expenditure Elasticities				*Robust Standard Errors*			
CEDS	0.98	1.26	0.51	0.72	*0.08*	*0.09*	*0.07*	*0.05*
LES	1.19	1.21	0.59	0.83	*0.05*	*0.05*	*0.06*	*0.04*
ITLM	1.01	1.14	0.84	0.99	*0.05*	*0.08*	*0.07*	*0.02*
DTLM	1.17	1.15	0.81	0.63	*0.13*	*0.07*	*0.17*	*0.21*
AIDS	1.23	0.84	0.76	1.06	*0.09*	*0.18*	*0.09*	*0.16*
S/AIDS	0.95	1.45	0.85	0.60	*0.12*	*0.13*	*0.13*	*0.15*
CEDS-w	1.23	0.86	0.78	1.08	*0.10*	*0.19*	*0.10*	*0.17*
LES-q	0.92	0.88	1.18	1.12	*0.04*	*0.15*	*0.19*	*0.20*
ITLM-w	1.01	1.14	0.84	0.99	*0.14*	*0.08*	*0.09*	*0.05*
AIDS-w	1.22	0.95	0.76	0.93	*0.08*	*0.18*	*0.11*	*0.10*
AIDS-q	1.08	1.29	0.80	0.62	*0.15*	*0.10*	*0.13*	*0.23*
S/AIDS-w	0.98	1.41	0.85	0.58	*0.12*	*0.14*	*0.12*	*0.15*
S/AIDS-q	0.87	1.55	0.92	0.51	*0.11*	*0.08*	*0.15*	*0.14*
	Own-price Elasticities				*Robust Standard Errors*			
CEDS	−0.96	−1.28	−0.53	−0.50	*0.09*	*0.12*	*0.08*	*0.06*
LES	−1.18	−0.93	−0.69	−0.92	*0.06*	*0.04*	*0.07*	*0.02*
ITLM	−0.78	−0.90	−0.64	−0.75	*0.08*	*0.07*	*0.10*	*0.11*
DTLM	−0.84	−0.52	−1.11	−0.45	*0.05*	*0.08*	*0.12*	*0.11*
AIDS	−0.93	−0.56	−0.55	−0.48	*0.08*	*0.12*	*0.10*	*0.10*
S/AIDS	−0.57	−0.69	−0.58	−0.35	*0.11*	*0.10*	*0.14*	*0.18*
CEDS-w	−0.94	−0.57	−0.55	−0.48	*0.09*	*0.13*	*0.10*	*0.12*
LES-q	−0.51	−0.41	−0.52	−0.43	*0.08*	*0.05*	*0.08*	*0.08*
ITLM-w	−0.78	−0.90	−0.64	−0.75	*0.15*	*0.07*	*0.13*	*0.13*
AIDS-w	−0.89	−0.80	−0.55	−0.89	*0.09*	*0.13*	*0.11*	*0.12*
AIDS-q	−0.63	−0.64	−0.49	−0.65	*0.06*	*0.13*	*0.11*	*0.21*
S/AIDS-w	−0.64	−0.69	−0.73	−0.65	*0.15*	*0.12*	*0.23*	*0.32*
S/AIDS-q	−0.49	−0.65	−0.58	−0.55	*0.08*	*0.05*	*0.14*	*0.20*
	Compensated Own-price Elasticities				*Robust Standard Errors*			
CEDS	−0.60	−0.96	−0.42	−0.59				
LES	−0.74	−1.23	−0.55	−0.80	*0.05*	*0.04*	*0.06*	*0.02*
ITLM	−0.41	−0.61	−0.44	−0.61	*0.08*	*0.08*	*0.09*	*0.11*
DTLM	−0.42	−0.24	−0.90	−0.36	*0.08*	*0.07*	*0.16*	*0.09*
AIDS	−0.48	−0.35	−0.37	−0.32	*0.06*	*0.11*	*0.09*	*0.12*
S/AIDS	−0.22	−0.33	−0.37	−0.26	*0.10*	*0.08*	*0.13*	*0.18*
CEDS-w	−0.48	−0.35	−0.37	−0.33				
LES-q	−0.17	−0.19	−0.24	−0.27	*0.03*	*0.03*	*0.05*	*0.06*
ITLM-w	−0.41	−0.61	−0.44	−0.61	*0.13*	*0.09*	*0.09*	*0.12*
AIDS-w	−0.45	−0.56	−0.37	−0.75	*0.07*	*0.10*	*0.09*	*0.13*
AIDS-q	−0.23	−0.31	−0.30	−0.56	*0.04*	*0.10*	*0.10*	*0.24*
S/AIDS-w	−0.28	−0.34	−0.53	−0.56	*0.15*	*0.11*	*0.22*	*0.32*
S/AIDS-q	−0.18	−0.27	−0.37	−0.48	*0.06*	*0.05*	*0.12*	*0.20*

The abbreviations for the models are those given in section 6.7.

7

THE ALMOST IDEAL DEMAND SYSTEM IN ERROR CORRECTION FORM

by Bengt Assarsson

7.1 INTRODUCTION

In this chapter we develop a dynamic AIDS model based on the error correction form. In their original paper, Deaton and Muellbauer (1980b) noted the apparent dynamic deficiency in the static demand system, as revealed by positively autocorrelated residuals in the estimated system. Later developments of dynamic systems encountered difficulties in introducing dynamics without violating some of the theoretical restrictions of a demand system, in particular the adding up condition.[1] Anderson and Blundell (1983) used the error correction form to analyse the long-run properties of the AIDS model. Their conclusion was that restrictive dynamic forms were rejected in favour of the more general error correction model. In this chapter we follow a similar strategy. We use the error correction model as a maintained hypothesis and test restrictions in the dynamic form. In addition, theoretical restrictions are tested. The tests are done for the Nordic countries, and differences are revealed among these countries. Contrary to Anderson and Blundell (1983), we find significant restrictions on the dynamic form, which considerably reduces the number of parameters to be estimated.

The chapter is organised as follows. In the next section we develop dynamic forms based on the error correction model. The third section presents results from unit root tests. The fourth section derives the hypothesis to be tested, theoretical restrictions in the short and long-run and dynamic restrictions on the error correction model. The fifth section presents the empirical results for the demand for non-durables and services in the Nordic countries. The last section summarises and concludes.

7.2 DYNAMIC AIDS IN ERROR CORRECTION FORM

In error correction form, the static model represents the long-run solution of the dynamic system. We reproduce the static AIDS given in Chapter 4 as (4.2), adding

[1] See the discussion in Chapters 5 and 11.

a stochastic disturbance term μ_{it}, which yields

$$w_{it} = \alpha_i + \sum_j \gamma_{ij} \ln p_{jt} + \beta_i (\ln x_t - \ln P_t) + \mu_{it} \tag{1a}$$

$$\ln P_t = \alpha_0 + \sum_k \alpha_k \ln p_{kt} + \tfrac{1}{2} \sum_k \sum_j \gamma_{kj} \ln p_{kt} \ln p_{jt} \,. \tag{1b}$$

A simple dynamic version of AIDS, suggested by Alessie and Kapteyn (1991) and Assarsson (1991), was also presented in Chapter 4 as (4.10). This was used in Chapter 5 as the common model for the Nordic countries, and in stochastic form is given by

$$w_{it} = \alpha_i + \sum_j \theta_{ij} w_{j,t-1} + \sum_j \gamma_{ij} \ln p_{jt} + \beta_i (\ln x_t - \ln P_t) + \mu_{it} \,, \tag{2}$$

where we impose $\Sigma_j \theta_{ij} = 0$ for identification and (4.3a) plus $\Sigma_i \theta_{ij} = 0$ for adding up.

Though the common model was shown in Chapter 5 to perform rather well empirically, since it is specified in level form it may suffer from the possible existence of unit roots in budget shares, prices and real income. If that is the case, statistical inference may be unreliable. A more general dynamic form of the system is the error correction model suggested by Davidson *et al.* (1978), and has been applied recently in a number of empirical studies. For the general dynamic model $y_t = a_1 + b_0 x_t + b_1 x_{t-1}$, the error correction form is given by

$$\Delta y_t = b_0 \Delta x_t + (a_1 - 1)(y_{t-1} - B x_{t-1}) + \varepsilon_t \,, \tag{3}$$

where b_0 is the impact effect, $(1 - a_1)$ the feedback effect and $B = (b_0 + b_1)/(1 - a_1)$ is the long-run response. $(1 - a_1)$ is thus that fraction of the deviation from the long-run equilibrium that is corrected by agents in each period, the disequilibrium being $(y_{t-1} - B x_{t-1})$ This disequilibrium may be directly estimated as μ_{it} using in the static AIDS demand system (1a). For a demand system the feedback effects are represented by a coefficient matrix with certain properties, and in particular this matrix should be restricted such that the adding-up condition is satisfied. A general specification is

$$\Delta w_{it} = \sum_j \aleph_{ij} \Delta \ln p_{jt} + \varphi_i \Delta \ln(x/P)_t + \sum_j \delta_{ij} \mu_{j,t-1} + \varepsilon_{it} \,, \tag{4}$$

for $i = 1, \ldots, n$. The residual vector $\boldsymbol{\varepsilon}_t$ is assumed to be multivariate normally, identically and independently distributed with zero mean vector and covariance matrix $\boldsymbol{\Sigma}$. The problem with singularity of $\boldsymbol{\Sigma}$ is solved in the usual manner by dropping one equation in the estimation. The equation that is left out can be then derived by using the following adding up conditions,

$$\sum_i \aleph_{ij} = \sum_i \varphi_i = \sum_i \delta_{ij} = 0 \,. \tag{5}$$

In addition, since budget shares identically sum to unity, then μ_{it} must identically sum to zero. For identification of (4) one of the error correction mechanisms ($\mu_{j,t-1}$) can be deleted or the system be estimated with the restriction

$$\sum_j \delta_{ij} = 0. \tag{6}$$

The long-run response is measured by the parameters in the static model (1a), the impact effect by the $\aleph$ and φ parameters, while the δ parameters estimate the feedback effects. The fraction of the disequilibrium in the jth good that is adjusted in the ith good in each period is given by $-\delta_{ij}$.

The matrix of the feedback parameters, $\boldsymbol{\delta}$, should have a negative diagonal. Restrictions on the dynamic form can be derived as restrictions on $\boldsymbol{\delta}$. In this system each budget share responds to disequilibrium in each of the goods in the system. A more restrictive formulation, but more similar to some previous dynamic formulations of the AIDS model[2], would use only the disequilibrium in the own budget share in each equation, $\boldsymbol{\delta}$ being diagonal. However, the adding up condition would then require δ_{ii} to be equal in each equation. This system is given by

$$\Delta w_{it} = \sum_j \aleph_{ij} \Delta \ln p_{jt} + \varphi_i \Delta \ln(x/P)_t + \delta \mu_{i,t-1} + \varepsilon_{it}, \tag{7}$$

where δ in this case is a negative scalar. The latter system can be derived from the expenditure function by writing (7) in level form as

$$w_{it} = \alpha_i + \sum_j \aleph_{ij} \ln p_{jt} + \varphi_i \ln(x/P)_t + (1+\delta) w_{i,t-1} + \sum_j \theta_{ij} \ln p_{j,t-1} + \psi_i \ln(x/P)_{t-1} \tag{8}$$

which can be derived from the AIDS expenditure function (4.1) by translating[3] the parameter α_i into

$$\alpha_i = \alpha_i^* + (1+\delta) w_{i,t-1} + \sum_j \theta_{kj} \ln p_{j,t-1} + \psi_i \ln(x/P)_{t-1}, \tag{9}$$

where the long-run parameters can be derived as

$$\gamma_{ij} = \frac{\aleph_{ij} + \theta_{ij}}{-\delta} \text{ and } \beta_i = \frac{\varphi_i + \psi_i}{-\delta}.$$

The last three terms in (9) may be interpreted as an adjustment cost in subsistence expenditure, due to the disequilibrium observed in the previous period.

In addition to the restricted dynamic form (7), Hendry and Richard (1983) derived a number of testable restrictions on the model (4). Some of these restrictions are of interest here, since they imply previously estimated demand systems. The partial adjustment model (no lagged independent variables) has been used by among others, Blanciforti and Green (1983, 1986), Ray (1985) and Assarsson

[2] See, for example, Blanciforti *et al.* (1986) or Ray (1985).

[3] See Pollak and Wales (1981) for a description of translating.

(1991). Another popular model is a system with autoregressive errors, see Berndt and Savin (1975), which is derived from (7) by imposing the restrictions $\aleph_{it} = \gamma_{it}$ and $\varphi_i = \beta_i$.

7.3 TESTING FOR UNIT ROOTS

The error correction form is especially attractive in the presence of unit roots in the variables of concern. To analyse whether the budget shares, the logarithm of prices or the logarithm of total expenditure contain a unit root, we perform the Dickey-Fuller test. This test uses the following auxiliary regressions

$$\Delta y_t = \kappa + \lambda y_{t-1} + \upsilon_t, \text{ or} \tag{10}$$

$$\Delta y_t = \kappa + \lambda y_{t-1} + \pi t + \upsilon_t \tag{11}$$

to test the null hypothesis that $\lambda = 0$ (y has a unit root) against the alternative hypothesis that y is stationary. This is done by computing the t-values for λ in (10) and (11). As shown by Dickey and Fuller (1979), this t-value has a non-standard distribution, and we use the small sample distributions tabulated in Dickey and Fuller (1981) to test for unit roots in all the variables in level form and for the dis-equilibrium term μ_{it}.

Data

The data required for estimating the model is budget shares and relative prices for various food items and the total outlay for these goods. We use the same data base as was used in the previous econometric analysis, *i.e.*, annual data for the Nordic countries.

However, since the unrestricted form of the error correction model implies the estimation of a large number of parameters, the number of goods in the system must be kept small due to limited availability of data. We therefore only use three goods: *food* (including meals at restaurants and cafés), *nondurable goods* and *services* as defined in Chapter 2. This is a slightly aggregated form of the first stage of the utility tree given in Figure 2.1.

The unit root tests show that practically all variables in level form have a unit root, whether (10) or (11) is used. Only a small fraction (about 10 per cent) of the error terms μ_{it} have a unit root. Hence, the error correction form of the system may be statistically appropriate.

7.4 TESTING RESTRICTIONS IN GENERALISED AIDS

We take (4) as the general AIDS form on which certain restrictions can be imposed, in order to obtain a parsimonious econometric model. There are two types of restrictions we are interested in. The first comprises restrictions imposed on the dynamic form, while the second consists of restrictions derived from economic theory. A number of restrictive dynamic forms can be derived from (4), as shown by Hendry and Richard (1983). However, we are particularly interested in those forms that have previously been used in estimating demand systems and forms that may consistently be derived from the expenditure function. The second class of restrictions are derived from economic theory; homogeneity in prices and total expenditure and symmetry of the Slutsky matrix. When using the error correction form we may distinguish between theoretical restrictions in the short and in the long-run, for instance the theoretical restrictions may hold in the long but not in the short-run. We therefore test the theoretical restrictions in both the short and the long-run, conditional on the dynamic form of the system.

7.4.1 Testing Dynamic Form

We have already derived certain restrictions on the δ matrix, *e.g.*, the diagonal model (7). Another possibility is to impose symmetry on δ, where the Slutsky conditions require the consumer to symmetrically adjust demand with respect to the most recently observed disequilibrium. This implies three forms for δ; unrestricted, symmetric and diagonal. With three goods in the system the symmetric δ gives two restrictions and the diagonal model three restrictions.

Other forms that have frequently been estimated in the literature are the partial adjustment model, the autoregressive error structure and the static model. The partial adjustment model may be derived by first rewriting (4) in level form and then imposing the restrictions by setting the parameters of the lagged independent variables to zero. These implies eight restrictions, defined by

$$\aleph_{ij} = -\sum_k \delta_{ik}\gamma_{kj} \text{ and } \varphi_i = -\sum_j \delta_{ij}\beta_j \qquad \text{partial adjustment.} \qquad (12)$$

The model with autoregressive error structure may be derived by setting the impact and the long-run parameters equal. These eight restrictions are given by

$$\aleph_{ij} = \gamma_{ij} \text{ and } \varphi_i = \beta_i \qquad \text{first order autoregressive errors,} \qquad (13)$$

i.e. six price restrictions and two real expenditure restrictions. Finally, the static model may be derived as

$$(12) \text{ and } \delta_{ii} = -1 \text{ and } \delta_{ij} = 0 \text{ for } i \neq j \qquad \text{static model.} \qquad (14)$$

7.4.2 Theoretical Restrictions

The theoretical restrictions to be tested are homogeneity and symmetry. These restrictions may hold in only the long-run or in both the short and the long-run. The long-run restrictions are given by (4.3b) and (4.3c), respectively. Short-run homogeneity is defined as

$$\sum_j \aleph_{ij} = 0 \qquad \text{short-run homogeneity,} \qquad (15)$$

and short-run symmetry by

$$\aleph_{ij} = \aleph_{ji}, \ \forall\ i \neq j \qquad \text{short-run symmetry.} \qquad (16)$$

Hence, (4.3b) and (15) imply homogeneity in both the short and the long-run. Similarly, (4.3c) and (16) imply symmetry in both the short and the long-run. However, an even stronger restriction would also require symmetry in the feedback matrix, *i.e.*,

$$\delta_{ij} = \delta_{ji}, \ \forall\ i \neq j \qquad \text{error correction symmetry.} \qquad (17)$$

The particular dynamic form of the system is not derived from economic theory, but economic behaviour is to a large extent governed by expectations about the future. Hence, dynamics are important. Also, short-run behaviour may be restricted by adjustment costs. For example, consumers may have shopping costs or costs for searching for the best offers, making them respond sluggishly. It therefore seems reasonable that the theoretical restrictions may hold only in the long-run, when equilibrium is derived from (the frictionless) economic theory.

7.5 EMPIRICAL RESULTS

The error correction model (4) can be estimated either by the simultaneous maximum likelihood estimation of the short-run and long-run parameters, or by using the two-step method suggested by Engle and Granger (1987). The two-step method first estimates the long-run parameters as the equilibrium relationship in level form as given in (1a). The estimate of disequilibrium vector μ_t thus obtained is then used in the second step estimation of the error correction mechanism (4).

In this study we use the first method, and estimate all parameters simultaneously. This yields efficient parameter estimates, see Johansen (1991).

7.5.1 Tests of Dynamic Form

The test strategy we use is to take the unrestricted long-run equilibrium model (4)

Table 1. Likelihood Ratio Tests of Dynamic Form and Theoretical Restrictions.

	df	Denmark	Finland	Norway	Sweden
Error correction model		315.39	353.03	261.87*§	227.84
Partial adjustment	8	289.67	318.09	234.66	216.33
		0.000	*0.000*	*0.000*	*0.003*
Autoregressive error	8	305.45	343.49	216.89	219.14
		0.011	*0.014*	*0.000*	*0.026*
Static model	12	264.66	299.58	223.21	205.06
		0.000	*0.000*	*0.000*	*0.000*
Symmetric ECM	1	315.28*	352.34	258.21	225.95
		0.639	*0.240*	*0.007*	*0.052*
Diagonal ECM	3	308.93	349.57*	252.62	225.95*§
		0.005	*0.074*	*0.000*	*0.286*
Long-run homogeneity	2	311.41	347.14	250.21	220.74
		0.021	*0.088*	*0.000*	*0.005*
Long-run symmetry	3	311.40	346.94	248.84	220.48
		0.051	*0.154*	*0.000*	*0.012*
Long and short-run homogeneity	4	310.90	345.35	246.42	218.12
		0.067	*0.077*	*0.000*	*0.005*
Long and short-run symmetry	6	310.48§	343.63§	244.85	218.12
		0.143	*0.065*	*0.000*	*0.016*

The values of the logarithm of the likelihood function are given in plain type and the *P*-values of the asymptotic likelihood ratio test are given in smaller italics. The preferred dynamic form is marked with *. Theoretical restrictions are tested against the preferred dynamic form, and the overall preferred model is marked with §.

as the maintained hypothesis, and to first of all test the restrictions concerning dynamic form, (*i.e.*, those described in section 7.4.1 plus (17) and the diagonal error correction model). These results are presented in the first part of Table 1, where we use the asymptotic likelihood ratio test, without any degrees-of-freedom correction, to calculate *P-values*.

As can be seen, the partial adjustment model, the autoregressive error model and the static model are rejected in all countries using a 5 percent significance level. The symmetric error correction model cannot be rejected for Denmark, however, whilst the diagonal ECM cannot be rejected for Finland and Sweden. These models are denoted as "preferred" for their respective countries, while the unrestricted model is preferred for Norway.

7.5.2 Tests of Homogeneity and Symmetry

The tests of economic theory are performed conditional on the preferred dynamic form. The results can be seen in the second part of Table 1. All the theoretical restrictions are rejected for Norway and Sweden, while for Denmark and Finland the results are somewhat mixed. The most restricted model, for which symmetry

Table 2. Goodness-of-fit and Diagnostic Tests for the Estimated Demand Systems.

	Food	Nondurables	Services	Food	Nondurables	Services
		Denmark			Finland	
R^2	0.997	0.921	0.997	0.995	0.900	0.995
R^2_Δ	0.734	0.733	0.495	0.780	0.655	0.789
ARCH	0.052	0.572	0.535	0.840	1.696	1.309
	0.819	*0.449*	*0.464*	*0.359*	*0.193*	*0.253*
CHOW	0.645	2.173	0.556	0.026	0.747	3.919
	0.534	*0.137*	*0.581*	*0.974*	*0.489*	*0.040*
HET	0.290	3.370	0.157	0.069	5.589	9.090
	0.865	*0.185*	*0.925*	*0.966*	*0.061*	*0.011*
JB	3.382	1.323	1.372	1.320	0.526	1.488
	0.184	*0.516*	*0.504*	*0.517*	*0.769*	*0.475*
		Norway			Sweden	
R^2	0.996	0.988	0.984	0.993	0.927	0.987
R^2_Δ	0.895	0.747	0.892	0.693	0.731	0.829
ARCH	0.955	0.436	0.148	0.075	0.432	1.191
	0.328	*0.509*	*0.700*	*0.784*	*0.511*	*0.275*
CHOW	0.210	0.141	0.022	0.894	0.859	0.084
	0.813	*0.870*	*0.978*	*0.433*	*0.446*	*0.920*
HET	1.122	0.947	1.421	0.741	6.697	1.947
	0.571	*0.623*	*0.491*	*0.690*	*0.035*	*0.378*
JB	3.274	0.263	1.255	0.916	0.311	0.834
	0.195	*0.877*	*0.534*	*0.632*	*0.856*	*0.659*

ARCH = Engle's test for autocorrelated residuals conditional on heteroscedasticity, CHOW = Chow's parameter stability test, HET = White's heteroscedasticity test, and JB = Jarque and Bera's test for residual normality. *P*-values are given in small type italics. R^2 is given for levels and differences (denoted Δ).

both in the short and long-run is imposed, cannot be rejected at the 5 percent level. However, homogeneity is rejected in the long-run for Denmark, indicating that it is primarily in the short-run that the theory works.

7.5.3 Goodness-of-Fit and Diagnostic Tests

In Table 2 we present the results of some single equation diagnostic tests for autocorrelation, heteroscedasticity, normality and parameter stability, as well as goodness-of-fit measured as the squared correlation coefficient between the actual and fitted values in level form. We use the asymptotic χ^2 versions of Engle's Arch test, White's heteroscedasticity test and Jarque and Bera's test for normality of the error terms. The usual version of Chow's parameter stability test is also used.[4]

[4] See Engle (1982), White (1980), Jarque and Bera (1980) and Chow (1960). The ARCH test uses one lagged squared residual the White test uses two squared independent variables in the auxiliary regression, and the Chow test lets two parameters vary between the first and second half of the sample.

The results seem rather satisfactory, since these tests give significant results (at the 5 percent level) in only a few of the equations. Heteroscedastic residuals are to be found for *nondurables* in Sweden and for *services* in Finland, while parameter instability is found for *services* in Finland. Hence, the equation for *services* in Finland seems to be misspecified.

7.5.4 Price and Total Expenditure Elasticities

The estimated long-run price elasticity in the AIDS model is given by (4.6a), that is

$$\hat{e}_{ij}^{L} = \frac{\hat{\gamma}_{ij} - \hat{\beta}_i[\hat{\alpha}_j + \frac{1}{2}\sum_k(\hat{\gamma}_{kj} + \hat{\gamma}_{jk})\ln p_k]}{\hat{w}_i^L} - \xi_{ij}, \tag{18}$$

where ξ_{ij} is Kronecker's delta, which equals 1 for $i = j$ and zero otherwise, and $\hat{w}_i^L$ refers to the estimated long-run solution for w_i, as defined by (1a). The short-run elasticity is not directly identified due to the loss of the constant term in difference form. However, as shown in Chapter 4, the constant α_i can be interpreted as the budget share for a household on the subsistence level. We assume that this subsistence budget share is equal in the short and in the long-run, and we thus define the short-run elasticity as

$$\hat{e}_{ij}^{S} = \frac{\hat{\aleph}_{ij} - \hat{\varphi}_i[\hat{\alpha}_j + \frac{1}{2}\sum_k(\hat{\aleph}_{kj} + \hat{\aleph}_{jk})\Delta\ln p_k]}{\hat{w}_i^S} - \xi_{ij}, \tag{19}$$

where $\hat{w}_i^S$ is the fitted value from (4) plus the actual budget share at time point $t-1$. The elasticities, as well as their standard errors, are functions of all the estimated parameters and independent variables in the system, and are thus likely to vary over time.

Short and long-run compensated price elasticities and total expenditure elasticities, evaluated at the mean values of the variables, are presented in Table 3. As can be seen, all own-price elasticities are negative, except for the long-run *food* elasticity in Norway and the short and long-run elasticities for *nondurables* in Sweden. All total expenditure elasticities are positive. *Food* is classified as a necessity in the long-run in all countries, while *Services* is a luxury in all countries except Sweden. The positive own-price elasticities for Sweden, and to some extent Norway, are peculiar, and cast doubts on the specification for these countries. It is likely that the *nondurables* equation for Sweden is misspecified, giving odd parameter estimates and heteroscedastic residuals.

The elasticities obtained in this chapter can be compared to those obtained, *e.g.*, with the common model in Chapter 5 or with the results of the more elaborated models in Chapter 6. It should be noted, however, that the system with only three goods was not used in the previous analysis. In addition, we distinguish here be-

Table 3. Short and Long-run Compensated Price and Expenditure Elasticities.

		Food	Nondurables	Services	Food	Nondurables	Services
		Denmark			Finland		
Food	SR	−0.122	0.243	0.093	−0.292	0.420	0.330
	LR	−0.126	0.233	0.015	−0.126	0.233	0.015
Non-durables	SR	−0.135	−0.320	0.315	−0.135	−0.320	0.315
	LR	0.282	−0.706	0.418	0.282	−0.706	0.418
Services	SR	0.211	0.223	−0.365	0.211	0.223	−0.365
	LR	−0.295	0.438	−0.364	−0.295	0.438	−0.364
Total expenditure	SR	0.907	1.345	0.880	1.329	0.570	0.818
	LR	0.445	0.987	1.800	0.640	0.872	1.402
		Norway			Sweden		
Food	SR	−0.270	0.026	0.004	−0.465	0.246	−0.032
	LR	0.128	0.166	0.415	−0.204	0.463	−0.198
Non-durables	SR	−0.233	0.022	−0.062	−0.024	0.196	−0.659
	LR	0.222	−0.193	0.533	−0.694	0.577	−0.956
Services	SR	0.519	0.364	−0.028	0.347	0.191	−0.015
	LR	−0.072	0.305	−0.823	0.468	0.730	−0.411
Total expenditure	SR	1.059	1.529	0.649	0.885	1.762	0.851
	LR	0.640	1.097	1.326	0.955	1.986	0.755

SR = Short-run elasticities, and LR = Long-run elasticities.

tween short and long-run elasticities, which was not done earlier (those elasticities being essentially of a short-run nature). Hence, it is difficult to compare the results of this chapter with our previous results. It seems nevertheless as if there are some large differences between the elasticities obtained here and those obtained earlier, *e.g.*, for *nondurables*.

7.6 CONCLUSIONS

Using U.K. data, Anderson and Blundell (1983) showed that the error correction form produced a much better fit than the more restrictive autoregressive or partial adjustment models. They used a two-step procedure in the estimation of the error correction model with auxiliary regressions for the AIDS model in difference form. Here we estimated the short-run (difference) and long-run (level) parameters simultaneously.

The results favour models with flexible functional as well as dynamic form. Restrictive dynamic forms are rejected by the data in all Nordic countries. In particular we show that symmetry in the dynamic form is rejected for Finnish and Norwegian data. The more restrictive dynamic form in which the feedback parameter matrix is diagonal cannot be rejected for Swedish data, however.

8

PROJECTIONS OF FUTURE CONSUMPTION IN FINLAND

by Ilkka Laurila*

8.1 INTRODUCTION

Thus far in the present study, the factors affecting consumption have been identified and quantified. In this chapter, our earlier results are employed to predict future consumption in Finland. Using predictions for future values of the exogenous variables, predictions are made for future values of endogenous variables. In the literature these *out-of-sample* predictions are called either projections (Deaton (1975)) or forecasts (Harvey (1990)). In the present chapter the terms projection and forecast are used interchangeably.

Since more detailed data is available for Finland than was used in the common model, the demand system used for forecasting purposes includes somewhat more categories than previously used (see Figure 1). The composition of the commodity bundles also differs somewhat from the composition used in the common model. Since the data allows the separation of various dairy products, *fresh milk* is included in *beverages*, instead of *animalia*. *Fruits and vegetables* are separated, but to avoid more than four goods in a group (a degrees-of-freedom restriction), *potatoes* are included in *vegetables*. *Fats and oils* are allocated under *animalia*, instead of *miscellaneous*, which is replaced by the single bundle *sugar and confectionery*.

The demand system is now composed of seven groups, and for each group an appropriate (or preferred) model specification is chosen. This choice between different specifications is based on hypothesis testing, where most of the hypotheses represent theoretical or statistical requirements. We use the *P*-values of the test statistics to judge which specification achieves the best representation of the data.

The preferred models for each group are used for projecting *per capita* food consumption patterns to the year 2000. Prices were not taken as given, but various hypotheses were made concerning the price paths. The consumption forecasts are thus conditional on the defined price and total expenditure developments. After predicting the growth path of population size, effects on demand at market level can be derived. The procedure thus describes how given changes in prices and expenditure affect the choice of different foodstuffs

* Special thanks are due to Anders Hummelmose for collecting the data concerning retail prices in Denmark.

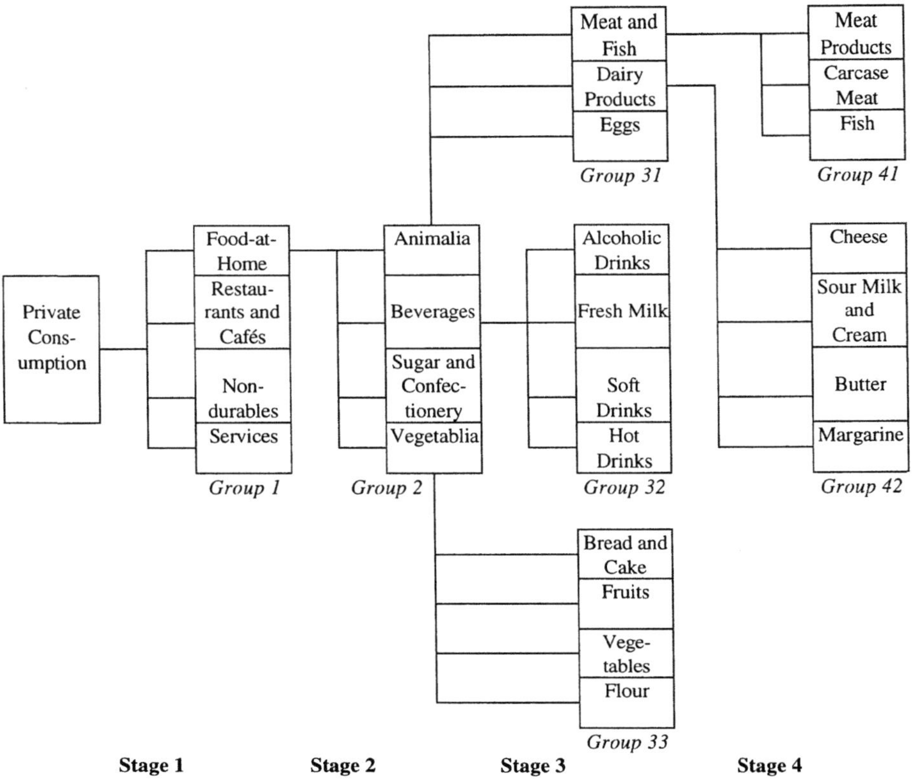

Figure 1. A Four-Stage Budgeting System for Forecasting in Finland

The quantities consumed are simulated under four scenarios regarding the development of prices over the period 1992-2000. Note that in the beginning of the period we expect a reasonable degree of reliability in the forecasts, whilst later on the predictions of consumer behaviour are conditional upon the specified development of the exogenous variables.

The purpose of this chapter is to try to answer the following questions:

1. What kind of effects can be foreseen in the household demand for food products during a period of transition to alternative price patterns, given certain changes in the total expenditure of households?
2. How do the alternative projections concerning the household demand affect the aggregate demand for food products, given certain changes in the size of the population?

8.2 SELECTION OF PREFERRED SPECIFICATIONS

Four versions of the AIDS were specified in Chapter 4: static AIDS, dynamic AIDS, switching static AIDS, and switching dynamic AIDS. Each version can be estimated in either unconstrained form (homogeneity and symmetry not imposed), homogeneity constrained form, and homogeneity and symmetry constrained form. Our strategy is to estimate all twelve specifications for each group in order to verify which version provides the best explanation of the observed changes in Finnish consumption. Along with the economic interest, the results can be used to justify a reduction in the number of parameters that are estimated.

The method of model selection is of critical importance, since results vary from one specification to another. The unrestricted switching dynamic AIDS is the most general model, the other eleven specifications are nested within it. Technically, four restrictions (static, non-switching, homogeneity, and symmetry including homogeneity) are nested directly within the switching dynamic AIDS. In order to choose between alternative specifications, tests of parameter restrictions and misspecification tests are used to judge whether the restrictions can be imposed. Two extra hypotheses, also of interest, are adding up and negativity. Adding up holds automatically in our estimation, however, and thus guarantees that the budget constraint is not violated.

Both likelihood ratio tests and Wald tests are used to test the restrictions. The "exact" Rao LR test (4.37 and 4.45a) is used for testing homogeneity, symmetry, and dynamics. An "exact" Wald test (4.45b) is available for the homogeneity and switching hypotheses, but a corrected Wald test (Chapter 4.4.3) is used to check symmetry and dynamics.[1] In Table 1 we present the *P*-values for all hypotheses for the unrestricted switching dynamic AIDS, which is the most general model specification. In addition, we also present results for the model that is chosen as the preferred specification for each particular group (in those cases where this is not the unrestricted model).

The unrestricted switching dynamic AIDS is accepted against all restrictions for four groups, *private consumption*, *food-at-home*, *vegetablia* and *dairy products*. Switching is accepted everywhere, but in *animalia* (Group 31), the switching static AIDS produces some peculiarities in own-price elasticities and, moreover, the Cusumsq test[2] indicates parameter instability. By rejecting the switching parameter, the problem is alleviated. Dynamics is rejected for *animalia* (Group 31) by the Wald and LR tests, and for *meat and fish* (Group 41) by the LR test.

The Reset, HW(tx), HW(di), and Cusumsq tests indicate serious misspecification in *beverages* (Group 32). This misspecification is alleviated by deleting the

---

[1] The "exact" tests are only truly exact for linear hypotheses in linear models. The AIDS models are only slightly nonlinear, however, and thus all LR tests except those for symmetry (which involves cross-equation restrictions) are very nearly exact. The Wald tests also use heteroscedastic consistent covariance estimates, which are only valid asymptotically.

[2] The misspecification tests were presented in Chapter 4.

Table 1. P-Values of Hypotheses for the Unrestricted and Preferred Specifications

Grp	Model	Homogeneity		Symmetry		Symmetry given homogeneity		No dynamics		No switch
		W^*	Λ^*	CW	Λ^*	CW	Λ^*	CW	Λ^*	W^*
1	SwDU	0.0091	0.0259	0.0000	0.0005			0.0000	0.0100	0.0000
2	SwDU	0.0000	0.0017	0.0000	0.0009			0.0000	0.0058	0.0000
31	SwDU	0.0000	0.0001	0.0000	0.0001			0.9151	0.9052	0.0020
31	TU	0.0001	0.0003	0.0000	0.0003					
32	SwDU	0.0000	0.0003	0.0000	0.0000			0.0000	0.0125	0.0000
32	DU	0.0001	0.0010	0.0000	0.0066			0.0000	0.1024	
33	SwDU	0.0010	0.0019	0.0000	0.0057			0.0000	0.0000	0.0003
41	SwDU	0.6029	0.5654	0.5595	0.4217	0.2555	0.1929	0.0179	0.0807	0.0000
41	SwDHS							0.0187		0.0000
42	SwDU	0.0001	0.0001	0.0000	0.0007			0.0000	0.0000	0.0000

The following abbreviations are used: W^* ("exact" heteroscedasticity consistent Wald test), CW (corrected heteroscedasticity consistent Wald test), Λ^* ("exact" likelihood ratio test), SwDU (switching dynamic AIDS, unrestricted), TU (static AIDS, unrestricted), DU (dynamic AIDS, unrestricted), and SwDHS (switching dynamic AIDS, homogeneity and symmetry restricted). The groups are as follows. Group 1: *private consumption*; Group 2: *food-at-home*; Group 31: *animalia*; Group 32: *beverages*; Group 33: *vegetablia*; Group 41: *meat and fish*; and Group 42: *dairy products*.

Table 2. Preferred Specification of AIDS, with Estimated Break Points

Group	Preferred specification	τ_1	τ_2
Private Consumption (Group 1)	Switching dynamic AIDS, unrestricted	1975	1984
Food-at-Home (Group 2)	Switching dynamic AIDS, unrestricted	1961	1984
Animalia (Group 31)	Static AIDS, unrestricted		
Beverages (Group 32)	Dynamic AIDS, unrestricted		
Vegetablia (Group 33)	Switching dynamic AIDS, unrestricted	1961	1989
Meat and Fish (Group 41)	Switching dynamic AIDS, homogeneity and symmetry restricted	1967	1975
Dairy Products (Group 42)	Switching dynamic AIDS, unrestricted	1965	1974

Break point τ_1 represents the end of the first regime and break point τ_2 is the start of the second regime.

switching parameter. After doing this, the LR test suggests a rejection of dynamics, while the Wald test does not. Replacing dynamic by static AIDS introduces serious misspecification in the HW(tx) and HW(di) tests, while other tests remained about the same. Consequently, the dynamic specification is chosen for *beverages*.

Both homogeneity and symmetry are rejected in all cases except *meat and fish* (Group 41). For this group the homogeneity and symmetry restricted specification of the switching static AIDS suffers from functional misspecification (Reset), group expenditure endogeneity (HW(tx)), and parameter instability (Cusumsq). The problems are alleviated if we accept dynamics which is, in fact, suggested by the Wald test but rejected by the LR test.

A summary of the preferred Finnish models can be found in Table 2. The break points, denoting the beginning and end of the gradually switching period, have been estimated by maximum likelihood, and are also given for the switching models. These estimated break points vary quite considerably from group to group.

8.3 FORECASTING ACCURACY

In this section model performance is studied, both *within-sample* and *out-of-sample*. As performance criteria we use the mean absolute percentage error (*MAPE*) and the squared coefficient of determination derived from the root-mean-square prediction error (*R^2-RMSE*), see Kennedy (1985, pp. 206-207) and Huang and Haidacher (1986). Both criteria measure the prediction error, that is the difference between the predicted and actual budget shares. The *MAPE* describes the average of the absolute values of the percentage prediction errors, *i.e.*,

$$MAPE = 100 \cdot \frac{\sum_t |\hat{w}_t - w_t|}{T\overline{w}}, \tag{1}$$

where $\hat{w}$ is the predicted budget share, $\overline{w}$ is the sample mean and T the number of observations. For the within-sample predictions the estimation and prediction periods are both 1961-1991, while for the out-of-sample predictions the estimation period is 1961-1990 and the prediction period 1991.

The root-mean-square prediction error (*RMSE*) is the square root of the average of the squared values of the prediction errors. This criterion gives greater weight to large prediction errors than *MAPE*. The *R^2-RMSE* measures the ability of the forecasting model to explain the data used to develop the forecasting model; it gives the proportion of the variation in the forecasted variable that is captured by the forecast, *i.e.*,

$$R^2\text{-}RMSE = 1 - \frac{(RMSE)^2}{Var(w)} = 1 - \frac{\sum_t (\hat{w}_t - w_t)^2}{\sum_t (\hat{w}_t - \overline{w})^2}, \tag{2}$$

where the estimation and prediction periods are as for *MAPE*.

To evaluate the accuracy of the out-of-sample predictions we introduce a benchmark model specification; the simple random walk. Applied to the present analysis, the random walk model implies that the best prediction of the next observation is the current observation,

$$\hat{y}_{T+1} = E(y_{T+1} | y_T) = y_T, \tag{3}$$

where in our case T is the year 1990. Because accuracy is evaluated for only one year (1991), we will not, for example, replace the AIDS with the random walk model, even if the random walk model shows better forecasting accuracy. This is

Table 3. Model Performance in Within-Sample and Out-of-Sample Predictions

Category	Within sample predictions		Predictions for 1991 (estimation period 1961-1990)			
	MAPE	*R^2–RMSE*	*MAPE*		*R^2–RMSE*	
	AIDS	AIDS	RW	AIDS	RW	AIDS
Private Consumption (Group 1)						
- Food-at-Home	0.6	0.996	4.0	0.9	0.936	0.997
- Restaurants and Cafés	1.5	0.996	5.4	6.3	0.918	0.888
- Nondurables	1.1	0.932	0.1	1.8	1.000	0.900
- Services	0.5	0.993	3.4	1.1	0.556	0.955
- AVERAGE	0.9		3.2	2.5		
Food-at-Home (Group 2)						
- Animalia	0.8	0.920	1.7	1.2	0.794	0.894
- Beverages	1.2	0.873	1.7	0.3	0.839	0.994
- Vegetablia	1.3	0.950	0.6	1.3	0.992	0.968
- Sugar and Confectionery	2.0	0.835	1.5	2.0	0.953	0.910
- AVERAGE	1.3		1.4	1.2		
Animalia (Group 31)						
- Meat and Fish	1.1	0.931	0.3	0.5	0.997	0.992
- Dairy Products	1.9	0.899	1.7	0.2	0.966	1.000
- Eggs	3.3	0.910	10.4	10.7	0.692	0.669
- AVERAGE	2.1		4.1	3.8		
Beverages (Group 32)						
- Alcoholic Drinks	1.6	0.991	1.7	1.6	0.987	0.989
- Fresh Milk	2.4	0.988	2.4	8.9	0.998	0.964
- Soft Drinks	2.9	0.975	0.9	3.5	0.997	0.957
- Hot Drinks	2.4	0.986	11.1	8.7	0.961	0.976
- AVERAGE	2.3		4.0	5.7		
Vegetablia (Group 33)						
- Bread and Cake	1.4	0.937	0.3	3.4	0.999	0.782
- Fruits	3.3	0.941	1.0	7.6	0.995	0.716
- Vegetables	2.6	0.936	0.7	2.3	0.997	0.967
- Flour	3.6	0.978	0.3	2.1	1.000	0.997
- AVERAGE	2.7		0.6	3.8		
Meat and Fish (Group 41)						
- Meat Products	1.5	0.937	0.5	1.3	0.994	0.965
- Carcase Meat	2.2	0.852	1.8	1.4	0.949	0.969
- Fish	4.6	0.259	3.8	1.6	0.881	0.978
- AVERAGE	2.8		2.0	1.4		
Dairy Products (Group 42)						
- Cheese	4.3	0.975	6.1	0.9	0.884	0.997
- Sour Milk and Cream	2.8	0.954	0.4	13.4	0.999	0.151
- Butter	3.3	0.975	13.5	16.9	0.946	0.915
- Margarine	3.9	0.820	1.9	7.5	0.979	0.684
- AVERAGE	3.6		5.5	9.7		

AIDS refers to the preferred Finnish model specifications that are named in Table 2. The abbreviated notations are MAPE (mean absolute percentage error), R^2–RMSE (coefficient of determination derived from the root-mean-square prediction error) and RW (random walk model).

because long-term (9 year) projections are being made, and the budget shares in most commodities have changed a good deal over a 10 year period (see Chapter 2). The assumption that budget shares will remain at the 1991 level for all of the 1990's is thus rather unjustified. The comparison between models is made in order to evaluate how well the AIDS performs, compared with the random walk model, as regards to short-term forecasting.

In Table 3 we present goodness-of-fit measures for the within-sample and out-of-sample predictions. These have been obtained by estimating the demand system stage by stage (subsystem by subsystem), without allowing for interaction between stages. The estimated expenditure at an upper level thus becomes the budget constraint at a lower level.

As previously mentioned, for the out-of-sample forecasts the AIDS models are estimated with the data covering 1960-1990, and the year 1991 is predicted. The performance criteria are thus based on the out-of-sample prediction errors. This is similar to the model selection procedure known as cross-validation, see Maddala (1992, pp. 504-506). Since only one period ahead is forecasted, the MAPE measures here the difference between the predicted and actual budget share in 1991, expressed as a percentage. In the case of the random walk model the MAPE measures the deviation of the 1990 actual budget share from the actual 1991 budget share, whereas in case of the AIDS model the MAPE measures the deviation of the AIDS projection for 1991 from the actual 1991 budget share. For example, the AIDS model predicted that the budget share of *food-at-home* should be 0.2675 in 1991, whereas the actual value is 0.2650. The absolute error is therefore 0.0025, which is 0.9 percent (the MAPE) of the actual value. The ratio of explained variation to the total variation is 0.997 (the R^2-*RMSE* in Table 3).

In Table 3 we can see that within sample mean absolute errors of 3 percent and above are recorded for *eggs, fruits, flour, fish, cheese, butter,* and *margarine*. In the groups *vegetablia, meat and fish,* and *dairy products* (Groups 33, 41, and 42) the errors are relatively large. In the out-of-sample predictions, the random walk model performs better than the AIDS for *beverages, vegetablia,* and *dairy products* (Groups 32, 33, and 42), and several low coefficients of determination are recorded for *vegetablia* and *dairy products*.

The results indicate that the preferred Finnish AIDS specifications are good forecasting models in a number of groups. Within *vegetablia* and *dairy products* (Groups 33 and 42), the prediction errors are large for both the within-sample and out-of-sample predictions. This suggests that the specified models should not be used for forecasting in these two groups. Some initial trials showed that if projections are made far enough into the future, then the budget shares of *flour* (within *vegetablia*) and *butter* (within *dairy products*) tended to zero, with the other goods taking up all of the group expenditure. This result is similar to that obtained by Wohlgenant (1986) in the context of a complete systems approach (the Fourier flexible functional form), and it is apparent that one has to exercise caution when using complete systems to forecast outside the sample.

Forecasts of the demand for *eggs* and *fish* must be interpreted with caution, since large prediction errors are recorded. Otherwise the models specified for Groups 31 and 41, to which *eggs* and *fish* belong, show such a good performance that the groups are included in our simulations. The model specified for *beverages* (Group 32) shows large prediction errors in the out-of-sample predictions but rather small prediction errors in the within-sample predictions. This group is thus also included in the simulations.

As a result of checking the forecasting accuracy, future consumption is projected for all groups except *vegetablia* and *dairy products* (Groups 33 and 42). Our forecasts are made using the preferred AIDS specifications given in Table 2. Note, however, that the prediction error tests stress the need to interpret the results with caution. The measured errors imply problems in the long-term projections, since prediction errors are cumulative over time and, thus the error is likely to be greater the longer the prediction period.

8.4 PROJECTIONS FOR THE EXOGENOUS VARIABLES

Predictions for future patterns of relative prices, total expenditure, and mean population are required to enable us to forecast the endogenous variables. Four alternative scenarios are used concerning prices, all of which employ the same budget constraint and size of population. The growth path of private consumption is mainly based on predictions made by the Ministry of Finance, whereas the growth path of the size of population is based on projections made by the Central Statistical

Table 4. Predictions for Private Consumption and Mean Population

Year	Private Consumption, yearly growth rate in percent	Mean Population, millions
1992	−2.5	5.037
1993	−4.5	5.054
1994	1.5	5.066
1995	3.5	5.075
1996	3.5	5.081
1997	3.0	5.087
1998	2.0	5.091
1999	2.0	5.093
2000	2.0	5.095

The 1992 growth rate excludes durables and semi-durables. Other growth rates refer to total private consumption (including durables and semi-durables). The figures refer to changes in aggregate demand; the *per capita* figures would be on average 0.1 percentage points lower.

Sources of private consumption: The 1992 figure is from the Statistical Office's national accounts (1993:4); The 1993-1997 figures are from the Finnish Ministry of Finance's 1993 prognosis; The 1998-2000 figures are from Vartia and Ylä-Anttila (1992, p. 297). The source of the mean population is the Statistical Office's population figures (1992:6).

Office of Finland (Table 4). An analysis that starts from total consumption has the advantage that one need not assume food expenditures to be exogenously determined. Thus, total expenditure is only needed for Stage 1, since in the following stages it is obtained from the preceding stage.

One scenario concerning the relative prices assumes that they remain at the 1991 level, two scenarios assume historical trends to continue, whereas the final scenario assumes a structural change in price patterns. The alternative predictions are obtained as follows.

1. The 1991 price scenario. Prices are assumed to remain at the 1991 level, which is the last year of observation. This scenario implies that there will be no changes in relative prices between the years 1991 and 2000.
2. The 1960-91 trend scenario. Relative prices are assumed to follow the Finnish 1960-1991 trend during 1992-2000. This implies, for example, a decrease of 4 percent in relative prices for *food-at-home* over the period 1992-2000 (see Table 5).
3. The 1980-91 trend scenario. Relative prices are assumed to follow the Finnish 1980-1991 trend during 1992-2000. This implies, *e.g.*, a decrease of 5 percent in

Table 5. Projected Changes in Relative Prices between 1991 and 2000. Percent

Category	Price change related to group price index			Price change related to general price index		
	Price scenario			Price scenario		
	1960-91 trend	1980-91 trend	Structural change	1960-91 trend	1980-91 trend	Structural change
Food-at-Home	–4	–5	–11	–4	–5	–11
- Animalia	–1	–2	1	–5	–7	–10
- Meat and Fish	–1	2	0	–6	–5	–10
- Meat Products	–0	2	–1	–6	–3	–11
- Carcase Meat	4	8	2	–2	2	–8
- Fish	–14	–37	0	–18	–41	–10
- Dairy Products	2	–4	–2	–3	–11	–11
- Eggs	–8	–8	10	–13	–14	–1
- Beverages	–4	5	–8	–8	–1	–18
- Alcoholic Drinks	–1	2	–11	–8	2	–27
- Fresh Milk	–0	–12	20	–8	–12	–1
- Soft Drinks	6	6	–1	–2	5	–19
- Hot Drinks	–2	–2	55	–9	–3	27
- Sugar & Confectionery	0	–6	1	–4	–11	–10
- Vegetablia	5	–1	7	1	–7	–5
Restaurants and Cafés	11	18	4	11	18	4
Nondurabless	1	–12	4	1	–12	4
Services	1	5	4	1	5	4

The general price index is the projected price of private consumption relative prices for *food-at-home* over the period 1992-2000 (see Table 5).

4. The structural change scenario. Relative prices are assumed to face a structural change during 1992-2000 . The relative prices in Denmark in 1992 are taken as expressions of how the relative prices could appear in Finland in 2000. The prices are assumed to change gradually, and the prices concerning the years between 1991 and 2000 are thus derived from a linear trend starting from prices in the year 1991 and ending with full adjustment in the year 2000 (see Table 5). This scenario can be seen as a potential price path if Finland joins the European Union.

As a benchmark for the structural change scenario, a comparison of price patterns in Denmark and Finland is used, where the average retail prices on forty food items are available. The aim is to choose representative goods for the commodity bundles presented in Figure 1. The Danish *krona* is converted to the Finnish *markka* at the exchange rate of DKK 1 = FIM 0.781.[3] The expenditure patterns found in the 1990 Finnish Household Expenditure Survey are used to weight both the Danish and Finnish prices, for example, the retail price for *fresh milk* is a combination of the 1992 prices for standard milk and skimmed milk, weighted by the mutual budget shares of the commodities in Finland in 1990. No reference prices concerning *restaurants and cafés*, *nondurables* and *services* are available. The structural change option implies, for example, that the price of *food-at-home* would decrease by 11 percent relative to the price of *private consumption*. No prediction concerning the development of the general price index is made. *Restaurants and cafés, nondurables* and *services* are thus assumed to become 4 percent more expensive relative to the price of *private consumption* by the year 2000, to offset the decrease of the relative price of *food-at-home*. No reference price concerning *fish* is available either, and thus the relative price of *fish* is assumed to remain at the 1991 level in the structural change scenario.

The variables h_t in (4.11) are set to unity over the prediction period. This is justified by the fact that the shifting parameters are not useful for projections, since one cannot both explain the cause of structural change and be able to forecast the direction and magnitude of that change (*c.f.*, Myers (1986, p. 180)).

In the simulations it is the relative prices within groups that are used, rather than prices relative to *private consumption*. For example, if one relative price in a group increases, then at least one other relative price has to decrease. Since the changes in relative prices - weighted by budget shares - must add up to zero, all the relative prices cannot be projected independently of one another and an adjustment must be carried out. In the first price scenario no price changes are predicted, and the size of the inconsistency is zero, *i.e.*, the above condition is automatically satisfied. For the other scenarios the following condition has to be imposed for goods within the rth group,

[3] Average of the Bank of Finland middle rates in 31 December 1991, 30 June 1992, 31 December 1992, and 30 June 1993.

$$\sum_i \frac{p_{i,2000}/p_{i,1991}}{\phi_{(r)}} w_{(r)i,1991} = \sum_i \frac{p^*_{i,2000}}{p_{i,1991}} w_{(r)i,1991} = 1, \tag{4}$$

where $p_{i,1991}$ is the ith price in 1991, $p_{i,2000}$ and $p^*_{i,2000}$ are the uncorrected and corrected predictions for the price in the year 2000, $w_{(r)i,1991}$ is the ith budget share within the rth group in 1991, and $\phi_{(r)}$ is the normalisation constant for the rth group.[4] Consequently, the condition says that Stone's price index remains the same for the whole forecast period, *i.e.*,

$$\sum_i p_{it} w_{(r)i,1991} = P, \tag{5}$$

for $t = 1992,\ldots,2000$. The condition implies that no change is predicted for the general price level between 1991 and 2000, and predicted changes in real expenditure can thus be interpreted without risk of any money illusion.

If the relative prices within groups are converted to price changes relative to the price of *private consumption*, then almost all food prices tend to decrease over the forecast period. For example, in the structural change option, only *hot drinks* and *restaurants and cafés* are predicted to become more expensive (see Table 5).

8.5 PROJECTIONS FOR THE YEAR 2000

8.5.1 Projected Volumes

The projected Finnish consumption volumes are derived by multiplying the estimated budget shares by the total expenditure in current prices. The outcome is then divided by the price index to obtain real consumption, and finally converted to *per capita* volumes by dividing with the predicted mean population for the corresponding year. Different projections of each category are obtained for each scenario. Note that consumption in terms of expenditure, which is presented here, is different from consumption in terms of physical units. In the case of food, changes in quality rather than changes in the quantity of raw materials, probably explain much of the changes in the expenditures allocated to individual bundles. The added value probably originates mainly from services, *i.e.*, the purchased good becomes more prepared before it reaches the consumer.

Looking at Table 6 we can see that if prices remain at the 1991 level, then *per capita* consumption of *meat products* and *restaurants and cafés* will increase by more than 20 percent. The consumption of *eggs, alcoholic drinks, soft drinks* and *sugar and confectionery* will also increase substantially, whereas the consumption of *carcase meat, fish, dairy products* and *fresh milk* will nearly stagnate. If prices

---

[4] The size of the inconsistency is very small in the 1960-91-trend and 1980-91-trend sceneraios. In these alternatives $\phi_{(r)}$ differs only slightly from 1, indicating that the initially derived relative prices are almost consistent. This is actually what one would expect due to the method we have used to predict the prices.

Table 6. Projected Changes in Food Consumption between 1991 to 2000. Percent

Category	*Per capita*				Aggregate			
	Price option				Price option			
	1991 price	1960-91 trend	1980-91 trend	Structural change	1991 price	1960-91 trend	1980-91 trend	Structural change
Food-at-Home	9	5	4	5	11	6	6	7
- Animalia	9	6	7	5	11	7	9	6
- Meat and Fish	14	9	12	6	16	11	14	7
- Meat Products	25	15	20	9	27	17	22	11
- Carcase Meat	2	–2	–10	2	4	0	–9	3
- Fish	2	16	46	3	3	18	48	5
- Dairy Products	1	–1	–2	3	3	1	–1	4
- Eggs	10	8	–2	4	12	9	0	5
- Beverages	12	5	1	9	14	7	3	11
- Alcoholic Drinks	17	7	5	8	19	9	6	10
- Fresh Milk	0	6	–4	8	2	8	–3	9
- Soft Drinks	13	–4	–2	1	15	–2	0	2
- Hot Drinks	4	1	–5	17	6	3	–3	19
- Sugar &Confectionery	12	9	6	10	14	11	8	12
- Vegetablia	4	2	2	0	6	3	4	1
Restaurants and Cafés	21	8	2	13	23	9	4	15

Consumption measured in real expenditure.

follow the 1960-91 trend, then the consumption of *meat products* and *fish* will increase by 15-16 percent until the year 2000. The consumption of *carcase meat, dairy products* and *soft drinks* will decrease, however. The 1980-91 trend scenario implies that the consumption of *meat products* and *fish* will increase strongly, while the consumption of *carcase meat, dairy products, eggs, fresh milk, soft drinks* and *hot drinks* will decrease.

If prices change according to the structural change scenario, then the consumption of *hot drinks* and *sugar and confectionery* will increase the most, while the consumption of *carcase meat, soft drinks* and *vegetablia* will nearly stagnate. For *hot drinks* the outcome is explained by two facts. Firstly, at the end of the 1980's, *hot drinks* became a Giffen good with positive own-price elasticity, and secondly, the structural change scenario implies a strong increase in the price of *hot drinks*. Since the verisimilitude of this outcome is doubtful, the projection concerning *hot drinks* in the structural change scenario will not be considered when deriving conclusions from the analysis.

The consumption of *food-at-home* faces the strongest increase if the price structure remained at the 1991 level until 2000, the other price scenarios leading to very similar results for this commodity group. Even the increase in the consumption of *restaurants and cafés* will be greatest for the 1991 price scenario (21 percent *per capita*). The structural change scenario generates a 13 percent increase in the *per capita* consumption of *restaurants and cafés*, whereas the 1980-91 trend scenario implies a nearly stagnate consumption of this group.

8.5.2 Projected Budget Shares

From Table 7 we find that the projected budget shares of the components of *food-at-home* (*animalia, beverages* and *vegetablia*) vary remarkably little under various price scenarios. The projected budget share of *animalia* varies between 33.5 and 34.0 percent in the year 2000, whereas it was 33.5 percent in 1991. The budget share of *beverages* and varies between 30.5 and 32.9 percent in the year 2000, while that of *vegetablia* varies between 24.3 to 26.0 percent. In 1991 these budget shares are 31.9 and 25.5 percent respectively. A greater variability is to be found in the disaggregated categories, however.

The structural change scenario causes the biggest changes in food consumption patterns. On average, shares would change 0.75 percentage points. In absolute terms, the largest increases in budget shares are projected for *fresh milk* and *hot drinks*. In both cases, the increase in the budget share is generated by increases in both total consumption and prices. The largest decrease in the budget share, caused

Table 7. Finnish Budget Shares in 1991 (Actual) and for 2000 (Forecast). Percent

Category (mutual dependency of categories in parentheses)	Share of Food-at-Home				
	Actual 1991	Forecasts for 2000, different scenarios			
		1991 price	1960-91 trend	1980-91 trend	Structural change
Food-at-Home (=1+8+13+14)	100.0	100.0	100.0	100.0	100.0
- Animalia (1=2+6+7)	33.5	33.6	33.6	33.5	34.0
- Meat and Fish (2=3+4+5)	21.3	22.2	21.8	22.6	21.8
- Meat Products (3)	11.4	12.8	12.2	13.3	11.8
- Carcase Meat (4)	7.8	7.3	7.5	7.3	7.8
- Fish (5)	2.2	2.1	2.1	1.9	2.2
- Dairy Products (6)	11.0	10.2	10.6	9.8	10.8
- Eggs (7)	1.2	1.3	1.2	1.1	1.4
- Beverages (8=9+10+11+12)	31.9	32.9	31.0	32.9	30.5
- Alcoholic Drinks (9)	21.6	22.7	20.8	23.1	18.1
- Fresh Milk (10)	5.1	5.1	5.4	4.8	6.3
- Soft Drinks (11)	2.7	2.8	2.6	2.9	2.4
- Hot Drinks (12)	2.5	2.3	2.2	2.2	3.8
- Sugar and Confectionery (13)	9.1	9.2	9.4	8.6	9.5
- Vegetablia (14)	25.5	24.3	26.0	24.9	26.0
Mean absolute deviation from 1991	0.00	0.53	0.35	0.66	0.75

The mean absolute deviation concerns the categories denoted with a single digit (11 altogether). It is computed as the sum of absolute departures from the respective actual shares in 1991, divided by 11.

by decreasing prices, is forecast for *alcoholic drinks*. In the structural change scenario, the budget shares of *carcase meat, fish, dairy products, eggs, fresh milk, hot drinks, sugar and confectionery* and *vegetablia* are higher in the year 2000 relative to the other scenarios. On the other hand, allocation to *meat products, alcoholic drinks* and *soft drinks* are relatively low.

In the 1980-91 trend scenario, the budget shares of *meat products* and *alcoholic drinks* will increase the most. Relative to the other scenarios, the 1980-91 trend option generates larger shares for *meat products, alcoholic drinks* and *soft drinks*, and lower shares for *carcase meat, fish, dairy products, eggs* and *fresh milk*. The average change in budget shares would be 0.66 percentage points by the year 2000 in this scenario. In the 1991 price scenario an average change of 0.53 percentage points in the budget shares is projected. In absolute terms, the largest increases in budget shares are to be found for *meat products* and *alcoholic drinks*. Compared to the other scenarios, the 1991 price scenario yields low budget shares for *carcase meat* and *vegetablia*.

Compared with the other scenarios, the 1960-91 trend scenario generates the smallest changes in the consumption patterns by the year 2000, *vegetablia* having a relatively high budget share and *hot drinks* a low one .

Under the 1991 price scenario, *food-at-home* will take 22 percent of the consumers' budget[5] during the whole forecasting period. Under the 1960-91 trend scenario, however, the allocation of *food-at-home* will start to decline in 1995, and end up at 20 percent in the year 2000. Similar developments can be seen for the 1980-91 trend and structural change scenarios, leading to shares of 19 and 18 percent respectively in the year 2000.

Looking at Figure 2, we can see that the combined consumption of food (*i.e.*, *food-at-home* and *restaurants and cafés*) took 28 percent of Finnish consumers' budget in 1991. The 1991 price scenario implies a gradual rise in the budget share, while other scenarios imply a gradual decline during the last half of the 1990's. The predicted shares in 2000 are between 27 percent (the structural change scenario) and 30 percent (the 1991 price scenario).

The budget share of *food-at-home excluding alcoholic drinks* is predicted to increase, or remain the same, during the first half of the 1990's, and to gradually decline thereafter. The resulting budget shares in 2000 are between 14 percent (the structural change scenario) and 17 percent (the 1991 price scenario). Expenditure on *restaurants and cafés* is predicted to be more or less the same for all scenarios, with a predicted budget share of 9 percent in 2000.

---

[5] The budget shares of *food-at-home* and *restaurants and cafés* are related to *total private consumption* (including *durables* and *semi-durables*). For that purpose, a projection of the development of *total private consumption* has to be made over the forecasting period. The changes are assumed to be equal to the changes in *private consumption* (excluding *durables* and *semi-durables*). There was one exception: in 1992, the actual recorded decrease in total expenditure of 5.7% has been used (instead of the forecasted 2.5%).

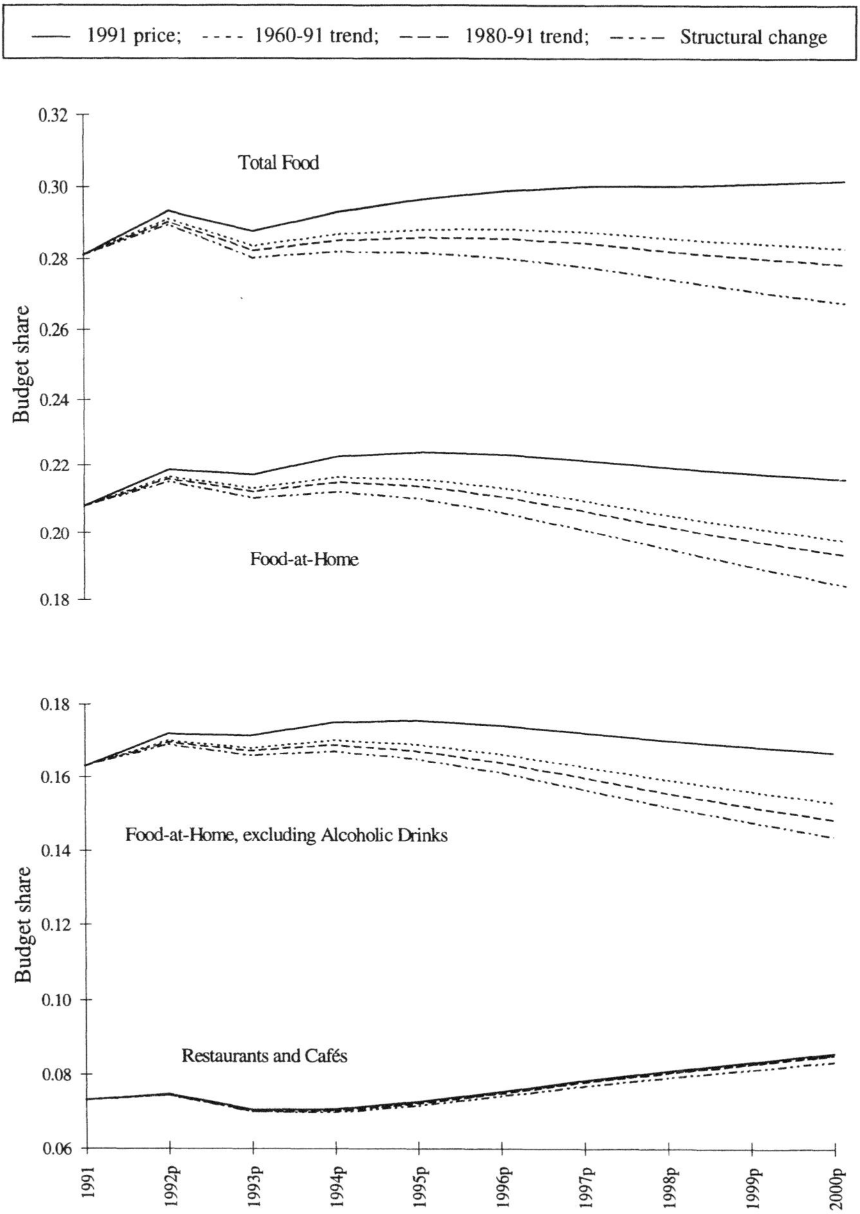

Note that (i) the abbreviation p denotes projections, and (ii) all expenditures are related to total private consumption (including durables and semi-durables).

Figure 2. Finnish Actual and Projected Budget Shares

8.6 CONCLUSIONS

The Finnish projections are sensitive to the choice of scenario concerning alternative price developments. The greatest variations in the projected volumes for the year 2000 are found for *meat products, fish, soft drinks* and *restaurants and cafés*, where the differences between the lowest and highest forecasts are 16 to 44 percent. In *food-at-home, animalia, dairy products, sugar and confectionery* and *vegetablia* these differences are 6 percent or less. The 1980-91 trend scenario generated the lowest forecasts in 10 of the 16 cases, whereas the 1991 price scenario generated the highest forecast in 13 of the 16 cases (see Table 8).

The 1991 price scenario implies that the *per capita* consumption of *meat products, alcoholic drinks, soft drinks, sugar and confectionery* and *restaurants and cafés* will increasesubstantially by the year 2000, whilst the consumption of *fresh milk* and *dairy products* will remain unchanged. The 1960-91 trend scenario implies that the *per capita* consumption of *meat products* and *fish* will increase substantially, whilst the consumption of *carcase meat, dairy products* and *soft drinks* will decrease. The 1980-91 trend scenario implies that the *per capita* consumption of *meat products* and *fish* will increase substantially, whilst the consumption of *carcase meat, dairy products, eggs, fresh milk, soft drinks* and *hot drinks* will decrease.

Finally, the structural change scenario implies that the *per capita* consumption of *sugar and confectionery* and *restaurants and cafés* will increase substantially, whilst the consumption of *soft drinks* and *vegetablia* will remain unchanged.

Table 8. Projected Per Capita Real Expenditure in 2000 (index: 1991 = 100)

Category	Lowest forecast	Highest forecast	Price option that generated lowest forecast	highest forecast
Food-at-Home	104	109	1980-91 trend	1991 price
- Animalia	105	109	Structural change	1991 price
- Meat and Fish	106	114	Structural change	1991 price
- Meat Products	109	125	Structural change	1991 price
- Carcase Meat	90	102	1980-91 trend	1991 price, structural change
- Fish	102	146	1991 price	1980-91 trend
- Dairy Products	98	103	1980-91 trend	Structural change
- Eggs	98	110	1980-91 trend	1991 price
- Beverages	101	112	1980-91 trend	1991 price
- Alcoholic Drinks	105	117	1980-91 trend	1991 price
- Fresh Milk	96	108	1980-91 trend	Structural change
- Soft Drinks	96	113	1960-91 trend	1991 price
- Hot Drinks	95	104	1980-91 trend	1991 price
- Sugar and Confectionery	106	112	1980-91 trend	1991 price
- Vegetablia	100	104	Structural change	1991 price
Restaurants and Cafés	102	121	1980-91 trend	1991 price

Table 9. Classification of Projected Changes in Per Capita Food Consumption

	Price option			
	1991 price	1960-91 trend	1980-91 trend	Structural change
Real expenditure projected to increase by 5 percent or more from 1991 to 2000	Meat Products Eggs Alcoholic Drinks Soft Drinks Sugar and Confectionery Restaurants and Cafés	Meat Products Fish Eggs Alcoholic Drinks Fresh Milk Sugar and Confectionery Restaurants and Cafés	Meat Products Fish Alcoholic Drinks Sugar and Confectionery	Meat Products Alcoholic Drinks Fresh Milk Sugar and Confectionery Restaurants and Cafés
Real expenditure projected to decrease by 2 percent or more from 1991 to 2000		Carcase Meat Soft Drinks	Carcase Meat Dairy Products Eggs Fresh Milk Soft Drinks Hot Drinks	

From Table 9 we can see that the projected *per capita* consumption of *meat products, alcoholic drinks* and *sugar and confectionery* increase by at least 5 percent until the year 2000 under all scenarios, while the projected consumption of *carcase meat, dairy products, hot drinks* and *vegetablia* did not increase by as much as 5 percent in any scenario.

The projections of the endogenous variables depend critically on the functional form and its specification (*e.g.*, which variables are included and what separability structure is used), the parameter estimates of the model and the projections of the exogenous variables. The procedure presented in the present chapter should be repeated regularly if up-to-date projections are required. In the short-run, new information concerning price developments, total expenditures and population growth may give rise to more exact forecasts. As consumer behaviour changes over time, new data will appear that allows the parameter estimates to be updated. In the long-run, the models also need to be respecified.

9

HOUSEHOLD AND AGGREGATE TIME-SERIES DATA

by Kyrre Rickertsen and Per Halvor Vale*

9.1 INTRODUCTION

The two most readily accessible data types for demand analyses are time-series and cross-sectional data. In this chapter, both data types are used to study Norwegian demand.

Cross-sectional and time-series data have several important differences. Firstly, the level of aggregation across consumers is different. The behaviour of (representative) households is measured by cross-sectional data while the behaviour of a market is measured by aggregate time-series data. Secondly, several aspects related to the time dimension are different. The period spanned by the data is, in general, longer for time-series data. Furthermore, each observation period is frequently longer. The observation period is also identical to the time interval between observations for time-series data while this is not necessarily the case for cross-sectional data. Thirdly, both data types have several specific statistical problems. Each of these differences may affect the interpretation of the estimation results.

The objectives of this chapter are twofold. Firstly, the effects of data type on the rejection rates of the testable restrictions of consumer theory is investigated. The constrained utility maximisation hypothesis implies certain restrictions on the estimated demand functions, as discussed in Chapter 3. These restrictions are, in principle, valid for one consumer. Both time-series and household budget data imply aggregation over consumers. In demand studies applying household data, the "consumer" is typically interpreted as the "household". This is assumed to act as a single rational decision unit, and conflicts and bargaining processes within the household is neglected. In demand studies applying aggregate market data, aggregation over consumers is typically completely neglected and the "representative consumer" argument is used. Neither of these assumptions are trivial, and both are frequently discussed in the literature, see for example Kirman (1992) and Stoker (1993). However, their empirical importance has not been investigated to any great extent. To study some implications for a typical demand study, we test the homo-

* Along with the other authors of this book, we would like to thank Michael Farmer for helpful comments in the preparation of this chapter.

geneity and symmetry restrictions at different levels of aggregation.

Secondly, some relationships between the numerical values of elasticities obtained by using the two data types are discussed. The parameters estimated in a demand study are usually used to calculate elasticities, which in turn are frequently used for forecasting demand and for policy decisions. The interpretation of the calculated elasticities is therefore very important. Furthermore, the distinction between the two data types is important when comparing different estimates with each other. There is usually no discussion, however, about the implications of the use of various data types in applied work.

Our time-series data is described in Chapter 2, although it should be noted that data from the period 1960 to 1991 was used in this chapter. The household data was collected as repeated cross-sections over the period 1982 to 1988. Each year, approximately 1500 households kept accounts of their expenses over a two-week period. Furthermore, expenses on durables during the last year were recorded in interviews. For each household, information about the quantities purchased of various goods and the corresponding expenditures were also collected. By dividing expenditure with quantity the implicit price per unit is obtained. The household data was collected evenly throughout the year.

The outline of this chapter is as follows. The restrictions in demand systems are discussed in Section 2 while factors affecting the values of elasticities are analysed in more detail in Section 3. Aggregation over individuals (households) in the almost ideal model and our empirical implementation are presented in Section 4. Finally, the empirical results are discussed in Section 5.

9.2 RESTRICTIONS IN DEMAND SYSTEMS

Restrictions concerning adding up, homogeneity of degree zero, symmetry and negativity must hold for any plausible demand system. Homogeneity and symmetry are tested in many studies and the hypotheses are frequently rejected. However, the rejections do not necessarily imply any rejection of the utility maximisation model. This is because the tested hypotheses are composite hypotheses, where aggregation over consumers, selected functional form, selected dynamic specification and separability assumptions all affect the results of the tests. For example, it is not *a priori* given that homogeneity or symmetry will hold for multi-person households or aggregate market data. Furthermore, the choice of functional form may be critical for the results obtained for a given data set, as discussed by Alston and Chalfant (1991a, 1991b). A dynamic specification may also be desirable when using time-series data as emphasised by Anderson and Blundell (1983). Finally, inappropriate use of asymptotically valid test criteria may cause rejections. However, Deaton (1986, p. 1794) concluded that "my reading of the literature is that the rejection of homogeneity in practice tends to be confirmed using exact tests and is not a statistical illusion based on the use of inappropriate asymptotics".

We will investigate the importance of aggregation level by testing for homogeneity and symmetry for single-person households, multi-person households, all households and aggregate market data. Moreover, the importance of dynamics is investigated for our time-series data. Rejections are expected to be more frequent for multi-person households and market level data than for single-person households.

9.3 ELASTICITIES AND THE TIME DIMENSION

9.3.1 The Conventional Interpretation of Time-series and Cross-sectional Elasticities

Time-series data measure variation in demand over time when average income and prices vary. Cross-sectional data measure variation in demand across consuming units with different incomes and facing varying prices within one period.

The difference in source of variation has frequently lead to two propositions, which are important for the interpretation of the elasticities. The first proposition is that time-series are interpreted as if they reflect short-run behaviour while cross-sections are interpreted as if they reflect long-run equilibrium behaviour. The second proposition is that the quantities of goods are treated as homogeneous over time in time-series, while the prices are treated as homogeneous at a point of time in cross-sections. This implies that there is no assumed change in (average) product quality over time and no price variation (for a given quality of a product) at a point of time.

The first proposition implies that elasticities estimated by using time-series data are interpreted as short-run while income elasticities estimated by cross-sectional data tend to be interpreted as long-run (*e.g.*, Kuh and Meyer (1957), George and King (1971) and Buse (1992, p. 149)). This long-run interpretation is based on the assumption that the majority of observed families have enjoyed their present income for some time. Given a stable aggregate income and only minor changes in income distribution prior to a cross-section survey, this assumption is reasonable. However, major fluctuations in aggregate income or changes in income distribution in the period(s) before the survey will cause the households to be in disequilibrium and the elasticities to be short-run of nature. The fluctuations in aggregate income (expenditure) were considerable during the 1980's. This is evident from Figure 1 that shows aggregate household consumption expenditure deflated by the consumer price index.

The second proposition implies that all cross-sectional price variation is interpreted as reflecting quality differences, which should be corrected for prior to estimation (*e.g.*, George and King (1971)). Consequently, there are no price elasticities to estimate. However, there are sources of price variation other than heterogeneous goods. Price variation may be the effect of regional and seasonal price variations or

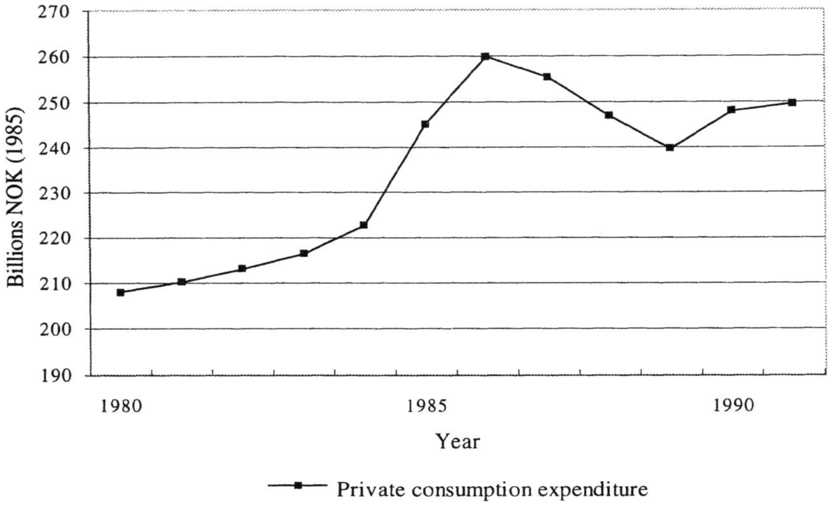

Figure 1. Norwegian Household Consumption Expenditure

different food pricing strategies for different types of stores. Cox and Wohlgenant (1986) used this argument to estimate price elasticities based on one expenditure survey. The relevance of the estimated price elasticities will, however, depend on the cause of price variation. Changes in demand caused by price variation of heterogeneous goods or different services purchased with the good are primarily of interest for the food processing and retailing industries and of little interest at the farm gate.

9.3.2 Observation Period and Average Interval Between Observations

The length of observation period and the interval between observations may be important for the calculated values of elasticities. As mentioned above, the observation period is identical to the interval between observations for time-series data. This is not necessarily the case for cross-sections, and especially not so for repeated cross-sections.

Consider a good which can be stored from one observation period to the next period without any reduction in quality (*e.g.*, wine). If the consumer expects price fluctuations for that good between the periods, then the intertemporal substitution will result in larger absolute values of short-run own-price elasticities than those of the long-run elasticities (see Pasour and Schrimper (1965) and Wohlgenant and Hahn (1982)). For example, given that the current price of wine is different from the expected price of wine, it will be profitable for the consumer to change his stock of wine. Given a short observation period, as for household data, many goods are suitable for storage over at least one observation period. The quantity effect of a given price change will thus be larger than those observed for annual time-series data.

On the other hand, a habit persistence hypothesis suggests that the desire for specific foodstuffs develop over a long period, and will not adjust completely, in the short-run, to current changes in income and prices (*e.g.*, Deaton and Muelbauer (1980a, pp. 373-377)). Habit persistence suggests that the absolute values of both own-price and income elasticities are larger in the long-run than in the short-run. This implies relatively larger elasticities with increasing period between observations. The average interval between each observation is about two and a half years for our household data that is randomly organised with respect to time.

Given the above arguments, the absolute values of own-price elasticities are expected to be U-shaped over time (see Manderscheid (1964), Pasour and Schrimper (1965), Wohlgenant and Hahn (1982) and Capps and Nayga (1990)) while income elasticities are expected to be relatively more elastic in the long-run than the short-run (see Kuh and Meyer (1957) and Houthakker and Taylor (1970)).

The hypothesised developments in values over time are shown in Figure 2. Let A and B denote two observations. Let the price of the observed good and the expenditure of the consumer both change at time A. The expenditure and own-price elasticities reach their new equilibrium simultaneously in the figure at time B. If the interval between the observations is shorter than the interval from A to B, then the

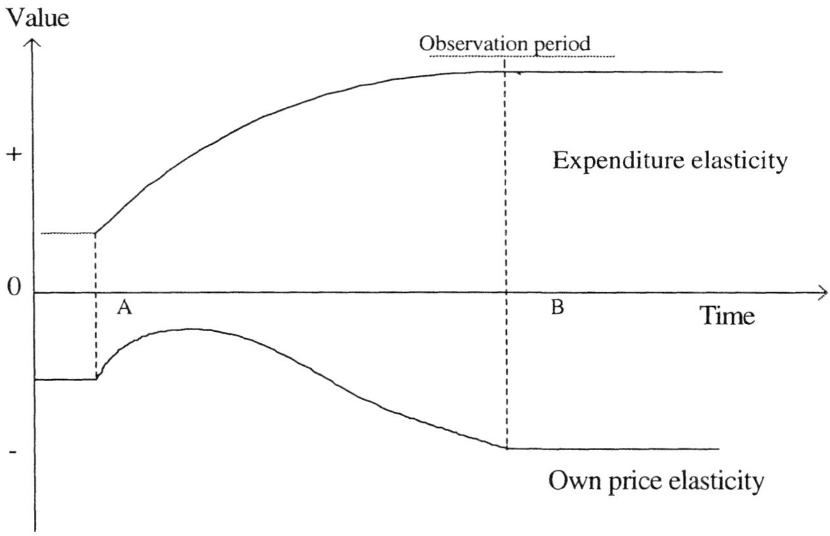

Figure 2. Elasticities Over Time

observed values will represent different short-run elasticities.

There has been a substantial increase in the number of goods available to the consumer over the past thirty years, and the consumption possibility set has expanded. In contrast, the set is relatively fixed for our cross-sectional data. Under the strong assumption that the expenditure on new goods accounts for an identical proportion of the commodity group under study as the expenditure on excluded goods, then the group expenditure elasticity obtained from a time-series will not, on average, be different from that obtained from a cross-section. The expenditure and price elasticities for any single good can be affected in either direction, however.

We do not, in general, know whether time-series or cross-sectional elasticities are most long-run in nature. It all depends on the specific data sets and it largely remains an empirical question. However, the brief observation period and relatively large average interval between observations, in our household data set, both suggest more elastic own-price elasticities for the household data.

We will estimate the price and expenditure elasticities using the almost ideal model. We assume homogeneous goods, *i.e.*, there is only one quality of goods at a point of time and over time. This assumption is made because we do not have any satisfactory variable measuring either quality changes or differences. Moreover, homogeneous goods are usually assumed in time-series studies and the effects of quality adjustments may be minor for cross-sectional data. For example, Cox and Wohlgenant (1986, p. 908) suggested that "parameter differences resulting from a failure to adjust cross-sectional prices for quality effects are likely to be small for relatively homogeneous, disaggregate food commodities."

9.4 AGGREGATION IN THE ALMOST IDEAL MODEL

According to Deaton and Muellbauer (1980b, p.314), the almost ideal demand system is based on a household expenditure function.[1] Exact nonlinear aggregation is applicable if individual household behaviour is described by

$$w_{ih} = \alpha_i + \sum_j \gamma_{ij} \ln p_j + \beta_i (\ln x_h - \ln k_h - \ln P), \tag{1}$$

where x_h is the hth household's expenditure on all goods included in the system. The variable k_h is a household specific expenditure deflator that can take account of age composition, economies of household size and other household characteristics. It further allows a limited taste variation across households. Given that there is price variation across households, equation (1) may be rewritten as

$$w_{ih} = \alpha_i + \sum_j \gamma_{ij} \ln p_{jh} + \beta_i (\ln x_h - \ln k_h - \ln P_h), \tag{2}$$

[1] This implies that Deaton and Muellbauer assume aggregation across household members to be of minor importance.

where the price index $\ln P_h$ is given either by the nonlinear price index (4.2b) or by Stone's approximate price index

$$\ln P_h = \sum_j w_{jh} \ln p_{jh}. \tag{3}$$

We use the linear form of the model, with Stone's index (*i.e.*, LAIDS), in this chapter.

The aggregate budget share of the ith good, (W_i) is defined in terms of the aggregate expenditure of all households (X), that is

$$W_i = \frac{\sum_h p_{ih} q_{ih}}{\sum_h x_h} = \frac{\sum_h w_{ih} x_h}{X}, \tag{4}$$

where q_{ih} is the hth household's consumption of the ith good. Substituting equation (2) into (4) yields the aggregate budget shares in terms of the micro variables, namely

$$W_i = \alpha_i + \frac{1}{X}\left[\sum_{h=1}^{H}\sum_{j=1}^{n} \gamma_{ij} x_h \ln p_{jh} + \beta_i \left(\sum_{h=1}^{H} x_h \ln x_h - \sum_{h=1}^{H} x_h \ln k_h - \sum_{h=1}^{H} x_h \ln P_h\right)\right]. \tag{5}$$

Accurate measurement of k_h is very difficult, and this variable must be approximated in empirical implementations. We use the following commonly applied procedure, which is outlined in Deaton and Muellbauer (1980a, p.195). A reference household, r, consisting of one adult and no children is selected, and the average expenditure of single adult households, x_r, is used as the corresponding reference expenditure. The variable k_h is calculated as

$$k_h = x_h / x_r = 1 + \sum_i \phi_i a_i, \tag{6}$$

where the a_i's are the number of additional household members in certain specified categories (such as adults, adolescents and children).

Following Chalfant's (1987) frequently used approximation, we assume that the budget shares are not affected by price changes, *i.e.*, $\partial w_j / \partial \ln p_j = 0$. The aggregate price elasticities, E_{ij}, are thus given as

$$E_{ij} = \frac{\gamma_{ij} - \beta_i W_j}{W_i} - \delta_{ij}, \tag{7}$$

where δ_{ij} is Kronecker's delta, equal to one when $i = j$ and zero elsewhere, and where it is assumed that price changes are proportional across households, such that the total partial derivatives $\partial p_{ih} / \partial p_i = p_{ih} / p_i$.

The aggregate expenditure elasticity for the ith good, E_i^*, is calculated as

$$E_i^* = 1 + \frac{\beta_i}{W_i}, \tag{8}$$

where it is assumed that expenditure changes are proportional across households, such that $\partial x_h / \partial X = x_h / X$. The parameters γ_{ij} and β_i are estimated using equation (2), and the W_i's are the predicted aggregate budget shares calculated using equation (4).

9.4.1 Empirical Implementation

The LAIDS model is used for both data sets. This version is selected to ease the computational burden for the household data while compatibility over the two data types is maintained. Both the static, (4.2a) and (4.4), and dynamic specifications, (4.10a) and (4.4), are estimated for the time-series data, whilst the static specification (2) and (3) is used for the cross-sectional data. The elasticities are calculated, for the appropriately defined budget shares, by using formulae (7) and (8).

Homogeneity and symmetry are tested for both data sets. We do not imposed the restrictions when computing the elasticities, however, since if the restrictions are valid the estimates will be almost identical for the restricted and unrestricted specifications. In this case there is therefore nothing to be gained by imposing homogeneity and symmetry. On the other hand, if the restrictions are not valid, then imposing them will lead to incorrect estimation of the parameters.

It is desirable to use the same commodity partitioning for both data sets, and the utility tree shown in Figure 3 is thus used in both cases. There are four major differences between this partition and the partition described in Figure 2.1. Firstly,

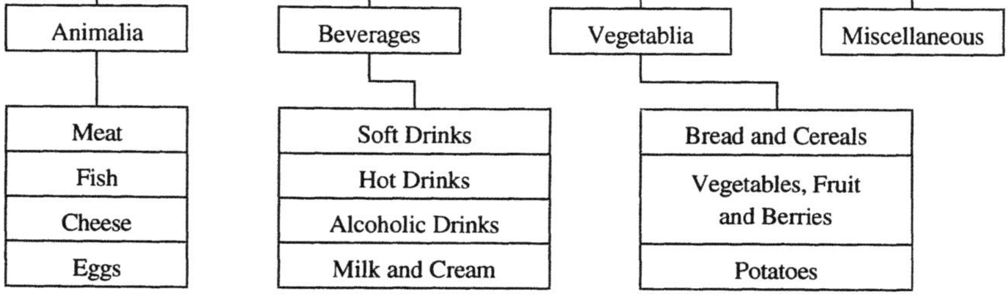

Figure 3. Commodity Partitioning

durables and semi durables are included in *private consumption*, this approach being dictated by the available commodity specification in the household data. Secondly, *expenses at restaurants* are included in *other goods and services*. Thirdly, *milk and cream* is included in the group *beverages* and not in *animalia*. Fourthly, the group *miscellaneous* is not estimated.

After some experimentation, three groups of additional household members were defined in equation (6); a_1 is the number of children aged zero to six years, a_2 is the number of children aged seven to seventeen years and a_3 is the number of additional adults.

In many of the sampled households we observe at least one good with zero purchase during the period of observation. Assuming that the cumulative probability of market participation is one, and that the most important reason for the observed zero purchase is the brief observation period, then the parameter estimates of a censored normal Tobit-model may be approximated by adjusting the OLS estimator so that

$$\hat{\beta} = \frac{m}{n} \hat{\beta}^{OLS}, \tag{9}$$

where n is the total number of households, m is the number of households with non-zero purchases in the given subsystem and $\hat{\beta}^{OLS}$ is the OLS estimate from the non-zero purchase observations. This procedure was selected after some experimentation with Heckman's two-stage procedure, which yielded very similar results.[2]

The model for time-series data is estimated in TSP version 4.2 as described in Chapter 4. The model for household data is estimated in the SAS programme, version 6.0. Seemingly unrelated regressions (SUR) was used in both cases

9.5 EMPIRICAL RESULTS

9.5.1 Goodness-of-Fit and Misspecification Tests

Parameter estimates, goodness of fit measures and the results of our diagnostic testing are not presented in any detail here due to space limitations, but may be found in Rickertsen (1994) and Vale (1995). A short summary is in order, however.

The goodness of fit is high for the time-series data. The systemwise R^2-values are above 0.9 for all the dynamic subsystems, and 10 percent or more of the unexplained variation in the static specification, adjusted for the degrees of freedom, is explained by the dynamic specification for four of the subsystems. The standardised standard errors of the regression are also below 4 percent in each equation, except for *potatoes*. The hypothesis of no autocorrelation is not rejected, except at stage one and for *potatoes*, in the dynamic specification. Durables represent a major

---

[2] See Heckman (1979) and Vale (1995).

theoretical problem at stage one, however. In the static specification, autocorrelation is especially prevalent for the *foodstuffs-at-home* and the *animalia* group, and significant results are found in six equations. Significant functional misspecification is found in two of the dynamic equations and in six of the static equations.

The R^2-values lie in the interval 0.05 to 0.37 for the household data. Such low R^2-values are not unusual, however, in studies at the household level. Furthermore, there are some problems regarding heteroscedasticity.

9.5.2 Tests of Homogeneity, Symmetry and No Dynamics

Our tests of restrictions are based on the F-statistic of the exact LRT given in Chapter 4 For the time-series data the SUR estimates of the household data an approximate F-test using sums of squares is used, see Greene (1993 p. 491). The probabilities of rejecting the null hypotheses given that they are true (the P-values) are reported in Tables 1 and 2. A given hypothesis is rejected at the 5 percent significance level, which is the level used in this chapter, if the P-value is below 0.05.

In Table 1 P-values for the test of homogeneity restrictions for the household and time-series data are reported. In addition, results for the hypothesis of no dynamics for the time-series data are reported in the column "No dynamics" in the table. The static model is rejected for three of the five subsystems. In the first stage, however, the dynamic specification represents no improvement compared to the

Table 1. Tests of the Homogeneity and No Dynamics Restrictions, P-Values

	Household data			Time-series data		
	Single-person households	Multi-person households	All households	Static	Dynamic	No dynamics
Private consumption	0.000	0.000	0.000	0.000	0.011	0.774
Food-at-home	0.000	0.000	0.000	0.001	0.001	0.029
Animalia	0.103	0.000	0.000	0.610	0.392	0.000
Beverages	0.513	0.000	0.000	0.001	0.002	0.015
Vegetablia	0.243	0.000	0.000	0.000	0.000	0.088

Table 2. Tests of the Symmetry Restriction, P-Values

	Household data			Time-series data	
	Single-person household	Multi-person household	All households	Static	Dynamic
Private consumption	0.000	0.000	0.000	0.000	0.011
Food-at-home	0.000	0.000	0.000	0.000	0.000
Animalia	0.004	0.000	0.000	0.002	0.103
Beverages	0.339	0.000	0.000	0.000	0.000
Vegetablia	0.067	0.000	0.000	0.000	0.000

static.

Furthermore, the aggregation from single-person to multi-person households causes homogeneity rejections. Homogeneity is not rejected for the single-person households in any of the groups *animalia*, *beverages* and *vegetablia*. However, homogeneity is rejected in each subsystem for the multi-person households and for the aggregate of all households. The time-series data represents a small improvement as compared with the aggregate household data and homogeneity is rejected in four of the groups. The dynamic specification does not improve the results regarding homogeneity.

The results in Table 2 show a similar pattern. The intra-household aggregation seems to cause rejections of symmetry. The aggregate time-series data with a dynamic specification fares somewhat better. Given the evidence in Tables 1 and 2, we conclude that the interpretation of a "household" as a "consumer" seems to cause rejections of the consumer theory.

The high rejection rates for the aggregate time-series data are not surprising, and are in line with most other studies, see Deaton and Muellbauer (1980a, pp. 67-80) and Johnson *et al.* (1986, pp. 13-16) for surveys of corresponding results. However, our results suggest that there is more than an aggregation problem behind the frequent rejections.

Negativity requires negative semidefiniteness of the Slutsky matrix. A necessary condition for negativity is that the diagonal terms of this matrix are negative. We checked for positive diagonal terms at the mean values. Violations of negativity occur in three of the 17 static equations, while no violations are detected in the dynamic specification of the time-series data, *i.e.*, the inclusion of dynamics represents a small improvement. Negativity was further checked for the aggregate of all households, and no breaks were detected.

9.5.3 Elasticities

The numerical values of within group elasticities and their standard errors are shown in Table 3, where the elasticities are calculated at the mean values of the input variables. It is important when interpreting the results to remember that quantities are measured as values in both data sets, and that they therefore include the effects of quality changes, such as shifts from low to high processed foodstuffs. For example, the data allows for the possibility that highly processed foods may be increasing the expenditure of total food consumption, although in some instances the quantity of food actually purchased may be decreasing. This may be viewed as either an advantage or disadvantage, depending on what part of the food chain one is primarily focusing on.

The elasticities are, in general, of reasonable magnitudes for the household data and, in the dynamic specification, also for the time-series data. One exception is the negative expenditure elasticity of *hot drinks*. This is not significantly different from zero, however, and furthermore, such factors as increased health concerns may

Table 3. Norwegian Within Group Own-Price and Expenditure Elasticities

	Own-Price Elasticities			Expenditure Elasticities		
	House-hold	Market Static	Market Dynamic	House-hold	Market Static	Market Dynamic
Other goods and services	−1.34	−0.94	−0.94	1.13	1.11	1.10
	0.01	*0.04*	*0.04*	*0.01*	*0.01*	*0.02*
Food and beverages at-home	−0.65	−0.58	−0.55	0.42	0.69	0.67
	0.05	*0.08*	*0.10*	*0.02*	*0.04*	*0.06*
Animalia	−0.94	−0.84	−0.94	1.05	1.11	1.18
	0.02	*0.17*	*0.15*	*0.01*	*0.11*	*0.17*
Meat	−1.20	−1.18	−1.10	1.24	1.67	1.11
	0.02	*0.22*	*0.09*	*0.01*	*0.11*	*0.08*
Fish	−1.00	−0.26	−0.75	0.91	−0.39	0.87
	0.03	*0.31*	*0.11*	*0.02*	*0.30*	*0.21*
Cheese	−0.78	−0.57	−0.91	0.44	−0.12	0.64
	0.06	*0.09*	*0.11*	*0.02*	*0.23*	*0.27*
Eggs	−0.90	0.01	−0.21	0.16	0.19	0.92
	0.08	*0.19*	*0.20*	*0.10*	*0.24*	*0.20*
Beverages	−0.50	−0.83	−0.86	0.94	1.48	1.26
	0.01	*0.08*	*0.12*	*0.03*	*0.12*	*0.16*
Soft drinks	−1.03	−0.70	−0.77	0.98	1.44	1.19
	0.02	*0.24*	*0.21*	*0.06*	*0.13*	*0.25*
Hot drinks	−0.94	−0.22	−0.19	0.53	−0.02	−0.11
	0.03	*0.05*	*0.08*	*0.02*	*0.19*	*0.26*
Alcoholic drinks	−0.89	−1.14	−1.06	1.09	1.63	1.51
	0.07	*0.07*	*0.06*	*0.05*	*0.05*	*0.07*
Milk and cream	−0.77	−0.10	−0.33	0.77	0.22	0.63
	0.05	*0.07*	*0.07*	*0.04*	*0.09*	*0.11*
Vegetablia	−0.90	−0.91	−0.94	1.00	0.49	0.59
	0.01	*0.08*	*0.08*	*0.02*	*0.07*	*0.10*
Bread and cereals	−0.91	−0.21	−0.59	0.94	0.65	0.86
	0.01	*0.10*	*0.11*	*0.01*	*0.26*	*0.14*
Vegetables, fruit, *etc.*	−0.98	−0.69	−0.86	1.05	1.36	1.18
	0.01	*0.17*	*0.20*	*0.01*	*0.23*	*0.13*
Potatoes	−0.96	−0.54	−0.53	0.23	−0.30	0.09
	0.05	*0.10*	*0.11*	*0.04*	*0.69*	*0.56*
Miscellaneous	−0.90	−0.26	−0.28	1.01	0.51	0.67
	0.01	*0.05*	*0.06*	*0.12*	*0.12*	*0.17*

Elasticities are given in large plain text and standard errors are given in small italics.

cause, for example, the demand for coffee to appear to be more inelastic than it is in reality.

There are several less intuitive elasticities in the static specification as applied on the market data. The expenditure elasticities for *fish, cheese, hot drinks* and *potatoes* are negative and the own-price elasticity for *eggs* is positive. Consequently, we concentrate on the comparison between the household data and the dynamic specification for the market data.

As discussed above, the brief observation period and relatively long average interval between observations, both suggest relatively more elastic own-price elasticities for the household data. This is because we believe that food and beverages, and especially basic foodstuffs, are habit forming. Most foodstuffs are also storable for some time. This hypothesis is confirmed, the own-price elasticities being relatively more elastic for 12 of the 17 goods. For three of the remaining goods the deviations are less than two standard errors (of the dynamic estimate).

The only surprising results for the group *beverages* and for *alcoholic drinks* are that the market elasticities are relatively more price elastic. However, it is important to note, that because of state regulation only small price fluctuations have taken place for alcohol, and the incentives for speculative inventory demand are removed. Furthermore, zero purchases and the corresponding parameter adjustment represent a special problem for alcoholic drinks. This because the approximation (9) relies on the assumption that zero purchases are due to the short survey period of two weeks. This is not completely true for alcoholic drinks, since 30 percent of households never consume alcohol. Finally, alcohol purchases may be underreported in the household data.

The own-price elasticities for the household data are substantially (more than two standard errors) more elastic for *other goods and services, fish, eggs, soft drinks, hot drinks, milk, bread, potatoes* and *miscellaneous. Other goods, hot drinks, potatoes* and *miscellaneous* (sugar, fats, etc) are commodities that are particularly well suited for storage, and the price fluctuations over time are considerable for these goods, see Rickertsen (1990). *Milk* and *bread* are basic foods in Norway, and it is reasonable to expect a rather strong habit persistence for these goods. The large effects for *eggs* and *fish* are more surprising, although, *eggs* and (frozen) *fish* may be stored from one two-week period to the next.

As discussed above, it is impossible to assign any *a priori* relationships for the expenditure elasticities because of the large expenditure fluctuations in the 1980's. The expenditure elasticities for the household data are relatively more *inelastic* for eight and more *elastic* for nine of the goods. The differences in values are more than two standard errors for five of the goods.

Given the different commodity grouping and observation period in this chapter, differences from the previously reported elasticities are to be expected, and this is indeed the case. The own-price and expenditure elasticities for *food and beverages at-home*, reported in Table 3, are –0.55 and 0.67. The corresponding values reported in Chapter 5 were –0.34 and 0.78. These differences have consequences for the values of the total elasticities that are shown in Table 4. It may be noted that the total expenditure elasticities are identical to the expenditure elasticities, given our commodity partitioning. The total elasticities are calculated at the mean values of the input variables and according to the procedure outlined in Chapter 4.2.4.

The correction from within group to total own-price elasticities reinforces to some extent the differences between the household and market data. Furthermore, it

Table 4. Norwegian Total Own-Price and Expenditure Elasticities

	Own-Price Elasticities			Expenditure Elasticities		
	House-hold	Market Static	Market Dynamic	House-hold	Market Static	Market Dynamic
Other goods and services	−1.34	−0.94	−0.94	1.13	1.11	1.10
Food and beverages at-home	−0.65	−0.58	−0.55	0.42	0.69	0.67
Animalia	−0.79	−0.67	−0.75	0.44	0.77	0.79
Meat	−0.86	−0.81	−0.93	0.55	1.28	0.88
Fish	−0.92	−0.28	−0.70	0.40	−0.30	0.69
Cheese	−0.73	−0.57	−0.89	0.19	−0.09	0.51
Eggs	−0.78	0.01	−0.20	0.07	0.15	0.73
Beverages	−0.36	−0.66	−0.69	0.40	1.02	0.84
Soft drinks	−0.95	−0.62	−0.72	0.39	1.47	1.00
Hot drinks	−0.89	−0.22	−0.19	0.21	−0.02	−0.09
Alcoholic drinks	−0.76	−0.86	−0.85	0.43	1.66	1.27
Milk and cream	−0.62	−0.08	−0.28	0.30	0.22	0.53
Vegetablia	−0.80	−0.87	−0.88	0.42	0.34	0.40
Bread and cereals	−0.74	−0.18	−0.55	0.40	0.22	0.34
Vegetables, fruit, *etc.*	−0.84	−0.59	−0.78	0.44	0.46	0.47
Potatoes	−0.86	−0.54	−0.52	0.10	−0.10	0.04
Miscellaneous	−0.87	−0.24	−0.24	0.42	0.35	0.45

may be noted that demand is inelastic with respect to prices for all goods for the market data. The pattern for the total expenditure elasticities is more unambiguous than for the within group expenditure elasticities. The expenditure elasticities estimated by the household data are relatively more inelastic for twelve of the goods. For four of the remaining goods there are only minor differences. The only exception is *hot drinks*, however, the expenditure elasticity is highly inelastic for both data sets.

Most of the values are reasonably close to those reported in Chapter 6.6, but a few differences are noticeable. Firstly, the own-price elasticities of *meat* and *vegetables, fruit and berries* are more price elastic in the current commodity partitioning. This is related to the more price elastic demand for *food and beverages-at-home* in this partitioning. Secondly, the expenditure elasticities of *cheese* and *alcoholic drinks* are substantially less elastic with respect to expenditure, as could be expected from the more inelastic expenditure elasticity for *food and beverages-at-home*.

9.6 CONCLUSIONS

A dynamic specification is superior to the static for the time-series data. It represents an improvement regarding specification and misspecification and for the intuitive appeal of the estimated elasticities.

Intra-household aggregation causes rejections of homogeneity and symmetry and the interpretation of a "household" as a "consumer" is questionable. The use of aggregate time-series data also causes rejections, although to somewhat less extent than in the multi-person households. The aggregation problem is evidently only one reason, however, and the rejections in single-person households must be explained in other ways. Our treatment of durables at stage one is probably too simplistic, our choices regarding functional form and separability may be incorrect and there may be measurement error in the data.

The values of the estimated elasticities are reasonable according to our hypotheses concerning stock behaviour and habits. The own-price elasticities for the household data are usually relative more elastic than the market data. Finally, the results contradict any long-run interpretation of expenditure elasticities estimated by our cross-sectional data, and a short-run interpretation is more plausible.

10

THE IMPORTANCE OF SOCIOECONOMIC VARIABLES

by Per Halvor Vale

10.1 INTRODUCTION

So far in the book, we have mainly estimated elasticities based on aggregate time-series data. In Chapter 9 we also applied household data, but the micro model used there only allowed a limited amount of taste variation across households. That model, for example, neglected any interaction between economic and socio-economic variables, and assumed identical marginal price responses, income responses and constant terms across the households.

In this chapter we estimate Norwegian elasticities at the household level, using a model characterised by a substantial amount of individual variation across the households. The purpose is to examine the assumption of identical marginal price and income responses across households, and to investigate potential problems related to the use of aggregate data or simplified micro-models.

10.2 THE MODEL

The model for the hth household is given by the following LAIDS demand system,

$$w_{ih} = \alpha_i^g + \sum_{j=1}^{n} \gamma_{ij}^g \ln p_{jh} + \beta_i^g (\ln x_h - \ln P_h) + \sum_{s=1}^{3} \phi_s^g d_s + \varepsilon_{ih}, \tag{1}$$

where w denotes the budget shares, p denotes prices, x denotes expenditure, d denotes a dummy variable representing seasonal effects, ε denotes a stochastic error term and P denotes Stone's approximate price index, where $\ln P_h$ is given by

$$\ln P_h = \sum_j w_{ih} \ln p_{jh}. \tag{2}$$

The subscripts of the variables are the same as defined in Chapter 9, while the superscript g $(= 1,\ldots, G)$ denotes specific household types.

Note that the households are grouped into G different household types. All the parameters in the demand equation are allowed to be group specific, and thus the values for each of the household types may be different from those of the other types. This implies that both price and income responses, as well as the constant term, are group specific. This technique gives a rather flexible demand system, capable of capturing household type heterogeneity. The advantage of this approach, as compared to the frequently applied techniques of scaling and translating, is that it is no longer necessary to apply a strict adult/children interpretation based on Barten's utility function, and one is free to include other socioeconomic dimensions. Note also the inclusion of three dummy variables, representing differences between the seasons.

10.3 EMPIRICAL RESULTS

10.3.1 Empirical Implementation

In applied demand analyses the most commonly used socioeconomic variables are : 1) the households' residential type (the rural/urban dimension), 2) the composition of the household members in terms of sex and age groups, 3) the number of household members, 4) the household member's family roles, *i.e.*, father, mother, *etc.* and 5) the occupation of the members of households (employee, employer, *etc.*). For more details see Salathe (1979), Sexauer (1979), Heien *et al.* (1989) and Blundell *et al.* (1993).

The household types used in this chapter are given in Table 1. The utility tree, estimation procedure and data are those described in Chapter 9.

10.3.2 Testing the Model for Misspecification

The model is tested at each of three stages of the utility tree, using the Jarque-Bera test to investigate non-normality of the error distribution and White's test to inves-

Table 1. Characteristics of the Household Types

Household type (g)	Adults	Children	Place of residence
1	2	No	Oslo, Bergen, Trondheim
2	2	No	Other urban areas
3	2	No	Rural areas
4	2	Yes	Oslo, Bergen, Trondheim
5	2	Yes	Other urban areas
6	2	Yes	Rural areas
7	1	No	Oslo, Bergen, Trondheim
8	1	No	Other urban areas
9	1	No	Rural areas

Oslo, Bergen and Trondheim are the three largest cities in Norway

Table 2. A Summary of the Test Results, 5 Percent Significance Level

		Stage 1	Stage 2	Stage 3	Total
Normality	Rejected	0	0	3	3
	Total	18	27	81	126
Homoscedasticitiy	Rejected	6	12	14	32
	Total	18	27	81	126

tigate homoscedasticity.[1] Table 2 shows the number of cases where the hypotheses of normal distribution and homoscedasticity are rejected at the 5 percent level. The model thus seems to be well specified in these respects.

10.3.3 Estimated Elasticities

The hypotheses of identical marginal price responses, identical marginal income (expenditure) responses and identical constant terms across households, are rejected. The urban/rural dimension, the number of household members and the demographic variables all affect these parameters.

The estimated within group own-price elasticities for the different household types can be found in Table 3. If we compare the elasticities for the different household types with those estimated for the first household type, we obtain the following results. At the first stage of the utility tree, the deviations of the elasticities are more than two standard errors of the first household type in nine cases (of 16). At stage two this occurs in eight (of 32) cases, while at stage three the differences are more than two standard errors in 21 (of 88) cases.

The within group expenditure elasticities are given in Table 4. Using the same procedure as for the price elasticities, we obtain the following results. At stage one of the utility tree the deviations of the elasticities are more than two standard errors of the first household type in three (of 16) cases, at the second stage this occurs in seven (of 32) cases, while at stage three the differences are more than two standard errors in 12 (of 88) cases.

Table 3 and 4 show that only a few commodities have the same elasticities across all household types, namely *miscellaneous* (fats and sugar, *etc.*), *eggs* and *potatoes*. For other commodities either the price elasticities, the expenditure elasticities or both of these differ by more than two standard errors for at least two household types.

The specific influence on consumption of rural residence, number of children and number of adults can be illustrated by moving from the first household type to the third, fourth and seventh household types, respectively. Compared with the first household type, the rural effects on consumption - other things equal - seem to give

[1] In White's test the squares and crossproducts of all the exogeneous variables are used in the auxiliary equation. The χ^2 versions of both tests are used.

Table 3. Norwegian Own-Price Elasticities for Different Household Types

	Within Group Elasticities for Household Type									Total
	1	2	3	4	5	6	7	8	9	
Food-at-home	–0.70	–0.85	–0.68	–0.66	–0.75	–0.93	–0.50	–0.99	–1.05	–0.73
	0.02	*0.01*	*0.02*	*0.02*	*0.01*	*0.02*	*0.02*	*0.01*	*0.02*	
Other products	–0.83	–0.82	–0.84	–0.85	–0.85	–0.68	–0.68	–0.92	–0.83	–0.84
	0.04	*0.02*	*0.03*	*0.03*	*0.03*	*0.02*	*0.02*	*0.03*	*0.02*	
Animalia	–0.82	–0.90	–1.05	–0.80	–0.94	–0.98	–0.83	–0.80	–0.87	–0.77
	0.01	*0.04*	*0.08*	*0.06*	*0.04*	*0.05*	*0.06*	*0.04*	*0.05*	
Meat	–1.14	–1.11	–1.26	–1.03	–1.12	–1.21	–1.07	–1.18	–1.11	–0.82
	0.06	*0.03*	*0.05*	*0.06*	*0.03*	*0.05*	*0.07*	*0.06*	*0.03*	
Fish	–1.03	–1.01	–1.32	–0.80	–1.04	–1.24	–0.95	–1.03	–1.10	–0.96
	0.11	*0.07*	*0.13*	*0.07*	*0.05*	*0.11*	*0.12*	*0.03*	*0.10*	
Cheese	–0.65	–0.97	–1.18	–1.66	–0.95	–0.53	–0.71	–0.9	–0.63	–0.87
	0.18	*0.12*	*0.21*	*0.18*	*0.13*	*0.16*	*0.20*	*0.16*	*0.26*	
Eggs	–1.03	–0.89	–1.71	–1.10	–1.08	–1.43	–0.56	–1.22	–1.08	–1.01
	0.75	*0.40*	*0.63*	*0.61*	*0.36*	*0.60*	*0.64*	*0.46*	*0.74*	
Beverages	–0.49	–0.50	–0.48	–0.44	–0.44	–0.68	–0.60	–0.55	–0.59	–0.46
	0.06	*0.03*	*0.06*	*0.03*	*0.03*	*0.05*	*0.03*	*0.03*	*0.05*	
Soft drinks	–1.16	–1.03	–0.88	–1.18	–0.73	–1.15	–1.21	–0.99	–1.38	–0.89
	0.17	*0.09*	*0.15*	*0.16*	*0.14*	*0.29*	*0.21*	*0.23*	*0.51*	
Hot drinks	–1.01	–1.02	–1.07	–1.00	–0.97	–1.03	–0.88	–0.83	–0.48	–0.89
	0.10	*0.06*	*0.12*	*0.11*	*0.06*	*0.13*	*0.17*	*0.12*	*0.24*	
Alco. drinks	–1.09	–1.05	–0.97	–1.19	–0.93	–1.10	–0.84	–1.16	–0.80	–1.01
	0.04	*0.03*	*0.06*	*0.03*	*0.023*	*0.07*	*0.04*	*0,04*	*0.13*	
Milk	–1.20	–0.90	–1.04	–0.88	–0.37	–0.60	–0.80	–0.36	–1.39	–0.63
	0.13	*0.13*	*0.06*	*0.11*	*0.17*	*0.10*	*0.19*	*0.22*	*0.32*	
Vegetablia	–0.93	–0.93	–1.04	–0.77	–0.94	–1.04	–0.81	–0.88	–1.00	–0.83
	0.06	*0.03*	*0.04*	*0.06*	*0.04*	*0.04*	*0.05*	*0.03*	*0.04*	
Bread and cereals	–0.91	–0.94	–1.12	–0.74	–0.87	–1.11	–0.58	–0.81	–0.76	–0.71
	0.08	*0.04*	*0.05*	*0.10*	*0.05*	*0.07*	*0.15*	*0.08*	*0.21*	
Vegetables, *etc.*	–0.96	–0.90	–0.86	–0.71	–0.70	–0.82	–1.04	–0.83	–0.84	–0.83
	0.07	*0.03*	*0.04*	*0.08*	*0.04*	*0.07*	*0.10*	*0.07*	*0.19*	
Potatoes	–0.67	–0.68	–0.83	–079	–0.71	–0.68	–0.72	–0.83	–0.77	–0.54
	0.12	*0.18*	*0.23*	*0.11*	*0.24*	*0.17*	*0.29*	*0.22*	*0.22*	
Miscellaneous	–0.76	–0.94	–1.00	–0.80	–0.99	–1.20	–0.69	–0.77	–1.06	–0.84
	0.25	*0.11*	*0.19*	*0.24*	*0.14*	*0.19*	*0.19*	*0.14*	*0.20*	

Elasticities are given in large plain text and standard errors are given in small italics.

more elastic prices for *animalia*, *fish*, *cheese*, *bread and cereals* and *food-at-home*, and a higher expenditure elasticity for *food-at-home* and a lower expenditure elasticity for *vegetablia*.

Compared with the first household type, a household with children - all other things equal - has more elastic prices for *cheese* and less elastic prices for *vegetablia*, *milk* and *bread and cereals*. The expenditure elasticities for the different food items are very much the same for these household types. If we compare single-

Table 4. Norwegian Expenditure Elasticities for Different Household Types

	Within Group Elasticities for Household Type									Total
	1	2	3	4	5	6	7	8	9	
Food-at-home	0.71	0.86	1.06	0.62	0.78	1.06	0.57	0.77	0.97	0.79
	0.12	*0.05*	*0.07*	*0.03*	*0.04*	*0.05*	*0.09*	*0.06*	*0.06*	
Other products	1.06	1.02	0.98	1.08	1.05	0.98	1.08	1.05	1.01	1.08
	0.16	*0.07*	*0.12*	*0.10*	*0.06*	*0.06*	*0.11*	*0.07*	*0.08*	
Animalia	0.91	0.94	1.02	1.03	1.01	1.04	0.93	0.95	0.80	0.81
	0.06	*0.03*	*0.04*	*0.04*	*0.02*	*0.03*	*0.04*	*0.03*	*0.04*	
Meat	1.17	1.19	1.20	1.12	1.21	1.25	1.16	1.06	1.10	0.91
	0.04	*0.02*	*0.03*	*0.04*	*0.02*	*0.03*	*0.05*	*0.04*	*0.06*	
Fish	1.05	0.94	0.95	1.13	1.01	0.92	1.14	1.21	1.03	0.80
	0.11	*0.06*	*0.10*	*0.07*	*0.01*	*0.08*	*0.10*	*0.06*	*0.12*	
Cheese	0.61	0.69	0.53	0.70	0.57	0.43	0.69	0.89	0.88	0.48
	0.09	*0.05*	*0.07*	*0.08*	*0.05*	*0.08*	*0.10*	*0.07*	*0.12*	
Eggs	0.52	0.30	0.45	0.46	0.56	0.60	0.47	0.59	0.75	0.39
	0.47	*0.23*	*0.33*	*0.36*	*0.222*	*0.33*	*0.44*	*0.27*	*0.50*	
Beverages	1.04	0.96	0.95	1.01	0.97	0.89	1.12	1.07	1.00	0.71
	0.06	*0.03*	*0.05*	*0.04*	*0.03*	*0.04*	*0.04*	*0.03*	*0.05*	
Soft drinks	1.23	1.22	1.19	1.02	1.26	1.10	0.54	1.08	0.98	1.08
	0.12	*0.07*	*0.12*	*0.13*	*0.10*	*0.15*	*0.17*	*0.12*	*0.27*	
Hot drinks	0.28	0.31	0.34	0.18	0.55	0.11	0.28	0.50	0.55	0.27
	0.14	*0.07*	*0.12*	*0.11*	*0.08*	*0.11*	*0.18*	*0.10*	*0.20*	
Alco. drinks	1.19	1.00	1.09	1.07	1.10	1.20	1.05	1.02	1.07	0.98
	0.07	*0.04*	*0.10*	*0.04*	*0.04*	*0.08*	*0.06*	*0.05*	*0.15*	
Milk	0.90	1.07	1.01	0.64	0.68	1.13	0.80	0.65	1.02	0.71
	0.15	*0.08*	*0.13*	*0.20*	*0.12*	*0.15*	*0.33*	*0.19*	*0.27*	
Vegetablia	1.17	1.16	1.05	1.00	1.14	1.10	1.05	1.14	1.15	0.89
	0.05	*0.02*	*0.04*	*0.04*	*0.03*	*0.04*	*0.04*	*0.03*	*0.04*	
Bread and cereals	0.92	0.95	0.86	0.79	0.90	0.94	0.91	0.97	0.86	0.84
	0.07	*0.03*	*0.05*	*0.09*	*0.05*	*0.09*	*0.14*	*0.07*	*0.13*	
Vegetables, *etc.*	1.05	1.00	1.18	1.07	1.15	1.03	0.94	1.14	1.04	1.08
	0.06	*0.03*	*0.04*	*0.07*	*0.04*	*0.07*	*0.09*	*0.07*	*0.12*	
Potatoes	0.61	0.41	0.47	0.69	0.59	0.54	0.47	0.49	0.53	0.62
	0.26	*0.10*	*0.12*	*0.23*	*0.09*	*0.31*	*0.16*	*0.21*	*0.16*	
Miscellaneous	0.82	0.91	0.93	0.90	0.76	0.86	0.81	0.72	0.93	0.66
	0.17	*0.18*	*0.14*	*0.18*	*0.11*	*0.15*	*0.16*	*0.11*	*0.17*	

Elasticities are given in large plain text and standard errors are given in small italics.

person households with the first household type, then the price elasticity is reduced for *food-at-home*, *other products*, *vegetablia*, *alcoholic drinks*, *milk* and *bread/cereals* and the expenditure elasticity is reduced for *vegetablia* and *soft drinks*.

The "total" column in Tables 3 and 4 represent average total elasticities, obtained as a weighted average of the *total* elasticities for the different household types, with weights given by the relevant expenditure shares. These average elasticities can be compared with those reported for household data in Table 9.4.

Firstly, note that the own-price elasticities in Tables 3 and 9.4 differ only slightly from each other for the following commodities; *animalia*, *beverages*, *vegetablia*, *miscellaneous*, *meat*, *fish*, *soft drinks*, *hot drinks*, *milk*, *bread and cereals* and *vegetables and fruit*. Secondly, the expenditure elasticities exhibit greater differences than the price elasticities. An important reason for this is the difference between the two estimated elasticities for *food-at-home*. If we calculate the total elasticities on basis of the same numerical value of the elasticity for *food-at-home*, then we would obtain approximately the same total expenditure elasticities for the different commodities.

10.4 CONCLUSIONS

Our results show that the marginal price responses, the marginal expenditure responses and the constant term vary across household types. This may indicate that it is difficult to capture individual heterogeneity with a small number of distributional variables. When the micro-model given in Chapter 9 (that allows exact aggregation over household members) does work, it may reflect a stable social structure throughout the sample period for household data (1982-1988).

Furthermore, a demand function in terms of prices and expenditure, that ignores socioeconomic variables, may exclude many important variables. Some implications for work on aggregate time-series data (macro-data) are:

- Since sociodemographic variables may change over time, and may also be correlated with real total expenditure and relative prices, it may be difficult to identify these separate effects when using aggregate data.

- Without the identification of these factors, it may be difficult to test theoretical hypotheses concerning price and income (expenditure) parameters.

- When total expenditure and price responses vary with household characteristics, then the conditions for exact aggregation do not hold.

11

TESTING ADDING UP IN THE COMMON MODEL

by David Edgerton*

11.1 INTRODUCTION

A system of equations must satisfy a number of requirements if it is to represent legitimate demand functions. The properties of *symmetry* and *negativity* are, for example, required to allow utility maximisation while *homogeneity* and *adding up* are needed to satisfy the budget constraint, see Chapter 3 and Deaton and Muellbauer (1980a).

According to the econometric philosophy of moving from the general to the particular, there has been a tendency in recent years to estimate flexible functional forms such as the popular AIDS demand systems. In particular homogeneity and symmetry have been tested within the framework of models that *allow* these properties to hold, but do not enforce them *a priori*.

The property of adding up is, in a sense, more basic than the properties derived from utility maximisation, and it is therefore natural that models that do not allow adding up to hold are considered with scepticism. Examples of such systems are the traditional double logarithmic (CEDS) model and a number of otherwise intuitively appealing dynamic models.[1] There is, however, no apparent point of principle that would prohibit us from testing adding up in a similar manner to that by which we test homogeneity and symmetry.

In practice adding up has not been tested empirically. Worswick and Champernowne (1954) gave conditions for when equation by equation least squares (OLS) will produce estimates that satisfy adding up, when applied to demand systems that are linear in the parameters. It can be shown that these conditions are exactly those needed to ensure that the linear model allows global adding up. Bewley (1986) has shown, however, that excluding variables from some equations, or applying other cross equation restrictions, can lead to estimated linear systems that do not automatically satisfy adding up even when the model allows adding up. He does this for OLS, systemwise least squares (SLS) and seemingly unrelated regressions (SUR).[2]

Maximum likelihood (ML) and generalised least squares (GLS) estimation are

---

* The theoretical results in this chapter are based on Edgerton (1995).

[1] See Anderson and Blundell (1982, 1983) and Blanciforti *et al* (1986).

[2] See Chapter 4 for a definition of these estimators. Note that SLS is sometimes called the minimum trace estimator.

essentially undefined in systems where adding up is assumed to hold, due to the singularity of the covariance matrix of the errors. Little attention has been given to the question of whether it is possible to obtain such estimates that do not automatically satisfy adding up. It has instead been the question of how to use ML and GLS in singular systems that has been addressed. Barten (1969), Powell (1969) and Berndt and Savin (1975) give some early results, while Bewley (1986), Dhrymes and Schwarz (1987) and McLaren (1990) are more recent contributions.

The concentration on the estimation of singular systems, together with the early results concerning adding up for unrestricted linear systems, has prompted the notion that estimation of demand systems that *allow* adding up will automatically produce estimates that *satisfy* adding up, whatever the functional form of the system and whatever the (consistent) estimation method chosen. When, for example, Deaton and Muellbauer (1980b) presented their Almost Ideal Demand System (AIDS), they stated that "since the data add up by construction, (adding up) is not testable".

The purpose of this chapter is to present (without proof) the conditions that determine when an estimated demand system will automatically satisfy adding up. Following Edgerton (1995), we will show that nonlinear AIDS does *not* fulfil these conditions when estimated by SLS or SUR, and it is thus possible to test if this model satisfies the adding up hypothesis. Using Swedish data, we apply such tests to the common model for the consumption of food described in Chapter 4. Our results are interpreted in terms of a misspecification analysis.

11.2 ADDING UP IN NONLINEAR DEMAND SYSTEMS

A general nonlinear demand system can be written in budget share form as

$$w_{it} = f_i(\mathbf{Z}_t;\boldsymbol{\theta}) + \varepsilon_{it}, \tag{1}$$

where w_{it} is the budget share of the ith good at time t, f_i is a function, $\mathbf{Z}_t$ is a vector of variables (usually containing at least the prices p_{jt}, the total expenditure x_t and a constant), ε_{it} is a stochastic error term and $\boldsymbol{\theta}$ is a vector of parameters. This system is an example of what is sometimes called an *allocation model*, and the results presented in this chapter are applicable to all such models.

Budget shares sum to one by definition, that is $\sum_i w_{it} = 1$ for $t = 1,\ldots,T$. If the function f_i is to represent a legitimate demand function which satisfies the budget constraint, then it too must satisfy the same *adding up* condition, namely

$$\textstyle\sum_i f_i(\mathbf{Z}_t;\boldsymbol{\theta}) = 1. \tag{2}$$

What happens if this condition fails to hold? Naturally, the observed budget shares will still sum to one. In this sense the adding up condition is therefore irrelevant. The condition is important in a couple of other senses, however. Firstly, the estimated and predicted budget shares will not sum to one if (2) does not hold, which has peculiar implications. Secondly, the identity $\Sigma_i f_i(\boldsymbol{Z}_t;\boldsymbol{\theta}) + \Sigma_i \varepsilon_{it} = 1$ always holds, and thus $\Sigma_i E(\varepsilon_{it}|\boldsymbol{Z}_t) = 1 - \Sigma_i f_i(\boldsymbol{Z}_t;\boldsymbol{\theta})$. If adding up does not hold then it is clear that $\Sigma_i E(\varepsilon_{it}|\boldsymbol{Z}_t) \neq 0$, and thus $\Sigma_i E(\varepsilon_{it}|\boldsymbol{Z}_t)$ cannot equal zero for all i for every t. This can be seen as a form of functional misspecification, since both omitted variables and simultaneous equation bias lead to nonzero conditional error expectations. A rejection of the adding up hypothesis can thus be interpreted as evidence in favour of a general misspecification problem.

The system of budget share equations can be written in matrix form as

$$\boldsymbol{W} = \boldsymbol{F}(\boldsymbol{Z};\boldsymbol{\theta}) + \boldsymbol{E}\,. \tag{3}$$

where $\boldsymbol{W}$, $\boldsymbol{E}$ and $\boldsymbol{F}$ are of order $(T \times n)$ and $\boldsymbol{Z}$ is of order $(T \times m)$. Let us also define the $(k \times 1)$ unit vector as $\iota_k = (1,\dots,1)'$ and the $(k \times k)$ identity matrix as $\boldsymbol{I}_k$. The budget shares thus automatically satisfy

$$\boldsymbol{W}\iota_n = \iota_T\,, \tag{4}$$

and the adding up condition (2) can thus be written

$$\boldsymbol{F}(\boldsymbol{Z};\boldsymbol{\theta})\iota_n = \iota_T\,. \tag{5}$$

In what follows it is important to distinguish between two questions:

(1) Can a demand model satisfy the adding up condition for all values of $\boldsymbol{Z}_t$ and for at least some values of $\boldsymbol{\theta}$? In this case the model is said to *allow* adding up.

(2) Given an affirmative answer to the first question, does estimation of the model by a certain estimation method always lead to parameter estimates that satisfy adding up? If this is so the method is said to *automatically satisfy* adding up.

To be more specific we introduce the following definitions.

Definition 1: Let Θ be the set of all admissible parameters and Ξ_Z the set of all values of $\boldsymbol{Z}$ with positive probability density. A set of demand equations is said to *allow* adding up if $\exists\, \boldsymbol{\theta}^* \in \Theta$ such that $\boldsymbol{F}(\boldsymbol{Z};\boldsymbol{\theta}^*)\iota_n = \iota_T$ for all $\boldsymbol{Z} \in \Xi_Z$.

If a model allows adding up we will denote by Θ^* the set of all $\boldsymbol{\theta}$ that satisfy adding up, that is for which (5) holds for all $\boldsymbol{Z} \in \Xi_Z$.

Definition 2: An estimation method $\hat{\boldsymbol{\theta}}(\boldsymbol{Z})$ is said to *automatically satisfy* adding up, when applied to a demand system, if $\boldsymbol{F}(\boldsymbol{Z};\hat{\boldsymbol{\theta}}(\boldsymbol{Z}))\iota_n = \iota_T$ for all $\boldsymbol{Z} \in \Xi_Z$. A necessary condition is obviously that the model allows adding up.

11.3 ADDING UP IN ESTIMATED DEMAND SYSTEMS

11.3.1 Maximum Likelihood Estimation

The theorems presented in this chapter are proven in Edgerton (1995).

Theorem 1: Maximum Likelihood (ML) estimation provides estimates that automatically satisfy adding up when applied to a model that allows adding up.

Intuitively this theorem is quite obvious since the error covariance matrix $\boldsymbol{\Sigma}$ is singular when adding up holds. The likelihood function thus grows without bound as the parameters approach values that satisfy adding up. If we maximise the unrestricted likelihood, then we will obtain estimates that satisfy adding up and produce a singular estimate of $\boldsymbol{\Sigma}$. An obvious way to obtain parameter estimates without running into numerical problems, is thus to impose the adding up conditions directly in the maximisation procedure. In many cases this is equivalent to the procedure of eliminating an arbitrary equation from the system, see Bewley (1986) and McLaren (1990).

11.3.2 Systemwise Least Squares Estimation

To study the properties of least squares estimates we shall introduce the following semilinear decomposition of the demand function.

$$f_i(\boldsymbol{Z}_t;\boldsymbol{\theta}) = \sum_{j=1}^{m} \theta_{1ij} k_j(\boldsymbol{Z}_t;\boldsymbol{\theta}_2) + g_i(\boldsymbol{Z}_t;\boldsymbol{\theta}_2), \tag{6}$$

where $\boldsymbol{\theta}' = (\boldsymbol{\theta}_1', \boldsymbol{\theta}_2') = (\boldsymbol{\theta}_{11}', \ldots, \boldsymbol{\theta}_{1n}', \boldsymbol{\theta}_2')$. This is a perfectly general decomposition, a total absence of (semi)linearities merely implies that $m = 0$ and $f_i = g_i$. The decomposition is, as we shall discuss later, not necessarily unique.

In what follows we shall use the abbreviated notation $f_{it} = f_i(\boldsymbol{Z}_t;\boldsymbol{\theta})$, $g_{it} = g_i(\boldsymbol{Z}_t;\boldsymbol{\theta})$ and $k_{jt} = k_j(\boldsymbol{Z}_t;\boldsymbol{\theta})$, whenever no confusion is caused. The equation (6) can now be written in matrix terms as

$$\boldsymbol{F} = \boldsymbol{K}\boldsymbol{\Theta}_1 + \boldsymbol{G} \tag{7}$$

where $\boldsymbol{F}$ and $\boldsymbol{G}$ are $(T \times n)$, $\boldsymbol{\Theta}_1$ is $(m \times n)$ and $\boldsymbol{K}$ is $(T \times m)$ of rank m for all $\boldsymbol{\theta}_2$. Using this notation the following theorem can be proven,

Theorem 2: The model allows adding up if and only if $\exists\, \boldsymbol{\theta}_2^*$ such that $(\boldsymbol{I} - \boldsymbol{G}^*)\boldsymbol{\iota}$ lies in the space spanned by the columns of $\boldsymbol{K}^*$ for all $\boldsymbol{Z} \in \Xi_Z$, where $\boldsymbol{G}^* = \boldsymbol{G}(\boldsymbol{Z}_t;\boldsymbol{\theta}_2^*)$ and $\boldsymbol{K}^* = \boldsymbol{K}(\boldsymbol{Z}_t;\boldsymbol{\theta}_2^*)$. In this case $(\boldsymbol{I} - \boldsymbol{G}^*)\boldsymbol{\iota} = \boldsymbol{K}^*\boldsymbol{\xi}$ for some $\boldsymbol{\xi}$, and $\boldsymbol{\Theta}_1^*\boldsymbol{\iota} = \boldsymbol{\xi}$.

In the simplest case of a linear system $\boldsymbol{G} = \boldsymbol{0}$ and $\boldsymbol{K} = \boldsymbol{Z}$. Theorem 2 now merely states that $\boldsymbol{\iota}$ must be a linear combination of the columns of $\boldsymbol{Z}$, which is usually satisfied by the model including a constant term (as say the first variable). In this case $\xi = (1,0,\ldots,0)'$, and adding up now implies that the columns of Θ_1 sum to ξ.

The systemwise least squares (SLS) estimator is defined as the value $\hat{\boldsymbol{\theta}}$ that minimises $\operatorname{tr} E(\boldsymbol{\theta})'E(\boldsymbol{\theta})$. The normal equations, obtained by differentiating these functions with respect to $\boldsymbol{\theta}$, can be expressed as

$$\hat{\Theta}_1 = (\hat{\boldsymbol{K}}'\hat{\boldsymbol{K}})^{-1}\hat{\boldsymbol{K}}'(\boldsymbol{W} - \hat{\boldsymbol{G}}), \tag{8}$$

together with the equations formed by differentiating with respect to $\boldsymbol{\theta}_2$. Using (8) and Theorem 2 leads to the following result.

Theorem 3: The systemwise least squares estimates automatically satisfy adding up if and only if $(\boldsymbol{I} - \boldsymbol{G}^*)\boldsymbol{\iota}$ lies in the space spanned by the columns of $\boldsymbol{K}$ for all $\boldsymbol{Z} \in \Xi_Z$ and $\boldsymbol{\theta}_2$.

The difference between Theorem 2 and Theorem 3 is whether $(\boldsymbol{I} - \boldsymbol{G})\boldsymbol{\iota}$ lies in the space spanned by the columns of $\boldsymbol{K}$ for *some* $\boldsymbol{\theta}_2$ or for *all* $\boldsymbol{\theta}_2$.

If the model is linear in the parameters and includes a constant term, then $\boldsymbol{G} = \boldsymbol{0}$ and $\boldsymbol{k}_1 = \boldsymbol{\iota}$. In this case $(\boldsymbol{I} - \boldsymbol{G})\boldsymbol{\iota} = \boldsymbol{\iota}$, which equals $\boldsymbol{K}\xi$ if $\xi = (1,0,\ldots,0)'$. This establishes Theorem 3 for this case. The parameter estimates satisfy $\hat{\Theta}_1\boldsymbol{\iota} = \xi$, that is

$$\sum_{i=1}^{n} \hat{\theta}_{1i1} = 1 \text{ and } \sum_{i=1}^{n} \hat{\theta}_{1ij} = 0 \text{ for } j \neq 1.$$

Models linear in the parameters include the Rotterdam model and the linearised version of AIDS. Another group of models that satisfy Theorem 3 are those where $\boldsymbol{K} = \boldsymbol{0}$ and $\Sigma_i g_{it} = 1$, such as the translog model. A further example is the linear expenditure system, which in budget share form has $\boldsymbol{k}_t = 1 - \Sigma_j \gamma_j(p_j/x_t)$ and $g_{it} = \gamma_i(p_i/x_t)$. In this case Theorem 3 is always fulfilled since $m = 0$ and $(\boldsymbol{I} - \boldsymbol{G})\boldsymbol{\iota} = \boldsymbol{k}$ identically. We return in Section 4 to an important case where systemwise least squares does not satisfy adding up.

11.3.3 Restricted Estimation

In many situations we wish to estimate a demand system under some conditions on the parameters. Imposing homogeneity or symmetry will, for example, often lead to such restrictions. If the (restricted) model allows adding up, then a simple adaptation of Theorem 1 shows that the maximum likelihood estimates will automatically satisfy adding up. Bewley (1986) and McLaren (1990) have shown that in these situations this is not necessarily equivalent to deleting an arbitrary equation.

The situation for systemwise least squares is less apparent, however. Assume that we wish to enforce h independent linear restrictions, $\boldsymbol{S}\boldsymbol{\theta}_1 = \boldsymbol{s}$, where we do not consider restrictions on $\boldsymbol{\theta}_2$ as these cannot affect adding up. The normal equations for the equality restricted systemwise least squares (ERSLS) estimates $\hat{\Theta}_1$ can be obtained by usual Lagrange differentiation. The following theorem can then be proven.

Theorem 4: If cross-equation restrictions are imposed, or if different restrictions are applied to different equations, then ERSLS estimates will in general not automatically satisfy adding up. If the same within-equation restrictions are imposed on each equation then we can write

$$\boldsymbol{S} = (\boldsymbol{I} \otimes \boldsymbol{B}) \text{ and } \boldsymbol{s} = (\boldsymbol{\iota} \otimes \boldsymbol{c}). \tag{9}$$

In this case ERSLS will satisfy adding up if (i) SLS satisfies adding up in the unrestricted model and (ii) $n\boldsymbol{c} = \boldsymbol{B}\xi$.

Imposing cross-equation restrictions (such as symmetry) or different within equation restrictions (such as exclusion restrictions) will thus lead to systemwise least squares estimation that can be applied to all n equations, and which does not satisfy adding up. It can be shown that the usual procedure of deleting one equation will neither yield the true SLS estimates nor be invariant to the equation deleted.

As regards identical within-equation restrictions, we can see that for systems that are linear in the parameters we have $\xi = (1,0,\dots,0)'$ and thus the condition of Theorem 4 becomes $n\boldsymbol{c} = \boldsymbol{b}_1$. The homogeneity restrictions of for example the Rotterdam and LAIDS models, do not involve the constant term and require that other parameter combinations shall sum to zero. That is they have $\boldsymbol{c} = \boldsymbol{b}_1 = \boldsymbol{0}$, which thus satisfies the theorem.

If the model is such that SLS does not automatically satisfy adding up, then we can naturally be interested in enforcing adding up explicitly.

As previously stated, SLS estimation is equivalent to minimising $\operatorname{tr}\boldsymbol{\Sigma}(\boldsymbol{\theta})$. If adding up holds, either automatically or because it is enforced, then the matrix $\boldsymbol{\Sigma}$ is singular and $\boldsymbol{\Sigma}\boldsymbol{\iota} = \boldsymbol{0}$. Let $\boldsymbol{\Sigma}_1$ be the $(n-1)\times(n-1)$ sub matrix consisting of the first columns and rows of $\boldsymbol{\Sigma}$, and σ_{nn} be the final element of $\boldsymbol{\Sigma}$. Minimising $\operatorname{tr}\boldsymbol{\Sigma}(\boldsymbol{\theta})$ is equivalent to minimising $\operatorname{tr}\boldsymbol{\Sigma}_1(\boldsymbol{\theta}) + \sigma_{nn}(\boldsymbol{\theta})$, which can only be equivalent to separately minimising $\operatorname{tr}\boldsymbol{\Sigma}_1(\boldsymbol{\theta})$ and $\sigma_{nn}(\boldsymbol{\theta})$ if these do not contain the same elements of $\boldsymbol{\theta}$, that is if no explicit or implicit cross-equation restrictions are imposed. The method of eliminating an arbitrary equation and then estimating using SLS is thus not invariant to which equation is eliminated when cross equation restrictions are imposed, see also Berndt and Savin (1975), Bewley (1986) and McLaren (1990). The correct procedure when imposing adding up is to use the singularity condition and note that in this case we minimise

$$\operatorname{tr}\boldsymbol{\Sigma} = \operatorname{tr}\boldsymbol{\Sigma}_1 + \operatorname{tr}\boldsymbol{\Sigma}_1\boldsymbol{\iota}_{n-1}\boldsymbol{\iota}'_{n-1} = \operatorname{tr}\boldsymbol{\Sigma}_1(\boldsymbol{I}_{n-1} + \boldsymbol{\iota}_{n-1}\boldsymbol{\iota}'_{n-1}),$$

which is obviously not the same as minimising $\operatorname{tr}\boldsymbol{\Sigma}_1(\boldsymbol{\theta})$.

11.3.4 Seemingly Unrelated Regression Estimation

Seemingly unrelated regression (SUR) estimates are obtained by minimising $\mathrm{tr}\boldsymbol{\Sigma}_0^{-1}\boldsymbol{E}(\boldsymbol{\theta})'\boldsymbol{E}(\boldsymbol{\theta})$, where $\boldsymbol{\Sigma}_0$ is an estimate of the error covariance matrix. If $\boldsymbol{\Sigma}_0$ is put equal to (a multiple of) the identity matrix then SUR reduces to SLS estimation, whilst letting $\boldsymbol{\Sigma}_0$ be a consistent estimate of $\boldsymbol{\Sigma}$ leads to SUR that has the same asymptotic properties as ML. Letting $\boldsymbol{\Sigma}$ be a function of $\boldsymbol{\theta}$ and iterating between estimation of $\boldsymbol{\Sigma}$ and $\boldsymbol{\theta}$ leads numerically to ML estimates (see Oberhoffer and Kmenta (1974)).

If $\boldsymbol{\Sigma}_0$ is non-singular, then the SUR estimates $\tilde{\boldsymbol{\Theta}}_1$ satisfies the normal equations

$$\tilde{\boldsymbol{\Theta}}_1 = (\tilde{\boldsymbol{K}}'\tilde{\boldsymbol{K}})^{-1}\tilde{\boldsymbol{K}}'(\boldsymbol{W}-\tilde{\boldsymbol{G}}). \tag{10}$$

Note that $\tilde{\boldsymbol{\Theta}}_1$ is not independent of $\boldsymbol{\Sigma}_0$ since $\tilde{\boldsymbol{K}}$ is a function of $\tilde{\boldsymbol{\theta}}_2$, nor is SUR equivalent to SLS if the model is nonlinear in the parameters. Equation (10) is of the same form as (8), and Theorems 3 and 4 will hold as for SLS.

If systemwise least squares does not automatically satisfy adding up, then unrestricted seemingly unrelated regressions estimates (USUR) can be obtained by using the unrestricted SLS estimate $\hat{\boldsymbol{\Sigma}}$ as $\boldsymbol{\Sigma}_0$. If, however, adding up is imposed (either automatically or explicitly) then the matrix $\hat{\boldsymbol{\Sigma}}$ obtained from the SLS/OLS estimates is singular. In this case SUR estimates are not defined. Alternative, if not totally satisfactory, procedures could either be to use merely the diagonal elements of $\hat{\boldsymbol{\Sigma}}$ or to use a non-singular estimate of $\boldsymbol{\Sigma}$ from the unrestricted model.

Methods that use generalised inverses when the covariance matrix is singular have been for applied to GLS (and thus SUR) by several authors, *e.g.*, Amemiya (1985 p 185). Dhrymes and Schwarz (1987) show that using the non-singular

$$\hat{\boldsymbol{\Sigma}}^{\circ} = \hat{\boldsymbol{\Sigma}} + k\iota_n\iota_n' \tag{11}$$

instead of the singular $\hat{\boldsymbol{\Sigma}}$ in ERSUR estimation with adding up explicitly imposed, yields the same results as using a generalised inverse $\boldsymbol{\Sigma}^{+}$, and that this holds for arbitrary nonzero k. These estimates are called generalised inverse SUR (GISUR).

11.4 ADDING UP AND NONLINEAR AIDS ESTIMATION

To prove that the SLS (and thus SUR) estimates of a model automatically satisfy adding up, it is sufficient to show that Theorem 3 holds for one decomposition (6). To prove that SLS does not automatically satisfy adding up we must, however, either construct a counter-example, or show that the conditions of Theorem 3 do not hold for *any* legitimate decomposition. The latter approach sounds laborious, since it involves an enumeration of all legitimate decompositions. This need not be too troublesome, however, due to the following lemma.

Lemma 1: Parameters that appear in more than one equation must belong to $\boldsymbol{\theta}_2$ if Theorem 3 is to hold.

The proof follows directly from the fact that if a parameter is an element of $\boldsymbol{\theta}_{1i}$ for two different equations, then a cross-equation relationship of the type described in Theorem 4 will hold, and adding up will not be automatically satisfied.

We can now consider the AIDS demand system defined by

$$f_{it} = \alpha_i + \sum_j \gamma_{ij} z_{jt} + \beta(v_t - P_t), \quad \text{with} \tag{12a}$$

$$P_t = \alpha_0 z_{0t} + \sum_j \alpha_j z_{jt} + \sum_j \sum_k \gamma_{jk} z_{jt} z_{kt} \,. \tag{12b}$$

where $z_{0t} = 1$, $z_{jt} = \ln p_{jt}$ and $v_t = \ln x_t$. Note first that α_0, α_i and γ_{jk} appear in all equations, and thus can only belong to $\boldsymbol{\theta}_2$ if adding up is to automatically be satisfied by least squares. The only possibly legitimate decompositions are to let β_i either belong to $\boldsymbol{\theta}_{1i}$ or to $\boldsymbol{\theta}_2$. Consider first the case where $\beta_i \in \boldsymbol{\theta}_2$, which is the trivial decomposition with $m = 0$ and $g_{it} = f_{it}$. If Theorem 3 is now to hold then $\Sigma_i g_{it}$ must equal 1 for all $\boldsymbol{Z}_t$ and $\boldsymbol{\theta}$. But

$$\sum_i g_{it} = \sum_i \alpha_i + \sum_j (\sum_i \gamma_{ij}) z_{jt} + (\sum_i \beta_i)(v_t - P_t), \tag{13}$$

which cannot equal 1 identically for all values of the parameters and variables.

The other possibly legitimate decomposition is when $m = 1$, $g_{it} = \alpha_i z_{0t} + \Sigma_j \gamma_{ij} z_{jt}$ and $k_t = y_t - P_t$. For Theorem 3 to hold then $\Sigma_i g_{it} + \xi k_t$ must equal 1 for some ξ and for all $\boldsymbol{Z}_t$ and $\boldsymbol{\theta}$. But

$$\sum_i g_{it} + \xi k_t = \sum_i \alpha_i + \sum_j (\sum_i \gamma_{ij}) z_{jt} + \xi(v_t - P_t), \tag{14}$$

which also cannot equal one identically for all values of the parameters and variables, whatever the value of ξ.

Deaton and Muellbauer's nonlinear AIDS model can thus be estimated by SLS and SUR without satisfying adding up. This implies that the validity of the model can be tested regarding adding up in the same manner for which it is customary to test for homogeneity and symmetry. Note, however, that the right hand side of (29) can be made equal to one for the specific values $\Sigma_i \alpha_i = 1$, $\Sigma_i \gamma_{ij} = 0$ and $\xi = \Sigma_i \beta_i = 0$, which establishes the well-known result that AIDS *allows* adding up.

11.5 TESTING FOR ADDING UP USING SWEDISH DATA

We will use the above results to estimate the static and dynamic three-stage AIDS models described earlier (see (4.2), (4.10) and Figure 2.1) using ML, GISUR, USUR, and SLS. Using Swedish data we apply ML to the reduced system excluding the first equation, while the other methods are applied to the complete system.

Table 1: Swedish Estimated Adding Up Conditions

	PRIVATE CONSUMPTION				FOOD-AT-HOME			
	Usur-dyn	Sls-dyn	Usur-st	Sls-st	Usur-dyn	Sls-dyn	Usur-st	Sls-st
$1-\Sigma\alpha$	-0.0098	-0.1234	-0.0019	-0.0453	0.0000	-0.0096	-0.0009	-0.0116
$\Sigma\beta$	-0.0051	-0.0577	-0.0014	-0.0331	0.0000	-0.0054	-0.0007	-0.0092
$\Sigma\gamma_1$	-0.0023	-0.0232	-0.0015	-0.0013	0.0000	0.0018	-0.0003	-0.0005
$\Sigma\gamma_2$	0.0030	0.0359	0.0013	0.0036	0.0000	-0.0022	-0.0006	-0.0505
$\Sigma\gamma_3$	0.0001	0.0028	0.0002	-0.0422	0.0000	0.0004	0.0010	0.0476
$\Sigma\gamma_4$	-0.0013	-0.0319	-0.0002	0.0338	0.0000	0.0002	-0.0002	0.0031
$\Sigma\theta_2$	0.0083	0.1688			0.0000	0.0024		
$\Sigma\theta_3$	0.0047	0.0341			0.0000	0.0048		
$\Sigma\theta_4$	-0.0013	0.0243			0.0000	0.0097		

	ANIMALIA				BEVERAGES			
	Usur-dyn	Sls-dyn	Usur-st	Sls-st	Usur-dyn	Sls-dyn	Usur-st	Sls-st
$1-\Sigma\alpha$	0.0186	0.3404	0.0121	0.3523	0.0000	0.0052	0.0000	-0.0527
$\Sigma\beta$	0.0069	0.2796	0.0098	0.2877	0.0000	0.0054	0.0000	-0.0409
$\Sigma\gamma_1$	0.0005	0.0103	0.0003	0.0054	0.0000	-0.0060	0.0000	0.0105
$\Sigma\gamma_2$	0.0004	-0.0919	-0.0033	-0.1052	0.0000	0.0007	0.0000	-0.0111
$\Sigma\gamma_3$	-0.0012	-0.0219	0.0021	-0.0034	0.0000	0.0040	0.0000	0.0059
$\Sigma\theta_2$	-0.0348	-0.0093			0.0000	0.0060		
$\Sigma\theta_3$	0.0177	0.0657			0.0000	-0.0033		

	VEGETABLIA				MISCELLANEOUS			
	Usur-dyn	Sls-dyn	Usur-st	Sls-st	Usur-dyn	Sls-dyn	Usur-st	Sls-st
$1-\Sigma\alpha$	0.0394	0.2172	0.0956	0.2555	0.0002	0.0029	-0.0003	-0.0527
$\Sigma\beta$	0.0360	0.2298	0.0808	0.2159	0.0001	-0.0299	-0.0002	-0.0409
$\Sigma\gamma_1$	-0.0187	-0.1438	-0.0721	-0.1844	0.0000	-0.0047	0.0001	0.0105
$\Sigma\gamma_2$	0.0126	0.0709	0.0516	0.1100	0.0000	0.0135	-0.0001	-0.0111
$\Sigma\gamma_3$	0.0041	0.0191	0.0165	0.0374	-0.0001	0.0092	0.0000	0.0059
$\Sigma\theta_2$	0.0183	0.0342			0.0000	-0.1209		
$\Sigma\theta_3$	0.0074	0.1392			0.0000	0.0407		

Usur and *Sls* denote estimation method, while *dyn* denotes the dynamic and *st* the static model.

Firstly we can note that estimating the unrestricted AIDS model with ML does indeed result in estimates that satisfied adding up (and a warning from the computer programme that the covariance matrix is singular). Using USUR and SLS leads, as expected, to estimates that do not satisfy adding up. The differences are in many cases small for USUR, however, especially in the dynamic model.

In Table 1 we see by how much the estimated parameters violate the adding up restrictions, and a number of points can now be made. Firstly, the dynamic model in general satisfies adding up better than the static model for both estimation methods. This is not surprising, since we know from our previous results that the static model is quite misspecified. Secondly we can see that the USUR estimates lie nearer the adding up condition than the SLS estimates. Again this is not surprising, since the change from SLS to USUR is equivalent to the first iteration of ML estimation. Repeated iterations would lead to estimates that satisfied adding-up. Finally we can see that USUR estimation of the dynamic AIDS model seems to lie quite close to the adding up conditions for all stages of the model.

In Table 2 we report the corrected Wald tests[3] for the adding up hypothesis in the dynamic model, using the USUR estimates. Other test statistics have also been calculated, but since we have used either Wald or LR tests in the rest of this book, and since LR tests are not applicable in non-ML situations, it seems natural to only report the Wald test. Homogeneity and symmetry are also tested, both conditionally and unconditionally, using USUR, GISUR and ML. Note that we use the same metric when estimating both restricted and unrestricted SUR, which is a necessary condition for most tests to be valid (although not the Wald tests). Note also that we do not report any tests for SLS, as these are based on the unrealistic assumption of identical error variances in all equations.

A number of things can be noticed from Table 2. Firstly we can see that adding up is not rejected for any of the subsystems in the dynamic model. A qualification to this result must nevertheless be given. In Chapter 6 we showed that AIDS estimation was quite insensitive to the choice of α_0. This result does not apply when adding up is not imposed, however, and the USUR and SLS estimates vary considerably as α_0 varies. The Wald statistic for the *food-at-home* equations (second stage) becomes extremely large when, for example, the value of α_0 is increased by 7.3.[4] This can be interpreted in a number of ways, but as suggested in section two, an eventual alternative of functional misspecification seems most plausible. Note also that the adding up hypothesis is rejected in the static model for the vegetablia subsystem (the P-value is 0.0017), even when using the same α_0 as in Table 2.

Secondly, the results for ML and GISUR are almost identical (the parameter estimates differ only in the second or third decimal). The difference noticed for the homogeneity restricted tests is merely due to different standard errors, which are themselves due to the use of the *unrestricted* error covariance matrix as metric for GISUR. We can also see that the homogeneity and symmetry tests are similar for GISUR and for adding up restricted USUR. A possible conclusion is that the choice between reasonable Σ matrices does not greatly affect on the estimation procedures (use of the unreasonable identity matrix (SLS) does have a considerable effect, however).

A conclusion of this chapter is that testing for adding up can be a useful com-

[3] The correction used is that named in Chapter 4, *i.e.*, $(T-k)/T$, where k is the average number of parameters per equation in the unrestricted model. This correction generally reduces the test bias. Note also that we do *not* use White's heteroscedasticity correction in this chapter, which explains the discrepancies for the ML tests of homogeneity and symmetry compared to previous results.

[4] The test statistics for the quasi LRT and other tests are not nearly so large, however.

Table 2: Corrected Wald Statistics in the Swedish Dynamic AIDS Model

(a) Unrestricted Seemingly Unrelated Regressions (USUR)

Hypothesis	d.f.	Priv Cons	Food	d.f.	Animalia	Beverages	Vegetablia	Miscellan.
A	9	0.1	0.0	7	0.1	0.1	1.8	0.0
		1.000	*1.000*		*1.000*	*1.000*	*0.972*	*1.000*
AH	12	27.4	8.4	9	22.5	9.2	21.5	0.5
		0.007	*0.754*		*0.007*	*0.417*	*0.010*	*1.000*
AHS	15	39.2	18.6	10	22.5	21.2	22.8	6.6
		0.001	*0.230*		*0.013*	*0.020*	*0.011*	*0.759*
H|A	3	27.6	8.4	2	24.1	9.2	24.0	0.5
		0.000	*0.039*		*0.000*	*0.010*	*0.000*	*0.795*
HS|A	6	38.6	18.6	3	24.1	21.2	25.9	6.6
		0.000	*0.005*		*0.000*	*0.000*	*0.000*	*0.084*
S|AH	3	11.9	10.9	1	0.0	10.4	1.9	6.5
		0.008	*0.012*		*0.947*	*0.000*	*0.166*	*0.011*

(b) Generalised Inverse Seemingly Unrelated Regressions (GISUR)

	d.f.	Priv Cons	Food	d.f.	Animalia	Beverages	Vegetablia	Miscellan.
H|A	3	28.2	8.4	2	18.9	9.2	18.8	0.5
		0.000	*0.039*		*0.000*	*0.010*	*0.000*	*0.793*
HS|A	6	39.0	18.6	3	18.9	21.2	20.4	6.6
		0.000	*0.005*		*0.000*	*0.000*	*0.000*	*0.087*
S|AH	3	11.6	10.9	1	0.0	12.4	1.7	6.4
		0.009	*0.012*		*0.948*	*0.000*	*0.196*	*0.011*

(c) *Maximum Likelihood (ML)*

	d.f.	Priv Cons	Food	d.f.	Animalia	Beverages	Vegetablia	Miscellan.
H|A	3	28.3	8.4	2	18.9	9.2	18.8	0.5
		0.000	*0.039*		*0.000*	*0.010*	*0.000*	*0.793*
HS|A	6	39.1	18.6	3	18.9	21.2	20.4	6.6
		0.000	*0.005*		*0.000*	*0.000*	*0.000*	*0.087*
S|AH	3	6.8	10.3	1	1.4	9.9	1.0	6.4
		0.079	*0.016*		*0.954*	*0.000*	*0.316*	*0.011*

A = Adding Up, H = Homogeneity, S = Symmetry. The symbol $x|y$ is to be read x conditional on y. The test statistics are given in plain face type and the P-values in italics.

plement to other misspecification tests. The dynamic three-stage budgeting process used in this study seems to work well for Swedish data as regards adding up, although the second stage (*food-at-home*) is open to some suspicion.

Part III

CONCLUSIONS

12

CONCLUSIONS*

12.1 METHODOLOGY

As stated in the introduction, the purpose of this book has been to analyse the demand for food in the Nordic countries. It is therefore natural to ask at the end of the book if we have succeed in performing such an analysis, and if so what results we have obtained.

The methodology we have used in our analysis has been quite specific. Flexible demand systems, consistent with the neoclassical theory of consumer demand, have been estimated and tested using modern econometric methods applied to aggregate time-series data. The success or failure of this approach depends partly on our ability to extract sufficient information from the data, and partly on our ability to use this information effectively in answering questions of economic interest. The quantity and quality of available data place an (unknown) limit on the amount of information at our disposal, but only our own ingenuity limits the way we use this information.

When considering the result of this study as a whole, we can naturally find a number of points where we have succeeded and a number where we have failed. Amongst our successes the following are especially worth noting.

1. The demand for food in the Nordic countries has previously hardly ever been rigorously investigated using a system approach. We have developed a common model, based on comparable data and time periods, which has been quite successfully applied to all the Nordic countries.

2. The most commonly used models in the demand analysis of aggregate time-series are in either *static* or *first difference* form. The *interrelated partial adjustment* model we have used succeeds in improving over these standard models, both in terms of misspecification analysis and goodness-of-fit.

3. Our models have been thoroughly checked for misspecification, using both single equation and system tests. To our knowledge, no previous demand study has been so closely inspected for misspecification. Furthermore, many of the tests at the system level have been specifically developed for this study. Our empirical results reveal the importance of such testing, and

* This chapter, which is the shared responsibility of all the authors, has been written by David Edgerton.

3. More sophisticated econometrics is a further possibility. Some improvements are of course possible, especially regarding testing and the calculation of estimation precision. Bootstrapping and other data intensive methods can maybe yield better *P*-values and standard errors. The use of an instrumental variable approach in the face of endogenous prices could also lead to some improvement, but the question of what instruments to use remains. The possibility of using GMM (Generalised Method of Moments) instead of maximum likelihood is another alternative. It seems unlikely, however, that substantial improvements can be obtained in this manner.

All the above suggestions could provide some improvements, but the basic problem would probably remain. There is quite simply a limit to the information that is available from aggregate annual time-series data! It seems reasonable to presume that while we may not have succeeded in extracting all this information, we have probably managed to use the major part. The introduction of new sources of data is thus paramount in a continued analysis.

The use of cross-sectional and/or panel data seems to be the only avenue available for further improvement in demand analyses. Note that this does not imply the replacement of time-series analysis, but rather provides a complementary approach. Cross-sectional and longitudinal data is, of course, better for the estimation of micro parameters, but macro models would still have their place in policy analyses, and attempts to only use cross-sectional data would mean replacing the aggregation problem by a disaggregation problem. Note also that the use of survey data introduces new statistical problems such as non-response.

The increased availability of survey data enables a future combination of aggregate and disaggregate models, which seems to be the only way forward for demand analysis.[2]

12.2 RESULTS: A GENERAL IMPRESSION

A wealth of information concerning the demand for food is given in this book, and these results can hardly be paraphrased in one short section. A few words concerning some general impressions may be appropriate, however.

In Table 1 we present what, in our opinion, are the best elasticity estimates available from this study. Note that these results are only given to one place of decimals, emphasising the limits of our inferences. The elasticities in the table have been calculated using the mean values of prices and expenditures in the different countries, but it must be remembered that elasticities in flexible demand models are in reality a function of time, and should therefore be judged as a series rather than as point estimates. This model consistent variation is for the most part not too great, however, which can be seen through the figures in bold type that indicate

[2] See Blundell *et al.* (1993) for a recent discussion on these topics.

Table 1. Total Elasticities at Mean Values for the Nordic Countries

	Expenditure Elasticities				Own-Price Elasticities			
	D	F	N	S	D	F	N	S
Food-at-home	0.7	1.1	0.8	0.5	–0.4	–0.4	–0.3	–0.6
Meat	0.9	1.1	1.0	0.6	–0.5	–0.2	–0.7	–0.4
Fish	0.9	0.5	0.5	0.2	–0.9	–0.3	–0.8	–0.3
Milk, Cheese and Eggs	0.6	0.3	0.5	0.5	–0.4	0.1	–0.2	0.0
Soft Drinks	0.7	1.7	1.1	0.3	–1.1	–1.2	–0.7	–0.6
Hot Drinks	**0.5**	**0.5**	**0.2**	0.2	**–0.2**	**–0.2**	–0.3	**–0.1**
Alcoholic Drinks	0.9	2.1	1.8	0.6	–0.5	–0.6	–0.9	–0.9
Cereals	0.3	0.4	0.4	0.6	–0.4	–0.1	–0.4	–0.7
Fruit and Vegetables	1.1	1.7	0.6	0.3	–0.5	–0.3	–0.6	–0.6
Potatoes	0.3	2.0	0.1	–0.1	–0.5	–0.5	**–0.5**	0.1
Fats and Oils	0.3	0.6	0.2	0.5	–0.6	–0.3	–0.2	–0.3
Sugar	0.3	1.2	0.8	**–0.2**	**–0.7**	**–0.3**	–0.2	**0.8**
Confectionery *etc*	0.5	1.5	0.5	0.4	–0.8	–0.4	–0.1	–0.4

D = Denmark, F = Finland, N = Norway and S = Sweden. This table is identical to Table 5.23.

those commodities for which the values at the mean differ by more than ±0.3 in absolute value from the elasticity at the last value. Another point to be remembered is that we concentrate on the *total* expenditure and price elasticities, that is where changes at one budgeting level are allowed to affect the allocation between groups at other levels.

The most obvious conclusion that can be drawn from Table 1, and our other results, is how *different* the Nordic countries are regarding food consumption. Expenditure elasticities vary considerably from country to country, even allowing for the imprecision due to estimation. Price elasticities vary somewhat less, but are still significant. The same impression is also obtained if we consider the degrees of misspecification and goodness-of-fit, which also vary considerably between countries. Yet again, an examination of the graphical presentation in Chapter 2 reveals substantial variations. In spite of considerable cultural similarities, the political and economic differences between the countries thus seem to be sufficient to lead to noticeable effects concerning the patterns of food consumption.

Looking in a bit more detail reveals that the estimates for *food-at-home* agree quite well with international results, with the exception of Finland that rather surprisingly makes food a luxury (the expenditure elasticity is greater than unity). This result is not statistically significant, however. The fact that the Finnish figure is twice as large as the one for Sweden affects the other results for those countries, however. The Swedish *sugar* results also seem rather strange, as do a number of other figures. It should be remembered, however, that over the sample period a change has occurred in the relative use of raw sugar and of prefabricated goods that include sugar in processed form. This means that the definition of the sugar commodity is changing, which causes problems when estimating aggregate elasticities. It should also be pointed out that the home production of, for example, *potatoes* is treated in different ways in different countries, and that these statistics are of poor quality especially in Sweden and Norway.

In Chapter 6 we report the findings of a large scale sensitivity analysis, where particular emphasis was placed on the Swedish models. In Table 6.10 a summary of these results is presented, which together with the other results in that chapter can allow us to draw a number of conclusions. Maybe the most important of these is that the common model seems to work relatively well. An interval of ±0.25 is, however, the *minimum* level of uncertainty that must be used in inferences concerning elasticities, if we are to take both stochastic and model consistent variation into account. In most cases the variability between different structures falls within this interval.

Two other more specialised analyses were also reported in Chapter 6. The first one considered different commodity partitions using Norwegian data, and the results indicate that choice of partitioning seems to be of minor importance for the elasticities of most goods. The second analysis used Danish data to estimate different functional forms. While no choice was clear cut, the results do not indicate that the common model should be discarded.

Chapters 7 - 11 take up a number of specific questions, and the reader is basically referred to the summaries that can be found in each chapter. Two general points are worth making, however.

Firstly, the comparison of cross-sectional and aggregate time-series data that is to be found in Chapters 9 and 10, shows that the rejection of the laws of demand cannot only depend on aggregation over households. Other factors, such as aggregation over commodities, treatment of durables and socioeconomic variation, can also be importance.

Secondly, from the 1st of January 1995, Sweden and Finland have joined Denmark as members of the European Union. Norway has remained outside the union and its common agricultural policy, however. An analysis of projected Finnish food consumption under this scenario is reported in Chapter 8, and this seems to indicate that consumption patterns will become more similar for those Nordic countries that are now members of the union. It will be interesting to follow up this result over the next few years, to see if increased economic integration does indeed lead to more homogenous patterns of demand.

Appendix 1

PUBLICATIONS AND WORKING PAPERS

PUBLICATIONS

PUB/1: Edgerton, D. L., "Hur mycket har matpriserna stigit? En jämförelse mellan nationalräkenskaperna och konsumentprisindex," *Ekonomisk Debatt,* 90:8, 766-771, 1990 (in Swedish).

PUB/2: Edgerton, D. L., "On the Estimation of Separable Demand Models," *Journal of Agricultural and Resource Economics*, 18, 141-146, 1993.

PUB/3: Edgerton, D. L., and C. Wells, "Critical Values for the Cusumsq Statistic in Medium Sized Samples," *Oxford Bulletin of Economics and Statistics*, 56, 355-365, 1994.

PUB/4: Rickertsen, K., "The Demand for Meat: Conditional and Unconditional Elasticities," *IAAE Occasional Paper* No. 7, 1995.

PUB/5: Rickertsen, K., "Etterspørsel etter matvarer," *Landbruksøkonomisk forum*, 12, 1-10, 1995 (in Norwegian)

PUB/6: Rickertsen, K., J. A. Chalfant, and M. Steen, "The Effects of Advertising on the Demand for Vegetables," *European Review of Agricultural Economics*, 22, 481-494, 1995.

PUB/7: Edgerton, D. L., and G. Shukur, "Some Questions Concerning Dynamic Almost Ideal Demand Systems," *Applied Economics Letters*, 1996 (forthcoming).

NORDIC FOOD DEMAND STUDY SERIES

Denmark

DK/1: Hummelmose, A., "Husholdingernes konsum," 1989 (in Danish).

DK/2: Hummelmose, A., "Analyser og prognoser for fødevareefterspørgslen i de nordiske lande," 1989 (in Danish).

DK/3: Hummelmose, A., "Brug af efterspørgselsmodeller på dansk nationalregnskapstal," 1990 (in Danish).

DK/4: Hummelmose, A., "Befolkningsforhold, indkomstudviklingen og omkostningsindex i Danmark," 1990 (in Danish).

DK/5: Hummelmose, A., "Udviklingen i prisen på og forbruget af fødevarer i Danmark, 1953-1987," 1990 (in Danish).

DK/6: Hummelmose, A., "Analyse af input i det privat konsum. Analyseperiode 1970-1986," 1990 (in Danish).

DK/7: Hummelmose, A., "Statisk og Dynamisk AIDS-Model for fødevareefterspørgslen i Danmark," 1991 (in Danish).
DK/8: Hummelmose, A., "Forbruget af fødevarer i Danmark, 1950-1989," 1991 (in Danish).
DK/9: Hummelmose, A., "Energi- og næringindholdet i fødevarerne i Danmark, 1970-1990," 1991 (in Danish).
DK/10: Hummelmose, A., "Komparative studier af efterspørgselssystemer," 1991 (in Danish).
DK/11: Hummelmose, A., "Sammenligning af forskellige efterspørgselssystemer og -modeller anvendt på danske data," 1992 (in Danish).
DK/12: Hummelmose, A., "Udgifterne til føde- og drikkevarer samt forbruget heraf i Danmark, 1950-1990," 1992 (in Danish).

Finland

FI/1: Laurila, I. P., "At the Beginning of the Nordic Project Some Points Worth Discussing," 1989.
FI/2: Laurila, I. P., "Food Consumption Data in Finland," 1989.
FI/3: Laurila, I. P., "Excerpts from the First Meeting. Lund 14/2/1989 General Model and Data," 1989.
FI/4: Laurila, I. P., "The Finnish Data I," 1989.
FI/5: Laurila, I. P., "The Finnish Data II," 1989.
FI/6: Laurila, I. P., "Elasticities of Demand for Food Products in Finland," 1989.
FI/7: Laurila, I. P., "Household Equivalence Scales," 1990.
FI/8: Laurila, I. P., "Demand for Food Products in Finland, 1960-1995," 1990.
FI/9: Laurila, I. P., "Food Consumption in Finland, 1950-1989," 1990.
FI/10: Laurila, I. P., "Static and Dynamic LAIDS Models of Demand for Food in Finland," 1991.
FI/11: Laurila, I. P., "Static and Dynamic AIDS Models of Demand for Food in Finland," 1991.
FI/12: Laurila, I. P., "Comparisons of Food Consumption in European Countries," 1992.

Norway

NO/1: Rickertsen, K., "Analys av efterfrågan på livsmedel - data til modellene," 1989 (in Norwegian).
NO/2: Rickertsen, K., "Norwegian Data to the Project," 1989.
NO/3: Vale, P. H., "Socioeconomic Variables in the Demand Function," 1990.
NO/4: Vale, P. H., "Spesifikasjon av funksjoner ved empiriske etterspørselanalyser," 1990 (in Norwegian).
NO/5: Rickertsen, K., "Food Demand in Norway - Description and Theory,"

Memorandum #5, Department of Economics and Social Sciences, Agricultural University of Norway, 1990.

NO/6: Rickertsen, K., "Static and Dynamic AIDS Models of Demand for Food in Norway," 1991.

NO/7: Vale, P. H., "Food Demand Studies on the Household Level," 1991.

NO/8: Rickertsen, K., "Norwegian Consumer Behavior - A Dynamic AIDS Model," 1992.

Sweden

SW/1: Assarsson, B., "Modelling and Forecasting Aggregate Consumption," 1989.

SW/2: Edgerton, D. L., "Food Consumption Data in Sweden," 1989.

SW/3: Assarsson, B., "The Stochastic Behaviour of Durables and Nondurables Consumption in Sweden," 1990.

SW/4: Assarsson, B., "Testing in the Life Cycle Hypothesis with Time Series Data Under Alternative Sampling Methods. A Monte Carlo Experiment," 1990.

SW/5: Edgerton, D. L., "Demand Functions - A Review," 1990 (Revised 1991).

SW/6: Edgerton, D. L., "Food Consumption in Sweden 1963-1989," 1990 (Revised 1991).

SW/7: Edgerton, D. L., "Hur mycket har matpriserna stigit? En jämförelse mellan nationalräkenskaperna och konsumentprisindex," 1990 (in Swedish).

SW/8 : Edgerton, D. L., "When Do Estimated Demand Systems Automatically Satisfy Adding Up?," 1991 (Revised 1995).

SW/9: Edgerton, D. L., "Estimating the Demand for Food in Sweden," 1991.

SW/10: Assarsson, B., "An Almost Ideal Demand System in Error Correction Form," 1992.

SW/11: Edgerton, D. L., "Estimating Elasticities in Multi-Stage Demand Systems," 1992.

OTHER RELEVANT PAPERS

Finland

P/F1: Laurila, I. P., "A Demand System Applied for Dairy Products: Implications for Future Consumption in an EC Applicant Finland," 1993.

P/F2: Laurila, I. P., "Demand for Food Products in Finland: A Demand System Approach," FD thesis, Department of Economics and Management, University of Helsinki, Finland, 1994.

Norway

P/N1: Rickertsen, K., and P. H. Vale, "Testing Restrictions in a Demand System: An Application to Norwegian Micro and Macro Data," Department of Economics and Social Sciences, Agricultural University of Norway, *Discussion Paper*, 1993.

P/N2: Rickertsen, K., "The Demand for Meat: Conditional and Unconditional Elasticities," *Discussion Paper #D13/1994*, Department of Economics and Social Sciences, Agricultural University of Norway, 1994.

P/N3: Rickertsen, K., "The Demand for Food and Beverages in Norway," *Report No. 13*, Department of Economics and Social Sciences, Agricultural University of Norway, 1994.

P/N4: Vale, P.H., "Micro Data in Demand Analysis. Theories, Applications and Empirical Findings," PhD thesis, Department of Economics and Social Sciences, Agricultural University of Norway, 1995.

P/N5: Rickertsen, K., and P. H. Vale, "Interpreting Measured Demand Elasticities," *Discussion Paper*, Department of Economics and Social Sciences, Agricultural University of Norway, 1995.

P/N6: Rickertsen, K., "Structural Change and the Demand for Meat and Fish in Norway," *Discussion Paper*, Department of Economics and Social Sciences, Agricultural University of Norway, 1995.

P/N7: Rickertsen, K., "The Demand for Food and Beverages in Norway," *Discussion Paper,* Department of Economics and Social Sciences, Agricultural University of Norway, 1995.

Sweden

P/S1: Shukur, G., "Demand for Meat and Fluid Milk in Sweden 1960-1989," MA thesis, Department of Statistics, Lund, Sweden, 1992.

P/S2: Shukur, G., "Demand for Meat and Fluid Milk in Sweden 1960-1989. Tests for Structural Change," FL thesis, Department of Statistics, Lund, Sweden, 1993.

P/S3: Edgerton, D. L., "Weak Separability and the Estimation of Elasticities in Multi-Stage Demand Systems," *Working Paper* 26/93, Department of Economics, Lund, Sweden, 1993.

P/S4: Edgerton, D. L., and C. Wells, "On the Use of the Cusumsq Statistic in Medium Sized Samples," *Working Paper* 22/93, Department of Economics, Lund, Sweden. 1993.

P/S5: Assarsson, B. and S. Johansson "Testing Hysteresis with Temporally Aggregated Data," *Working Paper,* Department of Economics, Uppsala, Sweden. 1994.

P/S6: Edgerton, D. L., and G. Shukur, "Testing Autocorrelation in a System Perspective," *Working Paper,* Department of Economics and Department of Statistics, Lund, Sweden, 1995.

P/S7: Edgerton, D. L., "Should Stochastic or Nonstochastic Exogenous Variables Be Used in Monte Carlo Studies?," *Working Paper*, Department of Economics, Lund, Sweden. 1995.

CONFERENCE CONTRIBUTIONS

Econometric Society's 6:th World Congress. Barcelona, Spain, 1990: SW/3.

The Econometric Days. Gothenburg, Sweden, 1991: SW/8.

Annual Meeting of the Nordic Society of Agricultural Researchers. Uppsala, Sweden, 1991: DK/7, FI/10, NO/6 and SW/9.

The Econometric Days. Lund, Sweden, 1992: SW/10.

The American Agricultural Economics Association's Meeting. Baltimore, USA, 1992: SW/11.

National Research Meeting for Economists. Oslo, Norway, 1992: NO/8.

Romanian-Swedish Economic Symposium. Bucharest, Romania, 1993. P/S3.

The Econometric Days, Stockholm, Sweden, 1993; P/S3 and P/S4.

European Congress of Agricultural Economists. Stresa, Italy, 1993; P/F1 and P/N1.

Econometric Society's European Meeting. Uppsala, Sweden, 1993; P/S3 and P/S4.

International Conference of Agricultural Economists. Harare, Zimbabwe, 1994; P/N2

The Econometric Days, Uppsala, Sweden, 1994; P/S5.

The Econometric Days, Umeå, Sweden, 1995; P/S6.

The American Agricultural Economics Association's Meeting. Indianapolis, USA, 1995: P/N5.

Econometric Society's 7:th World Congress. Tokyo, Japan, 1995: SW/8 and P/S6.

Appendix 2

DATA APPENDIX

The data and programmes used to estimate the models presented in this book are available in electronic form, and can be obtained through the usual international computer network system. Two main channels of communication are available; the *World Wide Web* (*WWW*), and *anonymous.ftp*. Readers should, if necessary, first consult the computer services department of their own institution for information on how to access the WWW or FTP servers of the School of Economics and Management at Lund University

1. Information concerning the Nordic Food Demand Study, including data and programme files, is available via the internet at the address:

http://www.ec.lu.se/~nekded/nordfood/

2. The compressed files *nordfood.exe* and *nordfood.zip* are available via FTP from the School of Economics and Management computer network system. The following commands should be issued after logging in to the School's network:

```
FTP       ftp.ec.lu.se
login:    anonymous
Password: [e-mail address] or [guest]       (do not type the brackets!)
FTP>      cd pub
FTP>      cd nek
FTP>      cd nordfood
FTP>      bin
FTP>      get nordfood.exe                  (file name must be in lower case)
FTP>      get nordfood.zip
FTP>      get pkunzip.exe
FTP>      bye                               (to log-off)
```

3. If difficulties are encountered with these channels, then the authors can be reached through the e-mail address "David.Edgerton@nek.lu.se". If all else fails, then a formatted 3½" DOS diskette can be sent to

David Edgerton, Department of Economics, Box 7082, S-220 07 Lund, Sweden.

The information found on the web is self-explanatory. PC users can fetch the file *nordfood.exe*, via FTP or diskette, which will self-decompress upon execution, while Mac and Unix users will have to decompress *nordfood.zip* using *pkunzip*. In both cases the following file and directory structure will be revealed:[1]

\README.TXT
\BIBLIOG\
\DATA\
\PROGRAMS\

The README.TXT file in the root directory contains general information. The DATA directory contains the data for Denmark, Finland, Norway and Sweden, that was used to obtain the results presented in this book. These files are available in Lotus (WK1) and ASCII (TXT) format, see the file DATA.TXT for details.

The PROGRAMS directory contains four subdirectories; DYNAMIC, DYN-BSW, X-DYN, and X-DY-BSW. The files in each of these subdirectories yields maximum likelihood solutions of the nonlinear AIDS model for the general dynamic, beta-switching general dynamic, diagonal dynamic, and beta switching diagonal dynamic models, respectively. These files are explained in the PROGRAMS.TXT file. The programmes are written in the TSP computer software package version 4.2.

Finally, the directory BIBLIOG contains an annotated bibliography. This covers recent titles (mainly from the 1980's and 1990's) concerning the analysis of food consumption using the demand systems approach and related topics, see the file BIBREAD.TXT for details.

[1] The directory structure will be lost if *nordfood.exe* is used, and PC users may therefore also wish to use *pkunzip* with the option "-d". Type *pkunzip* to obtain help on syntax if unsure.

BIBLIOGRAPHY

Alessie, R., and A. Kapteyn (1991): "Habit Forming and Interdependent Preferences in the Almost Ideal Demand System," *Economic Journal*, 101, 404-419.

Alston, J. M., and J. A. Chalfant (1987): "Weak Separability and a Test for the Specification of Income in Demand Models with an Application to the Demand for Meat in Australia," *Australian Journal of Agricultural Economics*, 31, 1-15.

Alston, J. M., and J. A. Chalfant (1991a): "Can We Take the Con Out of Meat Demand Studies?" *Western Journal of Agricultural Economics*, 16, 36-48.

Alston, J. M., and J. A. Chalfant (1991b): "Unstable Models from Incorrect Forms," *American Journal of Agricultural Economics*, 73, 1171-1181.

Alston, J. M., K. A. Foster and R. D. Green (1994): "Estimating Elasticities with the Linear Approximate Almost Ideal Demand System: Some Monte Carlo Results," *Review of Economics and Statistics*, 76, 351-356.

Amemiya, T. (1974): "The Nonlinear Two-Stage Least-Squares Estimator," *Journal of Econometrics*, 2, 105-110.

Amemiya, T. (1985): *Advanced Econometrics*, Cambridge Mass.: Harvard University Press.

Anderson, G., and R. Blundell (1982): "Estimation and Hypothesis Testing in Dynamic Singular Equation Systems," *Econometrica*, 50, 1559-1571.

Anderson, G., and R. Blundell (1983): "Testing Restrictions in a Flexible Dynamic Demand System: An Application to Consumers' Expenditure in Canada," *Review of Economic Studies*, 50, 397-410.

Andrews, D. W. K. (1991): "Heteroskedasticity and Autocorrelation Consistent Covariance Matrix Estimation," *Econometrica*, 59, 817-858.

Assarsson, B. (1991): "Alcohol Pricing Policy and the Demand for Alcohol in Sweden 1978-1988," *Nordic Food Demand Study* SW/9, Department of Economics, Uppsala University, Sweden.

Attfield, C. L. F. (1985): "Homogeneity and Endogeneity in Systems of Demand Equations," *Journal of Econometrics*, 27, 197-209.

Baccouche, R., and F. Laisney (1991): "Describing the Separability Properties of Empirical Demand Systems," *Journal of Applied Econometrics*, 6, 181-206.

Barnett, W. A. (1992): "A Test of Normality in Nonlinear Systems of Consumer Demand Equations," Chapter 2 in *Contributions to Consumer Demand and Econometrics*, edited by R. Bewley and Tran Van Hoa, London: Macmillan.

Barnett, W. A., and S: Choi (1989): "A Monte Carlo Test of Blockwise Weak Separability," *Journal of Business and Eonomic Statistics*, 7, 363-377..

Barten, A. P. (1969): "Maximum Likelihood Estimation of a Complete System of Demand Equations," *European Economic Review*, 1, 7-73.

Berndt, E. R., and N. E. Savin (1975): "Estimation and Hypothesis Testing in Singular Equation Systems with Autoregressive Disturbances," *Econometrica*, 43, 937-957.

Berndt, E. R., and N. E. Savin (1977): "Conflict Among Criteria for Testing Hypotheses in the Multivariate Regression Model," *Econometrica*. 45, 1263-1278.

Bewley, R. (1986): *Allocation Models: Specification, Estimation and Applications*, Cambridge Mass.: Ballinger.

Bickel, P. J. (1978): "Using Residuals Robustly I: Test for Heteroscedasticity, Nonlinearity," *Annals of Statistics*, 13, 13-25.

Blackorby, C., D. Primont, and R. R. Russell (1978): *Duality, Separability and Functional Structure: Theory and Economic Applications*, New York: North-Holland.

Blanciforti, L., and R. Green (1983): "An Almost Ideal Demand System Incorporating Habits: An Analysis of the Expenditure on Food and Aggregate Commodity Groups," *Review of Economics and Statistics*, 65, 511-515.

Blanciforti, L., R. Green, and G. King (1986): "U. S. Consumer Behavior over the Postwar Period: An Almost Ideal Demand System Analysis," *Monograph Number 40*, Giannini Foundation of Agricultural Economics, University of California.

Blundell, R., P. Pashardes, and G. Weber (1993): "What Do We Learn About Consumer Demand Patterns from Micro Data," *American Economic Review*, 83, 570-597.

Bowden, R. J., and D. A. Turkington (1981): "A Comparative Study of Instrumental Variable Estimators for Nonlinear Simultaneous Models," *Journal of the American Statistical Association*, 76, 988-995.

Bowden, R. J., and D. A. Turkington (1984): *Instrumental Variables*, Cambridge: Cambridge University Press.

Buse, A. (1992): "Alternative Data Sources for Demand Estimation," Chapter 9 in *Market Demand for Dairy Products*, edited by S. R. Johnson, D. P. Stonehouse, and Z. A. Hassan. Ames: Iowa State University Press.

Buse, A. (1994): "Evaluating the Linearized Almost Ideal Demand System," *American Journal of Agricultural Economics*, 76, 781-793.

Capps, O., and J. Havlicek (1987): "Concepts of Consumer Demand Theory," Chapter 1 in *Food Demand Analysis: Problems, Issues and Empirical Evidence*, edited by R. Raunikar and C. L. Huang, Ames: Iowa State University Press.

Capps, O., and R. M. Nayga (1990): "Effect of Length of Time on Measured Demand Elasticities: The Problem Revisited," Presented at the AAEA meeting, Vancouver.

Capps, O., and B. Senauer (1986): *Food Demand Analysis: Implications for Future Consumption*. Department of Agricultural Economics, Virginia Polytechnic Institute and State University, Blacksburg, Virginia.

Chalfant, J. A. (1987): "A Globally Flexible, Almost Ideal Demand System," *Journal of Business and Economic Statistics*, 5, 233-242.

Chalfant, J. A., and J. M. Alston (1988): "Accounting for Changes in Taste" *Journal of Political Economy*, 96, 391-410.

Chavas, J.-P. (1983): "Structural Change in the Demand for Meat," *American Journal of Agricultural Economics*, 65, 148-153.

Chavas, J.-P., and K. Segerson (1987): "Stochastic Specification and Estimation of Share Equation Systems," *Journal of Econometrics*, 35, 337-358.

Chiang, A. C. (1984): *Fundamental Methods of Mathematical Economics*, Third edition, New York: McGraw-Hill.

Chow, G. C., (1960): "Tests of Equality Between Sets of Coefficients in Two Linear Regressions," *Econometrica*, 28, 591-605.

Christensen, L. R., D. W. Jorgenson, and L. J. Lau (1975), "Transcendental Logarithmic Utility Functions," *American Economic Review*, 65, 367-383.

Cox, T. L., and M. K. Wohlgenant (1986): "Prices and Quality Effects in Cross-Sectional Demand Analysis," *American Journal of Agricultural Economics*, 68, 908-919.

Dahlgran, R. A. (1987): "Complete Flexibility Systems and the Stationarity of U S Meat Demands," *Western Journal of Agricultural Economics*, 12, 152-163.

Davidson, J. E. H., D. F. Hendry, F. Srba, and S. Yeo (1978): "Econometric Modelling of the Aggregate Time-Series Relationship Between Consumers' and Income in the United Kingdom," *Economic Journal*, 88, 661-692.

Davidson, R., and J. G. MacKinnon (1981): "Several Tests for Model Specification in the Prescence of Alternative Hypotheses," *Econometrica*, 49, 781-793.

de Janvry, A., J. Bieri, and A. Nuñez (1972): "Estimation of Demand Under Consumer Budgeting: An Application to Argentina," *American Journal of Agricultural Economics*, 54, 422-430.

Deaton, A. (1975): *Models and Projections of Demand in Post-War Britain*, London: Chapman and Hall.

Deaton, A. (1986): "Demand Analysis," Chapter 30 in *Handbook of Econometrics, Volume 3*, edited by Z. Griliches, and M. D. Intriligator. Amsterdam: North-Holland.

Deaton, A., and J. Muellbauer (1980a): *Economics and Consumer Behaviour*. Cambridge: Cambridge University Press.

Deaton, A., and J. Muellbauer (1980b): "An Almost Ideal Demand System," *American Economic Review*, 70, 312-326.

Dhrymes, P. J., and S. Schwarz (1987): "On the Invariance of Estimators for Singular Systems of Equations," *Greek Economic Review*, 9, 88-107.

Dickey, D. A., and W. A. Fuller (1979): "Distribution of the Estimators for Autoregressive Time Series with a Unit Root," *Journal of the American Statistical Association*, 74, 427-31.
Dickey, D. A., and W. A. Fuller (1981): "Likelihood Ratio Statistics for Autoregressive Time Series with a Unit Root," *Econometrica*, 49, 1057-1072.

Edgerton, D. L. (1972): "Some Properties of Two Stage Least Squares as Applied to Nonlinear Models," *International Economic Review*, 13, 26-32.
Edgerton, D. L. (1973): *Nonlinear Interdependent Systems*, FD thesis; *Selected Publications* 30, Department of Statistics, Uppsala, Sweden.
Edgerton, D. L. (1989): "Food Consumption Data in Sweden," *Nordic Food Demand Study* SW/2, Department of Economics, Lund University, Sweden.
Edgerton, D. L. (1992): "Estimating Elasticities in Multi-Stage Demand Systems," Presented at the AAEA meeting in Baltimore.
Edgerton, D. L. (1993a): "Weak Separability and the Estimation of Elasticities in Multi-Stage Demand Systems," *Working Paper* 26/93, Department of Economics, Lund, Sweden. To be published in revised form in the *American Journal of Agricultural Economics*, 1996/1997.
Edgerton, D. L. (1993b): "On the Estimation of Separable Demand Models," *Journal of Agricultural and Resource Economics*, 18, 141-146.
Edgerton, D. L. (1995): "When Do Estimated Demand Systems Automatically Satisfy Adding Up?" *Nordic Food Demand Study* SW/8, Department of Economics, Lund University, Sweden. Presented in revised form at the Econometric Society World Congress in Tokyo, 1995.
Edgerton, D. L., and G. Shukur (1995) "Testing Autocorrelation in a System Perspective," Department of Economics and Department of Statistics, Lund, Sweden. Presented at the Econometric Society World Congress in Tokyo.
Edgerton, D. L., and C. Wells (1993): "On the Use of the Cusumsq Statistic in Medium Sized Samples," *Working Paper* 22/93, Department of Economics, Lund, Sweden. Presented at the Econometric Society Meeting in Uppsala.
Edgerton, D. L., and C. Wells (1994): "Critical Values for the Cusumsq Statistic in Medium and Large Sized Samples," *Oxford Bulletin of Economics and Statistics*, 56, 355-365.
Engle, R. F. (1982): "Autoregressive Conditional Heteroscedasticity, with Estimates of the Variance of United Kingdom Inflations," *Econometrica*, 50, 987-1008.
Engle, R. F. (1984): "Wald, Likelihood Ratio, and Lagrange Multiplier Tests in Econometrics," Chapter 13 in *Handbook of Econometrics, Volume 2*, edited by Z. Griliches, and M. D. Intriligator. Amsterdam: North-Holland.
Engle, R. F., and C. W. J. Granger (1987): "Co-Integration and Error Correction: Representation, Estimation and Testing," *Econometrica*, 55, 251-276.

Gallant, A. R., and D. Jorgenson (1979): "Statistical Inference for a System of Simultaneous Non-linear, Implicit Equations in the Context of Instrumental Variable Estimation," *Journal of Econometrics*, 11, 275-302.
Georgakopoulos, T. A. (1990): "The Impact of Accession on Food Prices, Inflation and Food Consumption in Greece," *European Review of Agricultural Economics*, 17, 485-493.
George, P. S., and G. A. King (1971): "Consumer Demand for Food Commodities in the United States with Projections for 1980," *Monograph Number 26*, Giannini Foundation of Agricultural Economics, University of California.
Geweke, J. (1984): "Inference and Causality in Economic Time Series," Chapter 19 in *Handbook of Econometrics, Volume II*, edited by Z. Griliches, and M. D. Intriligator. Amsterdam: North-Holland.
Goddard, D. (1983): "An Analysis of Canadian Aggregate Demand for Food at Home and Away from Home," *Canadian Journal of Agricultural Economics*, 31, 289-318.
Godfrey, L. G. (1988): *Misspecification Tests in Econometrics*, Cambridge: Cambridge University Press.
Gorman, W. M. (1959): "Separable Utility and Aggregation," *Econometrica*, 27, 469-481.
Green, R. D., and J. M. Alston (1990): "Elasticities in AIDS Models," *American Journal of Agricultural Economics*, 72, 442-445.
Green, R. D., and J. M. Alston (1991): "Elasticities in AIDS Models: A Clarification and Extension," *American Journal of Agricultural Economics*, 73, 874-875.
Green, R., W. Hahn, and D. Rocke (1987): "Standard Errors for Elasticities: A Comparison of Bootstrap and Asymptotic Standard Errors," *Journal of Business and Economic Statistics*, 5, 145-149.
Greene, W. H. (1985): "Estimation of Limited Dependent Variable Models by Ordinary Least Squares and

the Methods Of Moments," *Journal of Econometrics*, 21, 120-132.
Greene, W. H. (1993): *Econometric Analysis*, Second Edition. New York: Macmillan.

Harvey, A. C. (1990): *The Econometric Analysis of Time Series*, Second Edition. New York: Philip Allan.
Heckman, J. J. (1979): "Sample Selection Bias as a Specification Error," *Econometrica*, 47, 153-161.
Heien, D., L. S. Jarvis, and F. Perali (1989): "Food Consumption in Mexico. Demographic and Economic Effects," *Food Policy*, 167-179.
Hendry, D. F., and J.-F. Richard (1983): "The Econometric Analysis of Economic Time Series," *International Statistical Review*, 51, 111-63.
Houthakker, H. S., and L. D. Taylor (1970): *Consumer Demand in The United States: Analyses and Projections*, Second edition. Cambridge, Mass.: Harvard University Press.
Huang, K. S. (1993): "A Complete System of U.S. Demand for Food," *Technical Bulletin No. 1821*. Economic Research Service, U.S. Department of Agricultural.
Huang, K. S., and R. C. Haidacher (1986): "Projecting Aggregate Food Expenditures to the Year 2000," pp. 67-85 in *Food Demand Analysis: Implications for Future Consumption*, edited by O. Capps and B. Senauer. Department of Agricultural Economics, Virginia Polytechnic Institute and State University, Blacksburg, Virginia.
Hummelmose, A. (1991): "Forbruget af fødevarer i Danmark 1950 -1989," (in Danish). *Nordic Food Demand Study* DK/8, Department of Economics, Royal Agricultural University, Copenhagen, Denmark.
Hummelmose, A. (1992): "Sammenligning af forskellige efterspørgselsystemer og -modeller anvendt på danske data," (in Danish). *Nordic Food Demand Study* DK/11, Department of Economics, Royal Agricultural University, Copenhagen, Denmark.

Jarque, C. M., and A. K. Bera (1980): "Efficient Tests for Normality, Homoscedasticity and Serial Inde pendence of Regression Residuals," *Economics Letters*, 6, 255-59.
Jarque, C. M., and A. K. Bera (1987): "A Test for Normality of Observations and Regression Residuals," *International Statistical Review*, 55, 163-172.
Johansen, S. (1991): "Estimation and Testing of Cointegration Vectors in Gaussian Autoregressive Models," *Econometrica*, 59, 1551-1580.
Johnson, S. R., R. D. Green, Z. A. Hassan, and A. N. Safyurtlu (1986): "Market Demand Functions," in *Food Demand Analysis: Implications for Future Consumption*, edited by O. Capps and B. Senauer. Department of Agricultural Economics, Virginia Polytechnic Institute and State University, Blacksburg, Virginia.
Johnston, J. (1984): *Econometric Methods*, Third edition. New York: McGraw-Hill.
Jorgenson, D. W., L. R. Lau, and T. M. Stoker (1982): "The Transcendental Logarithmic Model of Aggregate Consumer Behaviour," pp. 97-238 in *Advances in Econometrics, Volume 1*, edited by R. L. Basmann, and G. F. Rhodes. Greenwich: JAI Press.
Judge, G. G., W. E. Griffiths, R. Carter-Hill, H. Lütkepohl, and T.-C. Lee (1985): *The Theory and Practice of Econometrics*, Second Edition. New York: Wiley.

Kelejian, H. (1971): "Two-Stage Least Squares and Econometric Systems Linear in Parameters but Nonlinear in Endogenous Variables," *Journal of the American Statistical Association*, 66, 373-374.
Kendall, M. G., and A. Stuart (1963): *The Advanced Theory of Statistics, Volume 1*, Second Edition. London: Charles Griffin and Company.
Kennedy, P. (1985): *A Guide to Econometrics*, Second edition. Oxford: Basil Blackwell.
Kesavan, T., Z. A. Hassan, H. H. Jensen, and S. R. Johnson (1993): "Dynamics and Long-Run Structure in U.S. Meat Demand," *Canadian Journal of Agricultural Economics*, 41, 139-153
Keuzenkamp, H. A., and A. P. Barten (1995): "Rejection without Falsification: On the History of Testing the Homogeneity Condition in the Theory of Consumer Demand," *Journal of Econometrics*, 67, 103-128.
Kirman, A. P. (1992): "Whom or What Does the Representative Consumer Represent?," *Journal of Economic Perspectives*, 6, 117-136.
Kiviet, J. (1986): "On the Rigour of Some Specification Tests for Modelling Dynamic Relationships," *Review of Economic Studies*, 53, 241-262.
Klevmarken, N. A. (1979): "A Comparative Study of Complete Systems of Demand Functions," *Journal of Econometrics*, 10, 165-191.
Klevmarken, N. A. (1981): *On the Complete Systems Approach to Demand Analysis*, Stockholm: Almqvist and Wiksell.

Krinsky, I., and A. L. Robb (1986): "On Approximating the Statistical Properties of Elasticities," *Review of Economics and Statistics*, 68, 715-719.
Krinsky, I., and A. L. Robb (1990): "On Approximating the Statistical Properties of Elasticities: A Correction," *Review of Economics and Statistics*, 72, 189-190.
Krinsky, I., and A. L. Robb (1991): "Three Methods for Calculating the Statistical Properties of Elasticities: A Comparison," *Empirical Economics*, 16, 199-209.
Kuh, E., and J. R. Meyer (1957): "How Extraneous are Extraneous Estimates?," *Review of Economics and Statistics*, 39, 380-393.

LaFrance, J. T. (1991): "When Is Expenditure "Exogenous" in Separable Demand Models?" *Western Journal of Agricultural Economics*, 16, 49-62.
Lau, L. J. (1986): "Functional Forms in Econometric Model Building," Chapter 26 in *Handbook of Econometrics, Volume III*, edited by Z. Griliches, and M. D. Intriligator. Amsterdam: North-Holland.
Laurila, E. H. (1985): "Kulutus Suomen kansantaloudessa 1900-1975," (in Finnish with English summary: "Consumption in Finnish Economy in the Years 1900-1975"). Series B 42. The Research Institute of the Finnish Economy, Helsinki.
Laurila, I. P. (1991): "Static and Dynamic AIDS Models of Demand for Food in Finland," *Nordic Food Demand Study* F/11. Department of Agricultural Economics, University of Helsinki.
Lewbel, A. (1985): "A Unified Approach to Incorporating Demographic and Other Effects Into Demand Systems," *Review of Economic Studies*, 52, 1-18.
Lewbel, A. (1989): "Nesting the AIDS and Translog Demand Systems," *International Economic Review*, 30, 349-356.

MacKinnon, J. G. (1992) "Model Specification Tests and Artificial Regressions," *Journal of Economic Literature*, 30, 102-146.
Maddala, G. S. (1992): *Introduction to Econometrics*, Second Edition. New York: Macmillan.
Manderscheid, L.V. (1964): "Some Observations on Interpreting Measured Demand Elasticities," *Journal of Farm Economics*, 46, 128-136.
Manser, M. E. (1976): "Elasticities of Demand for Food: An Analysis Using Non-Additive Utility Functions Allowing for Habit Formation," *Southern Economic Journal*, 43, 879-891.
Mardia, K. V., and K. Foster (1983): "Omnibus Tests of Multinormality Based on Skewness and Kurtosis," *Communications in Statistics. Theory and Methods*, 12, 207-221.
Martin, W., and D. Porter (1985): "Testing for Changes in the Structure of the Demand for Meat in Australia," *Australian Journal of Agricultural Economics*, 29, 16-31.
McCabe, B. P. M., and M. J. Harrison (1980): "Testing the Constancy of Regression Residuals over Time Using Least Squares Residuals," *Applied Statistics*, 29, 142-148.
McGuirk, A. M., P. Driscoll, and J. Alwang (1993): "Misspecification Testing: A Comprehensive Approach," *American Journal of Agricultural Economics*, 75, 1044-1055.
McGuirk, A. M., P. Driscoll, J. Alwang and H. L. Huang (1995): "System Misspecification Testing and Structural Change in the Demand for Meats," *Journal of Agricultural and Resource Economics*, 20, 1-21.
McLaren, K. R. (1990): "A Variant on the Arguments for the Invariance of Estimators in a Singular System of Equations," *Econometric Reviews*, 9, 91-102.
Mergos, G. J., and G. S. Donatos (1989): "Consumer Behaviour in Greece: An Application of the Almost Ideal Demand System," *Applied Economics*, 21, 983-993.
Michalek, J., and M. A. Keyzer (1992): "Estimation Of a Two-Stage LES-AIDS Consumer Demand System for Eight EC Countries," *European Review of Agricultural Economics*, 19, 137-163.
Moschini, G. (1992): "A Non-Nested Test of Separability for Flexible Functional Forms," *Review of Economics and Statistics*, 74, 365-369
Moschini, G., and K. D. Meilke (1984): "Parameter Stability and the U.S. Demand for Beef," *Western Journal of Agricultural Economics*, 9, 271-282.
Moschini G., and K. D. Meilke (1989): "Modelling the Pattern of Structural Change in US Meat Demand," *American Journal of Agricultural Economics*, 71, 253-261.
Moschini G., D. Moro, and R. D. Green (1994): "Maintaining and Testing Separability in Demand Systems," *American Journal of Agricultural Economics*, 76, 61-73.
Myers, L. H. (1986): "Comments: Food Demand Analysis: Implications for Future Consumption," pp. 177-184 in *Food Demand Analysis: Implications for Future Consumption*, edited by O. Capps and B. Senauer. Department of Agricultural Economics, Virginia Polytechnic Institute and State University,

Blacksburg, Virginia.

Newey, W. K., and K. D. West (1987): "A Simple Positive Semi-Definite; Heteroskedasticity and Autocorrelation Consistent Covariance Matrix," *Econometrica*, 55, 703-708.

Oberhofer, W., and J. Kmenta (1974): "A General Procedure for Obtaining Maximum Likelihood Estimates in Generalized Regression Models," *Econometrica*, 42, 579-590.

Pasour Jr, E. C., and R. A. Schrimper (1965): "The Effect of Length of Run on Measured Demand Elastici ties," *Journal of Farm Economics*, 47, 774-788.

Phlips, L. (1983): *Applied Consumption Analysis*, Revised and enlarged edition. North Holland: Amsterdam.

Ploberger, W., and W. Krämer (1992): "The Cusum-Test with OLS Residuals," *Econometrica*, 60, 271-286.

Pollak, R. A. (1971): "Additive Utility Functions and Linear Engel Curves," *Review of Economic Studies*, 38, 401-414.

Pollak, R. A., and T. J. Wales (1978): "Estimation of Complete Demand Systems from Household Budget Data: The Linear and Quadratic Expenditure Systems," *American Economic Review*, 68, 348-359.

Pollak, R. A., and T. J. Wales (1981): "Demographic Variables in Demand Analysis," *Econometrica*, 49, 1533-51.

Pollak, R. A., and T. J. Wales (1992): *Demand System Specification and Estimation*. Oxford: Oxford University Press.

Powell, A. A. (1969): "Aitken Estimators as a Tool in Allocating Predetermined Aggregates," *Journal of the American Statistical Association*, 64, 913-922.

Pudney, S. E. (1981): "An Empirical Method of Approximating the Separable Structure of Consumer Preferences," *Review of Economic Studies*, 48, 561-577.

Rao, C. R. (1973): *Linear Statistical Inference and Its Applications*, Second edition. New York: Wiley.

Raunikar, R., and C. L. Huang (1987): *Food Demand Analysis: Problems, Issues and Empirical Evidence*. Ames: Iowa State University Press.

Ray, R. (1984): "A Dynamic Generalisation of the Almost Ideal Demand System," *Economics Letters*, 14, 235-239.

Ray, R. (1985): "Specification and Time Series Estimation of Dynamic Gorman Polar Form Demand Systems," *European Economic Review*, 27, 357-74.

Ray, R. (1986): "Demographic Variables and Equivalence Scales in a Flexible Demand System: The Case of AIDS," *Applied Economics*, 18, 265-278.

Rickertsen, K. (1990): "Food Demand in Norway," *Memorandum* No. 4, Department of Economics and Social Sciences, The Agricultural University of Norway, Ås.

Rickertsen, K. (1994): "The Demand for Food and Beverages in Norway," *Report* No. 13, Department of Economics and Social Sciences, The Agricultural University of Norway, Ås.

Rossi, N. (1988): "Budget Share Demographic Translation and the Aggregate Almost Ideal Demand System," *European Economic Review*, 31, 1301-1318.

Salathe, L. (1979): "The Effects of Changes in Population Characteristics on US Consumption of Selected Foods," *American Journal of Agricultural Economics*, 61, 1036-1045.

Sexauer, B. (1979): "The Effects of Demographic Shifts and Changes in the Income Distribution on 'Food-away-from-Home' Expenditure," *American Journal of Agricultural Economics*, 61, 1046-1057.

Spanos, A. (1986): *Statistical Foundations of Econometric Modelling*, Cambridge: Cambridge University Press.

Stoker, T. M. (1993): "Empirical Approaches to the Problem of Aggregation over Individuals," *Journal of Economic Literature*, 31, 1827-1874.

Swoffard, J. L., and G. A. Whitney (1988): "Comparison of Nonparametric Tests of Weak Separability for Annual and Quarterly Data on Consumption; Leisure and Money," *Journal of Business and Economic Statistics*, 6, 241-246.

Söder, L. (1984): "Kotitaloudet kansantalouden tilinpidossa" (in Finnish with English summary: "Households in National Accounts"). Studies, No. 109. Central Statistical Office of Finland, Helsinki.

Teklu, T., Z. A. Hassan, S. R. Johnson, and D. P. Stonehouse (1992): "Empirical Demand Systems," Chapter 4 in *Market Demand for Dairy Products*, edited by S. R. Johnson, D. P. Stonehouse and Z. A. Hassan. Ames: Iowa State University Press.

Theil, H. (1971): "An Economic Theory of the Second Moments of Disturbances of Behavioural Equations," *American Economic Review*, 61, 190-194.

Theil, H., and K. W. Clements (1987): *Applied Demand Analysis. Results from System-Wide Approaches.* Cambridge, Mass.:Balinger.

Thompson, G. D. (1988): "Choice of Flexible Functional Forms: Review and Appraisal," *Western Journal of Agricultural Economics*, 13, 169-183.

TSP (1990): *TSP User's Guide, Version 4.2*, Palo Alto, California: TSP International.

Vale, P. H. (1995): "Microdata in Demand Analysis. Theories, Application and Empirical Findings," *Dissertation*, Department of Economics and Social Sciences, The Agricultural University of Norway, Ås.

Varian, H. R. (1992): *Microeconomic Analysis*, Third edition. New York: Norton.

Vartia. P., and P. Ylä-Anttila (1992): Kansantalous 2017 (in Finnish with English summary: Abstract: "The Finnish Economy in 2017"). The Research Institute of the Finnish Economy: Helsinki.

Wahl, T. I., and D. J. Hayes (1990): "Demand System Estimation with Upward-Sloping Supply," *Canadian Journal of Agricultural Economics*, 38, 107-122.

White, H. (1980): "A Heteroskedasticity-Consistent Covariance Matrix Estimator and a Direct Test for Heteroskedasticity," *Econometrica*, 48, 817-838.

Wilks, S. S. (1938): "Weighting Systems for Linear Functions of Correlated Variables When There Is No Dependent Variable," *Psychometrika*, 3, 23-40.

Wohlgenant, M. K. (1986) "Global Behavior of Demand Elasticities for Food: Implications for Demand Projections," pp. 35-48 in *Food Demand Analysis: Implications for Future Consumption*, edited by O. Capps and B. Senauer. Department of Agricultural Economics, Virginia Polytechnic Institute and State University, Blacksburg, Virginia.

Wohlgenant, M. K., and W. F. Hahn (1982): "Dynamic Adjustment in Monthly Consumer Demands for Meats," *American Journal of Agricultural Economics*, 64, 553-557.

Woodland, A. D. (1979): "Stochastic Specification and the Estimation of Share Equations," *Journal of Econometrics*, 10, 361-383.

Worswick, G. D. N., and D. G. Champernowne (1954): "A Note on the Adding-up Criterion," *Review of Economic Studies*, 22, 57-60.

AUTHOR INDEX

a = non-named author in an "et al." reference
f = reference in footnote

Appendix 1

PUBLICATIONS AND WORKING PAPERS

PUBLICATIONS

PUB/1: Edgerton, D. L., "Hur mycket har matpriserna stigit? En jämförelse mellan nationalräkenskaperna och konsumentprisindex," *Ekonomisk Debatt,* 90:8, 766-771, 1990 (in Swedish).

PUB/2: Edgerton, D. L., "On the Estimation of Separable Demand Models," *Journal of Agricultural and Resource Economics*, 18, 141-146, 1993.

PUB/3: Edgerton, D. L., and C. Wells, "Critical Values for the Cusumsq Statistic in Medium Sized Samples," *Oxford Bulletin of Economics and Statistics*, 56, 355-365, 1994.

PUB/4: Rickertsen, K., "The Demand for Meat: Conditional and Unconditional Elasticities," *IAAE Occasional Paper* No. 7, 1995.

PUB/5: Rickertsen, K., "Etterspørsel etter matvarer," *Landbruksøkonomisk forum*, 12, 1-10, 1995 (in Norwegian)

PUB/6: Rickertsen, K., "Structural Change and the Demand for Meat and Fish in Norway," *European Review of Agricultural Economics*, 1996 (forthcoming).

PUB/7: Edgerton, D. L., and G. Shukur, "Some Questions Concerning Dynamic Almost Ideal Demand Systems," *Applied Economics Letters*, 1996 (forthcoming).

NORDIC FOOD DEMAND STUDY SERIES

Denmark

DK/1: Hummelmose, A., "Husholdingernes konsum," 1989 (in Danish).

DK/2: Hummelmose, A., "Analyser og prognoser for fødevareefterspørgslen i de nordiske lande," 1989 (in Danish).

DK/3: Hummelmose, A., "Brug af efterspørgselsmodeller på dansk nationalregnskapstal," 1990 (in Danish).

DK/4: Hummelmose, A., "Befolkningsforhold, indkomstudviklingen og omkostningsindex i Danmark," 1990 (in Danish).

DK/5: Hummelmose, A., "Udviklingen i prisen på og forbruget af fødevarer i Danmark, 1953-1987," 1990 (in Danish).

DK/6: Hummelmose, A., "Analyse af input i det privat konsum. Analyseperiode 1970-1986," 1990 (in Danish).

SUBJECT INDEX

Advanced Studies in Theoretical and Applied Econometrics

1. J.H.P. Paelinck (ed.): *Qualitative and Quantitative Mathematical Economics.* 1982 ISBN 90-247-2623-9
2. J.P. Ancot (ed.): *Analysing the Structure of Econometric Models.* 1984 ISBN 90-247-2894-0
3. A.J. Hughes Hallet (ed.): *Applied Decision Analysis and Economic Behaviour.* 1984 ISBN 90-247-2968-8
4. J.K. Sengupta: *Information and Efficiency in Economic Decision.* 1985 ISBN 90-247-3072-4
5. P. Artus and O. Guvenen (eds.), in collaboration with F. Gagey: *International Macroeconomic Modelling for Policy Decisions.* 1986 ISBN 90-247-3201-8
6. M.J. Vilares: *Structural Change in Macroeconomic Models.* Theory and Estimation. 1986 ISBN 90-247-3277-8
7. C. Carraro and D. Sartore (eds.): *Development of Control Theory for Economic Analysis.* 1987 ISBN 90-247-3345-6
8. D.P. Broer: *Neoclassical Theory and Empirical Models of Aggregate Firm Behaviour.* 1987 ISBN 90-247-3412-6
9. A. Italianer: *Theory and Practice of International Trade Linkage Models.* 1986 ISBN 90-247-3407-X
10. D.A. Kendrick: *Feedback.* A New Framework for Macroeconomic Policy. 1988 ISBN 90-247-3593-9; Pb: 90-247-3650-1
11. J.K. Sengupta and G.K. Kadekodi (eds.): *Econometrics of Planning and Efficiency.* 1988 ISBN 90-247-3602-1
12. D.A. Griffith: *Advanced Spatial Statistics.* Special Topics in the Exploration of Quantitative Spatial Data Series. 1988 ISBN 90-247-3627-7
13. O. Guvenen (ed.): *International Commodity Market Models and Policy Analysis.* 1988 ISBN 90-247-3768-0
14. G. Arbia: *Spatial Data Configuration in Statistical Analysis of Regional Economic and Related Problems.* 1989 ISBN 0-7923-0284-2
15. B. Raj (ed.): *Advances in Econometrics and Modelling.* 1989 ISBN 0-7923-0299-0
16. A. Aznar Grasa: *Econometric Model Selection.* A New Approach. 1989 ISBN 0-7923-0321-0
17. L.R. Klein and J. Marquez (eds.): *Economics in Theory and Practice.* An Eclectic Approach. Essays in Honor of F. G. Adams. 1989 ISBN 0-7923-0410-1
18. D.A. Kendrick: *Models for Analyzing Comparative Advantage.* 1990 ISBN 0-7923-0528-0
19. P. Artus and Y. Barroux (eds.): *Monetary Policy.* A Theoretical and Econometric Approach. 1990 ISBN 0-7923-0626-0

Advanced Studies in Theoretical and Applied Econometrics

20. G. Duru and J.H.P. Paelinck (eds.): *Econometrics of Health Care.* 1990
ISBN 0-7923-0766-6
21. L. Phlips (ed.): *Commodity, Futures and Financial Markets.* 1991
ISBN 0-7923-1043-8
22. H.M. Amman, D.A. Belsley and L.F. Pau (eds.): *Computational Economics and Econometrics.* 1992 ISBN 0-7923-1287-2
23. B. Raj and J. Koerts (eds.): *Henri Theil's Contributions to Economics and Econometrics.* Vol. I: Econometric Theory and Methodology. 1992
ISBN 0-7923-1548-0
24. B. Raj and J. Koerts (eds.): *Henri Theil's Contributions to Economics and Econometrics.* Vol. II: Consumer Demand Analysis and Information Theory. 1992
ISBN 0-7923-1664-9
25. B. Raj and J. Koerts (eds.): *Henri Theil's Contributions to Economics and Econometrics.* Vol. III: Economic Policy and Forecasts, and Management Science. 1992 ISBN 0-7923-1665-7
Set (23-25) ISBN 0-7923-1666-5
26. P. Fisher: *Rational Expectations in Macroeconomic Models.* 1992
ISBN 0-7923-1903-6
27. L. Phlips and L.D. Taylor (eds.): *Aggregation, Consumption and Trade.* Essays in Honor of H.S. Houthakker. 1992. ISBN 0-7923-2001-8
28. L. Mátyás and P. Sevestre (eds.): *The Econometrics of Panel Data.* Handbook of Theory and Applications. 1992 ISBN 0-7923-2043-3
29. S. Selvanathan: *A System-Wide Analysis of International Consumption Patterns.* 1993 ISBN 0-7923-2344-0
30. H. Theil in association with D. Chen, K. Clements and C. Moss: *Studies in Global Econometrics.* 1996 ISBN 0-7923-3660-7
31. P.J. Kehoe and T.J. Kehoe (eds.): *Modeling North American Economic Integration.* 1995 ISBN 0-7923-3751-4
32. C. Wells: *The Kalman Filter in Finance.* 1996 ISBN 0-7923-3771-9
33. L. Mátyás and P. Sevestre (eds.): *The Econometrics of Panel Data.* A Handbook of the Theory with Applications. Second Revised Edition. 1996
ISBN 0-7923-3787-5
34. B. Assarsson, D. Edgerton, A. Hummelmose, I. Laurila, K. Rickertson and P.H. Vale: *The Econometrics of Demand Systems.* With Applications to Food Demand in the North Countries. 1996 ISBN 0-7923-4106-6

Kluwer Academic Publishers – Dordrecht / Boston / London

9 780792 341062

GPSR Compliance

The European Union's (EU) General Product Safety Regulation (GPSR) is a set of rules that requires consumer products to be safe and our obligations to ensure this.

If you have any concerns about our products, you can contact us on ProductSafety@springernature.com

In case Publisher is established outside the EU, the EU authorized representative is:

Springer Nature Customer Service Center GmbH
Europaplatz 3
69115 Heidelberg, Germany

Batch number: 10620086

Printed by Printforce, the Netherlands